DRAMATIC RE-VISIONS

DRAMATIC RE-VISIONS

An Annotated Bibliography of Feminism and Theatre 1972–1988

Susan M. Steadman

American Library Association
Chicago and London 1991

Cover and text designed by The Wheetley Company, Inc.

Composed by Point West, Inc., in Garamond.

Printed on 50-pound Glatfelter, a pH-neutral stock, and bound in B-grade Holliston Roxite cloth by Edwards Brothers, Inc.

The paper used in this publication meets the minimum requirements of American National Standard for Information Sciences—Permanence of Paper for Printed Library Materials, ANSI Z39.48-1984. ∞

Library of Congress Cataloging-in-Publication Data
Steadman, Susan M.
    Dramatic re-visions : an annotated bibliography of feminism and
theatre, 1972–1988 / by Susan M. Steadman.
       p.   cm.
    Includes indexes.
    ISBN 0-8389-0577-3
    1. Feminism and theater—Bibliography.   2. Women in the
theater—Bibliography.   3. Drama—History and criticism—Bibliography.
4. Feminist criticism—Bibliography.   I. Title.
Z5784.F45S73   1991
[PN1590.W64]
016.792'09—dc20   91-16333

Printed in the United States of America.

95 94 93 92 91   5 4 3 2 1

Contents

❖
❖

Contents

Preface

❖
❖

The title of this work, *Dramatic Re-Visions,* was inspired by Adrienne Rich's much quoted statement:

> Re-vision—the act of looking back, of seeing with fresh eyes, of entering an old text from a new critical direction—is for women more than a chapter in cultural history; it is an act of survival. Until we can understand the assumptions in which we are drenched we cannot know ourselves. (35)
>
> —"When We Dead Awaken: Writing as Re-Vision," 1971.
> Rpt. in *On Lies, Secrets and Silence,* 1979

I borrow the hyphenated "re-vision" purposefully, to suggest not only the process of *changing* the practice of dramatic criticism, received notions of theatrical history, and the kind of performance presented on the stage but also the act of *looking* at theatre again—and again. It is, after all, the spectacle—the vision—of "woman" on the stage that has inspired the ongoing project of feminism's intersection with theatre.

The other bit of playfulness in the title entails a matter of extent: Ideas about theatre have been, are being, and will continue to be *dramatically* altered by feminist theory and practice. If the political goal of feminism is to re-vision and then seek ways to revise society—a society traditionally reflected in its cultural products—then theatre with its unique intimacy and immediacy presents itself as a potentially versatile, powerful tool: a "laboratory" for experimentation and social change.

While the impetus for a book-length annotated bibliography came from the receipt of a 1988 Whitney-Carnegie Grant from the American Library Association, the seeds actually lay in an act of volunteering. In 1981, at a meeting of the Women's Theatre Program of the American

Theatre Association (ATA), I raised my hand and offered to put together a bibliography of feminist dramatic criticism. Had I known that this simple gesture, this hand-raising, would lead to a decade of painstaking compilation of materials in an ever-expanding and inadequately indexed field, would I have done it so blithely?

The resultant bibliography, photocopied, stapled, and distributed at the following year's conference, was the first in a series of biennial bibliographies of "feminist dramatic criticism," a term now far too constricting. When the Women's Program weathered the chaos wrought by the demise of the ATA in 1985 to emerge as the renamed Women and Theatre Program affiliated with the new Association for Theatre in Higher Education (ATHE), I continued the project. As the program became less focused on women and their status in the theatre and more immersed in feminist theoretical issues, the enthusiastic reception of the bibliographies grew increasingly rewarding.

While my first bibliographic contribution was enjoyably executed with Janet Brown, author of *Feminist Drama: Definition and Critical Analysis,* subsequent installments were my sole responsibility. In performing this task, I have followed closely the change in quality and quantity of feminist writings on drama by men and women as well as reports on and analyses of feminist theatre and performance. However, when compiling the biennial (unannotated) bibliographies, I did not delve as deeply into all the available bibliographic sources as I did when conducting research for *Dramatic Re-Visions.* Furthermore, my original concentration on the dramatic text necessarily broadened as feminist criticism began to encompass all facets of theatre and theatrelike activity. The anticipated work of 400 annotated items mushroomed into this bibliography of approximately 850 entries.

If the persistent question for any bibliographer is "where to stop," then it is a particularly complex problem for the bibliographer in theatre. Unlike feminist literary criticism, a bibliography of feminism and theatre must take into account not just the written word, the published text, or even the readers' interaction with the script, but also performance aspects and, indeed, the ideological context in which a theatrical event is conceived, rehearsed, and produced, as well as its reception. The study of "theatre" must include the activities preceding the public viewing, the space in which the production takes place, the spectator-performer relationship, the signification of the physical body on the stage, the expectations of audience members and critics, and much more.

Unfortunately, none of the years of acting, directing, writing plays, or even teaching and publishing had prepared me for the task of compiling this bibliography. That I persisted in the face of constant frustration may be attributed to an inherent "teaching" drive—the need to share with others the vast resources that were proving so hard to find—plus the encouragement of feminist scholars, personal friends, and family members, as well as a good-sized element of sheer obstinacy.

Flashes of personal history rush by as I write this preface, fragments of my life and work . . . the experiences that brought me to this place. The impulse to give in to nonlinearity (a feminist aesthetic?), a musing linked by visceral and intellectual memory threads, becomes overwhelming when one has devoted three years to writing in a scholarly, "acceptable" mode, which is ironically phallocentric despite the feminist subject matter. So I shall indulge myself. This is, after all, the preface, my personal statement.

Fragments: poring over the first few copies of *Ms.,* borrowed from a sister graduate student at Louisiana State University in the early 1970s; scrapping my attempts at a dissertation dealing with images of career women in favor of studying family relationships in the Restoration comedy of manners and their subsequent changes in sentimental comedy; realizing, later, that family, especially women's roles in it as depicted in the male canon, has been a concern of feminist inquiry from its inception. My own family: my position(s) as a daughter and as the mother of two children; reading Rich, Dinnerstein, Chodorow; recognizing my mother's missed professional opportunities in the art world because women were supposed to be wives and mothers first.

More fragments: informal group efforts in Oxford, Ohio, to interpret Betsy Wing's draft of her translation of *La Jeune Née* (*The Newly Born Woman*) by Hélène Cixous and Catherine Clément; Betsy's patient attempts to explain Jacques Lacan's convoluted relationship to French feminism. The exhilaration at participating in a semester-long interdisciplinary seminar for feminist scholars led by Alison Jaggar at Douglass College in New Jersey—*but* as the only "theatre person" among the forty or so participants selected, some of whom traveled two or three hours to attend, wondering why feminist theatre scholarship was not better represented. Aside from the requisite bibliography, my contribution to the seminar was the reading of my first play, *The Milk Machine,* which addressed many of the issues under discussion (and fevered argument) during the sessions. Interviewing at a women's college in the mid-1980s and not being hired, the proffered reason being that my strengths would duplicate those of the other woman on the faculty . . . then learning, covertly, that one of the (male) faculty members "feared" my feminism. "Feared" it? At a women's college?

And finally, not long ago, watching my daughter's school play, a Christmas production involving all the second-grade classes, wherein the child playing the villain who would do away with the holiday, a dark-skinned boy, is thwarted by the blonde, blue-eyed, white-skinned good fairy. The issues of gender and race, of feminist pedagogy, of re-visioning the world through a feminist perspective—all that I had been working on in the privacy of my study thrown into chaos by the realization of what is still being taught to our children, even unconsciously... *particularly* unconsciously.

Even while indulging in these memory fragments, I can feel the pull to return to the work at hand—the bibliography, the mission. I shall resume the style of "the fathers," my teachers, my mentors (male and female alike): the formal, scholarly approach. Let the interval end.

In the Introduction I summarize the development of feminist criticism of drama/performance/theatre, as well as the historical publication aspects. Also included are explanations regarding the scope and use of the book.

Within the annotated bibliography itself, I have rigidly adhered to the years covered in the title of this work, 1972 to 1988. (Of course, there have been a number of significant works published since 1988; Appendix III provides a sampling of important books, anthologies, and special issues of periodicals published in 1989 and 1990.) I have repeatedly experienced enormous temptation to discard these limitations; but to get this book into print within my lifetime, and especially to make the materials available as quickly as possible to the scholars, students, teachers, and theatre practitioners to whom I offer this bibliography as a research aid, I maintained the original cutoff point.

There are many ways in which I wish I had approached this book differently. For example, over the years that I worked on this project I overhauled the Subject Index terms at least three times. Perhaps greater experience would have led me down an easier path. However, the separation of materials into chapters grouping similar subjects (if not critical perspectives and methodologies), as well as the availability of four different indexes, should provide users with the information they seek.

Despite the remarkable strides made in the development of feminist criticism of drama/performance/theatre and the more recent progress in eliminating the unfortunate schism that sometimes exists or is perceived to exist between theory and practice, as I look around me in my present metropolitan location I see all too little effect of the groundbreaking work. This theatrical market, like so many others dominated by male directors, playwrights, critics, and aesthetic criteria, with predictable gender representation on stage and, for the most part, "safe" play choices and interpretations, shows little evidence that feminism has influenced theatre. And this city is only one of hundreds of similar cities priding themselves on the vastness of their cultural offerings.

Feminism implies political activism, but I sometimes question if publishing feminist materials is in itself a *sufficient* activism. Some college and university professors throughout the country are managing to integrate feminism into the theatre curriculum in their institutions, but I suspect this is still a relatively small percentage. (I am not speaking here about advanced seminars in feminist dramatic theory for a select group of graduate students or courses on drama taught by committed feminists in English or Theatre departments who share their convictions within the safety of their tenure, but rather about "typical" courses in a "typical" curriculum.) Do most American drama survey classes, for example, still include Lillian Hellman as their sole female representative, with perhaps a nod to Megan Terry or Pulitzer Prize winners Beth Henley and Marsha Norman? Will Holly Hughes's subversive *The Well of Horniness,* a work that, in Lynda Hart's words, is coded "to empower lesbian spectators," even be mentioned? Will plays by African-American women such as Adrienne Kennedy be taught as part of the core of American drama? Broadening the query of American study: Will Sue-Ellen Case's *Feminism and Theatre* or Jill Dolan's *The Feminist Spectator as Critic* or any of the other provocative books and articles in this bibliography become required reading in the "typical" college theatre class? Will instructors introduce their students to feminist performance art's potential for deconstructing gender roles? Will Hélène Cixous's brilliant *Portrait de Dora* show up on the syllabus of a contemporary world drama course? Obviously, my questions—and aspirations for pedagogic reform—are endless.

I remain inspired by the concept of theatre as a vehicle for *change*. This is certainly not an original concept, if one thinks back to Brecht—or to any political theatre, for that matter, including the earliest suffrage plays. However, this topic is now being addressed in a serious, theoretical manner by women whose feminist discourse in theatre has become widespread currency. For example, as I mentioned earlier and will discuss in greater detail in the Introduction, there is the prospect of theatre as a "laboratory" for feminist change (explicated by Case and Dolan, among others). But change can be excruciatingly slow, and living through the last decade of political leadership in this country, with its reactionary treatment concerning both women and the arts, has been disheartening at times.

My hope is that this bibliography will contribute to the ongoing investigation into the nature of feminist drama, performance, and theatre, and the feminist critique of nonfeminist work, as well as the re-visioning of how we look at, teach, practice, and criticize our cultural productions. I hope, too, that it will inspire other feminist playwrights, helping to provide them with the courage to face the still overwhelming odds of attaining production and to confront their own mixed feelings about separatism and working in the mainstream.

Acknowledgments

❖
❖

Dramatic Re-Visions could not have been completed without the intellectual stimulation, reasoned feedback, emotional support, and research and clerical assistance from many individuals.

I want to express my gratitude to two remarkable women: Jean Vik, whose meticulous research proved invaluable during the final months of this project, and Sherry Searcy, who helped generate the Name and Title indexes. For their efforts in tracking articles and correct citation information, my thanks to Karen Temple, Janice Weiss, Beth Dandy, Jennifer Stephens, Lizz Roberts, Julie Watkins, Penny Reichard, Deborah Peifer, Meg Swanson, Tamara Bailey, Jean Bormett, and Arlene Arp. Jane Moss graciously clarified material pertaining to feminist theatre in Quebec. And Kendall lent her expertise in refining the Categorical Index.

The staff at the Richardson (Texas) Public Library gave above and beyond the call of duty. Librarians at Texas Woman's University's Blagg-Huey Library and the Dallas Public Library valiantly attempted to locate elusive items. In addition, I want to express my appreciation to countless reference librarians around the country who responded to my telephone inquiries. The search for ISIS publications was aided by R. Russell Maylone, Curator, Special Collections, Northwestern University Library.

At Texas Woman's University School of Library and Information Studies, Dr. Bernie Schlessinger's knowledgeable advice and enthusiasm sustained me throughout the initial stages of this project. It was also at TWU that I learned about the American Library Association's Whitney-Carnegie Grant, which provided funding for the annotated bibliography.

Once the American Library Association accepted my work for publication, Tina MacAyeal, my first editor, offered energetic faith in this undertaking and provided specific guidelines and information. Bonnie Smothers brought insight and objectivity to the book; her detailed notes on the draft of the Introduction evidenced her perceptiveness. Mary Huchting manifested a concern for detail which matched my own. I greatly enjoyed my long-distance friendship with all three editors.

I received invaluable input, encouragement, and feedback from many members of the Women and Theatre Program of the Association for Theatre in Higher Education, including but not limited to Jill Dolan, Judy Stephens, Gayle Austin, Rhonda Blair, Vicki Patraka, and Judith E. Barlow. Judith Piper and Marilyn Waligare at the University of Texas at Dallas answered my request for comment on the Introduction. Judith Piper also applied her keen intelligence in assisting in the reformulation of the Subject Index.

Several telephone calls to Canada elicited immediate responses to questions or supplied much-needed materials. I thank particularly Rota Herzberg Lister, pioneering feminist and founding editor of *Canadian Drama,* Jack David at ECW (publisher of *Canadian Literature Index*), and Sandra Haar of *Fireweed.*

Immeasurable gratitude goes to my husband Bill, for his unswerving support, willingness to accompany me to various libraries, and hours of proofreading; my fourteen-year-old son Jeremy, for his weeks of painstaking work, ranging from hunting down library materials to filing, proofreading, hole-punching, and fixing me endless glasses of iced tea—activities that took away from progress on his own book; and my nine-year-old daughter Paige, for her patience as I worked at my computer, her reordering of pages, and her excellent efforts at the copy machine. Finally, I wish to acknowledge my parents for their continuous encouragement throughout the vicissitudes of my careers.

Introduction

❖
❖

Theoretical and Historical Background

One is not born, but rather becomes, a woman. (267)
> —Simone de Beauvoir, *The Second Sex,* 1949

When a system of power [patriarchy] is thoroughly in command, it has scarcely need to speak itself aloud; when its workings are exposed and questioned, it becomes not only subject to discussion, but even to change. (58)
> —Kate Millett, *Sexual Politics,* 1970

Feminism implies that we recognize fully the inadequacy for us, the distortions, of male-created ideologies, and that we proceed to think, and act, out of that recognition. (207)
> —Adrienne Rich, "Conditions for Work: The Common World of Women," 1976. Rpt. in *On Lies, Secrets and Silence,* 1979

Feminism is the political theory and practice to free *all* women: women of color, working-class women, poor women, physically challenged women, lesbians, old women, as well as white economically privileged heterosexual women. Anything less than this is not feminism, but merely female self-aggrandizement.
> —Barbara Smith, 1979, talk given to NWSA Convention (quoted in Moraga and Anzaldúa 61)

Feminism defines itself as a political instance, not merely a sexual politics but a politics of experience, of everyday life, which . . . in turn enters the public sphere of expression and creative practice, displacing aesthetic

1

hierarchies and generic categories, and which thus establishes the semiotic ground for a different production of reference and meaning. That we see in feminist critical writings and other artistic practices, such as women's filmmaking. I would argue, in this regard, that the feminist critical text, the rereading against the grain of the "master works" of Western culture and the textual construction (written, filmic, etc.) of discursive spaces in which not Woman but women are represented and addressed as subjects, possessed of both a specificity (gender) and a history, is an original "cultural creation" of feminism; more, perhaps, than a new genre of (critical/fictional) creative expression, it can be thought of as a new aesthetic, a rewriting of culture. (10)

—Teresa de Lauretis, "Feminist Studies/Critical Studies," 1986

Feminist Criticism and Drama/Performance/ Theatre: The Development of a New Discourse

The five disparate quotations above, spanning almost forty years, contain the seeds of feminism's intersection with the multifaceted cultural product we call theatre. They also suggest the increasingly complex discourse that has come to characterize feminist theoretical writing on drama and performance. Patricia Meyer Spacks has noted that "feminist criticism faces a larger task than competing modes usually undertake: the task not only of enforcing new ways of seeing, but also of discovering new ways of saying" (16). Words, then, will be the place where I begin this introduction. Decisions must be made. *Which* words should I use? emphasize? define? redefine? Which issues will most succinctly convey the foci of feminism and theatre? The task is complicated by the multiplicity of perspectives informing the criticism.

Feminist Discourse

A feminist discourse employs words previously used in nonfeminist discourse as well as words created by necessity in forging new ground.[1] There are newly coined words such as "gynocritics"—the type of criticism focusing on the woman as writer.[2] And there are old words with emotionally charged association, such as "patriarchy," a term upon whose definition feminists are not always in agreement, but that refers

1. Teresa de Lauretis has interpreted the notion of a feminist discourse as "a configuration of rhetorical and interpretive strategies, a horizon of possible meanings that may be agreed upon as constituting and defining feminism at a given historical juncture...." ("Feminist Studies" 4).
2. "Gynocritics," used by Elaine Showalter in "Toward a Feminist Poetics," an essay first appearing in 1979, "begins at the point when we free ourselves from the linear absolutes of male literary history, stop trying to fit women between the lines of male tradition, and focus instead on the newly visible world of female culture" (*New Feminist Criticism* 131).

generally to the male control of family and society.[3] In addition, combinations of old words—such as "sexual" and "politics"—have spawned new meaning. In Kate Millett's ground-breaking book, she broadened the use of "politics" to "refer to power-structured relationships, arrangements whereby one group of persons is controlled by another" (23) and applied it to male-female relationships. As the criticism in this bibliography attests, "sexual politics" has been variously interpreted.

Obviously, some words are key in the project of feminist re-vision. As suggested by Millett's definition of sexual politics, one word consistently used or implied is "power." The issues that "power" entails include who assumes it, how it is wielded, how it is challenged, and how, as a concept, it is embedded in a society's ideology.[4] Annette Kolodny talks about "an acute and impassioned *attentiveness*" to how primarily male structures of power are encoded within our "literary inheritance." (For "literary inheritance" one can easily substitute "theatrical inheritance.") She points to the consequences of that encoding for women (as characters, readers, writers), "and, with that, a shared analytic *concern* for the implications of that encoding not only for a better understanding of the past but also for an improved reordering of the present and future" ("Dancing" 162). Reviewing feminist books on Shakespeare, Burton Hatlen discerns five fundamental assumptions regarding gender relationships and power. He concludes with the most significant, "an explicitly *moral* assumption: that inequalities of power are *wrong*, and that the domination of one human group by another inevitably warps the humanity of both groups, instilling habits of self-denigration in the subordinate group and a blindness to their own limits among members of the dominant group" (246).[5] Beyond doubt, power is a crucial issue in feminist criticism. But power is also the subject of other contemporary critical

3. According to Tuttle, "the personal is political" slogan of the women's movement reflects the impossibility of separation between private and public life in the patriarchal tradition: "It will never be enough for women to achieve economic and political equality if that equality is not reflected within the very structure of the family" (101). Maggie Humm remarks that no matter what historical form patriarchal society has taken, "a sex-gender system and a system of economic discrimination operate simultaneously. Patriarchy has power from men's greater access to, and mediation of, the resources and rewards of authority structures inside and outside the home" (*Dictionary* 159). Ania Loomba has recently noted: " 'Patriarchy', at best a functional term useful for referring to those social structures and ideologies that contribute to the subordination of women, has lately been dislodged from the status of a transhistorical and unitary phenomenon which was accorded it by varieties of essentialist feminism—the ongoing (and by no means conclusive) attempts to combine class and gender analysis have dismantled it into a historically and culturally variable, complex and even contradictory amalgam of institutions and attitudes" (1).

4. Gayle Greene and Coppélia Kahn define ideology as: "that system of beliefs and assumptions—unconscious, unexamined, invisible—which represents 'the imaginary relationships of individuals to their real conditions of existence' (Althusser 1971, p. 162); but it is also a system of practices that informs every aspect of daily life—the clothes we wear, the machines we invent, the pictures we paint, the words we use" (2–3).

5. The first four are (1) "gender relationships shape the character of human existence as deeply as—if not more deeply than—any other single force"; (2) "gender relationships are always inherently political," involving the power of one over the other; (3) these inequalities of power, at least in Western culture, have "issued in a legally and culturally sanctioned domination of men

discourses, such as the "new historicist" approach employed by numerous Renaissance scholars.[6] "Patriarchy" appears in almost all writing on the early modern period and in much dramatic criticism through the present. Even "sexual politics" has been utilized by writers whose intentions are not necessarily feminist in nature.

Feminist discourse on drama, performance, and theatre encompasses more than a few specific words or slogans—more than one way of "re-visioning." It critically reviews the entire theatrical apparatus, including our inherited beliefs of what "theatre" is and a recognition of its specific meaning in the historical moment. This discourse investigates previous and ongoing representations of the female as "object" *and* representations of the female as "subject."[7] It scrutinizes women's participation and authority (or lack of participation and authority) in the production process, and it raises new possibilities for women's critical and subversive abilities as readers and spectators. Feminist discourse reflects on the process of feminist collaboration in the development of a play. It deals with the challenge of explicating nontexted feminist scripts. It explores the differences between male and female in every theatrical context—not only in the debated psychoanalytical sense of "sexual difference" but also in practical terms: how men and women are directed to perform, read in the text, and treated by the critics. In addition, feminist discourse recognizes the differences *among* women and how these differences bear on the creation, presentation, and reception of the dramatic event.

A perusal of treatises on "feminism" will quickly prove that there is no universally accepted definition. Similarly, there is no single, unchallenged "feminist criticism," and certainly, *there is no one way of approaching the intersection of theatre and feminism.* Gayle Greene offered a framework for feminist criticism in a 1981 *Women's Studies* issue on Shakespeare:

> Feminist criticism is not necessarily criticism written by women or about women—though, of course, it may also be this. It is criticism which presupposes a feminist perspective, a perspective that both originates from

over women"; and (4) "the effects of these patterns of gender relationship infuse all the cultural products of any given historical epoch, so that any analysis of a cultural phenomenon which fails to take 'sexual politics' into consideration will necessarily remain incomplete" (245–46).

6. Peter Erickson clarifies a major distinction between feminist and new historicist approaches: "A significant difference remains between a position that asserts that the construction of genders is one among many factors, and a position that acknowledges gender is not the only factor but nonetheless claims it as absolutely central. The former will suspect the latter of overemphasizing gender, while the latter will suspect the former of not taking gender seriously enough" (329).

7. In the preface to *Technologies of Gender*, de Lauretis states that "a development may be seen to have taken place . . . with regard to the understanding of feminism as a radical *rewriting*, as well as a rereading, of the dominant forms of Western culture; a rewriting which effectively inscribes the presence of a different, and gendered, social subject" (xi).

and participates in the larger effort of feminism—the liberation of women from oppressive social structures and stereotypes. (30)

At its most basic level, Gayle Austin points out in her recent *Feminist Theories for Dramatic Criticism* that

> a feminist approach to anything means paying attention to women. It means paying attention when women appear as characters and noticing when they do not. . . . It means paying attention to women as writers and as readers or audience members. It means taking nothing for granted because the things we take for granted are usually those that were constructed from the most powerful point of view in the culture and that is not the point of view of women. (1–2)

Teresa de Lauretis comments in "Sexual Indifference":

> The question of address, of who produces cultural representations and for whom (in any medium, genre, or semiotic system, from writing to performance), and of who receives them and in what contexts, has been a major concern of feminism and other critical theories of cultural marginality." (168)

A synthesis of these statements, combined with the quotations that headed the introduction, reveals that women (or gender) and women's relationship to the society in which the cultural (artistic) product is produced provide a crucial focus of feminist inquiry. However, as Greene suggested, just because something is written by or about women does not make it feminist. Feminist criticism and theory (occasionally referred to as the "feminist project") are inseparable from political realities and the political goals of feminism. Maggie Humm asserts that "the growth of the feminist movement itself is inseparable from feminist criticism. Women become feminists by becoming conscious of, and criticising, the power of symbols and the ideology of culture" (*Feminist Criticism* 4). And in Tania Modleski's words: "The ultimate goal of feminist criticism and theory is female empowerment" (136).

The Interdisciplinary Nature of Feminist Research and Influences on Feminism and Theatre

Feminist criticism in all fields has developed and changed through the past two decades. While theatre emerged relatively late as a site of feminist research, it has produced an impressive body of work. My intention is to trace some of the means by which feminism has intersected drama (the text), performance (the act), and theatre (the institution, the working conditions, the historical record of symbolic communication organized as "theatrical events").[8] I use the unwieldy "drama/ performance/theatre" because each component, while interdependent with the others, is not identical to them. For example, performance criticism looks upon the text as simply one element in its investigation of complex processes that constitute the work as a whole.

Before addressing drama/performance/theatre criticism specifically, some general background about the interdisciplinary nature of feminist research is in order.[9] In the introduction to a 1989 special issue of *Modern Drama,* editors Jeannette Laillou Savona and Ann Wilson, writing about this phenomenon in which different fields enlighten one another, assert that

> both notions of "oppression" and "dominant ideology" informing its various approaches have produced important new theories in such diversified fields as political science, anthropology, sociology, philosophy, history, psychoanalysis, narratology, literature and the cinema. . . . They all seem to have two features in common. On the one hand, they strive to dismantle, or destabilize existing dominant viewpoints which have consistently ignored, devalued or silenced women. On the other, they attempt to create alternate visions and processes of thought which are meant to modify and even revolutionize so called "fundamental" knowledge in all disciplines. (1–2)

Annette Kuhn has written on the interdependency between politics and knowledge: "In the ordinary way, the link between them will often go unnoticed or be taken for granted; where feminism is concerned, however, this is impossible, precisely because knowledge has had to be self-consciously produced alongside political activity" (1–2).

It would be impossible to trace here all the influences on feminist criticism of drama/performance/theatre. The women's movement in the late 1960s had its initial impact on literary criticism, which would in turn affect the development of dramatic criticism, a phenomenon that

---

8. Josette Féral distinguishes three essential foundations of performance: "They are first, the manipulation to which performance subjects the performer's body—a fundamental and indispensable element of any performing act; second, the manipulation of space, which the performer empties out and then carves up and inhabits in its tiniest nooks and crannies; and finally, the relation that performance institutes between the artist and the spectators and the work of art, and between the work of art and the artist" (171).

9. An excellent example is afforded by Judith Butler's "Performative Acts and Gender Constitution: An Essay in Phenomenology and Feminist Theory," which editor Sue-Ellen Case chose to include not only in a 1988 *Theatre Journal* but in her 1990 compilation, *Performing Feminisms.*

preceded the more recent, growing body of performance theory.[10] Notably, feminist literary criticism infiltrated the halls of academe far earlier than feminist theatrical discourse. Maggie Humm claims that Simone de Beauvoir's *The Second Sex* and Kate Millett's *Sexual Politics* "appropriated literature for feminism" (*Feminist Criticism* 21). Showalter similarly notes that in the United States the literary and academic women who created a feminist criticism had participated in the 1960s women's movement and shared its activist commitment and sense of communal effort. She states that *Sexual Politics*, "the first major book of feminist criticism in this country, was at the same time a work of literary analysis and of impassioned political argument" ("Introduction," *The New Feminist Criticism* 5).[11]

According to Humm, feminism addresses three problems in literary criticism: a gendered literary history (addressed by reexamining male texts and noting their assumptions), the creation of a gendered reader (by offering her new methods and a fresh critical practice), and the creation of "new communities of writers and readers supported by a language spoken for and by women" (*Feminist Criticism* 14–15). Many feminist theatre critics have adapted such feminist literary devices as "reading against the text"—a way to avoid reading male texts in conventional fashion. The "resisting reader" may be transformed into the "resisting spectator," avoiding, in Jill Dolan's words, "the manipulation of both the performance text and the cultural text that it helps to shape" (*Feminist Spectator* 2).[12]

Special notice must be paid to the voluminous feminist work in Shakespearean criticism, much of which is included in this bibliography.[13] One might imagine that early feminist scholars desired to retain the investment of years studying Renaissance literature. (Although the problem of eliminating indoctrination by usually male professors and mentors is one beyond the scope of this introduction, it warrants mention.) A more important reason for the interest in English drama of the early modern period resides in the possibilities for gender examination that arise from the cross-dressing in the plays—particularly the sexual

10. I am certainly not dismissing performance criticism but am concentrating for the moment on the more prevalent dramatic criticism. A recent example of performance criticism appears in Judith Piper's review in *Theatre Journal* of Laura Farabough's *Bodily Concessions*. Piper cites Farabough's well-known iconographic and physical theatrical experimentations, wherein "sculpted objects, paintings, stylized dance, gestures, and narrative" combine to render her political aesthetic that "the body is the physical expression of the confines of culture; the body may also be an interpreter of that reality . . ." (261–62).

11. Sue-Ellen Case offers reasons for the comparative "tardiness" of the application of the feminist critique to university theatre studies in *Performing Feminisms* (2).

12. The phrase "resisting reader" was coined by Judith Fetterley.

13. One should keep in mind Lynda E. Boose's contention that "given the elevated status that Shakespeare occupies in American academia, the status of particular social issues within the field and scholarly disputes over them are never 'merely academic' in scope, but inescapably political" (707).

ambiguities that present themselves when men portray women disguised as men, and the potential for denaturalizing what has been assumed to be fixed: i.e., sexual identity and sexual difference.[14] Recently, Dympna Callaghan has posited that "gender opposition is probably the most significant dynamic of Renaissance tragedy, and . . . the gender categories produced both within and outside the dramatic text are precarious and problematic" (3).

Ann Thompson, in "The Warrant of Womanhood," has delineated several varieties of feminist Shakespearean critics. These include the apologists, who demonstrate that his female characters are not stereotypes and who emphasize the portrayal of friendship between women. Importantly, in terms of this book, apologists' studies of productions have revealed not only phallocentric (male-centered) critics who depict unfairly a misogynistic Shakespeare but also biased directors and adaptors as well.[15] Other feminist critics work within the historical context, relating "the ideas about marriage and the role of women in the family found in the plays to a general shift in thinking . . . which seems to have occurred in this period . . ." (80). A third group has provided a body of work based in psychoanalysis, an approach that paradoxically has allowed "feminist critics to write about male characters and tragedy as well as about female characters and comedy" (83).

Feminist psychoanalytic approaches, which have investigated issues of identity formation and subjectivity, revising traditional notions with object-relations theory and reformulations of mothering, have provided another major influence on the formulation of feminist theories of drama/performance/theatre.[16] More specifically, psychoanalytic literary criticism, mentioned above in the discussion of Shakespearean study and manifested in the work of such feminist critics as the prolific Coppélia Kahn, influences many items annotated in this bibliography.

14. In a different yet related context, Annette Kuhn sees cross-dressing as commenting ironically "on the conflation of body, gender, gender identity and subjectivity." I quote her argument, geared toward cinema, at some length because it bears strongly on theatrical issues. She maintains that cross-dressing "highlights the centrality of gender constructs in processes of subjectivity and comments upon a culturally salient means by which a would-be fixed gender identity is marked and constructed. It subverts the construct, offering at the same time ironic comment on its status as convention. By calling attention to the artifice of gender identity, crossdressing effects a 'wilful alienation' from the fixity of that identity; it has the potential, in consequence, to denaturalise it, to 'make it strange'. Crossdressing, then, may denaturalise that phenomenon held in our culture to be most evidently and pre-eminently natural: sexual difference" (54).

15. While most literary criticism of Shakespeare has not dealt with production variables, as early as 1981 Irene Dash's *Wooing, Wedding and Power: Women in Shakespeare's Plays* addresses this issue. I will return to this subject later in the section "On the Development of Feminist Criticism in Drama/Performance/Theatre."

16. "Object-relations theory explicates the child's development into a person, stressing the construction of the self in social relationships rather than through instinctual drives. In this terminology, 'objects' include everything that the self perceives as not itself. That is, the maternal object is not the mother but the child's mental representation of its mother" (Gardiner 130). Works by Nancy Chodorow, Dorothy Dinnerstein, and Adrienne Rich have been particularly important in this area.

Of particular significance among the psychoanalytic approaches has been the "new French feminisms," as Elaine Marks and Isabelle de Courtivron coin them in their 1980 anthology.[17] Summarizing the French feminists' impact on American feminism, Janet Todd remarks that "in their project they conversed endlessly with dominant men," employing Derrida's linguistic playfulness and interacting with the psychoanalytical theories of Jacques Lacan, the Freudian revisionist, "who at this point made an overwhelming entry into feminist polemics" (51–52).[18] Although influential French feminists, including Hélène Cixous, Luce Irigaray, and Julia Kristeva, cannot be simply lumped together—their differences are manifold—still, their celebration of femaleness and the distinctiveness of women's writing, their investigations into the "deep structures of culture and language" (Todd 51) have proven enormously influential (even though interpreting the mystical and dense style characterizing their own communication is sometimes difficult). The notion of *l'écriture féminine* (writing the body) has been hotly debated. Cixous urges in "Laugh of the Medusa": "Women must write through their bodies, they must invent the impregnable language that will wreck partitions, classes, and rhetorics, regulations and codes, they must submerge, cut through, get beyond the ultimate reserve-discourse . . ."(256). Despite the argument that this position is essentialist (i.e., based on the premise that there is an innate, uniquely feminine essence), it has been applied not only to the study of dramatic literature but even to performance. For example, Jane Moss, who has studied Quebec feminist theatre, relates *l'écriture féminine* to the "re-presentation" of the female body on stage "to be exposed, demystified, reclaimed, rehabilitated and reintegrated" (5).[19]

In addition to literary and psychoanalytical feminist theories, the impact of feminist film criticism on feminist theatre discourse cannot be

---

17. Elaine Marks and Isabelle de Courtivron generalize that the French feminists emphasize the difference between male and female more than Americans do, and note that one of the greatest focuses is on the description of woman's pleasure, "from Annie Leclerc's deification of woman's body to Monique Wittig's deconstruction and reconstruction of the lesbian body, from the post-Lacanian analyses of Luce Irigaray to the revised imagery of Hélène Cixous" (37).

18. In discussing the French feminists, Ann Rosalind Jones summarizes one aspect of Lacan that is particularly significant in terms of the development of feminist theories of drama and performance. "Lacanian psychoanalysis, extending Freud's exposure of the unconscious conflicts at work in any supposedly sovereign subject, intersects with certain deconstructive insights in its theory of the gendered speaking subject. For Lacan too the unified human subject is always a myth" (82–83).

19. Savona and Wilson discern that the division between French and American feminisms is reflected in the special issue of *Modern Drama* (1989), in which articles focusing on French plays show their search for "a new feminine theatrical language often based on the premise of sexual difference. The notion of gender, perceived by many American feminists as an oppressive sociopolitical construction underlying patriarchy, seems noticeably absent from the French playwrights studied (except for Michèle Foucher and Simone Benmussa). Most of them explore subversive forms of theatrical language through an assertion of the female body or the maternal experience or metaphor" (3).

underestimated.[20] This body of work, itself influenced by semiotics (the study of signs) and Lacanian psychoanalysis, has provided a vocabulary and approach for theatre feminists regarding notions of spectatorship, the "male gaze," and the female body as object. Barbara Freedman summarizes and expands these concepts for theatre:

> Since the male is traditionally envisioned as the bearer of the gaze, the woman represented as the fetishized object of the gaze (Mulvey), the gaze itself emerges as a site of sexual difference. The classic cinematic gaze splits us into male (voyeur) and female (exhibitionist). . . . Insofar as classic theatre incorporates not only spectacle but narrative—so that the male is represented as a mobile agent as well as a bearer of the gaze, the female as the object to be actively transformed by him—action as well as sight has implications for the study of gender ideology. (380)

Gayle Austin has devoted a chapter of her recent book to feminist film theory, applying Laura Mulvey's thesis of "man as bearer of the look" and ideas of scopophilia and narcissism to an analysis of Sam Shepard's *Tooth of Crime.*

Work in other fields such as history, sociology, and anthropology has influenced the discourse as well.[21] For example, the notion of "sex roles" was used by sociologists to define the social functions traditionally filled by men and women. When feminist theorists appropriated the term, the meaning changed, and "instead of considering the sex-role as something naturally dictated by biology, feminist analysis saw it as an assignment from society which linked certain psychological characteristics (such as aggression or passivity) with anatomical sex" (Tuttle 294). Gender, on the other hand, may be defined as "the socially imposed division between the sexes . . . the emotional and psychological attributes which a given culture expects to coincide with physical maleness or femaleness" (Tuttle 123).[22] Interestingly, one of the most frequently cited references in the criticism of drama/performance/theatre has been anthropologist Gayle Rubin's essay, "The Traffic in Women: Notes on the 'Political Economy' of Sex," in which she coins the term "sex/gender system," meaning "the set of arrangements by which a society transforms biological sexuality into products of human activity,

---

20. Among the notable theorists in this field are Teresa de Lauretis, E. Ann Kaplan, Annette Kuhn, and Laura Mulvey.

21. In fact, in 1990 *Women & Performance: A Journal of Feminist Theory* published a special issue on "Feminist Ethnography and Performance."

22. De Lauretis, in *Technologies of Gender*, proposes four considerations. In brief, they are: (1) "gender is (a) representation"; (2) "the representation of gender *is* its construction—and . . . high culture is the engraving of the history of that construction"; (3) the construction of gender continues today everywhere from the media to the family to the academy and avant-garde art and even in feminist theory itself; (4) "the construction of gender is also effected by its deconstruction; that is to say, by any discourse, feminist or otherwise, that would discard it as ideological misrepresentation" (3).

and in which these transformed sexual needs are satisfied" (159).[23] (The significance of "sex/gender roles" in the feminist criticism of drama/performance/theatre is reflected in the Subject Index to this bibliography, which includes four subheadings for this term: "deconstruction of," "rejection of," "reversal," and "satirized.")

Women, Theatre, and Culture

The traditionally male-dominated art of theatre provides a venue for feminists that is both particularly powerful and threatening to a male hegemony in the arts as well as in society as a whole. For example, Elin Diamond discusses cultural signs "that artists in the theater, perhaps more than in other areas, are best able to tackle, for the crucial medium of the theater artist is the performer's body that enters significations as soon as she/he steps on stage" ("Theoretically" 6).[24] In patriarchal society, women have been confined to the private sphere, yet theatre is the most public of arts—an arena from which for centuries women were excluded, unable even to portray female characters. Lesley Ferris makes a critical point in her recent book, *Acting Women:*

> Argument and discussion over the nature of women appears as one of the great recurrent themes of Western drama. . . . The controversy over women is an issue fundamental to the very nature of theatre, for the mimetic art of acting has produced the greatest of imaginative leaps required by the spectator: the theatrical illusion involved in witnessing men playing women. "Femininity," as a feminist theory has soundly argued, exists as a cultural and social construction; central to that construction, as far as the illusionistic art of theatre is concerned, remains the fact that women had absolutely no part in their own dramatic image-making. (19)

Even when women have been able to perform in certain cultures, "their bodies have generally been viewed as less capable of transformation than those of men, and sexual attractiveness, rather than the skills and techniques of effective disguise, has been regarded as their most essential talent" (Greenhalgh 172).

23. As summarized by Maggie Humm, Rubin uses insights from Freud, Lacan, Marx, and Lévi-Strauss to argue "that all societies organise the biological differences between men and women into specific social arrangements. This common sex-gender system is characterised by an asymmetrical exchange in which men always exchange women and not ever the other way around. Further, this sexual division of labour ensures that the interests of men, not women, are met in the act of exchange" (*Dictionary* 202).

24. Sue-Ellen Case and Jeanie K. Forte's comments in "From Formalism to Feminism" are also pertinent: "Relegated to the position of object, women have been exploited by the system of representation, serving only as boundaries of the male identity. To the extent that the stage is a reflection of this system of representation, the stage becomes a crucial arena for revealing this exploitation of women" (64).

Furthermore, theatre (as well as feminist criticism of it) is an art that demands *voice*. As recognized by feminist critics, Western culture has long prized women's silence as an appropriate attribute of "femininity." To find "our own voice" is a term repeatedly employed in feminist theatre discourse since its inception. Lynda Hart points out that theatre is the sphere most removed from domestic confinement, and that although the woman playwright who risks being heard here takes "a greater risk than the woman poet or novelist . . . it also offers her greater potential for effecting social change" (*Making a Spectacle* 2).[25]

Feminists working in theatre during the past two decades cannot be easily categorized. Their goals run a full range, from trying to raise the percentage of women's participation as playwrights, directors, designers, and high-ranking administrators in mainstream theatre to changing "not only theatrical conventions but society itself by bringing a feminist consciousness to bear on both the content and the form of drama" (Tuttle 320).

Hart and Tuttle echo the concerns quoted earlier in this introduction, particularly Greene's "the larger effort of feminism" and de Lauretis's "a rewriting of culture." One must not underestimate the importance of *effecting societal change*—as any political theatre intends—a point to which I will return in the section on the current status of feminism and theatre. As a political movement, feminism is committed to social transformation, not only advocacy of women's rights. As a theoretical approach (or, rather, a variety of theoretical approaches) feminism has had an uneasy but strengthening alliance with theatrical practice in the pursuit of this goal.[26]

A Summary of Feminist Issues Surrounding Drama/Performance/Theatre

Although a remarkably rich diversity of concerns marks the theory and criticism cited in this work as well as the actual texts and productions analyzed, there are many underlying common threads. This is not to imply that every book or article will address all of the following issues; indeed, some will take different, even *opposing*, attitudes. It is important to keep in mind that not only is feminist criticism interdisciplinary and eclectic but emphases vary according to the author's atten-

25. Many feminist scholars have discussed women's earlier success in writing novels (a private activity) contrasted to the difficulty of women playwrights' being heard. One practical condition that has interfered with an increased number of productions by women involves problems surrounding their participating in the production process (a public activity).

26. Teresa de Lauretis suggests that "theory is dialectically built on, checked against, modified by, transformed along with, practice—that is to say, with what women do, invent, perform, produce, concretely and not 'for all time' but within specific historical and cultural conditions" ("Left Hand of History" 23).

tion to text or performance. For example, those critics of performance art, which arose largely from the visual arts, will often be more concerned with the body—the physical, the nonverbal—than with the scripted text. Therefore, this list of aspects of feminist criticism is not intended to be inclusive but to suggest the range of investigation.

> The reclaiming of women whose contributions have been erased by male domination in the art of theatre and the recording of their history. The entire issue of who decides what constitutes the *canon*—the inherited list of "masterpieces" in traditional studies.[27]
>
> A sensitivity to women's oppression under a variety of societal and political structures, particularly capitalism, and the manifestations of this condition in drama and criticism.
>
> Attempts to undermine the privileging of the male viewpoint on stage and in criticism and the concomitant marginalization of women. Awareness of depictions of female protagonists in a "relational identity"—e.g., wife, daughter, "woman behind the man"—both in the plays themselves and in criticism of these works.
>
> The illumination of female experience through theatrical performance. The call for woman as a speaking subject; the female body as "politicized space."[28]
>
> The breaking of sexual taboos—what is talked about, what is not. Bringing to the forefront the recognition of women's sexuality and rejoicing in it.[29]
>
> The rejection of "compulsory heterosexism"—the premise that women do not have the freedom to choose their sexual orientation, the assumption of heterosexuality as the sole "norm,"

27. Humm defines "canon" as "a term for the list of literary *master*pieces in traditional literary studies. The canon is an informal institution of literature whose specific inclusions and exclusions, deletions and exceptions are nowhere codified" (*Dictionary* 23). In her introduction to *Modern American Drama: The Female Canon*, Schlueter comments that in the past twenty years the revisionist approaches of deconstruction and expansion "have been successful at opening a canon that the academic community once presumed closed and in questioning its admission standards" (11). Another challenge to the idea of canon is reading the canonized texts in "heretical ways," as noted by Margaret Ferguson and other editors in the introduction to *Rewriting the Renaissance* (xxi). According to Karen Newman: "The task of a political criticism is not merely to expose or demystify the ideological discourses which organize literary texts, but to *reconstitute* those texts, to reread canonical texts in noncanonical ways which reveal the contingency of so-called canonical readings, which disturb conventional interpretations and discover them as partisan, constructed, made rather than given, natural, and inevitable" (157).

28. Lynda Hart notes: "If the female body is at the root of male fear, the blank space that he must master, then it also has great power for the woman playwright as a medium for articulation" (*Making a Spectacle* 6).

29. The French feminists' use of *jouissance* is pertinent here. Ann Rosalind Jones remarks that *jouissance*, rich in connotations, is "the catalyst of a critical mini-industry. 'Pleasure' is the

and "the enforcement of heterosexuality for women as a means of assuring male right of physical, economical, and emotional access" (Rich, "Compulsory" 647).

An understanding and analysis of the social production of gender and how it has affected attitudes toward and the reception of live performance. The subversion of received idea(l)s of "femininity" and of sexist myths. The demystifying of what has been viewed as "natural."

The deconstruction of "Woman" (i.e., woman as a social construct, part of a patriarchal system of representation).[30] Explorations of the idea of woman as object, sign, or "Other," both in script and in production. Simultaneously, recognition of differences *among* women, in areas including race, class, and sexual preference.[31]

The reassessment of issues of spectatorship such as "the male gaze" and the (female) performer's body. Investigating "what does looking have to do with sexuality? With masculinity and femininity? With power? With knowledge?" (Kuhn 6).

The question of the existence of a feminist aesthetic or female sensibility that informs dramatic work by women, whether individual or collective.

A recognition of the connections between cultural productions—here, theatrical events—and the social, historical, and political conditions in which the text was written and/or performed.[32]

Again, I underscore that there is no *one* feminist criticism of drama/performance/theatre, no discrete ideology that places its stamp of approval on this body of writing.

Feminist writing on drama/performance/theatre ranges from narrowly focused critiques of the patriarchal structures informing canonized plays—e.g., pointing out the ways in which women have been

---

simplest translation. The noun comes from the verb *jouir*, to enjoy, to revel in without fear of the cost; also, to have an orgasm" (108n). The editors of *New French Feminisms* explain that the word is used by Hélène Cixous "to refer to that intense, rapturous pleasure which women know and which men fear" (95n).

30. For a complex treatment of this subject, see Butler's essay dissecting gender as constituted—a "performative act" within specific cultural conditions.

31. Of note is Luce Irigaray's oft-quoted title, "Ce sex qui n'en est pas un" or "This Sex Which Is Not One." The pun is significant. Not only is female sexuality multiple rather than singular but, because *"the feminine occurs only within models and laws devised by male subjects,"* there are not actually two sexes, but only one (86).

32. Helene Keyssar offers this perspective: "Meaning is made in the theatre by the interaction of two or more forms of communication (or semiotic systems). The performed drama is understood as simultaneously entire unto itself and part of the whole culture; the cultural material from which the drama is created is repeatedly mediated and revised as it interacts with the playwright, the performers, and, finally, the audience" (456).

oppressed by men—to praise of collaboration and collectivity in women's dramatic creations. It ranges from interviews in which women reflect on their depiction of female characters to theoretical essays attempting to rethink the theatrical apparatus and its relationship to gender. An example of the latter is Nancy Reinhardt's analysis of the politics of stage space and its connection to the male-defined *polis*, in which she discusses the reservation of stage center for men in the tragedy and serious plays of ancient, medieval, and early modern times. Noting that this has to do with the public nature of theatre, she argues that "tradition assumes for the most part a male audience and tends to create sexual imagery only for men" (375).

In combatting the notion of a sometimes unshakably patriarchal theatre, the issue of a feminine aesthetic or sensibility has been repeatedly addressed. According to Jan Stuart's introduction to articles by Maria Irene Fornes and Tina Howe in *American Theatre*:

> Women playwrights continue to ask the same questions in 1985 that troubled them in 1975: Is there a women's aesthetic that is distinct from men's? Do women censor themselves to get produced? Is there a different critical vocabulary that is used in addressing plays by women and plays on similar topics by men? What distinguishes a feminist perspective from a woman's perspective? (11)

On the other hand, in "The 'Woman' Playwright Issue," a collection of responses and objections to Mel Gussow's 1983 *New York Times* story on contemporary women playwrights, Anne Cattaneo asserts:

> I find the question of whether or not there exists a women's aesthetic in playwriting far less pressing than I did five or six years ago. I suspect that this is because it is an issue that may only exist when one is contemplating an aesthetic yet to come into being, a potentiality rather than a real body of work. . . . As the seasons have passed and the number of plays written by women has grown, it seems to me that the range of work is now so wide that the pretense of any unified aesthetic, the appearance even of an affinity of sensibility or style in the work of women writing today has been happily destroyed. (Austin 99)

As late as 1987, in their preface to the revised *Women in American Theatre*, Helen Krich Chinoy and Linda Walsh Jenkins list questions, including the existence of female aesthetic, still central concerning women and theatre. Below is an excerpt:

> Where do women fit in? Where can they make a living, have a career, and create authentic theatre art from women's lives? Is there a feminine sensibility in theatre creation? Is it the result of nature (some essential female

quality) or of nurture (the socialization that makes us feminine or masculine)? Do women directors approach their tasks in markedly different ways from the practices of male directors? Do women view the sacrifices and spoils of conventional success as men do? Can they or should they try to break the "Broadway barrier"? Do women playwrights have something special to say as women, not just as individual artists? Do they create in a distinctive way, use unique forms, speak a long-silenced "mother tongue"? (xii)

The topic continues to be debated through the date of this bibliography's publication. As far as I can foresee, any resolution is unlikely.

This brief survey of the dispute over a "female" or "feminist" aesthetic or sensibility makes obvious the need for some discussion of what constitutes "feminist drama" or "feminist theatre." Before embarking on that task, however, it is necessary to lay out the underlying dynamics that inform feminist approaches to theatre and determine the artist's and the critic's assessment of whether the product is, indeed, "feminist."

Types of Feminisms

Recognition of differences among the "feminisms" is crucial to understanding the various aims and approaches of feminist critics, theorists, and practitioners.

Political Feminisms

As reflected in the Subject Index as well as in the annotations themselves, several leading feminist writers in theatre and performance— Sue-Ellen Case and Jill Dolan in delineating American feminisms and Michelene Wandor in discussing the British variations—have differentiated among three main political dynamics informing the work: liberal (bourgeois), radical (cultural), and materialist (socialist).

Although the terms may differ somewhat from critic to critic, they generally have been used as indexed (in the Subject Index) and as indicated below. I wish to caution against oversimplification. In practice these tendencies or dynamics may overlap; furthermore, specific artistic works and critical approaches preclude neat pigeonholing. As Wandor points out in "Culture, Politics and Values," each feminist dynamic has both strengths and weaknesses. And in *Carry On, Understudies,* she emphasizes their similarities:

(1) All three tendencies seek to bring about some sort of change in the position of women. (2) All three tendencies challenge both the idea and the fact of male dominance. (3) All three tendencies assert the importance of self-domination for women. (131)

Keeping in mind the caveats, I will briefly summarize the three main political approaches.

1. *Liberal (bourgeois) feminism:* Here the emphasis is on women's equality with men. Liberal feminists in theatre have fought to gain more employment and positions of greater authority while working within the existing system. The liberal approach is reflected in the formation of such organizations as The Women's Project at the American Place Theatre. Dolan acknowledges that liberal feminists' persistent endeavor "to make visible the once-hidden talent of women in theatre has been primarily responsible for the growing number of women playwrights working in the professional arena" (*Feminist Spectator* 19). However, objections to this position have arisen because of its acceptance of the world as it is (Wandor, *Carry On, Understudies* 134). Liberal women playwrights have been criticized for buying into a system that has historically excluded them, because producing successfully for mainstream theatre means conforming to a model of "universality" that is still phallocentric.

2. *Radical (cultural) feminism:* Case employs the term "radical" feminism, identifying it as the predominant position in the United States, "based on the belief that patriarchy is the primary cause of the oppression of women" (*Feminism and Theatre* 63–64). On the other hand, Dolan uses "cultural" feminism for that branch whose analysis reifies "sexual difference based on absolute gender categories" (*Feminist Spectator* 5). Subjects addressed under this designation often include the idea of a female or feminist aesthetic and the difference between female and male writing (e.g., male style as linear, female style as circular). Criticism of this dynamic has come in the form of attacks against its "essentialism," which stresses not only the differences between women and men but often women's superiority, and its seeming inversion of the model of sexist values. It has also been recognized, however, that women working from the position of radical feminism were responsible for some of the earliest feminist theatre groups, including separatist lesbian companies organized for and by lesbians and playing to all-female audiences.[33]

33. Case's discussion of radical feminism in *Feminism and Theatre* (75–81) includes a description of lesbian acting and work toward a lesbian aesthetic.

3. *Materialist (socialist) feminism:* Although there are differences among materialist, Marxist, and socialist feminism, "materialist feminism" is used by Case and others as an umbrella term to distinguish it from liberal feminism and radical feminism. Case, Dolan, and Wandor, as well as many other contemporary theorists and critics, operate basically from this stance,[34] which sees gender as a culturally constructed product and analyzes the material conditions of production, proposing "changes both in the position of women as women, and in the power relations of the very basis of society itself" (Wandor, *Carry On, Understudies* 136). Dolan identifies the materialist feminist project in theatre as being "to disrupt the narrative of gender ideology, to denaturalize gender as representation, and to demystify the workings of the genderized representational apparatus itself" (*Feminist Spectator* 101). Moreover, Wandor explicitly argues in "Culture, Politics and Values" that "only socialist feminism can offer an analysis which provides for genuine, revolutionary change" (446).

It is from this position that such issues as class, race, and sexual preference have received the greatest treatment in the area of theatre.[35] As Linda Walsh Jenkins has observed:

Elaborate social, political, and economic systems have been constructed that separate, stereotype, and privilege or oppress not only according to sex, but also according to skin color, occupation, money and property ownership, beliefs, dialects, and other such factors. These systems, based on difference and privilege, are manifest in the material culture; all who participate in theatre (whether creators, audience, or teachers) must examine *how* theatre aids, challenges or "revisions" them. ("Matrix" 371)

Additional Perspectives

In addition to the three political positions outlined above, women theatre scholars and practitioners are also working from the perspectives of women of color and lesbians.

While "women of color" is defined by Kramarae and Treichler as a positive term, "designating women of many different ethnic and racial heritages . . . and emphasizing commonalities, sisterhood, and shared

34. What Austin says in her introduction to *Feminist Theories* seems to hold true for a number of individual women I have encountered as well as for the Women and Theatre Program of the Association for Theatre in Higher Education in general. She states: "My personal journey has taken me from the simple desire to see more female images on the stage and move more women into the mainstream of American theater, to a particular interest in women's playwriting, to a passion about the much broader issue of how drama and theater operate to represent women on the stage. In a political sense, I have moved from the position of liberal feminist to that of radical and then materialist feminist . . ." (3).

35. However, Loomba points out in the introduction to her 1989 book on Renaissance drama: "Sensitivity to race, class and gender in feminist criticism, despite being on its agenda for some time, is still in its infancy" (1).

oppressions," it has also been suggested that it "obscures diversity and specificity and lumps all racial and ethnic groups together, thus facilitating the tendency in language to universalize" (499). Case cogently points out: "Separating the position of women of colour from other feminist positions ghettoises these women and their work as they have been ghettoised traditionally. Ideally, the work of these women would be grouped with that of others around 'colour-blind' issues. The same might be said about the treatment of lesbian women. . . . However, women of colour have identified their position as a discrete issue within feminism, challenging the presumed homogeneity of voice and vision within the movement" (*Feminism and Theatre* 96).[36]

The reclaiming of black American women playwrights has been an expanding project. However, in contrast to black literary criticism, much of the writing pertaining to theatre has been more of a survey in nature than work incorporating feminist theory.[37] There are exceptions, of course, particularly in studies of Adrienne Kennedy's plays, analyses that demand a consideration of the interconnections of race and gender identity as well as of Kennedy's nonrealistic, highly imagistic dramatic techniques.

Yvonne Yarbro-Bejarano is notable for her numerous contributions to literature on Chicanas in theatre. In one article, "The Female Subject in Chicano Theatre: Sexuality, 'Race,' and Class," she explores the shift in female representation from the early texts embedded in cultural nationalism to more recent woman-centered and nonnarrative alternatives, including *Tongues of Fire*—a *teatropoesía* creating a collective female subject—and Cherríe Moraga's presentation of the Chicana lesbian "as desiring subject" in *Giving Up the Ghost*.[38] In an article centering on Moraga, Yarbro-Bejarano applauds her courageous and polemical

36. For first-hand visions by feminist women of color, see *This Bridge Called My Back: Writings by Radical Women of Color,* edited by Cherríe Moraga and Gloria Anzaldúa.

37. Barbara Smith's much-reprinted 1977 essay, "Toward a Black Feminist Criticism," represents one of the earliest attempts to break the "massive silence" surrounding black feminist criticism and black lesbian writers: "It is galling that ostensible feminists and acknowledged lesbians have been so blinded to the implications of any womanhood that is not white womanhood and that they have yet to struggle with the deep racism in themselves that is at the source of this blindness" (157). A more recent challenge to feminist literary criticism—and by extension, to feminist dramatic criticism—comes from Gayatri Chakravorty Spivak, who discerns a problem in American feminist criticism's "identification of racism as such with the constitution of racism in America" (81). She sees as the necessary object of investigation "not only the history of 'Third World Women' or their testimony but also the production, through the great European theories, often by way of literature, of the colonial object. As long as American feminists understand 'history' as a positivistic empiricism that scorns 'theory' and therefore remains ignorant of its own, the 'Third World' as its object of study will remain constituted by those hegemonic First World intellectual practices" (81–82).

38. Cherríe Moraga has said in an interview: "I feel that feminism which takes seriously the specific kinds of oppression suffered by women can also within that context take into consideration how class and racism complicate and increase the kinds of oppression suffered by women. The kind of movement that incorporates all those things is feminism to me. It has been my experience that unless you keep sticking in the word feminist, and I usually say that I'm a Chicana feminist, it is the first word to go in the context of another movement" ("Interview" 132).

writing "in both the Chicano and the feminist communities. Speaking from the position of one who is both lesbian and Chicana, she breaks taboos about sexuality and calls for a critique of sexism and homophobia in Chicano culture; within the feminist community she analyzes the racism and classism of the White women's movement and continues the dialogue on sexuality and sexual styles" (113).

Other theatre critics working from lesbian perspectives have addressed issues from both radical and materialist positions.[39] Lesbian theory's intersection with theatre has been particularly striking in the "re-visioning" of performance. For example, in "The Actor as Activator: Deconstructing Gender through Gesture," Sande Zeig explains the genderization of gestures according to two sex class systems, and argues for the lesbian actor's ability to influence contemporary theatre through gender-neutral presentation.

In summary, both lesbian feminist approaches and work by and about women of color challenge a concept of a unified feminist voice (i.e., white, middle-class, and heterosexual).[40]

A Multiplicity of Approaches?

Underlying the "feminisms" described above are varying attitudes pertaining to women's commonalities and differences. Perhaps the most productive feminist approach to the creation and analysis of drama/performance/theatre is one that admits of possibilities and values in *all* the perspectives. Lynda Hart, discussing problems surrounding canonization and practical decisions regarding course syllabi and anthology formations, concurs.

Avoiding formulations based on biological determinants that link all women writers together and flatten their multiplicities into a homogeneous mass is absolutely necessary. At the same time, however, we are reluc-

39. Here, too, the work began earlier in literary criticism. See, for example, Bonnie Zimmerman's "What Has Never Been: An Overview of Lesbian Feminist Literary Criticism," in Showalter's anthology, *The New Feminist Criticism* (200–224), reprinted from a 1981 issue of *Feminist Studies*. Savona and Wilson point out the impact of lesbian theories on feminist approaches to theatre, as in Adrienne Rich's analysis of the connections between compulsory heterosexuality, patriarchy, and women's oppression (both spiritual and economic), as well as her notion of a "lesbian continuum" (3–4). One should note, however, that this proposal of a "lesbian continuum," which Rich defines as "a range—through each woman's life and throughout history—of woman-identified experience" ("Compulsory" 648), has been criticized as seeming to include all women or being universalizing; other theorists have posed narrower definitions.

40. For further discussion, see pages 10–11 in de Lauretis's *Technologies of Gender*. Linda Alcoff offers a thoughtful examination of cultural feminism's definition of "women" and poststructuralism's rejection of the category and the necessity of transcending the limitations of each approach in an impressive 1988 *Signs* article. She proposes that "we can say at one and the same time that gender is not natural, biological, universal, ahistorical, or essential and yet still claim that gender is relevant because we are taking gender as a position from which to act politically" (433).

tant to give up the idea of women as a community; and we do so, I think, at our political peril. The problem can, and must, be successfully negotiated. Feminists are at risk when we reinstate a new either/or—the multiplicity of women's experience, differences between and among women, *or* women as a cultural community. We need both, but we must work together to challenge each other's tendencies to construct oppositional accounts of either. ("Canonizing" 279)

In addition, Elin Diamond, summarizing work in semiotics and psychoanalytic theory that demystifies cultural myths, citing differences between French and Anglo-American feminisms, and noting the importance to her own work of materialist analysis, argues that the vitality of cross-influences is needed "to conduct a gender critique that is not going to slip back into valorizing an ideologically normative identity" ("(Theoretically)" 6).[41]

Colliding Opinions: Attempts at Determining Definitions of "Feminist" Theatre and Drama

Depending on the individual critic's criteria, certain works, either by a single playwright or by a collective, have been considered feminist or not feminist; certain groups, composed of women, have also been considered feminist or not feminist. The immense variety and continuing development of feminist theatre(s), performances, and plays preclude a definitive answer. However, one of the purposes of this book is to provide access to the full range of views on what might constitute feminist drama/performance/theatre.

Feminist Theatre

"What is a feminist theatre group?" is a question that has been dodged as well as confronted head-on in the books and articles annotated in this work. The history of feminist theatre is not greatly argued. In the United States, for example, most writers acknowledge that the avant-garde 1960s theatre and the resurgence of the women's liberation movement—particularly in its consciousness-raising techniques—

41. Kolodny's notion of a "playful pluralism" rather than a prescriptive approach to some ideal nonsexist canon has received much attention, both positive and negative, as detailed by Showalter in the introduction to *The New Feminist Criticism* (13). In "Dancing through the Minefield," Kolodny writes that "our task is to initiate nothing less than a playful pluralism, responsive to the possibilities of multiple critical schools and methods, but captive of none, recognizing that the many tools needed for our analysis will necessarily be largely inherited and only partly of our own making" (161). Savona and Wilson point out that the only solution to the problem of feminist ventures starting from questionable sources or methodologies "is to proceed cautiously though a perpetual method of self-questioning and dialogue with others" (2).

combined to produce groups devoted to exploring and presenting women-centered issues.[42] My research has shown that most of the early writing on feminist theatre groups emphasized their collaborative approaches to creation, their experimentation with theatrical form, their attempts to avoid the hierarchical organization of male-dominated theatres (even the experimental theatres), and their special relationships with audience members.

Patti Gillespie's 1977 survey broadly describes feminist theatre as referring to "groups representing a wide range of theatrical, political, and sexual ideologies but sharing some degree of affiliation with feminism" ("Listing" 22). In another article, which focused on feminist theatre as a rhetorical phenomenon, Gillespie discerns that despite various groups' differences, they seem to share two convictions: "that women in this society have been subjected to unfair discrimination based on their gender, and that theatre can provide a least a partial solution to certain problems arising from such discrimination" ("Feminist" 286). In a 1987 essay on feminist theatre in Britain, which reflected the increased integration of feminist theoretical discourse into the writing about feminist theatre, Noëlle Janaczewska defines feminist theatre as "a form of theatre that incorporates an understanding of the social construction of femaleness and some analysis of the interactions of gender, class and power. . . . [T]his awareness is manifest in the content, form, perspective and processes of that theatre. . ." (107).

A number of writers, including Janaczewska, have commented that all "women's theatre" is not necessarily "feminist theatre." Not every theatre group composed of women has called itself "feminist." (For example, although the Omaha Magic Theatre has rejected that label, it is the home of feminist playwright Megan Terry and produces many plays widely considered feminist.) Therefore, the term in and of itself is not enough to distinguish a "feminist theatre" from a "women's theatre." Certainly, there are points of connection: Women make up all or most of the membership in both cases, and women are the focus of attention. Helen White considers theatre for or by feminists a subgenre of women's theatre, which she defines as "a vehicle for women's communication and creativity" (107). However, as Susan E. Bassnett-McGuire contends in "Towards a Theory of Women's Theatre," although reviewers tend to use the terms interchangeably, a distinction does exist. The following quotation reflects Bassnett-McGuire's British orientation, but it is applicable to feminist theatres elsewhere:

---

42. In England, much of the new feminist drama emerged from socialist theatre groups. Keyssar notes that "drawing from those origins, [they] either focused on local, topical issues presented in the form of social realism or took a didactic, Brechtian approach to problems such as birth control, economic equity and marriage" (459).

"Feminist theatre" logically bases itself on the established concerns of the organized Women's Movement, on the seven demands: equal pay; equal education and job opportunities; free 24-hour nurseries; free contraception and abortion on demand; financial and legal independence; an end to discrimination against lesbians and a woman's right to define her own sexuality; freedom from violence and sexual coercion. These seven demands, of which the first four were established in 1970, and the remainder in 1975 and 1978 show a shift towards a more radical concept of feminism that asserts female homosexuality and perceives violence as originating from men. The tendency therefore is not so much towards a re-evaluation of the role of women within society as we know it, but towards the creation of a totally new set of social structures in which the traditional male-female roles will be redefined. (447-48)

She has more difficulty defining "women's theatre"—theatre that deals with women's issues and perspectives, but that may still offer traditional statements about female identity or treat subject matter in traditional fashion. Eventually she ends up questioning whether the phenomenon of women's theatre is not an oxymoron—whether theatre itself is indeed *male* (462). Recently, Barbara Freedman has also questioned whether there can even be a feminist theatre, or if it is a contradiction in terms (378).

In terms of this bibliography, groups that have considered themselves or been treated as feminist by those writing about them, whether or not the groups conform to other critics' definitions of feminist theatre, have been included and indexed accordingly. (For additional information, see the introduction to the Categorical Index.)

Feminist Drama

Definitions of feminist plays have ranged around interrelated issues that include plot, themes, rhetoric, intention, and particularly form. Janet Brown's 1979 book provided an early working definition within a Burkean framework: A play is feminist when its central rhetorical motive is woman's struggle for autonomy within an unjust sociosexual hierarchy. While her definition aroused some dispute, it was significant as an early effort to formulate a theory that would help distinguish and validate feminist drama. In contrast, Rosemary Curb has rejected a narrow definition for what she calls "woman-conscious drama"—an encompassing term covering "all drama by and about women characterized by multiple interior reflections of women's lives and perceptions" (302). Acknowledging that it may be called feminist, lesbian, or postmodern, or eschew labels, she discusses its subversive potential in reflecting women's confinement and oppression, recognizing women's memories and visions, and representing women's conditioning to be complicit in their own diminishment (316). In short, its intention or at least its "subversive potential" seems to coincide with that of the feminist project in theatre.[43] Helene Keyssar argues that feminist drama's most distinctive attribute is "its resistance to traditional recognition scenes as the centerpost of dramatic structure." Rather than the pivotal finding of one's "true self," in feminist drama transformation (the process of change) is central, i.e., "there is no fixed, true self but human beings in the constant process of becoming other" (458).

Many themes are treated in feminist drama; in addition to women's oppression in a patriarchal society, there is an abundance of work on rape, mother-daughter relationships, rediscovered women in history, women and madness, lesbianism and "coming out," female-male relationships, and the opportunities for empowerment through female solidarity.

However, the treatment of such themes does not in itself establish the play's "feminism" for every feminist critic. Keyssar observes that "any serious approach to contemporary women's theatre must attempt to distinguish between productions that are merely elements of a new phase of the dominant culture and those that are genuinely emergent cultural forms" (454). She argues that in the 1980s American audiences could accept images of change in women's roles and gender relationships "as long as they celebrated the superwoman and the martyr but representations of angry women, of lesbian women and of men and women in transition have been minimalized by the concerted efforts of women and men to return to 'traditional American values' " (459). Keyssar uses Marsha Norman's Pulitzer Prize-winning 'night, Mother as a case in point, terming it "a product of the dominant culture," incorporating enough elements of the emergent feminist theatre to be mistaken for it while creating no disturbance in the social order (459).[44] Although Keyssar acknowledges the greater offerings of "women's drama" in England, she concludes that even a festival of "typical" plays by British women "would provide an education in women's issues and would have a palpable coherence of tone and commitment, but would cause no disturbance in the theatre or the culture" (460).

---

43. Jenkins interprets Curb's category as recognizing "the bind of gender polarity" but honoring women and bringing to the stage "the language of female experience" ("Matrix" 374).

44. Jill Dolan uses the same play to study the "gender-biased politics of reception" and canon formation in *The Feminist Spectator as Critic*. She recalls her initial negative review of 'night, Mother, which she saw "as coopted into a scheme of male dramatic and ideological values," and offers her current thinking that the play is typical of liberal feminist drama (35). She goes on to say that (like most typical American drama) its focus on individual suffering and "unwillingness to discuss Jessie's dilemma in terms of a wider social context make it weak as a political statement and inadequate from a materialist feminist perspective" (36).

With theme disallowed as the determining factor, the matter of form takes on greater significance. Early articles, mostly in women's periodicals, at first just observed how *different* were the offerings by women's groups (again, whether collectively or individually written) from those in mainstream theatre. In 1980, in *Feminist Theatre Groups,* Dinah Leavitt provided a list: "Plotless, circular, layered, poetic, choral, lyric, primal, ritual-like, multi-climactic, surreal, mosaic, collage-like and non-realistic are the terms often used to describe the bulk of feminist drama" (98). As theory has become more intricate and critics have adopted more politically sophisticated vantage points, the issue of form—which ties into the feminist aesthetic controversy discussed earlier—has become a heated focus.

Perhaps the most pressing question is whether realism is a usable (or "acceptable") form for the feminist playwright or director. In other words, can a play be both realistic *and* feminist? Is a realistic play "feminist" when it deals with issues of critical concern for women, features an all-female cast, or provides strong female role models? For a defense of realism's usability, the reader should consult Judith Stephens' "The Compatibility of Traditional Dramatic Forms and Feminist Expressions." However, the voices of critics of realism have been loud, indeed. In fact, this issue affected much of the discussion in the Women and Theatre Program "preconventions" in the late 1980s.[45] For a summary of some of the arguments against realism, see Jeanie Forte's recent essay in *Modern Drama*'s special "Women in the Theatre" issue. Forte explains that classic realism "supports the dominant ideology by constructing the reader as a subject (or more correctly, an 'individual') within that ideology" ("Realism" 115). As realism is "a reinscription of the dominant order," it bears no use for feminists wishing to subvert the patriarchal social structure (116). In that same issue, Elin Diamond's "Mimesis, Mimicry, and the 'True-Real' " analyzes feminist theatre theorists' interest in mimesis, which "posits a *truthful* relation between world and word, model and copy, nature and image or, in semiotic terms, referent and sign, in which potential difference is subsumed by sameness" (58). Diamond clarifies feminist resistance to theatrical realism, which itself "is more than an interpretation of reality passing as reality; it *produces* 'reality' by positioning its spectator to recognize and

45. These conferences precede the Association for Theatre in Higher Education's annual convention. Two specific articles that present a historical perspective on the contributions of this organization to the development of feminist criticism are Rhonda Blair's "A History of the Women and Theatre Program" and Judith L. Stephens' "Women and Theatre Program: Reactions and Reflections," both of which appear in the 1989 special issue of *Women & Performance: A Journal of Feminist Theory*.

verify its truths" and "mystifies the process of theatrical signification" (60).[46]

Much critical analysis has dealt with Hélène Cixous's *Portrait de Dora*. Its fragmentation of Freud's narrative and defiance of "the traditional system of representation which negates woman's sexual voice" (Case and Forte 65) have been heralded as hallmarks of exemplary feminist work. (The Subject and Title Indexes will provide the user with plentiful examples of criticism of this acclaimed play.)

On a practical level, the question of form—particularly realism—is associated with problematic issues surrounding women writing for mainstream theatre. Even aside from issues of the play's reinforcement of the dominant (nonfeminist) ideology, the question remains: Is it possible for a play to be feminist if the material conditions of production entail full participation in a male-dominated system?[47] Can a play be feminist when it excludes feminist spectators? As Jill Dolan points out about *'night, Mother*, there is little extant feminist press response available, in part "because Broadway prices generally keep these productions inaccessible to those outside a comfortable income bracket and therefore might not be of interest to many feminist press readers" (*Feminist Spectator* 36).

The relationship of feminist playwriting to feminist criticism is well articulated by Lynda Hart, whose words I borrow to end this section.

Language, space, and the body are loci for the woman playwright to dramatically challenge the images of women determined in dominant discourses. Not one, but all of these sites must be re-visioned for the feminist enterprise to succeed onstage. As more and more women begin to choose the stage as an arena for their visions, we, as critics, are called upon to discuss, analyze, and demonstrate their efforts. Our efforts combined are clearing public spaces for the foregrounding of women's realities. (*Making a Spectacle* 13)

---

46. Diamond's essay is far more intricate than can be summarized here. Suggesting that perhaps "mimesis can be retheorized as a site of, and means of, feminist intervention" (62), she considers Irigaray's reconfigurations of mimesis as mimicry and Kristeva's concept of the hysterical body's "true-real." She writes: "Why make this effort to recuperate mimesis? Because it tends, I think, to recuperate us. It is better perhaps to acknowledge certain mimetic desires, to militate for the complex, the *different* referents we want to see, even as we work to dismantle the mechanisms of patriarchal modeling" (62).

47. For a fuller consideration of the issue of feminism and mainstream theatre, I recommend Jill Dolan's second chapter in *The Feminist Spectator as Critic*. Another complication in the feminist-mainstream controversy stems from the fact that some women playwrights reject the label "feminist" despite the fact that their plays show a vision that many critics would easily accept as clearly feminist.

On the Development of Feminist Criticism in Drama/Performance/Theatre

A number of authors have remarked upon the relative slowness of dramatic criticism to develop or to acknowledge and incorporate feminist theories from many other disciplines.[48] Once again, an analysis of feminist literary criticism provides a good starting point.

Precedents in Literary Criticism

In the past decade, literary critics such as Elizabeth Abel and Elaine Showalter have formulated "stages" of feminist criticism. In *Writing and Sexual Difference*, Abel provides the following outline:

> Initially, feminist theorists bolstered claims for equality with claims of similarity. This perspective found expression in literary criticism which focused primarily on blind spots in male texts, cataloged masculine stereotypes of women, and documented the transmission of rigid and exaggerated notions of sexual difference. Feminist readings, overtly polemical, typically progressed from text to author to society in order to explain the limited array of female roles in literature. As feminist theorists began to reconceptualize sexual difference to women's advantage, however, feminist literary criticism shifted its focus to the reading of texts by women. Female experience displaced male bias as the center of analysis. . . . Recently, analyses of sexual difference have stressed interrelationship as well as opposition, difference *between* as well as difference *from*. Feminist critical attention has shifted from recovering a lost tradition to discovering the terms of confrontation with the dominant tradition . . . . [F]eminist critics now often strive to elucidate the acts of revision, appropriation, and subversion that constitute a female text. (1–2)

Showalter, in her introduction to *The New Feminist Criticism: Essays on Women, Literature, and Theory*, also traces three stages. In summary:

> The intellectual trajectory of feminist criticism has taken us from a concentration on women's literary subordination, mistreatment, and exclusion, to the study of women's separate literary traditions, to an analysis of the symbolic construction of gender and sexuality within literary discourse. (10)

---

48. See Austin's introduction to her book and my article in *Women & Performance*. As late as 1989 Hart states that "an abundance of books are now available about women poets and prose writers, while feminist critics still have much ground to break in our explorations of women's theatre" (*Making a Spectacle* 1).

27

Taking a slightly different approach, Wendy Frost and Michele Valiquette's introduction to *Feminist Literary Criticism: A Bibliography of
Journal Articles, 1975–1981* distinguishes two currents of feminist literary criticism: that of the alternative feminist culture and that of critics
working within the academy. They note that in the academy the earliest
feminist endeavors examined stereotypes of women in work by men,
concluding that they helped reinforce sexist stereotypes internalized by
women. The next move was to include women's writing in the curriculum, thereby paralleling the alternative feminist culture in moving from
using "the insights and techniques of consciousness-raising to expose
the political implications of mainstream cultural representations of
women. . . to a search for authentic representation" (15). Their ensuing
discussion of questions surrounding the canon and the realization of a
need for theory in feminist criticism warrants reading.

Feminist Criticism and Shakespeare—The Overlapping of the Literary and the Theatrical

One of the best-known analyses of the stages of feminist Shakespearean criticism is by Carol Thomas Neely. In "Feminist Criticism in
Motion" she acknowledges that her outline derives from the models of
feminist history proffered by Joan Kelly and Gerda Lerner. Neely's stages
include the compensatory—the study of assertive women characters as
a worthy project; the justificatory—the emphasis on women's oppression by a patriarchal society; and the transformational—the examination of "the multiple interactions between the commanding heroines
and the confining culture" (75) and "the relationship between gender
roles and generic structures" (76).

In analyzing the development of Shakespearean feminism, Claire
McEachern finds that until recently it "divided itself—and
Shakespeare—into two seemingly incompatible camps" (269). Pioneering critics viewed Shakespeare as "proto-feminist," with a commitment
to the portrayal of liberated women. Subsequently, this approach was
rejected as naive; the exposure of "patriarchal assumptions and structures that govern his drama and marginalize or contain its female energies" was substituted (270). McEachern sees problems in both
approaches because they posit a mimetic/deterministic relationship between art and society. She points out that more recent investigations
probe the "often contradictory, competing play of cultural texts" that
generates the "proto-feminist/patriarchal polarity" and reveal that patriarchy is not monolithic (270).

Significantly, several feminists associated with Shakespearean literary criticism have recently considered the idea of subversion through
production, expressing greater interest in the role of performance in

interpreting Shakespeare. For example, Joyce Wexler's 1988 article on *The Winter's Tale*, "A Wife Lost and/or Found," shows how Hermione's and Leontes' reunion does not necessarily have to be staged as displaying a reconciliation. She remarks that the text makes available several alternative versions of the ending, "but a performance can impose the director's interpretation. Because it recreates the circumstances of speech, drama offers a more fully defined context than the written text" (116). Kathleen McLuskie and Elaine Showalter are among others who have recently addressed the issue of performance.[49]

Drama/Performance/Theatre

From this point on, I will address the development of criticism specifically oriented to drama/performance/theatre, which in many ways parallels the path taken by feminist literary criticism. In its early stages, this writing attempted to correct traditional, phallocentric criticism (usually written by men), i.e., criticism that distorts or ignores female playwrights, the contributions of female performers, and the reactions of female audience members, as well as the significance of female characters in plays by men.

Many early works of "feminist" criticism (and some later ones as well) were not informed by a strongly grounded feminist theory, but attempted only to validate the importance of women as playwrights or to reexamine women's roles in the male canon in an investigation of these playwrights' feminism or antifeminism. For example, Caroline Lockett Cherry argues in her 1973 study, *The Most Unvaluedst Purchase: Women in the Plays of Thomas Middleton*, that Middleton's "female characters are the most impressive of the age in their variety, realism, and psychological insight" (208).

Although this kind of examination—what June Schlueter calls the "images-of-women approach" (*Feminist Rereadings* 12)—may still retain some value, interaction with other critical methods and other disciplines has resulted in an increasing complexity in the feminist discourse of drama/performance/theatre.[50] In my introduction to a bibliography published in *Women & Performance: A Journal of Feminist*

49. See McLuskie's "The Patriarchal Bard," which suggests the possibilities for reconstructing *Lear* in a production that subverts its misogynist meaning, and Showalter's proposal in "Representing Ophelia" that feminist revisions of Ophelia may come from the performer as well as from critics.

50. Schlueter finds its worth "as an expository device, designed to reveal the extent to which male-authorized fictional worlds portray mythical or stereotypical female characters and to which both author and reader, in failing to question those worlds, have endorsed the prevailing gender paradigm" (12). On the other hand, Judith L. Stephens remarks on the "outmoded" status of such criticism ("From Positive Image" 64).

Theory, a brief chronological survey of the materials is followed by this observation:

> Despite the complex strands of criticism and the multiplicity of "feminisms," the overlapping themes and diverse lines of inquiry shimmer into focus. We started with revision—the reclaiming of lost women, the reassessment of the canon for its treatment of female figures in Shakespeare or any lurking feminist tendencies in Ibsen's plays. At about the same time, we began to explicate, defend and analyze contemporary feminist performance and texts (e.g., publicizing and validating the work of feminist collectives in terms of process and product). We gradually began to employ deconstruction and other techniques to render a more rigorous discourse. Finally, among the most significant critical works of the mid- to late-1980s are those which have departed from studies of individual performers, groups, plays and playwrights to encompass a more theoretical approach, with suggestions for forming a new feminist theatre aesthetic. (119–20)

Other surveyors of the field have arrived at similar although not always identical assessments.[51]

Concentrating on American drama in "From Positive Image to Disruptive Apparatus," Judith L. Stephens writes that feminist critics have shifted focus from formalistic concerns to "concerns about mechanisms which tend to support or undermine conventional stage representations of women" (63). She notes the recent increased focus on "the discovery of a disruptive apparatus which offers feminists the possibility of a more fundamental challenge to conventional drama and its underlying assumptions" (63). Stephens provides several illustrations, including techniques that suggest a shared consciousness, the critique of the dominant ideology's ideas of self-determination, the questioning of assumptions about gender identity, and the challenging of "the very possibility of female *being* in patriarchy and hence, female representation in drama" (65). Similarly, Lynda Hart cites the change in the feminist perspective "from discovering and creating positive images of women in the content of the drama to analyzing and disrupting the ideological codes embedded in the inherited structures of dramatic representation . . ." (*Making a Spectacle* 4).

---

51. A footnote in Reinhardt's earlier publication, "New Directions for Feminist Criticism," presents a different chronology: "The first scholarly critical responses to the challenge of women's studies in theatre were from those who described and anthologized examples of the frontiers of the feminist-theatre movement. . . . The next step was for scholars to add a feminist slant to some recent biographical and sociological studies of women of the theatre, especially those caught in the star system. . . . Quite recently critics have begun applying a feminist perspective to great playwrights such as Shakespeare. . . . But these are, for the most part, thematic and character analyses, following the tradition of English literary criticism in which the text is primary" (385).

While this brief overview of the development of feminist criticism of drama/performance/theatre reinforces its diverse and expanding nature, one cannot help but wonder: How much criticism goes unwritten because feminist plays go unproduced or have been collaboratively produced and remain unscripted or have been produced in festival or workshop situations, and yet do not get published?[52]

The Publication History of Feminist Criticism and Theatre

In a work covering such a wide array of periodicals and books as *Dramatic Re-Visions*, parallels and distinctions must necessarily be drawn in tracing the history of publication of pertinent materials. Feminist periodicals of a nonacademic nature, many ephemeral and others, such as *Off Our Backs*, proving resilient, have covered theatre in a mostly minor fashion that has changed little through the years. The greater number of items in this bibliography come from scholarly journals, and their track is easier to follow. This is certainly not to suggest that feminist discourse has displaced phallocentric criticism within the academy (or for that matter, outside the academy), neatly shoving it aside; however, feminist concern with such issues as the social construction of gender has infiltrated the academy and its journals. In other words, the language and issues informing feminist inquiry are currently being employed in drama/performance/theatre studies—by both men and women—whose perspective is not necessarily "feminist." (I will return to this issue in the section below.)

In women's magazines or feminist newspapers, productions by feminist groups were reviewed sporadically almost from the beginning of feminist theatre. However, little has appeared in these publications tackling theoretical feminist issues surrounding theatre.[53] In addition to announcements of forthcoming productions, reviews of plays by individual women and collaborative projects, and interviews with members of feminist groups and women practitioners, writing on theatre in feminist nonacademic periodicals has often centered on discrimination against women in theatre and the efforts of specific organizations to

52. Keyssar reports a 1982 conversation with Michelene Wandor in which the latter asked whether publishers and producers reject plays by women or if the work does not exist in quantity and quality. While Keyssar had no definitive answer, she had conducted research showing "that there were hundreds of plays written by women in England and the United States that might get produced by a particular local company, 'off-Broadway' or on the Fringe and never get published. Data was beginning to emerge that showed that ten times as many plays by men were produced each year than by women and the publishing record was even worse" (452).

53. Dolan suggests: "Since the feminist canon is nascent at best, particularly in theatre, the feminist press tends to shy from the work and to concentrate instead on the woman" (*Feminist Spectator* 36).

provide greater opportunities for women's participation and recognition.

Whereas women/feminist/lesbian-focused periodicals as well as mainstream academic periodicals have offered some coverage of theatre since the early 1970s, theatre's late entry into the feminist project is again emphasized by contrasting the early establishment of feminist publications in other arts and literature: *Moving Out: Feminist Literary and Arts Journal* was begun in 1971, *Feminist Art Journal* was established in 1972, and *Camera Obscura: A Journal of Feminism and Film Theory* started in 1976. An informative discussion of early publication in feminist studies may be found in Cain, Hammell, and Pastine's "Library Research in Women's Studies," as well as in Frost and Valiquette's *Feminist Literary Criticism.*

In the following summary of the history of publication of materials on feminism and theatre, the chronological divisions provided are necessarily arbitrary.

From 1972 to About 1975

Despite the women's movement, which gathered steam in the late 1960s, subsequently affecting theatrical practice (as in the consciousness-raising techniques utilized by women's theatre groups), there was a notable lack of coverage of feminist theatrical enterprise in the general press and relatively little in specialized theatre journals. *The Drama Review* and, occasionally, other academic publications provided some peeps at the new feminist theatre, but these were infrequent at best. Somewhat more but still limited and erratic coverage was afforded by *Ms.* and other women's and feminist magazines. Although feminist periodicals began to reclaim women playwrights such as Aphra Behn, the far more dominant trend was the consideration of women characters in works by men. These studies appeared in a wide variety of scholarly periodicals. Even more noticeably, relevant books in these years ventured heavily into the reassessment of female characters in the male canon. Examples, all of which are annotated in the chapter titled "Feminist Reassessment of Men's Playwriting," include Marilyn L. Johnson's *Images of Women in the Works of Thomas Heywood* (1974), Malveena McKendrick's *Women and Society in the Spanish Drama of the Golden Age: A Study of the* Mujer Varonil (1974), Elizabeth Hardwick's discussion of Ibsen in *Seduction and Betrayal: Women in Literature* (1974), and especially Juliet Dusinberre's ground-breaking *Shakespeare and the Nature of Women* (1975).

From About 1975 to About 1980

These years saw a continuation of all of the trends described above, but particularly a flowering of Shakespearean criticism, mostly literary rather than theatre-oriented.[54] The influential collection, *The Woman's Part: Feminist Criticism of Shakespeare* (1980), edited by Carolyn Ruth Swift Lenz, Gayle Greene, and Carol Thomas Neely, examined both female and male characters and their relationship to social structures. Writers continued to approach other members of the male canon from a feminist perspective. For example, Rodelle Weintraub edited *Fabian Feminist*, a collection of essays on Shaw published in 1977.

The cataloging of women's and feminist theatre troupes and attempts to find common bonds among their endeavors made their way into a number of periodicals. As feminist inquiry began to infiltrate the work of academic theatre scholars (as opposed to literary scholars), a special issue of *Theatre News*, put out by the American Theatre Association in 1977, was devoted to "Women's Theatre."[55]

In a pioneering book on a pioneering woman playwright, Maureen Duffy offered *The Passionate Shepherdess*, a 1977 study of Aphra Behn. Publishers also began making collections of women's plays available, such as Honor Moore's *New Women's Theatre: Ten Plays by Contemporary American Women* (1977) and Rachel France's *A Century of Plays by American Women* (1979).

Most significantly, toward the end of this period two new books bearing single authorship boldly announced their feminism in theatre studies *not* focusing on the male canon: Janet Brown's *Feminist Drama: Definition and Critical Analysis* (1979) and Dinah Leavitt's *Feminist Theatre Groups* (1980).

From About 1980 to About 1985

During this time, criticism of Shakespeare and the early modern era became remarkably pervasive, with articles appearing not only in feminist journals such as *Signs* but in *Shakespeare Quarterly* and similarly established journals hardly noted for their feminist proclivities. (In fact, it has only been since 1984 that *Shakespeare Quarterly's* annual bibliography has included "feminism" as a term in its index to the previous

---

54. As early as 1978, the Modern Language Association of America offered a special session entitled "Feminist Criticism of Shakespeare" at its annual meeting.

55. This was a reflection of the formation of a women's caucus, which eventually became the Women's Theatre Program of the now-defunct American Theatre Association. As Rhonda Blair records, "The founding group believed that women as a class were not sufficiently included in ATA's governance and activities, particularly in terms of access to conference panels and the determination of their content. The first phase of the WTP was therefore geared toward increased integration of women into the mainstream of academic theatre and greater awareness of work being done by women in various theatrical venues" (5).

year's publications of Shakespearean criticism.) Among the abundance of significant books that did not simply reevaluate women characters in plays by men but contextualized their analysis within contemporary ideology and feminist issues such as sexual politics were Irene G. Dash's *Wooing, Wedding, and Power: Women in Shakespeare's Plays* (1981); Linda Bamber's *Comic Women, Tragic Men: A Study of Gender and Genre in Shakespeare* (1982); Lisa Jardine's *Still Harping on Daughters: Women and Drama in the Age of Shakespeare* (1983); Marianne Novy's *Love's Argument: Gender Relations in Shakespeare* (1984); Carol Thomas Neely's *Broken Nuptials in Shakespeare's Plays* (1985); Peter Erickson's *Patriarchal Structures in Shakespeare's Drama* (1985); and Catherine Belsey's *The Subject of Tragedy: Identity and Difference in Renaissance Drama* (1985).

Even more significant in terms of this bibliography, however, this period must be noted for its plethora of special issues of theatre publications based on either women in theatre or feminism and theatre. A year earlier, in fact, Rota Lister edited "Women in Canadian Drama," a 1979 special issue of *Canadian Drama*. The "Women and Performance" issue of *The Drama Review* appeared in 1980. A "Women in Theatre" issue of the British publication *Drama* came out in 1984, and in 1985 *Theatre Annual,* more scholarly in nature than *Drama*, produced an identically titled volume. What many feminists in theatre have come to call the "f word"—feminism—eventually appeared in the title of a special issue of *Canadian Theatre Review* (1985), "Feminism and Canadian Theatre," and the topic of "Staging Gender" was the subject of a *Theatre Journal* issue in the same year.

Whether such special issues of established (nonfeminist) journals constitute a kind of ghettoizing or simply fall into the same category as an issue devoted to, say, Brecht is controversial. While my own emotions remain mixed, I recognize that these special issues have been a necessity, gathering together multiple articles to manifest the extent of the work, articles to read both with and against one another. (That such special issues continue to be published on a frequent basis is apparent in Appendix III.)

In addition to the special issues, articles on feminist drama/ performance/theatre and feminist critical approaches to nonfeminist drama appeared more frequently in regular issues of mainstream theatre periodicals. Feminist periodicals also devoted special issues to theatre. The Canadian *Fireweed* produced two issues on performance in 1980, *Women's Studies* 9.1 and 9.2 (1981–82) focused on feminist criticism of Shakespeare, and *Heresies* offered "Acting Up: Women in Theater and Performance" in 1984.

Perhaps the most significant mark of the period, however, was the introduction in 1983 of a new semiannual periodical unambiguously entitled *Women & Performance: A Journal of Feminist Theory*. The initial editorial stated:

> We are tired of our absence from established media—an omission that prevents us from communicating. Creating this journal begins to give women a louder, more articulate voice everywhere in culture. *Women & Performance* will serve as a vehicle for discussion and analysis of our past, present and future activities. ("Editorial Voices" 3)

This journal has proved an invaluable forum for the feminist voice. Throughout the period covered by *Dramatic Re-Visions*, it remained the sole periodical consistently bridging feminist theory and drama/theatre/performance an unequaled source for researchers in the field.

An increasing number of articles that appeared during these years manifested concern with lesbian drama, black women playwrights, Chicanas in theatre, and attempts to find a theoretical framework for the new practice and scholarship. Whereas in the 1970s virtually nothing had appeared about women's excursions into performance art, in the 1980s this topic became an important factor in even the most traditional academic theatre journals.[56]

Several significant books provided overviews of feminism and its intersection with drama and performance. In 1981, Helen Krich Chinoy and Linda Walsh Jenkins produced their first edition of *Women in American Theatre: Careers, Images, Movements,* a compendium that would be expanded and updated in 1987. On the other side of the Atlantic, Michelene Wandor published *Understudies: Theatre and Sexual Politics*, later to be revised as *Carry On, Understudies* in 1986. Toward the end of the period, Helene Keyssar provided her wide-ranging *Feminist Theatre: An Introduction to Plays of Contemporary British and American Women*, and Elizabeth J. Natalle's *Feminist Theatre: A Study in Persuasion* offered a rhetorical perspective.

Books also were produced that dealt with feminism and historical theatre practitioners, such as Julie Holledge's *Innocent Flowers: Women in the Edwardian Theatre* (1981) and Albert Auster's *Actresses and Suffragists: Women in the American Theater, 1890–1920* (1984).

Methuen's yearly anthology of *Plays by Women*, featuring mostly British works, started in 1982, with the first four volumes edited and introduced by Michelene Wandor and the later volumes by Mary Remnant. A variety of other play collections were also published.

---

56. The 1983 publication of Moira Roth's book *The Amazing Decade*, annotated in the Performers/Performance Issues/Performance Art chapter, helped to publicize and validate feminist performance art.

From About 1985 to 1988

In the last few years covered by this bibliography, a surge of feminist writing in drama/performance/theatre encompassed theoretical issues and the development of a new feminist poetics. Moreover, all of the investigative trends that had begun earlier continued in various periodicals and in increasing proportions. Special issues included *Southern Quarterly*'s 1987 "Southern Women Playwrights," *Art & Cinema*'s 1987 "Work by Women," and *Theatre Journal*'s 1988 "Feminist Diversions."

Two influential although very different books by respected American feminist theatre theorists illuminated past feminist critical work and offered directions for the future: Jill Dolan's *The Feminist Spectator as Critic* and Sue-Ellen Case's *Feminism and Theatre*, both published in 1988. In addition, two collections of lesbian plays (separate from gay male works) claimed attention: Kate McDermott's *Places, Please! The First Anthology of Lesbian Plays* (1985) and Jill Davis's *Lesbian Plays* (1987). Interestingly, older works by women playwrights seemed increasingly anthologized in such volumes as Dale Spender and Carole Hayman's *How the Vote Was Won and Other Suffragette Plays* (1985); Bettina Friedl's *On to Victory: Propaganda Plays of the Woman Suffrage Movement* (1987); Judith E. Barlow's *Plays by American Women: Nineteen Hundred to Nineteen Thirty* (1985), a revised edition of her 1981 anthology; and Kendall's *Love and Thunder: Plays by Women in the Age of Queen Anne* (1988). Nor was there any lack of other, more contemporary anthologies of women's plays, including Margaret B. Wilkerson's *9 Plays by Black Women* (1986) as well as compilations of the works of individual feminist playwrights.

The history of the publication of feminist materials in drama/performance/theatre helps to demonstrate the great strides that have been made in this field as well as the diversity of venues. There will be users of *Dramatic Re-Visions* interested in the earlier, more "naive" studies of women in the male canon as well as users from a variety of disciplines other than theatre (women's studies, literature, and film, to name a few) who are more concerned with the aesthetic and theoretical issues presented in some of the more recent writing. It is hoped that through the use of the indexes, all users will be served.

Effects of Feminist Drama/Performance/Theatre Criticism, Current Status, and a Look to the Future

Among the contributions made by feminist criticism in general is the recognition of the multiplicity of interpretation and a striking body of studies showing that women matter.[57] Feminist criticism has affected what is known, questioned what is knowable, and changed notions of what is "appropriate" for scholarly attention.

In her recent compilation of feminist articles on performance, Case comments that feminist theory has brought to the academy and genre-based periodicals such as *Theatre Journal* "interdisciplinary work and a necessary bridging of scholarly study with the feminist social movement" (*Performing Feminisms* 3). She further states that questions have now been raised regarding the constitution of scholarship and epistemology, as the feminist critique "challenges the bourgeois code of manners that controls the kind of issues and materials that are suitable for study, bringing from the margins a variety of social transgressions into the halls of academia" (3). Ranging from lesbian representation to radical performance art and black folk theory, these subjects "push out the walls of the institution of theatre to a notion of performance . . . that blurs disciplinary and performative practices, metaphorizes practices, literalizes linguistic codes, and begs the very notion of what constitutes the topic of theatre" (3).

As far back as 1977, in "The Left Hand of History," de Lauretis underscored the necessary task of envisioning "a feminist theory of the process of textual production and consumption, which is of course inseparable from a theory of culture" (26). Citing Silvia Bovenschen's argument against a "feminine aesthetic" and her approval that no formal criteria could be definitively established for "feminine art," de Lauretis explained: "This enables us to reject the notion of artistic norms and facile labeling, and prevents cooptation and further exploitation of women's creativity" (26).

The theme of cooptation, exploitation, and appropriation has received attention in the 1980s. For Ann Wilson, the publication of the play itself is an act of appropriation by the dominant structure. In "The Politics of the Script," she demands that feminists working in theatre "fragment the authority of the script" and "assail the authority of logos" (175). Wilson discerns that feminist work is vulnerable to appropriation "because of the complexity of theatrical signification. To be deemed feminist it is not enough that a script deal with issues of concern to women nor that it subvert the formal conventions of linearity and closure. To be deemed feminist, a production should be born of a politically conscious theatre practice" (175). Wilson also goes on to state:

57. See Spacks' article, "The Difference It Makes," which centers on literary criticism, for further discussion of feminist criticism's diversity.

> Given that feminism is a political practice, it is important that we not lose sight of the material conditions of theatrical production. If the publication of a script marks its co-optation, it is the role of the critic to recuperate the script from its status as a commodity. The script which evolves from feminist theatre must never be accorded the status of a finished product for, if it is feminist, it is in process and is incomplete. (177)

Others have expressed fears about the appropriation of feminist *criticism* by that which it opposes. Neely finds that contemporary approaches to Shakespeare and Renaissance texts (new historicist, cultural materialist, Lacanian, and deconstructive) have actually appropriated, marginalized, or even erased the earlier feminist criticism (although they share areas in common). "All of the topoi of the new approaches. . . have the effect of putting woman in her customary place, of reproducing patriarchy—the same old master plot" ("Constructing the Subject" 7).[58] Neely suggests "over-reading" the texts with history, including the history of women (15).

Kathleen McLuskie comments on Neely's fears of the blurring of "the clear feminist commitment of earlier work" (*Renaissance Dramatists* 224). Emphasizing that problems still exist concerning reading the evidence of women's engagement with their culture (225), she suggests that "the relationship between women's experience and the construction of women in cultural representation is the most problematic area for feminist criticism. The feminist critic must place women at the centre of her enquiry, but feminist theory has taught her that 'women' is also an ideological category, the site of constant struggle" (227). Therefore, we can no longer simply view the representation of women on the Elizabethan stage (or any stage) as purely mimetic.[59]

The title of Annette Kolodny's 1988 article in *Chronicle of Higher Education* is in itself revealing: "Respectability Is Eroding the Revolutionary Potential of Feminist Criticism." She comments: "The male critics who would 'profess' feminism too often read only the same selective sampling, thus establishing for themselves their own 'feminist canon' and evading feminism's hard-won diversity of voices."

Undeniably, feminist discourse has infiltrated academe. However, as Dolan cautions in *The Feminist Spectator*, "the mainstream critical response to plays written by women continues to reveal deep-seated gender biases," and "mainstream criticism both shapes and reflects the

---

58. Boose makes a similar argument, particularly commenting on the dangers of new historicism.

59. McLuskie goes on to clarify: "The ways in which marriage and heterosexual relations held both the narrative structures of the drama and the institutions together may have been analogous but they were not the same" (338).

ideological workings of the dominant culture whose concerns it represents" (19).

We return here to my earlier emphasis on effecting social change, as well as the current theorizing about the interactionary process between theatre (art) and society. Helene Keyssar has written that "feminist theatre merits attention not because it addresses topical issues but because it encourages us to imagine a world transformed" (454). I am particularly intrigued by the notion of theatre as a laboratory.[60] As Dolan suggests: "If we stop considering the stage as a mirror of reality, we can use it as a laboratory in which to reconstruct new, non-genderized identities. And in the process, we can change the nature of theatre itself" ("Gender Impersonation" 10).

Case, in discussing possibilities for the future, hits a similar note in the ending of her book:

> The feminist in theatre can create the laboratory in which the single most effective mode of repression—gender—can be exposed, dismantled and removed; the same laboratory may produce the representation of a subject who is liberated from the repressions of the past and capable of signalling a new age for both women and men. (*Feminism and Theatre* 132)

The ideal goal has been recognized; it is its implementation that has yet to be realized as an ongoing process, rather than the rarified exception. Therefore, I return to practical considerations of pedagogy and the support of nontraditional (and noncommercial) art in our society.

As I remarked in the preface, this book is intended for use by scholars, critics, playwrights and other theatre practitioners, students and teachers. Let us turn for a moment to the last two. Elizabeth Langland and Walter Gove edited a 1981 volume of essays examining whether the feminist perspective has affected the academy in disciplines ranging from theatre to religious studies to political science. In their introductory notes to *A Feminist Perspective in the Academy: The Difference It Makes*, they acknowledge that while feminist analysis has begun to affect scholarship, "women's studies has yet to have a substantial influence on the traditional curriculum, principally because such analyses challenge fundamental assumptions in each discipline" (1). The important point they make, for theatre studies and all disciplines, is that of the effect of the feminist view on what we know—indeed, on what is "knowable"; and simultaneously, the failure of women's studies to change the curricula in higher education, and its challenge to the status quo. The preface of a more recently published work on feminist

---

60. Apparently Gayle Austin is as well. When I read her book after drafting this introduction, I found we had quoted much of the same material.

pedagogy, *Teaching Women: Feminism and English Studies,* edited by Ann Thompson and Helen Wilcox, admits that although the process "is exciting, diverse, demanding," it is sometimes difficult and not always successful.[61]

In that same book, Susanne Greenhalgh comments on her experiences with feminist pedagogy in the drama classroom. Noting such positive aspects as "the fusion of theory and praxis; interactive and collaborative learning and teaching; the breaking down of barriers among participants to create an atmosphere of trust and community" (178)—all of which could be considered part of most drama teaching— she also discerns the following:

> The drama teacher does not simply have to contend with her authority role as a teacher, but must often adopt the equally dominant persona of director whilst also acting as a receptive and responsive audience for her students' work. The conflicts, anger, and reversion to mother-daughter dynamics which may characterise the relationships between women students and teachers can have freer and more powerful scope within a classroom which is also—literally—an emotional and physical workshop, where feelings must be translated into performance images. Within that performance and within the classroom both students and teachers play many roles, and in the process may come to understand better how such roles are constructed. . . . [T]here are subtle and as yet unanalysed relationships between sex/gender, acting and power. . . . (178)

J. Karen Ray suggests in "The Ethics of Feminism in the Literature Classroom: A Delicate Balance" that "the appropriate uses of feminist inquiry are to help teacher and student: (1) to review the canon, (2) to re-vision the canon, and (3) to respond to the canon" (54). I would amend Ray's comments in this way: The feminist teacher's potential to bring into the "canon"—here in a very narrow meaning as those plays taught in the classroom—works by women, particularly feminist women, must be waged as a constant battle. Furthermore, students must be made aware of the process and dangers of canonization itself.[62]

Concerning Renaissance drama, Jeanne Addison Roberts, in "Making a Woman and Other Institutionalized Diversions," urges teaching *different* Shakespearean plays from those typically taught in secondary

61. This work concentrates on teaching literature in British institutions of higher learning.

62. In "Canonizing Lesbians?" Lynda Hart writes: "Few critics would dispute that women's plays have been neglected, lost, hidden, erased from the history of western theater. Most feminists . . . agree that canonization is a concept that has effectively permitted that erasure. Universality is evoked to justify excluding divergent and diverse viewpoints, and most of us know that heterosexuality is one of the primary terms of universality. The canon has been a white, male, heterosexual (or passing heterosexual) club that has mystified its terms for inclusion by establishing aesthetic criteria that suppress the sociohistorical context from which these aesthetic criteria emerge. Gaining admittance for marginalized others into that canon is slow, painstaking, and often results in token admissions" (279).

school, plays that "may highlight different gender configurations," and presenting the material differently, acknowledging and examining "the racist, sexist, chauvinist, elitist world which they inevitably reflect" (368).[63] Ann Thompson points out that the remaining challenges for Shakespearean feminists include making an impact on the editing of plays ("Warrant" 86). She also expresses disappointment that "feminist criticism has continued to follow traditional assumptions about the established hierarchy *within* the canon, privileging the tragedies above all, then the middle comedies and the problem plays" ("Warrant" 85).

In addition to the scholarly and pedagogical concerns cited above, I would like to propose several other issues: the need for increased publication of feminist plays; the making of space for women to work together without men, if desired; and continued efforts to raise the consciousness of the male (and sometimes female) reviewers who affect which plays audiences attend and of the theatrical administrators who determine what offerings are available. I would support the recommendation of Solange Collin, writing about Quebec theatre in the mid-1980s, to establish "theatre schools for women where the spirit of criticism [i.e., of societal conditions] would be encouraged, not stifled" (222). However, the possibilities for such a venture in the United States in this age of reduced funding for the arts, pervasive references to "postfeminism," and generally conservative atmosphere seem remote.

Specifics on the Scope, Methods, Organization, and Use of This Book

Scope

That only works written in English are included in this bibliography reflects limitations on the part of the bibliographer, unfortunately precluding the inclusion of illuminating materials in other languages. Furthermore, because I live and work in the United States, relying heavily on American public and academic libraries, the bibliography is heavily weighted with material accessible through these sources; i.e., American criticism and, secondarily, British and Canadian criticism. However, every attempt was made to locate criticism written in English that deals with theatrical activity in other cultures.

---

63. Typical offerings include *Macbeth*, *Hamlet*, and *Romeo and Juliet*. Roberts cautions: "Unless we are very careful, these plays reinforce for women their inherited and culturally sustained sense of their own insignificance, their fear of their own powers, their revulsion from their own sexuality, their masochism, their docility, and their confusion at their failure to meet an impossible ideal of female purity. Male students find reinforcement for their fears and suspicions of women, with object lessons in the perils of sexual entanglement" (367).

Materials Included

Although *Dramatic Re-Visions* relies heavily on American publications, articles from selected periodicals originating in other countries are also cited. Criteria for inclusion in the work included availability of the item in the United States (e.g., willingness of libraries to copy articles and send them via interlibrary loan) and whether the periodical is listed in indexes regularly consulted or easily located in the United States.

Academic publications in theatre, such as *Theatre Journal*, and in feminism, such as *Women's Studies*, were automatically considered. Also within the scope of this bibliography were other scholarly journals, such as *English Literary Renaissance*, and nonacademic feminist periodicals, such as *Ms.* and *Spare Rib.*

Although selected periodicals intended for special audiences, such as *Black World* or *Christopher Street* (directed toward gay readers), were allowed, general interest magazines such as *Newsweek* and daily newspapers were not. In fact, weekly, biweekly or daily periodicals of any sort were automatically excluded.[64]

Books written in English (or in which the pertinent chapters are written in English) have been included, regardless of place of publication. Juvenile books were excluded from this bibliography, as were unpublished dissertations.

Subject Matter

While the feminist study of dramatic texts, performance, and the institution of theatre provides a wide range for this bibliography, in terms of material choice and indexing depth, I have given preference to writing dealing with the work of feminist theatre groups and with feminist drama. However, the history and development of feminist criticism, as outlined earlier in this introduction, necessitate that a sizable portion of the book deal with feminist perspectives on the male canon, including investigations into manifestations of feminism or antifeminism in men's playwriting. As suggested earlier, the entire issue of canonization is itself a feminist concern, not only for those working within the academy but also for women actors, directors, playwrights, and other practitioners whose employment opportunities have been limited.[65]

---

64. I was particularly sorry to omit *The Village Voice* and other alternative weekly periodicals. Certainly there are plentiful materials for another bibliographer's endeavors.

65. Schlueter recognizes the value of questioning the inherited canon "in addressing the inevitable question of whether there should be any sacred texts at all, any institutionalized body of literature that is presumed to express values that speak to all cultures at all times" (*Modern American Drama* 11).

Work that discusses feminist dramatic/performance/theatre criticism itself, including critiques of its strengths and weaknesses, is also within the scope of this book.[66]

I have omitted for the most part articles or monographs that deal solely with feminist theory or feminist literary criticism and have no strong integration with drama or theatrical practice. However, in several borderline cases, I have included interdisciplinary articles published in *Theatre Journal* under the editorship of Sue-Ellen Case, who made invaluable contributions to enlarging that well-established periodical's scope.[67]

Although many of the cited works analyze plays by women, other items on women playwrights were relegated to my "N/A" file because they offered nothing "feminist" in the critical approach, the issues addressed, or the plays under discussion. Similarly, I did not include works about women theatre practitioners unless there was a feminist "angle" in terms of interpretation of a particular play with which the practitioner was associated or the effect of the women's movement on her career. Occasionally I came across articles on feminist playwrights—particularly interviews—that did not directly articulate feminist issues but did deal with the writing process (for example, the comments by Adrienne Kennedy, Maria Irene Fornes, and Megan Terry in the special "Playwrights and Playwriting" issue of *The Drama Review*). Assessing their revelations as being of potential importance to scholars, I did annotate them.

Interviews sometimes posed difficulty in the decision-making process. The following guidelines proved helpful in determining which ones to include:

1. If the interview were with a playwright usually considered to be a feminist or with members of a feminist theatre collective; or
2. If the interview were with a woman playwright, performer, performance artist, or theatre practitioner, and feminist criticism were offered or feminist issues raised either by the interviewer or by the interviewee. I broadly interpreted feminist issues in these cases, and considered the source of publication as well (e.g., whether the article appeared in a feminist periodical).

66. Feminist criticism of Shakespeare is particularly pertinent here. See, for example, Richard Levin's article, "Feminist Thematics and Shakespearean Tragedy," in which he points out problems with a particular feminist approach and suggests a more promising direction for feminist inquiry.

67. Case's introductory comments in the final 1988 issue of *Theatre Journal* (40.4) included an examination of the changes the journal had undergone from being a house organ for educational theatre to "a publication that influences and is influenced by theatre and drama scholars in many different disciplines. The readership and authorship of articles far exceeds previous disciplinary bounds to include those in anthropology interested in performance, those in art history who work on performance art, and those in the other language departments who work on international theatre." She recognizes that this approach "reflects the interdisciplinary move in theatre studies and the academy at large that has developed during the 1970s and 1980s" (452).

One of the most difficult aspects of preparing this bibliography was the determination of cutoff points. When I expanded my initial project to include not only dramatic criticism but performance issues (the best writing in the field often melding both areas), I opened the proverbial can of worms. For example, issues of female representation and male spectatorship in film and dance have had enormous bearing on and relationship to the problem of female representation (or its impossibility) in theatre. However, to set some boundaries on what could become a never-ending project, I boldly (and not without some pain) eliminated criticism that did not discuss drama/theatre explicitly, except as mentioned above. This in no way minimizes the value of works such as those comprising "The Body as Discourse," a special *Women & Performance: A Journal of Feminist Theory* issue on dance, particularly what Marianne Goldberg refers to in a footnote as her "performance piece for print" (31).[68]

While I did not include works about stand-up comics, I did consider performance art to fall within the designated boundaries. In addition to its ties to theatre, feminist performance art addresses many of the same issues as do collaborative and independently authored feminist plays (e.g., female subjectivity). Therefore, items about feminist performance artists can be found in the "Performers/Performance Issues/ Performance Art" chapter.

In the practice of contemporary "theatre," it is not at all uncommon for one art form to merge into another; for example, *tanztheater* blends theatre and dance.[69] Discussions of *tanztheater* are included in "Performers/Performance Issues/Performance Art," although, depending upon the author's slant, one could argue for their being included in "Twentieth-Century Women Playwrights." This overlapping, merging, and blending of theatrical practice, and my occasional difficulties in assigning items to appropriate categories, should not suggest a lack of conceptual differences in today's criticism regarding theatre and performance.[70]

A study that is mainly historical in nature—for example, the description of the work of a nineteenth-century actress or woman theatre

68. Writing of the "gendered body" in "Ballerinas and Ball Passing," Goldberg states: "I want to insert a different female body into representation, to bend the rules of the frame of the theatre to shift the way the woman's image is received by the spectator . . ." (13).

69. In the interview with Mechthild Grossmann, Carol Martin explains: "As a form which combines dance and theater, tanztheater uses a variety of techniques that have been developing in both Europe and America since the turn of the century. Unlike much American dance, pastiche, montage, and collage are primary vehicles for structuring tanztheater" (99).

70. Elin Diamond's discussion of this issue in "(In)Visible Bodies in Churchill's Theatre" provides a lucid distinction. She summarizes theatre as governed by the playwright's text, producing a unique dramatic world and encouraging spectators in "pleasurable narrativity," and performance as dismantling "textual authority, illusionism, and the canonical actor in favor of the 'polymorphous thinking body' of the performer, a sexual, permeable, tactile body, a 'semiotic bundle of drives' that scourges audience narrativity" (190).

manager—is generally not listed, even though it may focus on a redis-covered practitioner or provide an examination of conditions under which women workers in theatre (other than playwrights) labored. Only if the study explicated the subject's feminist approach to theatre or the writer worked within a feminist framework was the material con-sidered for inclusion. Again, there is a need for this kind of bibliographi-cal compilation in theatre history.[71]

Studies involving the status of contemporary women in theatre are cited if they entail a discussion of feminist plays or theatre groups or deal with an organization designed to promote women's work in the-atre. In the latter case they are listed in the "Reports" chapter, which also includes pieces on conferences and festivals.

Book and play reviews are excluded, as well as criticism dealing solely with radio or television scripts or productions, even if the femi-nist author of those scripts is also noted for writing stage plays.[72]

Exhaustivity

While the coverage of feminism's intersection with theatre is exten-sive in *Dramatic Re-Visions,* I make no claims for exhaustivity. Many articles proved inaccessible; too often, particularly in the earlier years, published indexes provided misleading or inadequate clues to the spe-cialized materials sought.

One area in particular bears witness to the impossibility of being to-tally exhaustive—the feminist Renaissance criticism that has appeared in countless articles and books since the late 1970s. It proved remark-ably difficult to choose and exclude studies among the outpouring of works on Shakespeare, because feminism has so greatly affected many current critical approaches to the early modern period. (See the discus-sion on appropriation on pp. 37–38.) This is especially apparent where

71. Chinoy and Jenkins' book contains a selected bibliography of women in American the-atre, which I edited. This bibliography in part includes such works.

72. Originally I intended to have an appendix of play reviews adhering to a number of very specific criteria; perhaps this project will be published separately at a later date. In formulating those criteria, I decided to omit "reviews" that were really only descriptions of a performance, such as those featured in the "Theatre Reports" section of *The Drama Review* (under its various name changes through the years). I later vacillated about including these descriptive pieces in the main part of the current bibliography, ultimately deciding to omit them. Among the most signifi-cant omissions was "Theatre Reports: An Evening in the East Village, 30 November 1984," *The Drama Review* 29.1 (1985): 25–56. Three of the many performances described bear directly on feminism and theatre: Jill Dolan's "Carmelita Tropicana Chats at the Club Chandalier," Amy C. Ward's "Beth Lapides' *A Good American Novel* at P.S. 122," and Kate Davy's "*Heart of the Scor-pion* at the WOW Cafe." Other descriptive pieces worth mentioning are Charlotte Rea's "The New York Feminist Theatre Troupe" in 18.3 (1974): 132–33; Stephanie Arnold's "Suzanne Lacy's *Whis-per, the Waves, the Wind*" in 29.1 (1985): 126–30; and Jill Dolan's "Teatro Viola's *Shoe-Show*" in 26.3 (1982): 111–14.

feminism and psychoanalytic theory connect concerning issues of family, identity, and sexuality.[73]

Those readers primarily interested in feminist criticism of Shakespeare should recall that since 1984, *Shakespeare Quarterly*'s annual bibliography has included "feminism" as a term in its index of the previous year's publications in the field of Shakespearean criticism. Other terms such as "women" and "gender" may also prove useful in using that source.

Methods

Numerous indexes were consulted, including the *Modern Language Association International Bibliography* (both in book form and online through Dialog), *Women Studies Abstracts, Humanities Index* (both printed and online), *Education Index, Magazine Index,* and *Alternative Press Index.* Other indexes were also checked, although they proved less productive. Compilations such as *New Books on Women and Feminism,* published by the University of Wisconsin System, provided additional "leads."

Perhaps the most fruitful sources came from the citations and bibliographies in feminist articles and books. Information also was presented via publishers' brochures and word-of-mouth at Women and Theatre Program conferences. Self-contained bibliographies in book and article form were consulted as well (see Appendix I).

A number of theatre and performance periodicals were examined issue by issue for the years covered by this bibliography. These included *American Theatre, Comparative Drama, Modern Drama, New Theatre Quarterly, Performing Arts Journal, Shakespeare Quarterly, Shakespeare Studies, Southern Theatre, TDR, The Drama Review: A Journal of Performance Studies* (formerly *The Drama Review*), *Theater, Theatre Journal,* and *Women & Performance: A Journal of Feminist Theory.* Other periodicals were examined as available for portions of the designated period (e.g., *Canadian Theatre Review* from 1979 through 1988).

When I could not personally examine a run of a periodical (as in the case of several small feminist publications) and the publication was not fully indexed for its duration, I took advantage of those years that were indexed or of specific citations in the work of other writers. I also looked through available issues of *Feminist Periodicals: A Current Listing of*

---

73. One source for those interested in this area is Murray Schwartz and Coppélia Kahn's *Representing Shakespeare: New Psychoanalytic Essays*, which contains 461 bibliographical items dating from 1964 to 1978, as well as an elucidating introduction.

Contents. In addition, I relied on a host of long-distance friends, relatives, and paid assistants to sort through materials for me. Occasionally, I called or wrote to the publishers, if they were still in existence. Despite these efforts, I cannot claim complete consistency in the inclusion of articles from certain periodicals.

Unfortunately, more frequently than I would have imagined, a request for an article in a relatively obscure periodical produced interlibrary loan feedback of "bad citation" or the article simply could not be located. Sometimes, even if an item was located, the holding institution refused to lend (or copy) the item, even for a fee. After at least three different sources (two large university libraries and one major public library) proved unable to locate a given citation, and when my contacts throughout the country could not find the material by searching runs of periodicals, I generally gave up the quest.

Style

For the most part, citations follow *The MLA Style Manual* (1985). Every guide contains a number of idiosyncrasies. A few examples that users of this bibliography may wish to note are listed below:

Interviews are alphabetized under name of interviewee. (Where most of the article's content is supplied by the author and not the subject, I did not consider it an "interview" per se and listed it under the author's name.)

When a journal has continuous pagination throughout the volume (which usually corresponds to the year), the issue number is omitted. *Theatre Journal* is a case in point.

Abbreviated versions of established publishers' names are used; i.e., words such as "Publishing Company" or "Books" are omitted.

"Rpt." ("Reprint") is used in two different ways in citations: If I am citing and annotating an article from a previously published collection, data will be given from the original publication, with the "Rpt. in" information following. If I am citing and annotating the original, the reprint information is enclosed in parentheses. For example:

Kahn, Coppélia. "*The Taming of the Shrew*: Shakespeare's Mirror of Marriage." *Modern Language Studies* 5.1 (1975): 88–102. (Rpt. in *The Authority of Experience: Essays in Feminist Criticism*. Ed. Arlyn Diamond and Lee R. Edwards. Amherst: University of Massachusetts Press, 1977. 84–100.)

When I felt it was necessary to add publication information to clarify a source so that a user could more easily obtain it, avoiding the delays and confusion I too often encountered, I did so. For example, *Fireweed* 7 and 8, both published in 1980, were special issues with the identical titles of "Women and Performance." Therefore, I added Summer and Fall (corresponding to issues 7 and 8) for clarification.

When a citation was uncovered and I received the article through interlibrary loan but follow-up efforts proved fruitless in establishing, for example, the month rather than the issue number for a monthly periodical (as required by MLA guidelines), I left intact whatever information was already available and sufficient to allow the user to locate the desired item.

All attempts at consistency have been made in writing the citations. However, over the course of time some periodicals changed their publication frequency, and what may appear to be an inconsistency is actually a reflection of the reality of publication circumstances. Furthermore, some periodicals are irregularly published and strangely numbered.[74]

A particular challenge presented itself in the materials published by ISIS, a resource and documentation center. ISIS produces a number of similarly titled periodicals, including *ISIS Women's World* and *ISIS International Women's Journal*.[75] Unfortunately, sources such as the *Alternative Press Index* did not always differentiate among these periodicals; tracking them down and getting the correct citations took the better part of two years.

Organization

Each chapter is divided in books (and chapters in books) and monographs, and periodicals, serials, and annuals. I have generally followed the most usual procedures in assigning material to one section or another. For example, *Shakespeare Quarterly* cites *Shakespeare Survey* in abbreviated, periodical, rather than book, form, and I followed suit. Common sense and the economical use of space also influenced my decision.

Some serials are published annually with a consecutive numbering system, each with a separate title indicating its subject matter. I have

---

74. I ran into one such problem with *Theatre News*, normally published nine times a year, usually with a month designated; however, in citing the Freydberg article in the "Reports" chapter, the issue was designated "Fall 1981." I chose to include all information, including volume and issue number, to allow easier access to it.

75. I eventually discovered that Northwestern University is an excellent source for these materials.

found these works shelved in libraries in chronological order and available for interlibrary loan, unlike a "regular" periodical, which is not lent out (although articles may be copied and sent to the requesting institution through interlibrary loan). For instance, I annotated many articles from the annual publication *Themes in Drama*. Because each year's issue has its own focus and title, I could not call the 1985 *Drama, Sex and Politics* a "special" issue. Therefore, I elected to formulate my own system, placing the annual title in parentheses after the journal title and number. In book form, it would read (following the author's name and essay title, and preceding the article's page numbers):

Drama, Sex and Politics. Ed. James Redmond. Themes in Drama 7. Cambridge, England: Cambridge University Press, 1985.

However, essays from this work are listed in the periodicals section, with *Themes in Drama* as the title listed first and *Drama, Sex and Politics* in parentheses. For example:

Carlson, Susan L. "Women in Comedy: Problem, Promise, Paradox." *Themes in Drama* 7 (*Drama, Sex and Politics*) (1985): 159–71.

Other annuals, such as *Theatre Annual,* only occasionally have a "special issue," and thus are treated like any other periodical in this bibliography.

The overall organization of the book categorizes the materials into eight chapters and three appendixes.

1. *Theories and Overviews.* Intended to provide general perspectives on feminist approaches to theatre, this chapter includes a variety of theoretical bases for feminist assessment of drama and performance (whether the work itself is inherently feminist or not), as well as overviews of feminist theatre practice and criticism. Examinations of gender bias in criticism, debates over the existence of a female aesthetic, comprehensive histories of women's endeavors in the male-dominated world of theatre—these are among the efforts falling within this chapter's parameters.

2. *Feminist Theatres and Theatre Groups.* Here, materials that focus on feminist companies and their work are annotated. The reason for the two-faceted title is that theatre groups, which are usually collectives with a fairly consistent membership, may be formed and exist without a specific theatrical space or home. A feminist theatre, such as New York's WOW Cafe, is not necessarily one cohesive group, but may welcome many kinds of performers and performances (although, in this case, WOW presents productions from a lesbian-feminist perspective).

3. *Pioneering Women Playwrights.* "Rediscovered" women authors (writing prior to the twentieth century) are examined, and the tradition of female playwriting is reclaimed.

4. *Twentieth-Century Women Playwrights.* Women playwrights from around the world are included in works of criticism and numerous interviews.

5. *Feminist Reassessment of Men's Playwriting.* Plays by canonized playwrights such as Shakespeare and Ibsen as well as contemporary male writers are reevaluated through feminist methodologies and concerns.

6. *Performers/Performance Issues/Performance Art.* Critical pieces on performance art and artists, women actors and feminist acting theories, the contributions of women directors, and such special types of performance as *tanztheater* are located in this chapter. Also included are historical studies of actresses whose work both inside and outside the theatre manifested their struggle to promote women's rights.

7. *Selected Play Collections.* Not all anthologies of plays by women are included. A collection has been selected if it adheres to at least some of the following criteria:
    1. It has a useful introduction.
    2. It includes plays that are not widely available separately.
    3. It contains at least three plays when the plays are by the same author. In addition, plays by an individual woman collected in one volume are *not* included unless there is an introduction of note, the plays are overtly feminist in nature, or the plays are otherwise hard to locate.[76]
    4. The title is not helpful as a finding device (e.g., *Plays by Women*).

8. *Reports: Conferences, Festivals, and Organizations.* This catch-all chapter features news about and commentary on theatre conferences, play festivals, and organizations supportive of the goals of women in theatre. Note that transcripts of papers and panels (dealing with a playwright's or performance artist's work, for example) are listed in the chapters pertinent to the subject matter. Here the user will find items that deal with the conference (or festival or organization) *itself,* including the issues raised through discussions and presentations. Festival reports that are in reality just reviews of the productions have been excluded.

---

76. For example, Marsha Norman's *Four Plays* (TCG, 1988) is excluded. Norman is a famous and popular writer, and even a beginning researcher would have no trouble gaining access to her works.

Appendix I. *Resources: Bibliographies and Directories.* These selected bibliographies and directories have been annotated only as necessary to demonstrate their relevance to the study of feminist dramatic criticism or feminist drama and performance. Introductory material is summarized and broadly indexed. Contents are indexed only if specific; e.g., a bibliography of Aphra Behn would be indexed in the Name Index under Behn.

Readers should remember that they will find other useful bibliographies in the books and articles listed in this work, particularly those included in the "Theories and Overviews" chapter.

Appendix II. *Special Issues of Journals, Including Selected Annuals.* This appendix acts as a locating device for significant periodicals that are cited in full or in part in the main sections of the book. While relevant articles—those fitting the criteria of this bibliography—are individually annotated in the appropriate chapter (e.g., "Performers/ Performance Issues/Performance Art"), other related articles on women in theatre or excerpts from plays or performance art pieces are noted here as well. The unannotated articles and excerpts mentioned are broadly indexed.

Appendix III. *A Sampling of Works Published after 1988.* Appendix III comprises a list of selected books, play collections, bibliographies, and special issues of periodicals. These items are neither annotated nor indexed.

Not surprisingly, many periodical articles, books, or essays in books fit into more than one category. I have tried to organize the materials in a way that indicates their main thrust. Therefore, a work on American women playwrights that briefly surveys early writers and then concentrates on the last few decades would be placed in the "Twentieth-Century Women Playwrights" chapter. When the discussion pertains to the production or script of a collaborative effort of a specific company (e.g., the Women's Experimental Theater with its three collaborators), I have placed the work in the "Feminist Theatres and Theatre Groups" chapter.

Sometimes the appropriate categorization of an item was extremely problematic, as when an individual playwright formed a *temporary* collective-type arrangement with others to create a piece under her inspiration or direction. (I ultimately determined that such a study would be placed in the "Twentieth-Century Women Playwrights" chapter.) At other times an item fit equally well in two, or even three, categories. (However, if a piece discussed both male and female playwrights in about equal proportion, I placed the item in the appropriate women playwrights' chapter.)

The user should recognize the importance of the four indexes—Name, Title, Categorical, and Subject—in providing access to specific information, no matter how I have chosen to classify the item as a whole (i.e., the chapter in which the item has been placed). The most direct way to use this bibliography, when possible, is to look up playwrights' names or play titles. In no way are these suggestions meant to diminish the joys of browsing!

Presentation of the Material

My technique is descriptive rather than evaluative. That is, I have tried not to pass judgment on the "correctness" of the writer's views or the size of the contribution she or he has made to the literature. However, I recognize that there is no such thing as "objective" reporting, and surely my own biases must creep in, both in terms of the selections included and in the critical arguments I have chosen to emphasize.

My aim from the beginning has been to provide resources for independent thought and scholarship, and to do so as much as possible without imposing arbitrary restrictions. Therefore, I did not impose strict number-of-words limits on the length of annotations, although I did attempt to edit them to be as short as possible while conveying the salient points. In addition, as many subject terms as deemed necessary have been used to enable access to an item.

Within the annotations, I have maintained a standardized spelling of names such as Hrotsvitha and Delariviere Manley, both of which appear in a number of forms. However, an author's original spelling of discrepant or disputed names was not altered in citing titles of books and articles.

Within the main body of the book, special issues of journals or collections of essays in book form that concentrate on one particular playwright (e.g., Shakespeare) from a feminist standpoint are cited only once. The contents are then listed or described, according to space considerations. When such a collection of essays was not strictly feminist in its scope, I individually annotated the pertinent articles.

In general, articles that have been reprinted, whether in books or in other periodicals (or articles that appear elsewhere in revised or expanded versions), are listed with "see" reference for the fuller or more updated version. Such entries, which lack full summaries, are at least broadly indexed, with the subject index terms listed in the annotation itself for the reader's convenience. If the subject of the piece is not reflected in its title (e.g., if the title does not indicate the work or playwright discussed), that information is also included in the annotation. For example:

Rose, Mary Beth. "Moral Conceptions of Sexual Love in Elizabethan Comedy." *Renaissance Drama* ns 15 (1984): 1–29.

This article, which deals with works by Lyly, Greene, and Shakespeare, appears in a revised version as the first chapter in Rose's book, *The Expense of Spirit*. See E58. *Terms:* desire, heterosexual; marriage; sexuality, female; sexuality, male.

If the article is reprinted without change, this fact appears in the citation itself, per MLA format.

Very occasionally, an article of great significance or one that when incorporated into a book did not receive its own chapter may be fully annotated.

The Nature and Use of the Indexes

Of course, it is impossible to index a book in as much detail as an article. Therefore, there is a discrepancy between the amount of material in an article and the amount of material in a book that signifies a "substantive" discussion. Books, simply because of their length, tend to have a great many more index terms associated with them.

The Name Index, Title Index, Categorical Index, and Subject Index provide various means of gaining access to the materials. Their general attributes are briefly noted below. Additional and more explicit information regarding their use may be found preceding each index.

Name Index

Playwrights, performance artists, theatres, women's and feminist theatre groups, organizations, festivals, projects, and theatre practitioners such as directors are listed here.

Title Index

In general, titles are included here when the discussion of the play or performance art piece is substantive in the item. However, I have privileged the generally less accessible feminist works by reducing criteria for indexing them, compared with the criteria applied to, say, Shakespeare's plays.

In a piece where play discussions are briefly interwoven within studies of themes or where plot summaries are provided with no overt feminist criticism, plays are not listed separately. These studies are indexed by the playwrights' names, however, if warranted. Therefore, if the user has not found sufficient information under a play title, she or he should consult the Name Index for the playwright. Interviews exemplify items for which play titles are rarely indexed, because interviewees tend to touch upon their individual works only briefly.

Categorical Index

This index includes a breakdown of women playwrights by nationality and minority groupings, geographical and other cataloging of feminist theatre companies, a listing for lesbian plays, and a guide to studies of drama and theatrical practice by country and time period.[77]

Subject Index

It will probably prove helpful for the user to take some time to browse through this index. Every subject index has its quirks, and this one is no exception.

As a *selective* index derived from the works read, rather than conforming to a predetermined system, it may not contain every term used or issue addressed in feminist drama and criticism. A vast network of cross-indexing, however, should help the user find whatever she or he seeks. While I have tried to be as consistent as possible in assigning Subject Index headings, variations in the writers' use of words and shifting nuances of individual terms due to the evolving nature of feminist criticism mitigate the possibility of complete consistency.[78]

The Subject Index provides an excellent means of locating materials pertaining to such wide-ranging themes as androgyny, critical bias, domesticity, *l'écriture féminine*, the influence of various feminisms on theatrical criticism and practice, overviews of minority theatre, the connection between gender and genre, images of women in drama, lesbian desire, misogyny, the issue of representation, male fear of female power, psychoanalytic theory and feminist methodology, self-realization, sexual difference, and many other areas of concern to scholars investigat-

77. Potential problems arise with anonymously authored works, such as *Swetnam, the Woman-Hater Arraigned by Women*. Linda Woodbridge in *Women and the English Renaissance: Literature and the Nature of Womankind, 1540–1620* uses "s/he" once, then refers to the author as he. While the main candidates are Dekker and Heywood, Woodbridge suggests Webster as well. It is possible that the play was penned by a woman, but nothing I uncovered strongly suggested this, although Lesley Ferris states that "so much of the unattributed material in the play finds a source in the pamphlets of the three women [Rachel Speght, Ester Sowernam, and Constantia Munda] that it is tempting to speculate that a woman could have possibly written the script" (12). (I have categorically indexed *Swetnam* under nation and period, not under women playwrights.)
78. Professor Bernie Schlessinger of Texas Woman's University has told me that studies have shown only about an 80-percent level of consistency in indexing. I have tried to keep the notion of human fallibility firmly in mind as I debated, redesigned, and reassigned terms for the Subject Index.

ing feminism's intersection with theatre. Nearly 400 headings and subheadings are included.

References Cited

Abel, Elizabeth, ed. *Writing and Sexual Difference.* Chicago: University of Chicago Press, 1982.

Alcoff, Linda. "Cultural Feminism Versus Post-Structuralism: The Identity Crisis in Feminist Theory." *Signs* 13 (1988): 405–36.

Austin, Gayle, ed. "The 'Woman' Playwright Issue." *Performing Arts Journal* 7.3 (1983): 87–102.

Austin, Gayle. *Feminist Theories for Dramatic Criticism.* Ann Arbor: University of Michigan Press, 1990.

Bassnett, Susan. "Women Experiment with Theatre: Magdalena 86." *New Theatre Quarterly* 3.11 (1987): 224–34.

Bassnett-McGuire, Susan E. "Towards a Theory of Women's Theatre." *Semiotics of Drama and Theatre: New Perspectives in the Theory of Drama and Theatre.* Ed. Herta Schmid and Aloysius Van Kesteren. Amsterdam: Benjamins, 1984. 445–66.

Beauvoir, Simone de. *The Second Sex. Le Deuxième Sexe.* 1949. Trans. and ed. H. M. Parshley. New York: Knopf, 1953.

Blair, Rhonda. "A History of the Women and Theatre Program." *The Women and Theatre Program.* Spec. issue of *Women & Performance: A Journal of Feminist Theory* 4.2 (1989): 5–13.

Boose, Lynda E. "The Family in Shakespeare Studies; or—Studies in the Family of Shakespeareans; or—The Politics of Politics." *Renaissance Quarterly* 40 (1987): 707–42.

Brown, Janet. *Feminist Drama: Definition and Critical Analysis.* Metuchen, N.J.: Scarecrow, 1979.

Butler, Judith. "Performative Acts and Gender Constitution: An Essay in Phenomenology and Feminist Theory." *Theatre Journal* 40 (1988): 519–31.

Cain, Melissa McComb, Kathryn A. Hammell, and Maureen Pastine. "Library Research in Women's Studies." *For Alma Mater: Theory and Practice in Feminist Scholarship.* Ed. Paula A. Treichler, Cheris Kramarae, and Beth Stafford. Urbana: University of Illinois Press, 1985. 423–41.

Callaghan, Dympna. *Women and Gender in Renaissance Tragedy: A Study of* King Lear, The Duchess of Malfi *and* The White Devil. Atlantic Highlands, N.J.: Humanities, 1989.

Case, Sue-Ellen. "Comment." *Theatre Journal* 40 (1988): 452.

Case, Sue-Ellen. *Feminism and Theatre.* New York: Methuen, 1988.

Case, Sue-Ellen. *Performing Feminisms: Feminist Critical Theory and Theatre.* Baltimore, Md.: Johns Hopkins University Press, 1990.

Case, Sue-Ellen, and Jeanie K. Forte. "From Formalism to Feminism." *Theater* 16.2 (1985): 62–65.

Cherry, Caroline Lockett. *The Most Unvaluedst Purchase: Women in the Plays of Thomas Middleton.* Salzburg Studies in English Literature; Jacobean Drama Studies 34. Salzburg, Austria: Institut für Englische Sprache und Literatur, Universität Salzburg, 1973.

Chinoy, Helen Krich, and Linda Walsh Jenkins, eds. *Women in American Theatre: Careers, Images, Movements.* Rev. ed. New York: Theatre Communications Group, 1987.

Cixous, Hélène. "Laugh of the Medusa." Trans. Keith Cohen and Paula Cohen. *New French Feminisms.* Ed. Elaine Marks and Isabelle de Courtivron. Amherst: University of Massachusetts Press, 1980. 245–64.

Collin, Solange. "An Alternative to the Traditional Theatre in Québec." Trans. Dympna Borowska. *In the Feminine: Women and Words/Les Femmes et les mots: Conference Proceedings 1983.* Ed. Ann Dybikowski, et al. Edmonton, Canada: Longspoon, 1985. 219–23.

Curb, Rosemary K. "Re/cognition, Re/presentation, Re/creation in Woman-Conscious Drama: The Seer, the Seen, the Scene, the Obscene." *Staging Gender.* Spec. issue of *Theatre Journal* 37 (1985): 302–16.

Dash, Irene G. *Wooing, Wedding, and Power: Women in Shakespeare's Plays.* New York: Columbia University Press, 1981.

de Lauretis, Teresa. "Feminist Studies/Critical Studies: Issues, Terms, and Contexts." *Feminist Studies/Critical Studies.* Theories of Contemporary Culture 8. Bloomington: Indiana University Press, 1986. 1–19.

de Lauretis, Teresa. "The Left Hand of History." *Heresies* 1.4 (1977-78): 23–26.

de Lauretis, Teresa. "Sexual Indifference and Lesbian Representation." *Feminist Diversions.* Spec. issue of *Theatre Journal* 40 (1988): 155–77.

de Lauretis, Teresa. *Technologies of Gender: Essays on Theory, Film, and Fiction.* Bloomington: Indiana University Press, 1987.

Diamond, Elin. "(In)Visible Bodies in Churchill's Theatre." *Feminist Diversions.* Spec. issue of *Theatre Journal* 40 (1988): 188–204.

Diamond, Elin. "Mimesis, Mimicry, and the 'True-Real.'" *Women in the Theatre.* Spec. issue of *Modern Drama* 32.1 (1989): 58–72.

Diamond, Elin. "(Theoretically) Approaching Megan Terry: Issues of Gender and Identity." *Work by Women.* Spec. issue of *Art & Cinema* ns 1.3 (1987): 5–7.

Dolan, Jill. *The Feminist Spectator as Critic.* Theater and Dramatic Studies 52. Ann Arbor, Mich.: UMI Research Press, 1988.

Dolan, Jill. "Gender Impersonation Onstage: Destroying or Maintaining the Mirror of Gender Roles." *Women & Performance: A Journal of Feminist Theory* 2.2 (1985): 5–11.

"Editorial Voices." *Women & Performance: A Journal of Feminist Theory* 1.1 (1983): 3–4.

Erickson, Peter. "Rewriting the Renaissance, Rewriting Ourselves." *Shakespeare Quarterly* 38 (1987): 327–37.

Feminist Ethnography and Performance. Spec. issue of *Women & Performance: A Journal of Feminist Theory* 5.1 (1990).

Féral, Josette. "Performance and Theatricality: The Subject Demystified." *Modern Drama* 25 (1982): 170–81.

Ferguson, Margaret W., Maureen Quilligan, and Nancy J. Vickers, eds. *Rewriting the Renaissance: The Discourses of Sexual Difference in Early Modern Europe.* Women in Culture and Society. Chicago: University of Chicago Press, 1986.

Ferris, Lesley. *Acting Women: Images of Women in Theatre.* New York: New York University Press, 1989.

Fetterley, Judith. *The Resisting Reader: A Feminist Approach to American Fiction.* Bloomington: Indiana University Press, 1987.

Fornes, Maria Irene, and Tina Howe. "Women's Work: Tina Howe and Maria Irene Fornes Explore the Woman's Voice in Drama." *American Theatre* Sept. 1985: 10–15.

Forte, Jeanie. "Realism, Narrative, and the Feminist Playwright—A Problem of Reception." *Women in the Theatre.* Spec. issue of *Modern Drama* 32.1 (1989): 115–27.

Freedman, Barbara. "Frame-Up: Feminism, Psychoanalysis, Theatre." *Theatre Journal* 40 (1988): 375–97.

Frost, Wendy, and Michele Valiquette. *Feminist Literary Criticism: A Bibliography of Journal Articles, 1975–1981.* New York: Garland, 1988.

Gardiner, Judith Kegan. "Mind Mother: Psychoanalysis and Feminism." *Making a Difference: Feminist Literary Criticism:* Ed. Gayle Greene and Coppélia Kahn. New York: Methuen, 1985. 113–45.

Gillespie, Patti P. "Feminist Theatre: Rhetorical Phenomenon." *Quarterly Journal of Speech* 64 (1978): 284–94.

Gillespie, Patti [P.]. "A Listing of Feminist Theatres." *Women's Theatre.* Spec. issue of *Theatre News* Nov. 1977: 22–24.

Goldberg, Marianne. "Ballerinas and Ball Passing." *The Body as Discourse.* Spec. issue of *Women & Performance: A Journal of Feminist Theory* 3.2 (1987–88): 7–31.

Greene, Gayle. "Feminist and Marxist Criticism: An Argument for Alliances." *Feminist Criticism of Shakespeare.* Spec. issue of *Women's Studies* 9.1 (1981): 29–45.

Greene, Gayle, and Coppélia Kahn. "Feminist Scholarship and the Social Construction of Woman." *Making a Difference: Feminist Literary Criticism.* Ed. Gayle Greene and Coppélia Kahn. New York: Methuen, 1985. 1–36.

Greenhalgh, Susanne. "Occupying the Empty Space: Feminism and Drama." *Teaching Women: Feminism and English Studies.* Ed. Ann Thompson and Helen Wilcox. Manchester, England: Manchester University Press, 1989. 170–79.

Grossmann, Mechthild. Interview. "Mechthild Grossmann: The Art of Anti Heroes." With Carol Martin. *The Drama Review* 30.2 (1986): 98–106.

Hart, Lynda. "Canonizing Lesbians?" *Modern American Drama: The Female Canon.* Ed. June Schlueter. Rutherford, N.J.: Fairleigh Dickinson University Press; London: Associated University Presses, 1990. 275–92.

Hart, Lynda. *Making a Spectacle: Feminist Essays on Contemporary Women's Theatre.* Ann Arbor: University of Michigan Press, 1989.

Hatlen, Burton. "Five Feminist Studies of Shakespeare." *Review* [Blacksburg, Va.] 8 (1986): 241–64.

Humm, Maggie. *The Dictionary of Feminist Theory.* Columbus: Ohio University Press, 1990.

Humm, Maggie. *Feminist Criticism: Women as Contemporary Critics.* New York: St. Martin's, 1986.

Irigaray, Luce. *This Sex Which Is Not One. Ce Sexe qui n'en pas un.* 1977. Trans. Catherine Porter with Carolyne Burke. Ithaca, N.Y.: Cornell University Press, 1985.

Janaczewska, Noëlle. "'Do We Want a Piece of the Cake, or Do We Want to Bake a Whole New One?': Feminist Theatre in Britain." *Hecate* 13.1 (1987): 106–13.

Jenkins, Linda Walsh. "Matrix: New Intersections of Gender, Identity and Politics." *Women in American Theatre.* Ed. Helen Krich Chinoy and Linda Walsh Jenkins. Rev. ed. New York: Theatre Communications Group, 1987. 371–76.

Jones, Ann Rosalind. "Inscribing Femininity: French Theories of the Feminine." *Making a Difference: Feminist Literary Criticism.* Ed. Gayle Greene and Coppélia Kahn. New York: Methuen, 1985. 80–112.

Keyssar, Helene. "Hauntings: Gender and Drama in Contemporary English Theatre." *English Amerikanische Studies* 3–4 (1986): 449–68.

Kolodny, Annette. "Dancing through the Minefield: Some Observations on the Theory, Practice, and Politics of a Feminist Literary Criticism." *The New Feminist Criticism: Essays on Women, Literature, and Theory.* Ed. Elaine Showalter. New York: Pantheon, 1985. 144–67.

Kolodny, Annette. "Respectability Is Eroding the Revolutionary Potential of Feminist Criticism." *Chronicle of Higher Education* 4 May 1988: A52.

Kramarae, Cheris, and Paula A. Treichler, with assistance from Ann Russo. *A Feminist Dictionary.* Boston: Pandora, 1985.

Kuhn, Annette. *The Power of the Image: Essays on Representation and Sexuality.* London: Routledge & Kegan Paul, 1985.

Langland, Elizabeth, and Walter Gove. *A Feminist Perspective in the Academy: The Difference It Makes.* Chicago: University of Chicago Press, 1981.

Leavitt, Dinah Luise. *Feminist Theatre Groups.* Jefferson, N.C.: McFarland, 1980.

Levin, Richard. "Feminist Thematics and Shakespearean Tragedy." *PMLA* 103 (1988): 125–38.

Loomba, Ania. *Gender, Race, Renaissance Drama.* Cultural Politics Series. Manchester, England: Manchester University Press, 1989.

McEachern, Claire. "Fathering Herself: A Source Study of Shakespeare's Feminism." *Shakespeare Quarterly* 39 (1988): 269–90.

McLuskie, Kathleen. "The Patriarchal Bard: Feminist Criticism and Shakespeare: *King Lear* and *Measure for Measure*." *Political Shakes-*

peare: New Essays in Cultural Materialism. Ed. Jonathan Dollimore and Alan Sinfield. Ithaca, N.Y.: Cornell University Press, 1985. 88–108.

McLuskie, Kathleen. *Renaissance Dramatists.* Atlantic Highlands, N.J.: Humanities, 1989.

Marks, Elaine, and Isabelle de Courtivron, eds. *New French Feminisms: an Anthology.* Amherst: University of Massachusetts Press, 1980.

Millett, Kate. *Sexual Politics.* Garden City, N.Y.: Doubleday, 1970.

Modleski, Tania. "Feminism and the Power of Interpretation: Some Critical Readings." *Feminist Studies/Critical Studies.* Ed. Teresa de Lauretis. Theories of Contemporary Culture 8. Bloomington: Indiana University Press, 1986. 121–38.

Moraga, Cherríe. "Interview with Cherríe Moraga." With Norma Alarcón. *Third Woman* 3.2 (1986): 127–34.

Moraga, Cherríe, and Gloria Anzaldúa, eds. *This Bridge Called My Back: Writings by Radical Women of Color.* Watertown, Mass.: Persephone, 1981.

Moss, Jane. "The Body as Spectacle: Women's Theatre in Quebec." *Women & Performance: A Journal of Feminist Theory* 3.1 (1986): 5–16.

Neely, Carol Thomas. "Constructing the Subject: Feminist Practice and the New Renaissance Discourses." *Women in the Renaissance II.* Spec. issue of *English Literary Renaissance* 18 (1988): 5–18.

Neely, Carol Thomas. "Feminist Criticism in Motion." *For Alma Mater: Theory and Practice in Feminist Scholarship.* Ed. Paula A. Treichler, Cheris Kramarae, and Beth Stafford. Urbana: University of Illinois Press, 1985. 69–90.

Newman, Karen. "'And Wash the Ethiop White': Femininity and the Monstrous in *Othello.*" *Shakespeare Reproduced: The Text in History and Ideology.* Ed. Jean E. Howard and Marion F. O'Connor. New York: Methuen, 1987. 141–62.

Parker, Patricia, and Geoffrey Hartman, eds. *Shakespeare and the Question of Theory.* New York: Methuen, 1985.

Piper, Judith A. "*Bodily Concessions.*" *Theatre Journal* 40 (1988): 260–63.

Ray, J. Karen. "The Ethics of Feminism in the Literature Classroom: A Delicate Balance." *English Journal* 74.3 (1985): 54–59.

Reinhardt, Nancy. "New Directions for Feminist Criticism in Theatre and the Related Arts." *Soundings: An Interdisciplinary Journal* 64 (1981): 361–87.

Rich, Adrienne. "Compulsory Heterosexuality and Lesbian Existence." *Signs* 5 (1980): 631–60.

Rich, Adrienne. "Conditions for Work: The Common World of Women." *On Lies, Secrets and Silence: Selected Prose 1966–1978.* New York: Norton, 1979. 203–14.

Roberts, Jeanne Addison. "Making a Woman and Other Institutionalized Diversions." *Shakespeare Quarterly* 37 (1986): 366–69.

Rubin, Gayle. "The Traffic in Women: Notes on the 'Political Economy' of Sex." *Toward an Anthropology of Women.* Ed. Rayna R. Reiter. New York: Monthly Review Press, 1975. 157–210.

Savona, Jeannette Laillou, and Ann Wilson. "Introduction." *Women in the Theatre.* Spec. issue of *Modern Drama* 32.1 (1989): 1–4.

Schlueter, June, ed. *Feminist Rereadings of Modern American Drama.* Rutherford, N.J.: Fairleigh Dickinson University Press; London, Associated University Presses, 1989.

Schlueter, June, ed. *Modern American Drama: The Female Canon.* Rutherford, N.J.: Fairleigh Dickinson University Press; London: Associated University Presses, 1990.

Schwartz, Murray, and Coppélia Kahn, eds. *Representing Shakespeare: New Psychoanalytic Essays.* Baltimore: Johns Hopkins University Press, 1980.

Showalter, Elaine, ed. *The New Feminist Criticism: Essays on Women, Literature, and Theory.* New York: Pantheon, 1985.

Showalter, Elaine. "Representing Ophelia: Women, Madness and the Responsibilities of Feminist Criticism." *Shakespeare and the Question of Theory.* Ed. Patricia Parker and Geoffrey Hartman. New York: Methuen, 1985. 77–94.

Showalter, Elaine. "Toward a Feminist Poetics." *The New Feminist Criticism: Essays on Women, Literature, and Theory.* New York: Pantheon, 1985. 125–43.

Smith, Barbara. "Toward a Black Feminist Criticism." *All the Women Are White, All the Blacks Are Men, but Some of Us Are Brave: Black Women's Studies.* Ed. Gloria T. Hull, Patricia Bell Scott, and Barbara Smith. Old Westbury, N.Y.: Feminist, 1982. 157–75.

Spacks, Patricia Meyer. "The Difference It Makes." *A Feminist Perspective in the Academy: The Difference It Makes.* Ed. Elizabeth Langland and Walter Gove. Chicago: University of Chicago Press, 1981. 7–24.

Spivak, Gayatri Chakravorty. *In Other Worlds: Essays in Cultural Politics.* New York: Methuen, 1987.

Steadman, Susan. "Feminist Dramatic Criticism: Where We Are Now." *The Women and Theatre Program.* Spec. issue of *Women & Performance: A Journal of Feminist Theory* 4.2 (1989): 118–48.

Stephens, Judith L. "The Compatibility of Traditional Dramatic Forms and Feminist Expressions." *Women in Theatre.* Spec. issue of *Theatre Annual* 40 (1985): 7–23.

Stephens, Judith L. "From Positive Image to Disruptive Apparatus: Feminist Perspectives in American Plays and Dramatic Criticism." *The Pennsylvania Speech Communication Annual* 44 (1988): 59–67.

Stephens, Judith L. "Women and Theatre Program: Reactions and Reflections." *The Women and Theatre Program.* Spec. issue of *Women & Performance: A Journal of Feminist Theory* 4.2 (1989): 14–19.

Thompson, Ann. "The Warrant of Womanhood: Shakespeare and Feminist Criticism." *The Shakespeare Myth.* Ed. Graham Holderness. Manchester, England: Manchester University Press, 1988. 74–88.

Thompson, Ann, and Helen Wilcox, eds. *Teaching Women: Feminism and English Studies.* Cultural Politics Series. Manchester, England: Manchester University Press, 1989.

Todd, Janet. *Feminist Literary History.* New York: Routledge, 1988.

Tuttle, Lisa. *Encyclopedia of Feminism.* New York: Facts on File, 1986.

Wandor, Michelene. *Carry On, Understudies.* London: Routledge & Kegan Paul, 1986.

Wandor, Michelene. "Culture, Politics and Values in Plays by Women in the 1980s." *English Amerikanische Studies* 3–4 (1986): 441–48.

Wexler, Joyce. "A Wife Lost and/or Found." *The Upstart Crow* 8 (1988): 106–17.

White, Helen. "Paths for a Flightless Bird: Roles for Women on the New Zealand Stage Since 1950." *Australasian Drama Studies* 3.2 (1985): 105–43.

Wilson, Ann. "The Politics of the Script." *Feminism and Canadian Theatre.* Spec. issue of *Canadian Theatre Review* 43 (1985): 174–97.

Woodbridge, Linda. *Women and the English Renaissance: Literature and the Nature of Womankind, 1540–1620.* Urbana: University of Illinois Press, 1984.

Yarbro-Bejarano, Yvonne. "Cherríe Moraga's *Giving Up the Ghost:* The Representation of Female Desire." *Third Woman* 3.1–2 (1986): 113–20.

Yarbro-Bejarano, Yvonne. "The Female Subject in Chicano Theatre: Sexuality, 'Race.' and Class." *Theatre Journal* 38 (1986): 389–407.

Zeig, Sande. "The Actor as Activator: Deconstructing Gender through Gesture." *Women & Performance: A Journal of Feminist Theory* 2.2 (1985): 12–17.

Theories and Overviews

❖
❖

Books and Monographs

A1

Bassnett-McGuire, Susan E. "Towards a Theory of Women's Theatre." *Semiotics of Drama and Theatre: New Perspectives in the Theory of Drama and Theatre.* Ed. Herta Schmid and Aloysius Van Kesteren. Amsterdam: Benjamins, 1984. 445-66.

Bassnett-McGuire examines the assumptions behind the idea of "women's theatre," grapples with terminology issues, and demonstrates how the phenomenon calls into question the very nature of theatre. Specifically, she uses works by Ruth Wolff and Pam Gems to illustrate her contention that historical plays about great women are inherently nonfeminist; she discusses the organizational structures of women's theatres and their attempts to counter stereotypical stage images of women; and she examines women's discussion theatre aimed at challenging social attitudes. Offering a critique of Roberta Sklar's concept of theatre as a process of consciousness-raising for actor and audience, she raises questions about boundaries between theatre and nontheatre. She also addresses the crucial issue of form, including the male nature of linearity, and cites Dacia Maraini's *Dialogo d'una prostituta col suo cliente* as achieving a genuinely new, fragmentary theatre.

A2

Brown, Janet. *Feminist Drama: Definition and Critical Analysis.* Metuchen, N.J.: Scarecrow, 1979.

Applying Burkean methodology, Brown defines a play as feminist when its central rhetorical motive is woman's struggle for autonomy within an unjust sociosexual hierarchy. She studies five dramas in terms of their patterns of symbolic action and associational clusters: Rosalyn Drexler's *The Bed Was Full,* David Rabe's *In the Boom Boom Room,* Alice Childress's *Wine in the Wilderness,* Tina Howe's *Birth and After Birth,* and Ntozake Shange's *for colored girls who have considered suicide/ when the rainbow is enuf.* Brown also describes rhetorical strategies common to the works of feminist theatre groups—sex-role reversal, use of historical role models, satire of sexual stereotypes, and direct portrayals of women's oppression—with examples drawn from the Westbeth Playwrights Feminist Collective, the B & O Theatre, the Rhode Island Feminist Theatre, Circle of the Witch, and the Boulder Feminist Theatre. She points out ways in which the groups' plays differ from those by individual playwrights, including the use of several protagonists and the proposal of group solidarity to achieve autonomy, less sophisticated rhetorical devices, and more advanced feminist ideology.

A3
Case, Sue-Ellen. *Feminism and Theatre.* New York: Methuen, 1988.

Case's overview of the relationship between feminism and theatre history, practice, and theory is organized as a "sampler," with each chapter relatively complete in itself. Deconstructing the classical canon, she considers issues ranging from the misogyny of *The Oresteia* and the complete exclusion of women from theatre to gender-crossing and homoeroticism in Shakespeare. In addition to reclaiming early women performers and playwrights, Case examines "personal theatre," including the salon and contemporary performance art. To delineate the political implications and impact on theatre of the various "feminisms," she offers separate chapters on radical feminism, materialist feminism, and women of color. Case concludes with a discussion of feminist theory and the application of the "new poetics" to selected plays. She explicates the relationship of such approaches as semiotics and psychoanalytic theory to feminist dramatic criticism and practice and explores the arguments for and against a feminine morphology.

A4
Chinoy, Helen Krich, and Linda Walsh Jenkins, eds. *Women in American Theatre: Careers, Images, Movements.* Rev. ed. New York: Theatre Communications Group, 1987.

This extensive collection of essays, interviews, and sources on the contributions of women to theatre and theatre-like activity is introduced by Chinoy's essay on women's theatrical heritage, which stresses that women seem to have found especially congenial "the sharing, collective, creative, community aspects." Seven sections are each preceded by an editorial overview. "Female Rites" explores women's role in the ritual/theatre continuum, ranging from Native American tribal events to political organizations and Adrienne Kennedy's plays. "The Actress" provides pieces on individual performers, as well as on the actress as harlot, women in male roles, and mimes. "Where Are the Women Playwrights?" includes studies on Mercy Warren, Rachel Crothers, Anne Nichols, Sophie Treadwell, Mary Chase, Gertrude Stein, Lillian Hellman, and Lorraine Hansberry, as well as on the folk play and forms in contemporary works. "If Not an Actress, What . . . ?" considers women in areas of theatrical production other than performance or playwriting. "Images" surveys work on gender display: women in melodrama, in Pulitzer Prize plays, in Glaspell's *Trifles,* and in works by black playwrights. Also in this section are articles on the tragic mulatto figure, sexism in creative drama, and Suzan Zeder's female characters. "Feminist Theatre" contains a discussion of its rhetorical aspects as well as descriptions of specific groups; reflections by Martha Boesing, Roberta Sklar, and Megan Terry; and pieces on Karen Malpede's *Rebeccah,* Maria Irene Fornes's *Fefu and Her Friends,* and consciousness-raising techniques in feminist drama. "New Problems, Practices and Perspectives" is an "eclectic gathering of voices," which offers a survey of experiences, opinions, and data that reveals current concerns ranging from the pragmatic to the theoretical. The "Sourcebook" catalogs lists of awards; organizations, studies, conferences, and festivals; selected reference works; dissertations; film, video, and audio resources; and plays by women.

A5
Curtin, Kaier. *"We Can Always Call Them Bulgarians": The Emergence of Lesbians and Gay Men on the American Stage.* Boston: Alyson, 1987.

With an emphasis on Broadway theatre, Curtin investigates the depiction of gay male and lesbian characters since the 1920s within its theatrical, cultural and political context. In addition to his well-documented analysis of (frequently homophobic) critical reaction, he details censorship issues, legal harassment, audience responses, and the effects of writing/acting/directing choices in the representation of gays and lesbians. He also looks at "closeted gays" in the works of Eugene O'Neill, Michael Arlen, and Noel Coward. The following plays, which deal with lesbian themes, are among those receiving in-depth discussion: Sholom Asch's *The God of Vengeance,* Edouard Bourdet's *The Captive,* William Hurlbut's *Hymn to Venus* (retitled *Sin of Sins*), Thomas H. Dickerson's *Winter Bound,* Christa Winsloe's *Girls in Uniform,* Lillian Hellman's *The Children's Hour,* Stephen Powys' (Mrs. Guy Bolton's) *Wise Tomorrow,* Aimee McHardy Stuart and Philip Stuart's *Love of Women,* and *Trio* by Dorothy and Howard Baker. Mae West's antigay bias in *The Drag* and *Pleasure Man* is also examined, as is Rose Franken's ambiguous treatment of intolerance in *Outrageous Fortune.*

A6

Dolan, Jill. *The Feminist Spectator as Critic.* Theater and Dramatic Studies 52. Ann Arbor, Mich.: UMI Research Press, 1988.

Building on feminist film criticism, Dolan's theoretical essays deconstruct the position of the ideal, white, middle-class heterosexual male spectator whose ideology is reflected in all aspects of theatrical production. Distinguishing among liberal, cultural, and materialist feminism, she outlines critical approaches to many performance situations. She illustrates her scrutiny of canon formation with Marsha Norman's *'night, Mother,* a case study of gender-biased reception. Drawing upon Lacan's treatment of subjectivity, she demonstrates how gender polarization structures Richard Foreman's postmodernist work despite claims of nonideology. Delineating the politics of the pornography debate, she considers issues of sexuality and gender, power and desire, in performance art, erotica, lesbian performance (particularly the WOW Cafe), and lesbian pornography. Dolan criticizes cultural feminist theatre and its focus on mother-daughter relationships, contending that despite formal experimentation it fails to tackle the issue of women's place in representation and narrative. Instead, she offers materialist feminist performance strategies influenced by Brechtian techniques, especially the model of the lesbian subject as the "not . . . but" to subvert representation and effect cultural change.

A7

Janz, Mildred. "Ours Is a Theater of and by Man: And Now We Need a Theater of Woman." *Playwrights, Lyricists, Composers on Theater.* Ed. Otis L. Guernsey, Jr. New York: Dodd, Mead, 1974. 301–4.

Calling twentieth-century woman the "last unexplored territory of the theatre," Janz urges women to look *inside* themselves to find Everywoman for presentation on stage. In contrast she cites Lillian Hellman as holding an outside viewpoint in *The Little Foxes.*

A8

Keyssar, Helene. *Feminist Theatre: An Introduction to Plays of Contemporary British and American Women.* London: MacMillan, 1984. New York: Grove, 1985.

Keyssar's analysis of feminist theatre as a genre begins by tracing its emergence in political activism and theatre experimentation of the 1960s and surveying such precursors as Lillian Hellman (a "negative model of women's theatre"), Alice Childress, Lorraine Hansberry, Joan Littlewood, Shelagh Delaney, and Ann Jellicoe. Separate chapters are devoted to Megan Terry, the "mother of American feminist drama," and to the "politics of possibility" in the work of Caryl Churchill. Keyssar also examines playwrights of the 1960s and 1970s (Myrna Lamb, Adrienne Kennedy, Rochelle Owens, Maria Irene Fornes, and others) and their theatrical networks; communities of women in the works of Pam Gems, Michelene Wandor, and Ntozake Shange; and the commercial successes of women dramatists, including Mary O'Malley, Catherine Hayes, and Marsha Norman. A final chapter exploring the "nooks and crannies" (collective works, lesbian drama, and feminist drama by men) concludes with an analysis of Wendy Kesselman's exemplary study of the abuse of power, *My Sister in This House*. Keyssar theorizes that "for theatre to remain authentic it must offer not just recognition but images of individuals and relationships in the process of transformation."

A9

Malpede, Karen, ed. *Women in Theatre: Compassion and Hope*. New York: Drama Book, 1983.

In her introduction to this volume of theoretical writings, Malpede reflects upon the meaning of being simultaneously a woman and a creative artist. Maintaining that each of the women represented here has "touched the ancient life-affirming origins of theatre and has made her art from this deeply felt imperative," she contrasts the ancient rituals in which women played major roles as creators and performers with a patriarchal theatre characterized by violent conflict. The book is organized into six parts: acting (Fanny Kemble, Ellen Terry, Eva Le Gallienne, Angna Enters), criticism (Emma Goldman on Strindberg, Rosamond Gilder on Hrotsvitha), dance (Isadora Duncan, Martha Graham, Katherine Dunham), playwriting (Augusta Gregory, Susan Glaspell, Gertrude Stein, Lorraine Hansberry), producing and directing (Hallie Flanagan, Judith Malina, Barbara Ann Teer), and feminist plays and performances (Clare Coss, Sondra Segal, and Roberta Sklar on the W.E.T.; Eleanor Johnson on the process of art and feminism and Emmatroupe; Karen Malpede on three of her plays; Dolores Brandon on acting; and an interview with percussionist Edwina Lee Tyler).

A10

Natalle, Elizabeth J. *Feminist Theatre: A Study in Persuasion*. Metuchen, N.J.: Scarecrow, 1985.

Writing from a rhetorical perspective, Natalle defines feminist theatre as a "multi-locational" communication process designed to influence the beliefs of both audience and theatre members. Through the examination of feminist arguments and proofs in specific plays, she investigates the nature of the persuasive process and categorizes works performed by ten groups into three areas of concern: sexual politics (Myrna Lamb's *But What Have You Done for Me Lately?;* Rhode Island Feminist Theatre's *The Johnnie Show, Persephones* [sic] *Return, Taking It Off,* and *Paper Weight;* Karen Malpede's *The End of War;* Megan Terry's *Babes in the Bighouse;* and *How to Make a Woman* by Bobbi Ausubel with Stan Edelson), the woman-identified woman (Calliope Feminist Theatre's *Make Up by Mother Nature;* Martha Bocsing's *Love Song for an Amazon* and *The Web;* Ausubel's *Focus on Me!; Electra Speaks* by Clare Coss, Sondra Segal, and Roberta Sklar; and Jane Chambers' *A Late Snow*), and family roles and relationships (Joan Holden's *The Independent Female (or, A Man Has His Pride);* Boesing's *River Journal* and *The Story of a Mother;* Ausubel's *Tell Me a Riddle;* Rhode Island Feminist Theatre's *Internal Injury;* and Terry's *American King's English for Queens*). Natalle also compares the rhetoric of feminist theatre to that of the women's movement and assesses feminist theatre's potential impact.

A11

Neely, Carol Thomas. "Feminist Criticism in Motion." *For Alma Mater: Theory and Practice in Feminist Scholarship.* Ed. Paula A. Treichler, Cheris Kramarae, and Beth Stafford. Urbana: University of Illinois Press, 1985. 69–90.

This survey of the development of feminist criticism is blended with an account of Neely's personal journey within the field. Included is a detailed discussion of the three modes of feminist criticism of Shakespeare: compensatory, justificatory, and transformational. Outlining the conflicts within feminist theory, criticism, pedagogy, and her own feminism, she argues for both separation from and assimilation with the dominant culture.

A12

Thompson, Ann. "The Warrant of Womanhood: Shakespeare and Feminist Criticism." *The Shakespeare Myth.* Ed. Graham Holderness. Manchester, England: Manchester University Press, 1988. 74–88.

Approaching feminist criticism of Shakespeare within the wider context of feminist literary criticism, Thompson surveys the range of interpretative approaches. In addition, she emphasizes the importance of production choices and suggests challenges remaining for feminist critics.

A13

Todd, Susan, ed. *Women and Theatre: Calling the Shots.* London: Faber & Faber, 1984.

This collection contains nine essays by British women who discuss their creative work in theatre and address such issues as the representation of women onstage and the ways in which masculinist notions of women's behavior can be challenged. The contributors include actor-director Harriet Walter, playwright-director Bryony Lavery, designer Di Seymour, director Pam Brighton, actor Maggie Steed, playwright Catherine Hayes, playwright Ann Jellicoe, technical stage manager Mari Jenkins, and playwright-director Liane Aukin.

A14

Wandor, Michelene. *Carry On, Understudies.* London: Routledge & Kegan Paul, 1986.

Continuing her materialist analysis of theatre, Wandor expands upon and updates to the 1980s her earlier work, *Understudies: Theatre and Sexual Politics* (see A16). Her intention to shift from a historical thrust to a greater balance between documentation and commentary is exemplified by the addition of separate chapters on cross-dressing and on the feminisms. She has also added sections on several other women playwrights, including herself, to those examined in the earlier work. An appendix by Noel Grieg describes the takeover of the General Will (a Bradford theatre) by gay activists.

A15

Wandor, Michelene. *Look Back in Gender: Sexuality and the Family in Post-War British Drama.* London: Methuen, 1987.

Starting with the thesis that gender is a fundamental variable in the creation of the imagined world, Wandor compares and contrasts key postwar British plays from the period before 1968 when statutory censorship was in effect and the period after its abolition. Setting the plays within their social and political contexts, she investigates not only the portrayal of sexuality and the family but also such related issues as the representation of men and women in drama, the recurring image of the mother figure, the relative balance of domestic and public settings, and the connections between the interpersonal and the political. In addition, she considers the differing gender foci of male and female playwrights in each period. Wandor concentrates on works by such playwrights as John Osborne, Arnold Wesker, Harold Pinter, John Arden, Shelagh Delaney, Ann Jellicoe, Doris Lessing, Joe Orton, Edward Bond, Frank Marcus, Bertolt Brecht, Jane Arden, Maureen Duffy,

Theories and Overviews   A17

Howard Brenton, Trevor Griffiths, David Hare, Caryl Churchill, David
Edgar, G. F. Newman, and Stephen Lowe. She also briefly looks at plays
by Mary O'Malley, Pam Gems, and Nell Dunn featuring all-women casts.
Kenneth Tynan's 1965 essay condemning censorship serves as an "Interval" between the studies of pre- and post-1968 works.

A16
Wandor, Michelene. *Understudies: Theatre and Sexual Politics.* Lon-
    don: Methuen, 1981.

Wandor's exploration of the theatre-class-gender relationship addresses
the influence of feminist and gay activism on women's position as theatre practitioners and on drama's representation of women and treatment of homosexuality. Her opening chapter summarizes the historical,
political, and aesthetic contexts surrounding feminist and gay theatre.
Subsequent chapters trace the development of British alternative theatres concerned with sexual politics (the Women's Theatre Group, Gay
Sweatshop, Monstrous Regiment, and others) and the sources from
which they sprang. Other sections examine the ways in which feminist
and gay consciousness affect women theatre practitioners; individual
women playwrights (particularly Pam Gems and Caryl Churchill) and
the difficulty of defining plays as "feminist"; radical plays written before 1968 that express uneasiness with the state of family and sexual
roles; and men writers of the 1970s whose perspective on women remains male-determined.

Periodicals, Serials, and Annuals

A17
Austin, Gayle. "Women/Text/Theatre." *Performing Arts Journal* 9.2–3
    (1985): 185–90.

Austin urges women playwrights to reject the creation of conventional,
realistic works; find models in contemporary women innovators; and
create new shapes for theatre. She contrasts the work of individual playwrights with that of collaborative feminist theatres, and points out connections between the groups and the 1960s' avant-garde. Austin also
encourages writers and groups to seek each other out and to pursue
more intensely a sound theoretical basis for feminist performance.

A18

Boose, Lynda E. "The Family in Shakespeare Studies; or—Studies in the Family of Shakespeareans; or—The Politics of Politics." *Renaissance Quarterly* 40 (1987): 707–42.

Arguing that scholarly disputes over social issues in Shakespearean study are never merely academic but inescapably political, Boose examines the context for the discourse on family, marriage, and sex. She sets contemporary research against challenged traditions, reviews the development of Shakespearean feminism, and discusses at length the issue of Shakespeare's attitude toward patriarchy's subordination of women. Boose also delineates the dangers of marginalization faced by feminist inquiry, the erasure of women in the new historicism, the relationship of feminism within the academy to applied politics, and related topics.

A19

Butler, Judith. "Performative Acts and Gender Constitution: An Essay in Phenomenology and Feminist Theory." *Theatre Journal* 40 (1988): 519–31.

In an essay drawing from anthropological, theatrical, and philosophical discourses, Butler argues that gender is not a stable identity but "an identity tenuously constituted in time—an identity instituted through a *stylized repetition of acts.*" Noting that the acts constituting gender are similar to performative acts within theatrical contexts, she sets her task as investigating "in what ways gender is constructed through specific corporeal acts, and what possibilities exist for the cultural transformation of gender through such acts."

A20

Case, Sue-Ellen. "The Personal Is [Not] Political." *Work by Women.* Spec. issue of *Arts & Cinema* ns 1.3 (1987): 4.

Case contends that radical feminism, based on the belief that patriarchy is the cause of women's oppression, obfuscates differences among women that stem from class and race. She maintains that radical feminist drama's focus on white middle-class women, family relationships, and psychological problems "replicates the ways women have always been represented in sexist societies," and that the emphasis on gender rather than female sexuality "has produced aberrant departures from the representation of lesbian desire." Case also decries women playwrights' abandonment of the feminist movement.

A21

Case, Sue-Ellen, and Jeanie K. Forte. "From Formalism to Feminism."
   Theater 16.2 (1985): 62–65.

Pointing out the failures of the politicized theatre of previous decades to
dethrone the status quo, Case and Forte offer as "a gateway to the future
political stage" the current feminist appropriation of deconstruction's
critique of the self to illuminate the cultural oppression of women. Citing work by Hélène Cixous and Caryl Churchill, they suggest that the
combination of desiring female subject with homosexuality "disrupts
the center of traditional drama, which seems obsessively focused on the
male/female polarization."

A22

Chinoy, Helen Krich. "Art Versus Business: The Role of Women in American Theatre." *Women and Performance*. Spec. issue of *The Drama
   Review* 24.2 (1980): 3–10.

This is an abridged version of the introduction to Chinoy and Jenkins'
book, *Women in American Theatre*. See A4. *Term:* discrimination in
theatre practice.

A23

Cixous, Hélène. "Aller à la mer." *Modern Drama* 27 (1984): 546–48.

Cixous poses the question: "How, as women, can we go to the theatre
without lending our complicity to the sadism directed against women
. . .?" She envisions a new theatre that reclaims the "living, breathing,
speaking body" and in which woman's voice is heard.

A24

Daniels, Sarah. "There Are Fifty Two Percent of Us." *Women in Theatre*.
   Spec. issue of *Drama* 152 (1984): 23–24.

The author of *Masterpieces* briefly comments on women's current reactions against a patriarchal theatre.

A25

Davy, Kate. "Constructing the Spectator: Reception, Context, and Address in Lesbian Performance." *Performing Arts Journal* 10.2
   (1986): 43–52.

Drawing on reception theory, Davy explores lesbian theatre's potential
to effect radical change by rupturing the traditional representational apparatus grounded in the dynamics of sexual difference. She distinguishes between (1) lesbian-made feminist theatre, which conflates

lesbian with "woman," positing a female rather than male spectator/ subject and falling into the trap of generalized, universal subjectivity, and (2) renegade lesbian performance, which undercuts the heterosexual model and addresses a lesbian spectator. *The Search for Signs of Intelligent Life in the Universe* and Holly Hughes's *Lady Dick* at the WOW Cafe are used in illustration.

A26

de Lauretis, Teresa. "Sexual Indifference and Lesbian Representation." *Feminist Diversions.* Spec. issue of *Theatre Journal* 40 (1988): 155–77.

De Lauretis acknowledges that despite its limitations, the initial feminist critique of Western discourse with its emphasis on sexual difference opened up a space where "in the very act of assuming and speaking from the position of subject, a woman could concurrently recognize women as subjects *and* as objects of female desire." De Lauretis examines lesbian representation within the history of lesbian literature and its reception, framing her essay with Irigaray's distinction between *homosexuality* and *hommo-sexuality*. Discussing the project of lesbian performance, theatre, and film to devise "strategies of representation which will, in turn, alter the standard of vision, the frame of reference of visibility, of *what can be seen,*" she cautions against predicating redefinitions of conditions of vision and modes of representation "on a single, undivided identity of performer and audience."

A27

Diamond, Elin. "Brechtian Theory/Feminist Theory: Toward a Gestic Feminist Criticism." *TDR, The Drama Review: A Journal of Performance Studies* 32.1 (1988): 82–94.

Diamond proposes an intertextual reading of feminist theory and Brechtian theory to produce "a recovery of the radical potential of the Brechtian critique and a discovery, for feminist theory, of the specificity of theatre." Her approach brings together gender critique and *verfremdungseffekt;* sexual difference and the Brechtian "not, but"; women's history and historicization; and issues of spectatorship/the performer's body and historicization. Producing a proposal for "gestic feminist criticism," Diamond provides illustration of a gestic moment joining actor-subject, character, spectator, and author—all female—in the prologue to Aphra Behn's *The Forced Marriage.*

A28

Dolan, Jill. "Gender Impersonation Onstage: Destroying or Maintaining the Mirror of Gender Roles." *Women & Performance: A Journal of Feminist Theory* 2.2 (1985): 5–11.

With reference to Lacanian theory, Dolan extends "the analogy between the mirror stage and the social mirror to the stage as mirror of sexual difference." She briefly traces women's invisibility in Western theatre, noting that even gay male drag reflects women's socially constructed roles. She suggests that feminist perspectives, which expose and deconstruct underlying gender assumptions, should question theatre's representational apparatus.

A29

Dolan, Jill. "Is the Postmodern Aesthetic Feminist?" *Work by Women.* Spec. issue of *Art & Cinema* ns 1.3 (1987): 4–5.

Dolan argues that "postmodernism has deproblematized feminism essentially by trivializing the feminist project." Citing works by Elizabeth LeCompte, Richard Foreman, and Robert Wilson, she shows that although the traditional aesthetic values of text and authority may be subverted, the representation of sexual difference remains intact. She contrasts postmodernism's empty formalism with the WOW Cafe lesbian performers' use of postmodern elements in politically intentioned works that "resist the founding of representation on the binary opposition of heterosexuality."

A30

Dolan, Jill. "The Politics of Feminist Performance." *Theatre Times* July-Aug. 1986: 1+.

Finding that the label "women in theatre" has obscured political and aesthetic differences, Dolan distinguishes between such camps as feminist theoreticians who view the performer-spectator exchange as privileging the male perspective and precluding women's representation on stage and those women in theatre who see the main issue as one of discrimination. After discussing the limitations of the model of consciousness-raising that inspired such groups as the Women's Experimental Theater, she suggests that the most important issue for feminist theatre today is not sex (male-female opposition) but gender (masculine-feminine polarization). WOW Cafe's gender-bending work is described.

A31
Ellenberger, Harriet. "The Dream Is the Bridge: In Search of Lesbian
Theatre." *Trivia* 5 (1984): 17–59.

Ellenberger writes about the "synchronicity/attraction/connection" between lesbian lives and experimental theatre. Dividing theatre-making
into three interacting processes of enacting, freeing, and shaping, she
provides numerous illustrations, including presentations at the National
Festival of Women's Theatre, Catherine Nicholson's direction of Martha
Boesing's *Ashes, Ashes, We All Fall Down,* and Peter Schumann's Bread
and Puppet Theatre. Specific issues addressed include lesbians' need to
create new dramatic structures, audience response to feminist and lesbian theatre, releasing women's voices, the collaborative process, and
cross-dressing. She offers productions of Monique Wittig's *The Constant Journey* and Brecht's *Galileo* as examples of a moving simplicity
achieved through complexity, asserting that both Wittig and Brecht "attempt to make art a weapon of freedom struggle."

A32
Erickson, Peter. "Rewriting the Renaissance, Rewriting Ourselves."
Shakespeare Quarterly 38 (1987): 327–37.

Assessing the current relations between new historicism and feminist
criticism, Erickson notes their disagreement about the relative importance of gender and conflicting attitudes toward the present and explores the possibilities for future collaboration. He also details new
historicism's failure to include a satisfactory conception of politics.

A33
Freedman, Barbara. "Frame-Up: Feminism, Psychoanalysis, Theatre."
Theatre Journal 40 (1988): 375–97.

In an article influenced by feminist film criticism and entailing a critique of Lacan and his (mis)appropriation by feminists, Freedman inter-
weaves complex issues surrounding sexual difference, narrativity,
subjectivity, and the constitutive gaze. She probes "how theatre figures
difference," a topic that involves "the problem of the frame and framing
behavior as intrinsic to theatre, the extent to which theatre is always already determined by the frames it puts onstage, and the extent to which
theatre provides a means for reframing." Freedman proposes that theatre, quintessentially deconstructive, provides a path for psychoanalytic
and feminist theories to follow if they are willing "to reread Lacan
against himself, to accept how feminism's gaze has been purloined, to
interrogate the political implications of psychoanalysis."

A34

Gelderman, Carol W. "The Male Nature of Tragedy." *Prairie Schooner* 49 (1975): 220–27.

This investigation into why women have not written great tragedy focuses largely on the beginnings of Western drama, particularly the changes in the structure of Greek society dramatized in *The Oresteia*. Gelderman maintains that even today, "all the conditions of [a woman's] life are hostile to the state of mind which is needed to create great tragedy." Following Gelderman's essay, a section entitled "Symposium: Women and Tragedy" contains other viewpoints on the issue. See A39.

A35

Hollingsworth, Margaret. "Why We Don't Write." *Feminism and Canadian Theatre.* Spec. issue of *Canadian Theatre Review* 43 (1985): 21–27.

After emphasizing the historical suppression of women's work in the arts, Hollingsworth focuses on the English-Canadian theatre's domination by male artistic directors unwilling to risk producing unsanctioned women's plays. She discusses the socialization of women to identify with a male world view and the discomfort of men—and some women—in watching a work lacking male characters or wherein women speak candidly. Contending that women's opportunities to express themselves in their own theatrical style require more women in leadership roles, Hollingsworth suggests affirmative action as a solution.

A36

Janaczewska, Noëlle. " 'Do We Want a Piece of the Cake, or Do We Want to Bake a Whole New One?': Feminist Theatre in Britain." *Hecate* 13.1 (1987): 106–13.

The author's overview of feminist theatre in Britain since 1970 places its development within an artistic, social, political, and economic context. Stating that not all women's theatre is feminist theatre, Janaczewska defines the latter as incorporating "an understanding of the social construction of femaleness and some analysis of the interactions of gender, class and power," and expressing such awareness "in the content, form, perspective and processes of that theatre." She also argues against a female aesthetic and looks at feminist theatre's success as an innovative force.

A37

Jenkins, Linda Walsh. "Locating the Language of Gender Experience." *Women & Performance: A Journal of Feminist Theory* 2.1 (1984): 5–20.

In this wide-ranging essay, which attempts to lay the groundwork for further study of gender significance in dramatic criticism and theory, Jenkins stresses the need to find the authentically female aspects of dramatic art. She centers her discussion around gender differences in perception and naming and issues of domestic (female) vs. public (male) spheres. She defines as "female" those dramatic actions that emphasize relational crises and movement toward communion and those forms that are associational or circular. In addition, she examines misogyny within and outside selected plays, and women's restrictions in patriarchal theatre.

A38

Jenkins, Linda Walsh. "Women in Theatre Today." *Women's Theatre.* Spec. issue of *Theatre News* Nov. 1977: 4.

Jenkins emphasizes the increased visibility of women outside the heavily institutionalized aspects of theatre. She directs attention to the investigation of theatre from a feminist perspective within academia and the creation of single projects, such as *Not as Sleepwalkers,* which explore "a new theatrical language of women's experiences."

A39

Keilstrup, Lorraine M., et al. "Symposium: Women and Tragedy." *Prairie Schooner* 49 (1975): 227–36.

Several writers respond to the question posed by Gelderman in "The Male Nature of Tragedy": "Why is it that no woman has ever written great tragedy?" (See A34.) *Terms:* gender, influence on writing; women playwrights, status and conditions, difficulty or underrepresentation in attaining production.

A40

Keyssar, Helene. "Hauntings: Gender and Drama in Contemporary English Theatre." *English Amerikanische Studies* 3–4 (1986): 449–68.

In her effort to define feminist theatre, Keyssar reflects on the necessity of distinguishing "between productions that are merely elements of a new phase of the dominant culture and those that are genuinely emergent cultural forms." After delineating the meaning of gender differences in classical Greek drama and patriarchal theatre's resistance to "its elemental multi-voicedness," Keyssar considers feminist theatre's specific attributes. Arguing that its most distinctive feature is the rejection of traditional recognition scenes and self-discovery, she underscores its dramaturgy of transformation, in which "there is no fixed, true self but human beings in the constant process of becoming other." She then focuses on the diverse contributions by Pam Gems, Louise Page, and especially Caryl Churchill to the creation of a true alternative drama, finding a commonality in their plays' "insistence on dramatizing historical moments in which dominant concepts of gender are called into question."

A41
Lamb, Margaret. "Feminist Criticism." *The Drama Review* 18.3 (1974): 46–50.

Lamb outlines three general areas of potentially valuable inquiry: research on women in theatre history; the examination of creative work presently being done by women and its relation to feminism; and reassessment of the critical approaches used to explore work by, for, or about women. Surveying the lack of regular coverage by the feminist press and the mixed quality of response in the *New York Times* and other periodicals, she suggests specific ways for feminists to engage in theatre criticism.

A42
Levin, Richard. "Feminist Thematics and Shakespearean Tragedy." *PMLA* 103 (1988): 125–38.

Levin restricts his critique to one trend of feminist criticism: the interpretative approach, which assumes that character and action serve a theme relating to the role of gender in the individual and in society. He takes issue with critics' locating the cause of the tragic outcome in "masculinity" or "patriarchy," and outlines distortions involved in thematic readings. He then details the results of this approach in terms of the characters, the tragic effect, the conception of tragedy, and authorial intention. Levin suggests as a more promising line of feminist inquiry the actual nature of the gender assumptions in the plays.

A43
Lushington, Kate. "Fear of Feminism." *Feminism and Canadian Theatre.* Spec. issue of *Canadian Theatre Review* 43 (1985): 5–11.

Incorporating frequent quotations from and references to Rina Fraticelli's "Any Black Crippled Woman Can!" (see D89) and to the government-solicited report on "The Status of Women in Canadian Theatre," Lushington dissects the failure of feminism to affect Canadian theatre. She addresses issues that include misconceptions about feminism, the marginalization of women's theatre, the powerlessness inherent in the acting profession, and the anti-intellectualism intrinsic to Canadian theatre.

A44

McKewin, Carole. "Shakespeare Liberata: Shakespeare, the Nature of Women, and the New Feminist Criticism." *Mosaic* 10.3 (1977): 157–64.

Surveying the development of feminist criticism of Shakespeare, McKewin cites the particular significance of Dusinberre's *Shakespeare and the Nature of Women*. She notes that the more recent criticism "has become less self-conscious about the polemic of the movement, and more involved with the work of art itself." The variety of methodologies used by feminists, the process of re-visioning Shakespeare's women, and the need to distinguish between antifeminism in playwrights and in critics also are discussed.

A45

Mael, Phyllis. "Beyond Hellman and Hansberry: The Impact of Feminism on a Decade of Drama." *Kansas Quarterly* 12.4 (1980): 141–44.

Attributing women's previous silence in dramatic literature to exclusion from the collaborative efforts of theatre, Mael considers several reasons for the recent proliferation of drama by women, including women's greater participation in 1960s nontraditional theatre, the development of networks, and the effects of feminist theory. She comments briefly on the variety of content and structures emerging in feminist drama.

A46

Neely, Carol Thomas. "Constructing the Subject: Feminist Practice and the New Renaissance Discourses." *Women in the Renaissance II.* Spec. issue of *English Literary Renaissance* 18 (1988): 5–18.

Neely contends that despite all that the current theoretical approaches—new historicist, cultural materialist, Lacanian, and deconstructive—seem to have in common with feminist criticism, their effect has actually been "to oppress women, repress sexuality, and subordinate gender issues." She recommends "over-reading" Shakespeare and other Renaissance texts as if for the first time, to uncover "the possibility of human (especially female) gendered subjectivity, identity, and agency, the possibility of women's resistance or even subversion." She urges that methods be constructed to contextualize canonical texts with new work by women's historians, social historians, and feminists working to construct a Renaissance that includes women.

A47

Neely, Carol Thomas. "Feminist Criticism and Teaching Shakespeare." *ADE Bulletin* 87 (1987): 15–18.

While declining to offer an authoritative definition of feminist criticism, Neely suggests some of its aspects. Drawing illustrations from *Hamlet,* she delineates three modes of feminist criticism of Shakespeare: compensatory, justificatory, and transformational. She also explores the implications of feminist criticism in her teaching.

A48

Reinhardt, Nancy. "New Directions for Feminist Criticism in Theatre and the Related Arts." *Soundings: An Interdisciplinary Journal* 64 (1981): 361–87. (Rpt. in *A Feminist Perspective in the Academy: The Difference It Makes.* Ed. Elizabeth Langland and Walter Gove. Chicago: University of Chicago Press, 1981. 25–51.)

After analyzing why feminist scholarship in theatre has lagged behind that in film, Reinhardt discusses the application of feminist perspectives to theatre criticism and history. In considering dramatic genre, she examines the authority of Aristotle's *Poetics* and the male nature of tragedy's characters, structure, and moral framework. To show how a gender analysis of visual imagery helps describe the social and ideological content of drama, she employs examples from historical staging, including blocking, costuming, and audience seating, all of which evidence the distinction between central male and peripheral female space.

A49

Roth, Martha. "Notes Toward a Feminist Performance Aesthetic." *Women & Performance: A Journal of Feminist Theory* 1.1 (1983): 5–14.

Roth seeks new images of women on stage to replace the old, pornographic, exemplary representations that embody male fantasies about women. She investigates such topics as the tradition of male performance, which requires cross-dressing and male imitation of women; stage images as a reflection of the political economy of sex; and the interrelationships of sex, class, and age in the portrayal of female characters.

A50
Savona, Jeannette Laillou. "French Feminism and Theatre: An Introduction." *Modern Drama* 27 (1984): 540–45.

Serving as a conceptual framework to articles by Hélène Cixous (see A23) and Josette Féral (see D77), this short piece outlines French approaches to feminist criticism and defines major strategic issues confronting feminist critics of theatre. Cixous's playwriting career is summarized.

A51
Schechner, Richard. "Women and Ma." *TDR, The Drama Review: A Journal of Performance Studies* 32.1 (1988): 4–6.

Briefly discussing the call for a new performance-audience relationship by feminists rejecting phallocentric art, Schechner suggests that other cultures offer applicable alternatives to Western practice.

A52
Segal, Sondra, and Roberta Sklar. "The Women's Experimental Theater." *The Drama Review* 27.4 (1983): 74–75.

The group's artistic directors note that their goals from the early 1970s—the evolution of a feminist aesthetic and the establishment of women's theatre as a form of expression—still pertain. Reflecting on women's relationship with major theatre institutions, they call for "a theatre that has been revolutionized by feminism and women's vision."

A53
Sisley, Emily L. "Notes on Lesbian Theatre." *The Drama Review* 25.1 (1981): 47–56.

Borrowing from William Hoffman's definition of gay theatre, Sisley defines lesbian theatre "as a production that implicitly or explicitly acknowledges that there are [lesbians] on both sides of the footlights." She reconstructs the history of feminist theatre, noting the few groups specifically identifying themselves as lesbian and pointing out similarities between lesbian and feminist groups. In addition, she compares lesbian with "just plain" theatre, citing the commercial successes of Jane Chambers, and discusses Keltie Creed and the Atthis Theatre (Toronto), as well as the work of other current lesbian groups.

A54
Stasio, Marilyn. "The Night the Critics Lost Their Cool." *Ms.* Sept. 1975: 37–41.

In this examination of gender bias in criticism, Stasio cites as examples reaction to three recent plays: Anne Burr's *Mert & Phil,* David Rabe's *In the Boom Boom Room,* and Ray Aranha's *My Sister, My Sister.*

A55

Stephens, Judith L. "From Positive Image to Disruptive Apparatus: Feminist Perspectives in American Plays and Dramatic Criticism." *The Pennsylvania Speech Communication Annual* 44 (1988): 59–67.

Emphasizing the diversity and changing nature of feminist thought as reflected in American drama and criticism, Stephens distinguishes three feminist dynamics—liberal, cultural, and materialist—and their manifestations in selected plays. She then differentiates between early feminist criticism, which involved assessments of female images and attempts to define feminist drama and/or characters, and recent criticism, which presents a more fundamental challenge to traditional drama by scrutinizing the concept of dramatic character and the notion of identity itself.

A56

Stummer, Peter O. " 'I Go to the Theatre a Lot Because I Care So Much about Anarchy': The Problems of Contemporary 'Women's Theatre.' " *Mid-American Review* 8.2 (1988): 53–70.

Stummer's comparison of feminist discourse on political, theoretical, and aesthetic levels provides the context for a brief survey of women dramatists from several countries. He identifies three characteristics of feminist playwriting: inversion (e.g., role reversal), affirmation (placing women in the center), and extension (including such phenomena as countercasting and overstepping genre limits).

A57

Wandor, Michelene. "Culture, Politics and Values in Plays by Women in the 1980s." *English Amerikanische Studies* 3–4 (1986): 441–48.

Wandor establishes that women began making a visible impact on the British playwriting community only in the early 1980s, and underscores the need to place their work within the legacies of 1970s feminism and to consider the current ideological approaches toward their presence. Cautioning that simply because a play is by a woman or features women characters does not mean it is feminist, she summarizes three dominant feminist tendencies—radical, bourgeois and bourgeois radical, and socialist—and applies them to women's theatre work. The strengths and weaknesses of each position are specified, as well as the commonalities and differences among them.

A58
Wandor, Michelene. "The Impact of Feminism on the Theatre." *Feminist Review* 18 (1984): 76–92.

Scrutinizing feminism's influence on British theatre since 1968, Wandor analyzes three oppositional sexual-political groups, the Women's Theatre Group, Monstrous Regiment, and Gay Sweatshop, to assess the connection between "forms of organizing the work process, and the content and aesthetic possibilities these forms generate." She discusses the relationship between level of radicalism and commercial success, investigates women playwrights' patronage problems, distinguishes current bourgeois feminist efforts and their contradictory effects, and stresses two preconditions for healthy interaction between feminism and theatre: the press for employment parity and "a lively and critical self-awareness among feminists which will continue to push the boundaries of content and form."

A59
Wandor, Michelene. "Sexual Politics and the Strategy of Socialist Theatre." *Theatre Quarterly* 9.36 (1980): 28–30.

Wandor specifies the influences of feminist ideology on socialist theatre, which has generally viewed males as the protagonists of the class struggle and the site of struggle as the workplace. She notes that the primary job of feminist and gay theatre groups is "to reclaim women and gays from their secondary or ghettoized position in theatre, and assert their experiences as valid subject matter for political theatre work."

A60
Wilson, Ann. "The Politics of the Script." *Feminism and Canadian Theatre.* Spec. issue of *Canadian Theatre Review* 43 (1985): 174–97.

Maintaining that a script is not feminist simply because it sympathetically represents women's issues, Wilson contends that feminists must also recognize "the social relations which inscribe the politics of the play as well." She sees the feminist project in theatre as attempting to dismantle the hierarchical structure that privileges the script. In illustration, she contrasts the appropriation by the dominant social structure of *Cloud Nine,* a published play (and therefore a commodity), with *This Is for You, Anna,* an ongoing work engaged with its audience and resisting closure.

A61

Yarbro-Bejarano, Yvonne. "The Female Subject in Chicano Theatre: Sexuality, 'Race,' and Class." *Theatre Journal* 38 (1986): 389–407.

Yarbro-Bejarano, in a review of the history of Chicano theatre, explores the shift in representation of the subject from the early texts, embedded in cultural nationalism, to more recent alternatives. She analyzes Luis Valdez and El Teatro Campesino's influential works, in which ordered narratives reinforce heterosexual hierarchy, perpetuating the male as subject and the female as *La Malinche* or *La Virgen*. She describes Chicanas' responses to male-dominated theatre, such as the formation of all-women *teatros*, and details the materialist analysis of Teatro de la Esperanza, whose docudramas illustrate "the difficulty of decentering the male subject of representation in narrative forms." She also examines two nonnarrative works: *Tongues of Fire*, a *teatropoesía* creating a collective female subject, and Cherríe Moraga's *Giving Up the Ghost*, which presents the lesbian as desiring subject.

Feminist Theatres and Theatre Groups

Books and Monographs

B1

Bassnett-McGuire, Susan [E.]. "Women's Theatre—Notes on the Work of Monstruous [sic] Regiment." *British Drama and Theatre from the Mid-Fifties to the Mid-Seventies*. Rostock, Germany: Wilhelm-Pieck Universität, 1979. 89–101.

The author outlines the group's purpose of redressing theatre's imbalance weighted toward men, collective method of working, and struggle to find new forms for their portrayal of "women as women, rather than as the adjuncts of men." *Floorshow, Vinegar Tom*, and *Kiss and Kill* are discussed.

B2

Collin, Solange. "An Alternative to the Traditional Theatre in Québec." Trans. Dympna Borowska. *In the Feminine: Women and Words/Les Femmes et les mots: Conference Proceedings 1983*. Ed. Ann Dybikowski, et al. Edmonton, Alberta, Canada: Longspoon, 1985. 219–23.

Collin concisely depicts the fight of women in theatre "to speak their minds and take their place." She reminisces about her work with Le Théâtre des cuisines, cites several subversive feminist plays, and cautions that while women have gained ground, power in the theatre, as elsewhere, is still held by men.

B3

Coss, Clare, Sondra Segal, and Roberta Sklar. "Separation and Survival: Mothers, Daughters, Sisters—The Women's Experimental Theater." *The Future of Difference*. Ed. Hester Eisenstein and Alice Jardine. Boston: G.K. Hall, 1980. 193–235.

An explanation of the Women's Experimental Theater's goals precedes excerpts from *Daughters* and *Sister/Sister*, two parts of *The Daughters Cycle*, a trilogy focusing on women in the family. Following the excerpts, a summary of the postperformance discussion with the audience touches on such topics as feminist acting and the collaborative approach.

B4

Fido, Elaine. "Radical Woman: Woman and Theatre in the Anglophone Caribbean." *Critical Issues in West Indian Literature: Selected Papers from West Indian Literature Conferences, 1981–1983*. Ed. Erika Sollish Smilowitz and Roberta Quarles Knowles. Parkersburg, Iowa: Caribbean, 1984. 33–45.

Stressing that women's radicalism requires innovative aesthetic form, Fido offers a brief look at women's theatrical activity in the West Indies, then focuses on two Jamaican contributions to women's theatre: Sistren's *Bellywoman Bangarang*, which makes extensive use of African-style ritual and dance, and Pat Cumper's *The Rapist,* a more conventionally structured play with an innovative approach to the theme of rape.

B5

It's All Right to Be Woman Theatre. Interview with Karen Malpede Taylor. *People's Theatre in Amerika*. New York: Drama Book Specialists, 1972. 325–28.

In this interview with eight of the group's members, the comments of individuals are not differentiated. The theatre's goals, collaborative working processes, and enactment of audience members' dreams are among the subjects addressed.

B6

Itzin, Catherine. *Stages in the Revolution: Political Theatre in Britain Since 1968*. London: Eyre Methuen, 1980.

Three individual essays tracing the development of the Women's Theatre Group, Gay Sweatshop, and Monstrous Regiment, and another describing the plays of Caryl Churchill are of particular interest. A chronology of productions of works by playwrights, companies, and theatres is included.

B7
Leavitt, Dinah Luise. *Feminist Theatre Groups*. Jefferson, N.C.: Mc-Farland, 1980.

In this first book-length study of American feminist theatre, Leavitt provides an in-depth analysis of four Minneapolis groups (Alive and Trucking, Lavender Cellar, Circle of the Witch, and At the Foot of the Mountain), examining their structure, objectives, finances, creative processes, playwrights, productions, impact on audiences, and critical responses elicited. Stressing the multiplicity of perspectives on feminist theatre and drawing upon the work of other theatres and nonaffiliated feminist playwrights, Leavitt traces the development of feminist theatre and its relationship to the women's movement and the avant-garde theatre of the 1960s. She also evaluates the drama in terms of the emergence of common themes, the representation of women, the search for new forms, and the use of ritual. A separate chapter compares and contrasts feminist theatre activity with the 1930s political theatres and the black theatre movement.

B8
Suntree, Susan. "Women's Theatre: Creating the Dream Now." *Women's Culture: The Women's Renaissance of the Seventies*. Ed. Gayle Kimball. Metuchen, N.J.: Scarecrow, 1981. 106–16.

Suntree provides a brief overview of a number of interrelated topics, including the creation of new theatrical images of women through new forms, the limitations of realism, the role of ritual in women's theatre, and the relationship between women's theatre groups and their audiences. Her discussion of the creative process of women's theatre collectives is enhanced by the description of her own work on *Antigone Prism* with the Women's Ensemble of the Berkeley Stage Company.

B9
Wandor, Michelene. "The Personal Is Political: Feminism and the Theatre." *Dreams and Deconstructions: Alternative Theatre in Britain*. Ed. Sandy Craig. Derbyshire, England: Amber Lane, 1980. 49–58.

Noting the historical lack of sexual equality in theatrical practice and the exclusion of women as subjects of drama, Wandor summarizes the development of feminist theatre in England within a social and political context. Four strands are delineated: agit-prop, Theatre-in-Education, professional theatre practitioners, and the socialist theatre movement. Wandor reviews work by such companies as the Women's Theatre Group, Monstrous Regiment, and several small, all-women groups who subvert the bourgeois images of female sexuality.

Periodicals, Serials, and Annuals

B10

Ausubel, Bobbi. " 'Liberated' American Woman Meets 'Emancipated' Polish Woman." *The Second Wave* 1.4 (1972): 34–37.

A member of the Caravan Theatre, which participated in the Polish International Festival of Festivals, Ausubel reports on her personal encounters with and observations of Polish women and their role in Poland's society, as well as audience reactions to the feminist ideology of *How to Make a Woman*.

B11

Bardsley, Barney. "The Young Blood of Theatre: Women's Theatre Groups." *Women in Theatre*. Spec. issue of *Drama* 152 (1984): 25–29.

In this survey of British women's theatre companies that have survived despite marginalization, male critical prejudice, and financial difficulty, Bardsley categorizes thirteen widely varied groups as follows: those using an agit-prop style—Sensible Footwear, Spare Tyre, Sadista Sisters; those that use a more conventional, narrative approach—the Women's Theatre Group, Monstrous Regiment, Mrs Worthington's Daughters, Little Women, Theatre of Black Women; those concerned with visual imagery and physical theatre—Three Women Mime, Bloodgroup; and those with a more radical premise—Siren, Scarlet Harlets, Burnt Bridges.

B12

Bessai, Diane. "Women, Feminism and Prairie Theatre." *Feminism and Canadian Theatre*. Spec. issue of *Canadian Theatre Review* 43 (1985): 28–43.

Reporting on the growing feminist undercurrent in contemporary prairie theatre, Bessai divides her piece into two sections: (1) companies (e.g., Nellie McClung Theatre and Hecate's Players), productions (e.g., *Rock and a Hard Place*), and organizations (e.g., Celebration of Women in the Arts) and (2) individual artists. Varying reactions to feminism are expressed in commentary from many women theatre practitioners, including playwrights Wendy Lill and Sharon Pollock.

B13

Bustos, Nidia. Interview. "Art and Culture a Revolutionary Force in Nicaragua." With Coco Fusco. *Womanews* Mar. 1986: 8+.

Bustos, founder and national director of the Movement for Campesino Artistic and Theatrical Expression (MECATE), a grassroots consciousness-raising organization involving eighty groups throughout Nicaragua, talks about performances designed to eliminate machismo and restraints on campesino women's self-expression. She also addresses questions regarding MECATE's structure, educational efforts, and independence from the state, as well as women's participation in the groups.

B14

Caravan Theatre. "A Conversation with Caravan Theatre." With members of Female Liberation. *The Second Wave* 1.4 (1972): 18–25.

Four interviewers from Female Liberation speak with several women and men involved in the Boston troupe's play *How to Make a Woman*, which underwent profound changes during its five years of performance. The effect of the women's liberation movement on the play, the performers, and the audience reaction is discussed.

B15

Carlson, Susan. "Process and Product: Contemporary British Theatre and Its Communities of Women." *Theatre Research International* 13 (1988): 249–63.

Carlson views women's groups as distinguished by their goal of giving women a voice in the theatre and their nurturing of plays featuring communities of women. Detailing the movement of women's groups from attempts at democratic collectives to experimentation with skills specialization, she describes two ventures offering "a foretaste of how women's community-produced theatre may develop": the Women's Playhouse Trust and the Colway Theatre Trust. Carlson also explores the main expressions of the communal presence in women's plays: the use of group protagonists, the depiction of women's relationships with one another, and the reconstruction of the family, particularly in the endings of comedies.

B16

Carrington, Patricia. "Sistren Back in Britain." *Spare Rib* 171 (Oct. 1986): 46.

Announcing the Jamaican women's theatre collective's London visit, Carrington describes the group's working class background and its focus on issues of racism and sexism.

B17

Chhachhi, Amrita. "Media as a Political Statement: Two Attempts by Women's Groups." *ISIS International Women's Journal* 2 (Dec. 1984): 94-100.

Chhachhi concentrates on a street play and an exhibition produced by a small, independent group to illustrate the Indian women's movement's creativity in using alternative (noninstitutional) forms for consciousness-raising. She relates how the collectively created *Om Swaha,* dealing with women's victimization in marriage, drew audience members into the performance, ending with a chant of solidarity, and how the visual presentation of the roots of dowry served as a forum for discussion.

B18

Collins, Robert. "A Feminist Theatre in Transition: Its Multi-Cultural Ideals Intact, At the Foot of the Mountain Confronts Some Difficult Changes." *American Theatre* Feb. 1988: 32–34.

Collins reports on the efforts of the Minneapolis theatre to transcend its essentially white middle-class feminist orientation and form a new multicultural acting company. *The Story of a Mother*, a reworked collaborative piece (with playwright Martha Boesing), is discussed.

B19

Coss, Claire, Sondra Segal, and Roberta Sklar. "Why Do We Need a Feminist Theatre?" *Women & Performance: A Journal of Feminist Theory* 1.1 (1983): 15–18.

The founders-artistic directors of the Women's Experimental Theater (W.E.T.) set forth the group's collaborative efforts, underscoring the distinctiveness both of women's experience and of the relationship between feminist actor and female spectator.

B20

de Lauretis, Teresa. "The Left Hand of History." *Heresies* 1.4 (1977–78): 23–26.

The author's witnessing of a performance of *Nonostante Gramsci (Despite Gramsci)* by the militant Rome feminist collective, La Maddalena, and analysis of the subsequently published text of the production and its underlying research, provide a basis for her theorizing about "women as subjects—not commodities but social beings producing and reproducing cultural products, transmitting and transforming cultural values."

B21

Emberley, Heather. "Millie Lamb: A Lifetime of Issues." *Herizons* Apr. 1984: 40.

This profile includes feminist activist Lamb's reminiscences on the birth of Winnipeg's Nellie McClung Theatre and explanation of the group's ongoing relationship with grassroots audiences.

B22

Ford-Smith, Honor. "Jamaican ♀ Theatre: An Interview with Honor Ford-Smith." With Esther Figueroa. *Off Our Backs* Apr. 1987: 10–12.

Ford-Smith talks about Sistren, a Jamaican women's cultural organization that expanded from its start as a theatre group into research, textiles, and other ventures. In part the interview focuses on the collective process in creating theatre pieces based on actual life experiences.

B23

Franey, Ros. "Women in the Workshop." *Plays and Players* Nov. 1973: 24–27.

This article on the Women's Theatre Group and its relationship with the women's liberation movement includes interviews with playwright Pam Gems and actress Alexandra Berlin.

B24

Freilicher, Elizabeth. "Feminist Troupe Opens on Coast." *New Directions for Women* 5.1 (1976): 15 + .

The author describes the Theatre of Process, an all-woman group in Santa Barbara, California.

B25

French, Joan. "Organizing Women through Drama in Rural Jamaica." *ISIS International Women's Journal* 6 (1986): 104–10.

French writes about Sistren's use of drama based on real-life experiences to motivate and organize a group of Sugartown women.

B26

Fuller, Janine. "Working Together on Feminist Theatre." *Herizons* July–
Aug. 1985: 34–35.

Declaring that "feminist work has found its niche within the broader category of alternative theatre," while noting its financial constraints, Fuller uses interviews with playwright Amanda Hale, Cynthia Grant of Toronto's Nightwood Theatre, and actor-playwright Gay Bell to explore the effects of the collaborative process and issues surrounding the re-structuring of theatre and society.

B27

Furer, Jessica. "WOW: Anarchy on the Lower East Side." *Womanews*
June 1986: 15.

Furer tracks the history of WOW Cafe, beginning with the international Women's One World festivals from which it sprang, and praising it as a rich cultural resource for the women's community. She explains WOW's philosophy of providing a permanent space for women without the pressures and restrictions of mainstream theatre and delineates the sensitive, changing, and increasingly difficult process of deciding what gets performed.

B28

Gillespie, Patti P. "Feminist Theatre: Rhetorical Phenomenon." *Quarterly Journal of Speech* 64 (1978): 284–94.

Gillespie interprets the development of feminist theatre in the 1970s as a vigorous grassroots movement offering an excellent medium for over-coming feminists' particular rhetorical problems. She outlines feminist theatre's appropriation of strategies previously used by the 1960s artistic avant-garde and political Left, and distinguishes two major kinds of groups: those committed to promoting women theatre artists, and those committed to improving women's condition in general.

B29

Gillespie, Patti P. "Feminist Theatres of the 1970s." *Women's Theatre*.
Spec. issue of *Theatre News* Nov. 1977: 5 + .

Gillespie provides a more fully developed version of this article in "Feminist Theatre: Rhetorical Phenomenon," annotated in B28. *Terms:* feminist drama, rhetorical aspects; feminist theatre, history of.

B30

Gragen, Coleen, Janet Aalfs, and Madeleine Gladu. Interview. "Women in Martial Arts." With Becca Harber. *Off Our Backs* Apr. 1987: 14–16.

In part this interview deals with a women's martial arts theatre group whose performances both demonstrate the arts and provide insight into their meaningfulness for the participants.

B31

Grant, Cynthia, et al. "Notes from the Front Line." *Feminism and Canadian Theatre*. Spec. issue of *Canadian Theatre Review* 43 (1985): 44–51.

In individual sections of the article, the founders of Toronto's Nightwood Theatre—Grant, Kim Renders, Margo Vingoe, and Maureen White—comment on the group's history, struggle to survive, collective working process, goals, and accomplishments. Nightwood's categorization as a "women's theatre" is discussed.

B32

Greenfield, Myrna. "Acting, Pregnant?" *Spare Rib* 110 (Sept. 1981): 6–8.

Interviewing two members of the British feminist theatre Beryl and the Perils and two former members who were fired because of pregnancy, Greenfield comments on the relationship between feminism and motherhood.

B33

Hall, Katherine Ekau Amoy. "Theatre: A Tool for Change." *Womanews* May 1986: 10.

The author announces the uniting of three lesbian/women groups, Cuarto Creciente (a shelter-library-theatre in Mexico City), Whirling Women of Colors (a New York theatre ensemble), and Nightsage (a Swiss international media company), to form an ensemble of activist artists. Individual participants are briefly profiled.

B34

Hanna, Gillian. Interview. "Feminism and Theatre." With Peter Hulton. *Theatre Papers* 2nd ser. 8 (1978): 1–14.

Hanna, a founder-member of Monstrous Regiment, discusses the need for social change, the relationship between socialism and feminism, and the role of theatre within this framework. She talks about the group's plays, with reference to their collective processes and creation of new forms, and contrasts male and female approaches to theatre.

B35
Hanson, Lori, and Jan Mandel. "Alive and Trucking Theatre." *Women: A Journal of Liberation* 3.2 (1972): 8–9.

The authors discuss the history and work of the Minneapolis company.

B36
Ives, L. Patricia. "*The Last Will and Testament of Lolita*: The Very Best Bad Girls Create . . . ." *Canadian Theatre Review* 55 (1988): 30–33.

Citing Toronto's Nightwood Theatre as one of the numerous feminist companies working collectively to deal with social and political issues, Ives details the creation and performance of as well as the reaction to *The Last Will and Testament of Lolita*, a multimedia production inspired by *Re-Visions*, Marcia Resnick's book exploring female adolescence.

B37
"Jamaica: Women's Theatre." *ISIS: An International Bulletin* 21 (1982): 26–27.

This brief article on Sistren, a collective, working-class theatre, describes its development and themes.

B38
Khuri, Suzanne Odette, et al. "Fragments." *Feminism and Canadian Theatre*. Spec. issue of *Canadian Theatre Review* 43 (1985): 167–73.

Members of the Toronto-based collective, the Anna Project—Khuri, Anne-Marie MacDonald, Banuta Rubess, Tori Smith, and Maureen White—reflect on the creation of *This Is for You, Anna*.

B39
Killian, Linda. "Feminist Theatre." *Feminist Art Journal* 3.1 (1974): 23–24.

In an overview of the development of feminist theatre, Killian suggests that despite its myriad styles and ideologies, it can be defined as women-authored drama "which tries to explore the female psyche, women's place in society and women's potential." She focuses on the work of the Westbeth Playwrights Feminist Collective and the Women's Interart Center and their difficulties in obtaining funding.

B40

Kingsbury, Marty. "Way Off Broadway: A Feminist Response to The-atre." *The Second Wave* 5.3 (1979): 32–38.

Kingsbury profiles four women's theatre groups: Rhode Island Feminist Theatre, Circle of the Witch, Spiderwoman, and the Muse Conceptions.

B41

Kishwar, Madhu, et al. "A Women's Theatre Workshop." *Manushi* 4 (Dec. 1979/Jan.–Feb. 1980): 24.

This report on the collective efforts by a group of women in Delhi to evolve a theatrical performance from their concerns highlights the par-ticipants' discovery of shared feelings of imprisonment as women in their society. The group's hope for expansion is expressed.

B42

LoMonaco, Martha Schmoyer. "Of, By and For Women: The Women's Playhouse Trust." *Women & Performance: A Journal of Feminist Theory* 2.2 (1985): 59–64.

The author discusses the formation of a London women's collective, Women's Playhouse Trust (WPT), in reaction to discrimination against women in theatre. She also describes WPT's first production, a revival of Aphra Behn's *The Lucky Chance*.

B43

Lowell, Sandra. "New Feminist Theater." *Ms.* Aug. 1972: 17–23.

Surveying the development of a feminist alternative to male-dominated theatre throughout the country, Lowell looks at offerings by such com-panies as the Westbeth Playwrights Feminist Collective and the Painted Women Ritual Theater. Lowell also acknowledges efforts by playwright Myrna Lamb and other individual theatre practitioners.

B44

McGauley, Laurie-Ann. "Super(stack) Inspiration." *Canadian Theatre Review* 53 (1987): 35–38.

In an account of Sudbury (Ontario) residents' tumultuous relationship with the International Nickel Company's acid plant, McGauley reveals how the working class's struggle has fed other struggles for minority rights, a cleaner environment, and adequate living conditions. She describes the use of theatrical techniques in these protests, focusing on the intersection of the women's movement and dramatic experimentation, particularly in the collective work of Sticks and Stones.

B45

Martin, Carol. "Charabanc Theatre Company: 'Quare' Women 'Sleggin' and 'Geggin' the Standards of Northern Ireland by 'Tappin' the People." *The Drama Review* 31.2 (1987): 88–99.

Martin describes the work of the Charabanc Theatre Company, a collaborative group performing within Catholic and Protestant working-class communities. She includes an interview with three of the founders—Marie Jones, Carol Scanlan, and Eleanor Methven—who discuss women portraying men and the real-life bases for their plays.

B46

Massimino, Mickie. "Collectively Speaking." *Gold Flower* Mar.–Apr. 1977: 11.

Massimino, one of the mother-originators of Circle of the Witch Theatre, points out the gap between theory and practice, the difficulties of creating an effective collective working process "*without* sacrificing working relationships or personal lives." She focuses on the problem of reducing the collective structure into a "leader" outside its members—i.e., "the theatre" as entity.

B47

Massimino, Mickie. "Collectively Speaking: Part II." *Gold Flower* May–June 1977: 6–7.

Massimino discusses the decision to work within an all-women theatre collective and the trap of creating a play in angry reaction to men.

B48

Massimino, Mickie. "Collectively Speaking: Part III." *Gold Flower* Nov.–Dec. 1977: 6–7.

After briefly describing Circle of the Witch Theatre's *Lady in the Corner* and men's reaction to its all-women context, Massimino concerns herself with the nature of women's art collectives functioning outside the patriarchal overculture. Writing about the patriarchal bias that dismissed women's arts as "crafts," and the "herstorical context of women's collectives," she concludes that "a women's art was born long before the second wave of the feminist movement."

B49
Moss, Jane. "Women's Theater in France." *Signs* 12 (1987): 548–67.

Moss surveys French feminist theatre companies and playwrights since the 1970s, describing the socioeconomic focus of La Carmagnole, the milestone productions of Théâtre de l'aquarium's *La Soeur de Shakespeare* and Michèle Foucher's *La Table*, the lesbian militancy of Lilith Folies, the feminist/Occitanist work of Lo Teatre de la carriera, and Le Théâtre du campagnol's ethnic drama. She distinguishes revisionist pieces on women from myth, legend, and history in works by Hélène Cixous, Anne Roche, Jeanne Fayard and Anne Delbée, and others. Examining such feminist themes as *prise de parole*, Moss discusses additional playwrights, including Emma Santos, Mona Thomas, Denise Chalem, Catherine Derain, Anne-Marie Kraemer, Elisabeth Janvier, Denise Bonal, and Loleh Bellon. She also explores the adaptation of earlier women's texts and the phenomenon of *humour au féminin*.

B50
"Nightwood Theatre Tells the True Story of *The True Story of Ida Johnson*." *Women and Performance*. Spec. issue of *Fireweed* 7 (Summer 1980): 30–35.

This chronicle of the challenges and setbacks in creating, funding, and producing the play based on Sharon Riis's novel concludes with a statement regarding the group's continuing preoccupation—"collective adaptation with an emphasis on a style approaching montage"—and current endeavors. Scenes from the drama follow the article.

B51
Parrish, Sue. "The Women's Playhouse Trust." *Women in Theatre*. Spec. issue of *Drama* 152 (1984): 13.

The inception, aims, and policies of the London theatre company are presented.

B52
Pelletier, Pol. Interview. "Pol Pelletier, March 1985." With Banuta Rubess. *Feminism and Canadian Theatre*. Spec. issue of *Canadian Theatre Review* 43 (1985): 179–84.

Feminist actor, writer, director, teacher and administrator Pelletier reflects on the history of Le Théâtre expérimental des femmes, as well as her increasing dissatisfaction with the collective process, her venture into playwriting, and her dream of founding a theatre school.

B53

Pelletier, Pol. Interview. "Talking to Pol Pelletier." With Joanne Gormley.
    Women and Performance. Spec. issue of *Fireweed* 7 (Summer
    1980): 88–96.

A founding member of Le Théâtre expérimental de Montréal, Pelletier
relates how her desire to work solely with women, who would have
"the possibility and the habit of being self-generating, creative persons,
instead of sitting back and expecting men to take over," led to her formation of Le Théâtre expérimental des femmes. She expresses women's
need for knowledge about their condition and history before doing
plays, to avoid reproducing the conditions of oppression.

B54

Rea, Charlotte. "Women for Women." *The Drama Review* 18.4 (1974):
    77–87.

Rea assesses women's theatre groups in terms of their development of a
feminist aesthetic, creation of new content based on real-life experience, and (especially) their relationship with all-women and mixed audiences. Exploring such issues as the interaction between development
of materials and intended audience and the impact of performances on
spectators' lives, she focuses on the ideas of Sue Perlgut (It's All Right to
Be Woman Theatre), Roberta Sklar (the Women's Unit), and Lucy Winer
and Claudette Charbonneau (the New York Feminist Theatre).

B55

Rea, Charlotte. "Women's Theatre Groups." *The Drama Review* 16.2
    (1972): 79-89.

Delineating variations in performance style, goals, and internal structure, Rea highlights several feminist groups, including the New Feminist
Theatre, directed by Anselma dell'Olio; It's All Right to Be Woman Theatre, a collective whose members use their own lives as material; and
the Women's Guerrilla Theatre, which has created "Elevator Plays." She
also discusses the Westbeth Playwrights Feminist Collective, a group of
playwrights working within a nonauthoritarian structure; Roberta
Sklar's women's acting class; and skits by the Vancouver Women's Caucus.

B56

Rhode Island Feminist Theatre. "*Persephones Return.*" *Frontiers* 3.2
    (1978): 60-74.

An afterword to the script describes the collaborative effort resulting in the work, the research responsible for production choices, and the play as "an exorcism of the patriarchy."

B57
Roth, Stephanie, et al. Interview. "Bread and Roses." With Solo. *Sister* Oct.–Nov. 1975: 11+ .

Members of Bread and Roses converse about the Los Angeles company's formation for the purpose of communicating feminist ideas in a lively way, their relationship with their audiences, and the role of humor in dealing with women's oppression.

B58
Rouyer, Marie-Claire, and Ann Cipriani. "Women's Theatre in Great Britain." *Women and Performance*. Spec. issue of *Fireweed* 8 (Fall 1980): 46–61.

Tracking the development of British women's theatre groups and their varied relationships to feminism, the authors stress the importance of festivals, differentiate among the formats and styles of collective works, and mark the use of humor in undermining sexist clichés. They find that while the early years were marked by "carefully documented plays concerned with scrupulous information," the newer emphasis is on developing women's creative potential. Reference is made to the frequent collaborative efforts between professional women playwrights and collective groups, and an annotated list of companies and productions is provided.

B59
Schwartz, Barbara, and Mara Shelby. "A Survey of Women's/Feminist/ Lesbian Theater Groups in New York." *Christopher Street* June 1978: 28–32.

In addition to describing the varied approaches and productions of a number of companies—It's All Right to Be Woman, Womanrite Theater Ensemble, Spiderwoman, Cutting Edge, New Cycle, and Medusa's Revenge—the authors examine the contributions of playwright-director Maria Irene Fornes to the growth of women's theatre. Issues addressed include the problem of theatrical standards versus feminist values and the inclusion or exclusion of male performers and audience members.

B60
Sherman, Deborah. "*The Paris Project* and the Art of Lesbian Relationships." *Heresies* 6.2 (1987): 9–13.

Sherman chronicles the collaborative creation of *The Paris Project*, based on Natalie Barney and her circle of lesbian artists, by the Paris Project theatre group, organized by Stephanie Glickman. An account of Sherman's personal journey during the period of the play's development is interwoven.

B61
"Sistren Street Theatre." *ISIS Women's World* 1 (Mar. 1984): 4.

This overview of the Jamaican working-class women's collective summarizes its achievement in productions and workshops as transforming women's role as preservers of culture into authors of a new culture, breaking the silence about women's exploitation through drama, stimulating discussion, and experimenting with solutions to social problems. Also noted is their promotion of Caribbean cultural traditions through language and ritual.

B62
Sklar, Roberta. " 'Sisters' or Never Trust Anyone Outside the Family." *Women & Performance: A Journal of Feminist Theory* 1.1 (1983): 58–63.

Sklar considers "sisterhood," the creation of *The Daughters Cycle* trilogy by the Women's Experimental Theater (Sklar, Clare Coss, and Sondra Segal), and the pain and joy of writing the Quadrologue section of *Sister/Sister* (Part II of *The Daughters Cycle*). The Quadrologue, a fugue for the voices of four adult sisters, follows the article.

B63
Solomon, Alisa. "The WOW Cafe." *The Drama Review* 29.1 (1985): 92–101

This article depicts the history of the "anarchic organizing collective" in whose productions feminism and lesbianism are givens. Included are comments by Lois Weaver, Peggy Shaw, and other members. Part One of Holly Hughes's *Well of Horniness* follows.

B64
Spunner, Suzanne. "Since Betty Jumped: Theatre and Feminism in Melbourne." *Meanjin* 38 (1979): 368–77.

Investigating the effect of the women's movement on Melbourne theatre, Spunner traces in particular the history and influence of the Women's Theatre Group, which "changed audience expectations of the role of women in the theatre." She examines the collaborative process as well as the vexing issue of hierarchies and the consequences of separatism as it affected the group's work. She also notes the increase in male playwrights who deal with women's lives.

B65
Sugarman, Nancy. "Circle of the Witch: A Collective Feminist Theatre." *Gold Flower* Mar.–Apr. 1977: 6–7.

Sugarman reports on the significant changes in Circle of the Witch's "process as a collective and as a theatre" during the past year. Included is a discussion of *Time Is Passing*, which reveals the stories of women in turn-of-the-century Minnesota, and the diverse reactions to the piece.

B66
Thomas, Elean. "Lionhearted Women." *Spare Rib* 172 (Nov. 1986): 14–19.

Outlining the origin and accomplishments of the Jamaican women's collective, Sistren, Thomas describes its development of drama reflecting working-class women's lives, use of historical materials, concern with issues of colonialism, participation in the women's movement, and expansion into cultural ventures other than theatre.

B67
Thomas, Elean. "Lion Hearted Women: The Sistren Theatre Collective." *Race and Class* 28.3 (1987): 66–72.

This is a condensed version of Thomas's *Spare Rib* article, annotated in B66. *Terms:* class/classism, relationship to race/racism; colonialism.

B68
Tregebov, Rhea. "Company of Sirens Entices Audiences." *Herizons* Dec. 1986: 11.

Discussing the new Toronto feminist theatre group, Tregebov details the issue of union-oriented work on which the Company of Sirens is currently focusing, its financial limitations, the backgrounds of individual members, and plans to nurture other women theatre artists.

B69
Tsui, Kitty. "Lilith and the Hired Help." *Acting Up!* Spec. issue of *Heresies* 5.1 (1984): 50–51.

Recounting her experience in a collaborative production about maids with Lilith, A Women's Theatre, Tsui expresses shock at her firing, which resulted from her speaking out about the racist and classist stereotyping characterizing the effort.

B70

Van Kleef, Deborah. "Pillbox Hats, White Gloves and Ladies Against Women." *Theater* 13.3 (1982): 74–75.

The author reports on a guerrilla theatre-type rally organized by the Pro-Choice Action Committee, which transformed itself into Ladies Against Women, designed to upstage Phyllis Schlafly during her visit to Cleveland.

B71

Warren, Nancy. "*Downpression Getablow*: Jamaican Women's Theatre." *Womanews* May 1985: 16.

Warren sketches the history of Sistren, the Jamaican working-class women's theatre collective.

B72

Williams, Gail Ann, and Selma Vincent. Interview. "Ladies Against Women." With Tricia Lootins, Alice Henry, and Ruth Wallsgrove. *Off Our Backs* June 1986: 20–22.

Ladies Against Women members Williams and Vincent talk about their stage appearances, in-character demonstrations at such events as the Republican Convention in Dallas, and street theatre performances; the effect of having men in the group and in the audience; their political content; the workshops they conduct; and their relationship to the right-wing women they parody.

B73

Wilshire, Donna. "Feminist Theater Melds Politics with Art." *New Directions for Women* Mar.–Apr. 1981: 6–7.

The author defines feminist theatre as an aesthetic-political movement that dramatizes the lives of ordinary women. Specific companies discussed are At the Foot of the Mountain, Emmatroupe, and Light and Shadow: A Company of Women.

B74

Winer, Lucy. "Staging for Consciousness-Raising." *Emergency Librarian* 2.4–5 (1975): 18–23.

Winer contrasts the creation of a new women's theatre informed by a feminist vision with patriarchal theatre. She describes specifically the collective approach of the New York Feminist Theatre Troupe, of which she is a member.

B75

Wolff, Ruth. "The Aesthetics of Violence: Women Tackle the Rough Stuff." *Ms.* Feb. 1979: 30-36.

The author looks at three plays that explore–not exploit–violence in women's lives: *Hey Rube*, conceived by Janet McReynolds and presented at the Women's Interart Center in New York City; the Rhode Island Feminist Theatre's *Internal Injury*; and Emmatroupe's *A Girl Starts Out . . . .*

B76

Yarbro-Bejarano, Yvonne. "Chicanas' Experience in Collective Theatre: Ideology and Form." *Women & Performance: A Journal of Feminist Theory* 2.2 (1985): 45-58.

Yarbro-Bejarano examines the options available to Chicanas in theatre. Tracing Chicano theatre collectives to the Chicano movement's efforts "to validate popular and oral forms of cultural expression," she describes their commitment in both structure and function to oppose the ideologies of the dominant society. The San Francisco Mime Company and the Teatro de la Esperanza are cited as offering opportunities for Chicanas and Latinas, and the assimilationist Teatro Campesino is criticized for stereotyping females. She also discusses the sexist double standard of many groups, the collaborative process and its problems, formal experimentation, and the work of individual Chicanas and Latinas in commercial theatre.

Pioneering Women Playwrights

Books and Monographs

C1

Clark, Constance. *Three Augustan Women Playwrights.* American University Studies, Series 4; English Language and Literature 40. New York: Peter Lang, 1986.

Clark's introduction describes theatre in late seventeenth-century England, women's position in society, and the activity of female writers, especially Aphra Behn, who preceded and was emulated by the subjects of this study. Individual chapters focusing on Catharine Trotter, Delariviere Manley, and Mary Griffith Pix are divided into three sections: biography, critical overview, and synopses of works and criticism. Clark details the sources of and influences on their plays, depicts the conditions surrounding the original productions, and considers staging problems. She draws occasional attention to the writers' feminist arguments. Among the plays discussed are Trotter's *Agnes de Castro, The Fatal Friendship, Love at a Loss, The Unhappy Penitent,* and *The Revolution of Sweden;* Manley's *The Lost Lover, The Royal Mischief, Almyna; or, the Arabian Vow,* and *Lucius, The First Christian King of Britain;* Pix's *Ibrahim, The Thirteenth Emperor of the Turks, The Spanish Wives,* and *The Innocent Mistress.* Clark also provides a summary and explication of *The Female Wits,* which satirized the three playwrights.

C2

Cotton, Nancy. *Women Playwrights in England, c. 1363–1750.* Lewisburg, Pa.: Bucknell University Press, 1980.

Cotton's biographical and critical survey also attempts to focus on social and historical factors surrounding the playwrights, most of whom have suffered scholarly neglect. She first deals with medieval and Renaissance noblewomen who wrote closet dramas, masques, and pastoral entertainment, including Mary Sidney Herbert, Countess of Pembroke; Elizabeth Cary, Viscountess Falkland; Queen Henrietta Maria; Margaret Cavendish, Duchess of Newcastle (termed England's first feminist playwright); Katherine Philips; and others. A chapter each is devoted to Behn and Susanna Centlivre, while other chapters center on the female wits—Catharine Trotter, Delariviere Manley, and Mary Pix—and minor women playwrights (1670–1750) such as Anne Finch, Countess of Winchilsea; Mary Davys; Eliza Fowler Haywood; and Charlotte Cibber Charke. Cotton also examines the "Salic Law of Wit," which excluded women from Parnassus, and the varied contemporary responses to women writers. A final chapter explores the widely imitated personae of Astrea (unorthodox female adventuress) and Orinda (deferential lady writer) adapted by Behn and Philips in reaction to the critical double standard.

C3
Duffy, Maureen. *The Passionate Shepherdess: Aphra Behn (1640–89).* London: Jonathan Cape, 1977.

Duffy reclaims England's first professional woman playwright (who was also a novelist, poet, and spy) from fictionalized accounts of her life and gender-biased interpretation of her works, which were frequently attacked for their frank treatment of sex. Presenting conflicting documentary evidence and filling in the gaps with reasoned conjecture, Duffy re-creates Behn within Restoration theatre, social, and political life. In her brief discussion of Behn's plays, including *Sir Patient Fancy* and *The Rover,* she delineates sources and touches upon such issues as cross-dressing, the treatment of marriage, and Behn's defense of women's rights.

C4
Goreau, Angeline. *Reconstructing Aphra: A Social Biography of Aphra Behn.* New York: Dial, 1980.

Using Behn's writings and numerous other seventeenth-century documents to place her within the context of her times, Goreau emphasizes Behn's double bind, in which the strictures of a dependent feminine role, as dictated by the period (a role that she could not totally discard), vied with her desire to act autonomously in a "masculine" sphere that ranged from spying for the king to writing bawdy Restoration plays. She examines Behn's plays, poems, and novels for their feminine perspective and reactions to a patriarchal system disastrous to women in all aspects of life.

C5

Moriarty, David J. "Michael Field (Edith Cooper and Katherine Bradley) and Their Male Critics." *Nineteenth-Century Women Writers of the English-Speaking World.* Ed. Rhoda B. Nathan. Contributions in Women's Studies 69. New York: Greenwood, 1986. 121–42.

Recounting the collaboration of two nineteenth-century women using a male pseudonym who wrote twenty-five plays, a masque, and poetry, Moriarty stresses the critical gender bias they encountered. *A Question of Memory* (their only produced play) and *Attila, My Attila* are among the works discussed. Moriarty notes the recurrent figure of the captive woman in their writing.

C6

Pearson, Jacqueline. *The Prostituted Muse: Women Dramatists and Images of Women, 1642–1737.* New York: St. Martin's, 1988.

Pearson sets out to explore the contradictory stories of women playwrights who argued for their rights to engage in literary pursuits but "absorbed enough of their culture's misogyny to feel guilt, or anxiety, or ambivalence about these claims," and who expressed a female vision while working within the conventional dramatic forms of the male-dominated theatre. The first part of the book surveys contemporary views on women writers and the feminist debate; details women's involvement in theatre as performers, managers, and audience members; and analyzes images of women in the works of male playwrights. The second part studies individual women writers (Margaret Cavendish, Aphra Behn, Mary Pix, Catharine Trotter, Delariviere Manley, Susanna Centlivre, and numerous minor dramatists), their relationship to feminism, and their treatment of gender roles. In her discussion of both male and female playwrights, Pearson investigates the visibility and language of female characters and addresses such specific topics as the sexual double standard, female sexuality, women's friendships, unconventional women characters, and rape.

C7

Weaver, Elissa. "Spiritual Fun: A Study of Sixteenth-Century Tuscan Convent Theater." *Women in the Middle Ages and the Renaissance: Literary and Historical Perspectives.* Ed. Mary Beth Rose. Syracuse, N.Y.: Syracuse University Press, 1986. 173–205.

Weaver describes theatrical productions by Italian nuns that provided expression for the feelings and artistic talents of this female subculture and united them, at least temporarily, with their friends and relatives outside the convent. Focusing on the *commedia sacra,* a form combining religious and secular elements, she examines Sister Maria Grazia Centelli's *Tragedia di Eleazzaro ebreo* and particularly Sister Beatrice del Sera's *Amor di virtù,* which protests society's mistreatment of women.

Periodicals, Serials, and Annuals

C8

Aston, Elaine. "Feminism in the French Theatre: A Turn-of-the-Century Perspective." *New Theatre Quarterly* 2.7 (1986): 237–42.

In her investigation of the stage depiction of women's issues in the late 1890s, Aston examines the offerings of the short-lived Théâtre féministe, a group dedicated to promoting plays by women, as well as the "new woman" drama by male playwrights. She notes the period's optimistic view of theatre as an instrument of social change, challenging capitalism and reflecting the struggle for female emancipation.

C9

Bank, Rosemarie K. "Theatre and Narrative Fiction in the Work of the Nineteenth-Century American Playwright Louisa Medina." *Theatre History Studies* 3 (1983): 55–67.

Bringing to light the work of professional playwright Medina, Bank examines her techniques, the reasons her adaptations of novels persisted over those of her rivals, and her significance in American theatrical history. The plays discussed—*The Last Days of Pompeii, Nick of the Woods, or the Jibbenainosay,* and *Ernest Maltravers*—represent the three subjects Medina dramatized: historical, American frontier, and contemporary romance/adventure.

C10

Beilin, Elaine. "Elizabeth Cary and *The Tragedie of Mariam.*" *Papers on Language & Literature* 16 (1980): 45–64.

The author speculates that Cary's work (the first English play definitely attributable to a woman), which treats the question of obedience to authority in marriage and affirms the Christian ethic, stems partly from her own experiences as a wife.

C11

Case, Sue-Ellen. "Re-Viewing Hrotsvit." *Theatre Journal* 35 (1983): 533–42.

In her articulation of Hrotsvitha's seminal role in women's dramatic history, Case investigates pertinent issues surrounding the constitution of the canon. She discusses the centrality of women characters in *Dulcitius* and *Callimachus,* reinterprets Hrotsvitha's plays in the context of semiotics and reception theory, and applies a feminist morphology to *Paphnutius.* Case also details the problems and choices involved in and the critical response to her own 1982 production of Hrotsvitha's works.

C12

Cotton, Nancy. "Katherine of Sutton: The First English Woman Playwright." *Educational Theatre Journal* 30 (1978): 475–81.

This article is reprinted in chapter 1 of Cotton's book, *Women Playwrights in England.* See C2. *Term:* women playwrights, status and conditions, rediscovered.

C13

Frankforter, A. Daniel. "Hroswitha of Gandersheim and the Destiny of Women." *Historian* 41 (1979): 295–314.

Frankforter focuses on Hrotsvitha's examination of traditional feminine roles (virgin, wife, and whore), suggesting that despite her acceptance of male dominance, "she seems to have seen in the Christian dynamics of sin and salvation a destiny which gave women great worth and a basis for self-respect."

C14

Frankforter, A. Daniel. "Sexism and the Search for the Thematic Structure of the Plays of Hroswitha of Gandersheim." *International Journal of Women's Studies* 2 (May–June 1979): 221–32.

Analyzing gender bias in the criticism of Hrotsvitha's work, the author notes that most interpretations have ignored her sex and her claim that her plays are about women. Frankforter argues that Hrotsvitha's six plays—*Gallicanus, Dulcitius, Callimachus, Abraham, Paphnutius,* and *Sapientia*—have a common theme pertaining to female virtue and constitute an integrated cycle.

C15

Gallagher, Catherine. "Who Was That Masked Woman? The Prostitute and the Playwright in the Comedies of Aphra Behn." *Last Laughs:*

Perspectives on Women and Comedy. Ed. Regina Barreca. Spec. issue of *Women's Studies* 15 (1988): 23–42.

Gallagher examines Behn's introduction of the persona of the professional woman writer as a whore and the issues of female selfhood it raises. Analyzing *The Lucky Chance,* she maintains that its crisis moments "are not those in which a woman becomes property but those in which a woman is burdened with a selfhood that can be neither represented (a self without properties) nor exchanged."

C16
Gethner, Perry. "Melpomene Meets Women Playwrights in the Age of Louis XIV." *Neophilologus* 72 (1980): 17–33.

The author underscores the historical significance of several tragedies by French women playwrights, who broke through a major barrier by being produced in the second half of the seventeenth century. Gethner contends that in addition to shedding light on tragedy's evolution—particularly because the playwrights, "with the additional handicap of sex to overcome, had to be attuned to the public's desires"—an analysis of three works (*Nitétis* by Marie-Catherine Desjardins, *Genséric* by Mme Deshoulières, and *Laodamie, reine d'Epire* by Catherine Bernard) within the context of historical sources and dramatic tradition suggests how conventional views of femininity and role models for heroines were reexamined and modified.

C17
Grundy, Isobel. "Sarah Gardner: 'Such Trumpery' or 'A Lustre to Her Sex'?" *Tulsa Studies in Women's Literature* 7 (1988): 7–25.

Identifying eighteenth-century performer Gardner, who wrote one produced comedy, *The Advertisement,* as "a classic case of a woman whose own witness has been suppressed, while a competing version has been inscribed in history by male persons in authority," Grundy details the vicissitudes of Gardner's career. Refuting charges of plagiarism, she shows how Gardner's female viewpoint subverts audience expectations of stock characters.

C18
Katz, Candace Brook. "The Deserted Mistress Motif in Mrs. Manley's *Lost Lover,* 1696." *Restoration and 18th Century Theatre Research* 16.1 (1977): 27–39.

Katz studies Manley's "overtly feminist" approach in reversing the typical depiction of the cast-off mistress figure, whom she makes the center of interest and sympathy, rather than merely "a difficulty which the hero must overcome in order to marry his chaste heiress."

C19

Kendall, Kathryn. "From Lesbian Heroine to Devoted Wife; Or, What the Stage Would Allow." *Historical, Literary, and Erotic Aspects of Lesbianism.* Spec. double issue of *Journal of Homosexuality* 12.3–4 (1986): 9–22.

Kendall contrasts the treatment of a tragic fourteenth-century love triangle in Catharine Trotter's 1696 *Agnes de Castro,* which features a lesbian heroine, to that in Mary Russell Mitford's 1841 *Inez de Castro,* which depicts the heroine as a self-sacrificing, heterosexual wife. She argues that because both Trotter and Mitford would now be defined as lesbians, the heroine's portrayal reflects the audience rather than the playwright.

C20

Kramer, Rita. "Lost Women: Aphra Behn: Novelist, Spy, Libertine." *Ms.* Feb. 1973: 16–18.

This brief account of Behn's life and career notes critical reaction to her plays and novels.

C21

Langdell, Cheri Davis. "Aphra Behn and Sexual Politics: A Dramatist's Discourse with Her Audience." *Themes in Drama* 7 (*Drama, Sex and Politics*) (1985): 109–28.

Contending that Behn's writing and her attitude toward it are acts of "sexual politics" in Restoration terms (i.e., women's use of power to redress the social balance), Langdell relates Behn's assertion in the plays proper of a woman's need for freedom to choose her marriage partner to her assertion in the prefaces, epilogues, etc., of the woman writer's need to have her work judged without gender bias.

C22

Pearse, Nancy Cotton. "Elizabeth Cary, Restoration Playwright." *Texas Studies in Literature and Language* 18 (1977): 601–8.

This article is reprinted in the first chapter of Cotton's book, *Women Playwrights in England.* See C2. *Term:* women playwrights, status and conditions, rediscovered.

C23
Pearse, Nancy Cotton. "Mary Pix, Restoration Playwright." *Restoration and 18th Century Theatre Research* 15.1 (1976) 12–23.

This article appears in Chapter 3 of Cotton's book, *Women Playwrights in England*. See C2. *Terms:* marriage; women playwrights, status and conditions, rediscovered.

C24
Pearson, Jacqueline. " 'Women May Discourse . . . As Well As Men': Speaking and Silent Women in the Plays of Margaret Cavendish, Duchess of Newcastle." *Tulsa Studies in Women's Literature* 4 (1985): 33–45.

Pearson examines Cavendish's female characters and analyzes her ambivalence about women—Cavendish's strong belief in both a woman's potential and the impossibility of her controlling her own life—and her central theme of women's access to language in a male-dominated world. *Youths Glory and Deaths Banquet* and *Loves Adventure* are among the plays considered. Some of this material appears in Pearson's book, *The Prostituted Muse.* See C6.

C25
Roberts, Vera Mowry. "Bright Lights and Backstage: Women Playwrights in the Theatre." *Furman Studies* 34 (Dec. 1988): 26–35.

Roberts traces the emergence of women playwrights, noting how often work as an actress legitimized other theatrical activity. After surveying the pioneers in English theatre, particularly Aphra Behn, Roberts refutes the popular view of the scarcity of American women playwrights, noting the largely unknown status of numerous nineteenth-century authors. She also comments on the increasing number of women playwrights in contemporary theatre and the influence of feminism.

C26
Root, Robert L., Jr. "Aphra Behn, Arranged Marriage, and Restoration Comedy." *Women and Literature* 5.1 (1977): 3-14.

Root establishes Behn's uniqueness among her contemporaries in her awareness that adultery may stem from real love and social injustice as well as from licentiousness. He illustrates her indictment of arranged marriage and her sympathy with women in such plays as *The Lucky Chance.* Behn is also contrasted with the women playwrights claiming to be her disciples in the mid-1690s, when the exemplary approach replaced the satirical.

C27
Showalter, English, Jr. "Writing off the Stage: Women Authors and Eighteenth-Century Theatre." *The Politics of Tradition: Placing Women in French Literature.* Spec. issue of *Yale French Studies* 75 (1988): 95–111.

Detailing the relative exclusion of women from playwriting due to social and institutional barriers in this period, Showalter focuses on the careers and plays of four produced dramatists: Marie-Anne Barbier, Madeleine de Gomez, Marie-Anne Du Boccage, and Françoise de Graffigny. Their pathetic heroines are discussed.

Twentieth-Century Women Playwrights

Books and Monographs

D1

Betsko, Kathleen, and Rachel Koenig. *Interviews with Contemporary Women Playwrights.* New York: Beech Tree-Morrow, 1987.

The introduction by Koenig underscores the "radical act" of the woman playwright who tries to communicate her vision. Attacking the notion that art is genderless or transcends gender, Koenig characterizes the woman playwright's art as stemming from a female sentience. Betsko's afterword discusses gender bias in theatre criticism and tracks reasons why women playwrights have historically been overlooked or forgotten. Betsko illustrates her points by contrasting critical responses to Caryl Churchill with those to David Mamet. A brief background sketch precedes each of the thirty interviews with playwrights Liliane Atlan, Bai Fengxi, Betsko, Alice Childress, Churchill, Anne Commire, Gretchen Cryer, Donna de Matteo, Rosalyn Drexler, Laura Farabough, Maria Irene Fornes, Mary Gallagher, Griselda Gambaro, Pam Gems, Beth Henley, Tina Howe, Corinne Jacker, Adrienne Kennedy, Karen Malpede, Emily Mann, Eve Merriam, Janet Neipris, Marsha Norman, Rochelle Owens, Louise Page, Ntozake Shange, Megan Terry, Michelene Wandor, Wendy Wasserstein, and Susan Yankowitz. An extensive index provides access to subjects covered in the interviews.

D2

Brown-Guillory, Elizabeth. *Their Place on the Stage: Black Women Playwrights in America.* Contributions in Afro-American and African Studies 117. New York: Greenwood, 1988.

Brown-Guillory's study of black women playwrights begins with a discussion of the Black Renaissance and the contributions of Angelina Weld Grimké, May Miller, Georgia Douglas Johnson, Alice Dunbar-Nelson, Mary Burrill, Ruth Gaines-Shelton, Marita Bonner, and others. The rest of the book focuses on Alice Childress, Lorraine Hansberry, and Ntozake Shange. The author explores issues of racism, sexism, and poverty as revealed through symbols in *Florence, Trouble in Mind, Mojo: A Black Love Story, A Raisin in the Sun, for colored girls who have considered suicide/when the rainbow is enuf,* and *spell #7* and delineates how dramatic structure is shaped by African-American "initiation and survival rituals" experienced by heroines searching for wholeness in *Wedding Band: A Love/Hate Story, Wine in the Wilderness, Raisin,* and *a photograph: lovers in motion.* Brown-Guillory also examines images of black men and women and the playwrights' portrayal of the black family as the progeny of Africa.

D3

Cheney, Anne. *Lorraine Hansberry.* Twayne's United States Authors Series 430. Boston: Twayne, 1984.

This first full-length study of Hansberry chronicles her life and career. Separate chapters are devoted to *A Raisin in the Sun* (of particular interest is a discussion of Hansberry's respect for strong women and its manifestation in *Raisin*), *The Sign in Sidney Brustein's Window,* and her last plays, including *Les Blancs, The Drinking Gourd,* and *What Use Are Flowers?* Robert Nemiroff's *To Be Young, Gifted and Black,* a "dramatic testament of black life" based on Hansberry's writing, is the subject of the final chapter.

D4

Chinoy, Helen Krich. "Suppressed Desires: Women in the Theater." *Women, the Arts, and the 1920s in Paris and New York.* Ed. Kenneth W. Wheeler and Virginia Lee Lussier. New Brunswick, N.J.: Transaction, 1982. 126–32.

Surveying women's contributions to American theatre of the 1920s, Chinoy distinguishes between the commercial Broadway fare and the alternative theatres in which "more revealing insights about women were offered in experimental forms that seemed invented to express the troubled spirit of modern woman." Rachel Crothers, Susan Glaspell, and Sophie Treadwell are among the dramatists discussed.

D5

Coates, Carrol F. "From Feminism to Nationalism: The Theater of Françoise Loranger, 1965–1970." *Traditionalism, Nationalism, and*

Feminism: Women Writers of Quebec. Ed. Paula Gilbert Lewis. Westport, Conn.: Greenwood, 1985. 83–94.

Investigating the themes of domination and self-discovery in Loranger's full-length plays, Coates traces her shift from traditional theatre techniques in the exploration of the bourgeois family to her more experimental approach in expressing the theme of national identification. Five plays are analyzed: *Une Maison, un jour, Encore cinq minutes, Double Jeu, Le Chemin du Roy,* and *Médium saignant.*

D6

Cohn, Ruby. *New American Dramatists, 1960–1980.* New York: Grove, 1982.

Although Cohn's analysis of American theatre treats mainly male playwrights, the book does include a concise overview of the works of Megan Terry, Maria Irene Fornes, Joan Holden and the San Francisco Mime Troupe, Adrienne Kennedy, and Rochelle Owens.

D7

Cotnoir, Louise. "Woman/Women on Stage." Trans. A. J. Holden Verburg. *A Mazing Space: Writing Canadian Women Writing.* Ed. Shirley Neuman and Smaro Kamboureli. Edmonton, Alberta, Canada: Longspoon, 1986. 307–11.

Tracing the convergence of the theoretical and the theatrical in Quebec's developing feminist theatre, Cotnoir underscores women's inscription on stage of "a language which testifies to their own preoccupations and their own imaginary [sic]." She concentrates on five works: *Môman travaille pas, a trop d'ouvrage!* by the Théâtre des cuisines; *La Nef des sorcières,* with texts by twelve women; *Les Fées ont soif* by Denise Boucher; *Un reel ben beau, ben triste* by Jeanne-Mance Delisle; and *A ma mère, à ma mère, à ma mère, à ma voisine* by Dominique Gagnon, Louise Laprade, Nicole Lecavalier, and Pol Pelletier.

D8

Curb, Rosemary K. "Pre-Feminism in the Black Revolutionary Drama of Sonia Sanchez." *The Many Forms of Drama.* Ed. Karelisa V. Hartigan. The University of Florida Department of Classics Comparative Drama Conference Papers 5. Lanham, Md.: University Press of America, 1985. 19–29.

Examining three black revolutionary plays produced or published in the 1960s, Curb finds that although none asserts a conscious feminism, their portrayals of women's victimization "constitute a preliminary raising of consciousness."

D9

Gillespie, Patti P. "America's Women Dramatists, 1960–1980." *Essays on Contemporary American Drama*. Ed. Hedwig Bock and Albert Wertheim. Munich, Germany: Hueber, 1981. 187–206.

Gillespie investigates trends in women's playwriting, including (1) the clustering of women dramatists in alternative theatres and their abandonment of structures associated with realism, (2) the emergence and success of black women playwrights, and (3) the increasing importance of feminism as a distinguishing characteristic. While surveying the work of numerous playwrights, she focuses on Lillian Hellman's *Toys in the Attic,* Myrna Lamb's *The Mod Donna,* and Ntozake Shange's *for colored girls who have considered suicide/when the rainbow is enuf.*

D10

Gottlieb, Lois C. *Rachel Crothers.* Twayne's United States Authors Series 322. Boston: Twayne, 1979.

The author reviews Crothers' career within the context of a developing American theatre. In addition to tracing the playwright's themes, forms, use of conventions, and individual style, Gottlieb examines the nature of Crothers' feminism in the plays, their reflection of social concerns, and critical responses. She draws particular attention to the depiction of the New Woman, whose desire for economic and sexual freedom conflicts with the traditional goals of romance and marriage. Gottlieb's final chapter offers an overview of Crothers' achievements and debates labeling her a "feminist" playwright. Plays analyzed include *As Husbands Go, The Coming of Mrs. Patrick, Expressing Willie, He and She, Let Us Be Gay, A Little Journey, A Man's World, Mary the Third, Myself Bettina, Nice People, Ourselves, Susan and God, The Three of Us,* and *When Ladies Meet.*

D11

Jacker, Corinne. "Better Than a Shriveled Husk: New Forms for the Theater." *Toward the Second Decade: The Impact of the Women's Movement on American Institutions.* Ed. Betty Justice and Renate Pore. Contributions in Women's Studies 25. Westport, Conn.: Greenwood, 1981. 25–34.

This informal essay deals with the problems women playwrights have faced in the exclusively male "club" of theatre as well as their recently increased visibility. Jacker also discusses her own playwriting and addresses the issue of female sensibility, differentiating "women's theatre" from theatre created through a woman's vision.

D12

Kennedy, Adrienne. *People Who Led to My Plays.* New York: Knopf, 1987.

Kennedy's memoirs take the form of a scrapbook depicting the many influences on her writing since early childhood, such as fairy tales, friends and relatives, characters from literature, religious figures, her mother's dreams, famous actors, and other playwrights.

D13

Lamb, Myrna. "Female Playwright: Confessions of a Fallen Woman." *Woman as Writer.* Ed. Jeannette Webber and Joan Grumman. Boston: Houghton-Mifflin, 1978. 134–36.

In this essay, which is preceded by introductory notes explaining that Lamb is carving her identity as a playwright in an "atmosphere of moved and responsive audiences, a hostile reception from the conservative theater establishment, and avoidance by segments of the women's movement," Lamb reflects on the impossible position of the daring female artist.

D14

Levin, Tobe, and Gwendolyn Flowers. "Black Feminism in *for colored girls who have considered suicide when the rainbow is enuf."* *History and Tradition in Afro-American Culture.* Ed. Günter H. Lenz. Frankfurt, Germany: Campus, 1984. 181–93.

Contending that Shange's choreopoem deals both with concerns specific to blacks and with "tensions and misunderstandings between humans of both sexes, regardless of racial origin, pitted against one another within phallocratic culture," the authors (one black and one white) offer "independent but mutually supportive" readings. A theoretical introduction to black feminism is provided.

D15

Lister, Rota Herzberg. "Erika Ritter and the Comedy of Self-Actualization." *Gynocritics/La Gynocritique.* Ed. Barbara Godard. Toronto, Ontario, Canada: ECW, 1987. 143–55.

This study of Ritter's preoccupation with the possibilities for young womanhood draws upon Northrop Frye's classification of comic structure in analyzing *A Visitor from Charleston, The Splits, Winter 1671,* and *Automatic Pilot.* Lister ascertains that in all four plays the protagonist's essential dramatic task is "a redefinition of herself that takes her beyond relational identity and also creates for herself a satisfactory future goal and role."

D16

McKay, Nellie. " 'What Were They Saying?': Black Women Playwrights of the Harlem Renaissance." *The Harlem Renaissance Re-Examined.* Ed. Victor A. Kramer. New York: AMS, 1987. 129–47.

In a survey of the themes in black women's plays between 1918 and 1930, McKay focuses on race and gender issues in the work of Angelina Weld Grimké, Alice Dunbar-Nelson, Mary Burrill, Georgia Douglas Johnson, Marita Bonner, and others.

D17

Marranca, Bonnie, and Gautam Dasgupta. *American Playwrights: A Critical Survey.* New York: Drama Book Specialists, 1981.

Among the eighteen independent essays contained in this book are pieces on Maria Irene Fornes, Rochelle Owens, Megan Terry, and Rosalyn Drexler. Each essay provides a general overview of the playwright's themes and techniques, a discussion of the individual plays, and a critical assessment.

D18

Mitchell, Carolyn. "A Laying on of Hands: Transcending the City in Ntozake Shange's *for colored girls who have considered suicide/when the rainbow is enuf." Women Writers and the City: Essays in Feminist Literary Criticism.* Ed. Susan Merrill Squier. Knoxville: University of Tennessee Press, 1984. 230–48.

Mitchell explores the play's paradox of "the modern American city as a place where black women experience the trauma of urban life, yet find the strength to transcend the pain."

D19

Moss, Jane. "Women's Theatre in Quebec." *Traditionalism, Nationalism, and Feminism: Women Writers of Quebec.* Ed. Paula Gilbert Lewis. Westport, Conn.: Greenwood, 1985. 241–54.

Citing dissatisfaction with traditional female roles as a major motivation for the new women's theatre, Moss traces its development, including both the work of individual playwrights and feminist groups. She observes that although much of women's theatrical activity of the 1970s takes the form of the collective *spectacles de femmes* (which "bear witness to a strong desire for solidarity") and widely employs the monologue form (reminding us of "the loneliness and estrangement of many women"), more recent trends include conventionally structured plays reexamining women's past and present roles, and poetic dramas glorifying female culture. She also notes the inclusion of male characters by several women playwrights attempting to "reintegrate newly liberated female characters into their conjugal and familial roles" and the growing presence of lesbian writers and actors.

D20

Olauson, Judith. *The American Woman Playwright: A View of Criticism and Characterization.* Troy, N.Y.: Whitson, 1981.

Olauson's chronologically ordered work focuses on women playwrights' depiction of women from 1930 to 1970. Her introduction, which outlines the neglect and sex-based criticism suffered by women writers, examines four women critics with male-oriented standards. She then analyzes plays by and critical reactions to Susan Glaspell, Rose Franken, Lillian Hellman, Zoe Akins, Clare Boothe, Rachel Crothers, Sophie Treadwell, Elsa Shelley, Fay Kanin, Carson McCullers, Jane Bowles, Lorraine Hansberry, Adrienne Kennedy, Rosalyn Drexler, Megan Terry, Rochelle Owens, and Myrna Lamb. Keeping sight of changing American attitudes toward women's social roles, she detects a gradually freer expression of themes and characters as well as a change in characterization from passive, subjugated women to more active women seeking autonomy.

D21

Owens, Rochelle, Crystal Field, and Rosalyn Drexler. "Women and the Avant-Garde Theatre: Interviews with Rochelle Owens, Crystal Field, Rosalyn Drexler." With Joan Goulianos. *Woman: An Issue.* Ed. Lee Edwards, Mary Heath, and Lisa Baskin. Spec. issue of *The Massachusetts Review* 13.1–2 (1972). Boston: Little, Brown, 1972. 257–67.

Playwrights Owens and Drexler and actor-director Field discuss their lives and work in relation to the women's liberation movement. Specific topics include female stereotypes and discrimination against women in the theatre.

D22

Pavlides, Merope. "Restructuring the Traditional: An Examination of Hélène Cixous' *Le Nom d'Oedipe.*" *Within the Dramatic Spectrum.* Ed. Karelisa V. Hartigan. University of Florida Department of Classics Comparative Drama Conference Papers 6. Lanham, Md.: University Press of America, 1986. 151–59.

The author demonstrates how Cixous's hymnic opera creates new archetypal images of Jocasta and Oedipus that radically differ from those presented by Sophocles.

D23

Pelletier, Pol. "Myth and Women's Theatre." *In the Feminine: Women and Words/Les Femmes et les mots: Conference Proceedings 1983.* Ed. Ann Dybikowski, et al. Edmonton, Alberta, Canada: Longspoon, 1985. 110–13.

Pelletier, a playwright, director, actor, teacher and administrator, comments on her changing interest from collective creation to "the visionary capacity of the solo writer." She stresses the need for women both to reclaim established myths and to discover their own personal mythology.

D24

Randall, Phyllis R., ed. *Caryl Churchill: A Casebook.* Garland Reference Library of the Humanities 736; Casebooks on Modern Dramatists 3. New York: Garland, 1988.

Nine original essays on Churchill divide themselves chronologically into three groups. The initial set includes Randall's "Beginnings: Churchill's Early Radio and Stage Plays," in which the themes and techniques from the earliest plays are shown to carry over to more recent works; Mark Thacker Brown's "'Constantly Coming Back': Eastern Thought and the Plays of Caryl Churchill"; and Michael Selmon's "Reshuffling the Deck: Iconoclastic Dealings in Caryl Churchill's Early Plays." The three essays that follow, which exhibit varying perspectives on specific reputation-making plays, are Lisa Merrill's "Monsters and Heroines: Caryl Churchill's Women," an analysis of *Owners, Vinegar Tom,* and *Top Girls* in the context of current socialist-feminist theory; John M. Clum's "'The Work of Culture': *Cloud Nine* and Sex/Gender Theory," an examination utilizing both feminist and gay critical writings; and "Caryl Churchill's *Top Girls* Catches the New Wave," in which Janet Brown suggests that "the play proposes a re-definition of feminism itself." The final group of essays contains Helene Keyssar's "Doing Dangerous History: Caryl Churchill and *A Mouthful of Birds";* Kimball King's "*Serious Money:* A Market Correction?"; and "Closing No Gaps: Aphra Behn, Caryl Churchill, and Empire," in which Elin Diamond appropriates "Brechtian historicization to conceptualize better the monolithic, history-erasing habits of the I/eye of Empire," focusing primarily on *The Widow Ranter* and *A Mouthful of Birds.* In addition, Randall provides a bibliography of primary sources and an annotated bibliography of secondary materials.

D25

Savran, David. *In Their Own Words: Contemporary American Playwrights.* New York: Theatre Communications Group, 1988.

Savran interviews twenty playwrights, including Maria Irene Fornes, Joan Holden, Emily Mann, Marsha Norman, and Megan Terry. The interviews, each preceded by short critical introductions, explore the playwrights' early experiences in theatre, influences, working methods, attitude toward critics, view of American theatre, relationship between "aesthetic and moral mission," and related topics.

D26
Shange, Ntozake. Interview. "Ntozake Shange." *Black Women Writers at Work*. Ed. Claudia Tate. New York: Continuum, 1983. 149–74.

Shange identifies personal, social, and aesthetic issues affecting her work. *For colored girls who have considered suicide/when the rainbow is enuf* and other pieces are discussed.

D27
Terry, Megan. "Exercise." *Convocation! Women in Writing*. Ed. Valerie Harms. Tampa, Fla.: United Sisters, 1975.

In Megan Terry's address at the 1975 conference for writers sponsored by NOW, she talks about her own theatrical work, the conditions of playwrights and other artists in the United States, and the need for women to back other women in their projects.

D28
Wallace, Robert, and Cynthia Zimmerman. *The Work: Conversations with English-Canadian Playwrights*. Toronto, Ontario, Canada: Coach House, 1982.

Margaret Hollingsworth, Sharon Pollock, Carol Bolt, and Erika Ritter are among the interviewees. Following each "conversation" are—as applicable—lists of published and unpublished stage plays, writing about the theatre by the playwright, and selected criticism and commentary on the playwright.

D29
Wilkerson, Margaret. "The Sighted Eyes and Feeling Heart of Lorraine Hansberry." *Essays on Contemporary American Drama*. Ed. Hedwig Bock and Albert Wertheim. Munich, Germany: Hueber, 1981. 91–104.

Wilkerson underscores Hansberry's importance in exposing the troubled American culture and provides detailed biographical information. Works discussed include *A Raisin in the Sun, The Sign in Sidney Brustein's Window,* and *The Drinking Gourd* (a never-produced television script dealing with slavery), as well as two essentially unfinished plays, *What Use Are Flowers?* and *Les Blancs.*

Periodicals, Serials, and Annuals

D30

Abramson, Doris E. "Angelina Weld Grimké, Mary T. Burrill, Georgia Douglas Johnson, and Marita O. Bonner: An Analysis of Their Plays." *Sage: A Scholarly Journal on Black Women* 2.1 (1985): 9–13.

Abramson discusses four serious, relatively unknown plays dealing with the black experience: Grimké's *Rachel,* Burrill's *They That Sit in Darkness,* Johnson's *Plumes,* and Bonner's *The Purple Flower.*

D31

Abramson, Doris, et al. "Women in the Theatre." *Centerpoint* 3.3–4 (1980): 31–37.

In this transcript of a session of the 1979 "American Women in the Arts" symposia, Abramson, Maria Irene Fornes, Carolee Schneemann, Florence Falk, Bonnie Marranca, and Rosette C. Lamont (moderator) address the conference's subtheme—"the dialectic between public and private spaces"—in relation to women's theatrical contributions, ranging from the work of early twentieth-century playwrights to Fornes's plays (particularly *Fefu and Her Friends*) and Schneemann's performance art.

D32

Anbinder, Adrienne. "She's Got Her Act Together." *TABS: Aids for Ending Sexism in Schools* 3.3 (1980): 14–15.

Anbinder proposes *I'm Getting My Act Together and Taking It on the Road* by Gretchen Cryer (book and lyrics) and Nancy Ford (music) as a potential teaching tool. The play's depiction of a woman's taking command of her life and audience reactions to the production are examined. In a brief interview with Cryer, the playwright talks about sexism.

D33

Anderlini, Serena. *"The Advertisement:* New-Feminist Re-Readings and Old-Fashioned Triangles in the Dramaturgy of Natalia Ginzburg." *Carte Italiane: A Journal of Italian Studies* 8 (1986–87): 1–13.

Drawing numerous comparisons between Ginzburg and Lillian Hellman, Anderlini studies the Italian writer's relationship to feminism, use of the absurdist model, and exploration of the dynamics of gender. She outlines the depiction of women and unacknowledged physical attraction of the women friends in *L'inserzione.*

D34
Anderlini, Serena. "Franca Rame: Her Life and Works." *Theater* 17.1 (1985): 32–39.

Anderlini discusses playwright-actor Rame's early career, collaboration with Dario Fo, and concern with women's issues beginning in the 1970s. She investigates the feminist dimensions of *Tutta casa letto e chiesa,* whose nine monologues underscore women's oppression, and *Coppia aperta, quasi spalancata,* comprising three pieces about male-female relationships.

D35
Anderson, Mary Louise. "Black Matriarchy: Portrayal of Women in Three Plays." *Negro American Literature Forum* 10 (1976): 93–95.

Anderson focuses on Lorraine Hansberry's *Raisin in the Sun,* James Baldwin's *The Amen Corner*, and Alice Childress's *Wine in the Wilderness.*

D36
Austin, Gayle. "Alice Childress: Black Woman Playwright as Feminist Critic." *Southern Women Playwrights.* Spec. issue of *The Southern Quarterly: A Journal of Arts in the South* 25.3 (1987): 53–62.

Trouble in Mind and *Wine in the Wilderness* are studied in terms of the three stages of feminist literary criticism and the concept of absence. Austin praises Childress as a pathfinder playwright-critic who breaks down binary oppositions (male-female, black-white, etc.) and provides nonstereotypical black female roles.

D37
Austin, Gayle, ed. "The 'Woman' Playwright Issue." *Performing Arts Journal* 7.3 (1983): 87–102.

This article consists of responses to Mel Gussow's May 1, 1983, *New York Times Magazine* cover story on contemporary women playwrights. His "generalizations, acts of commission and omission, his lack of historical and critical perspective" elicited a variety of viewpoints and concerns from the contributors, who include Colette Brooks, Maria Irene Fornes, Elizabeth Wray, Julia Miles, Marjorie Bradley Kellogg, Karen Malpede, Joan Schenkar, Anne Cattaneo, and Roberta Sklar. They deal with such issues as the (male) American canon, the existence of a female aesthetic, and women playwrights working within and outside the patriarchal theatre.

D38
Barthelemy, Anthony. "Mother, Sister, Wife: A Dramatic Perspective." *The Southern Review* 21 (1985): 770–89.

The author's analysis of three plays centering on racism and the black family considers Lorraine Hansberry's *A Raisin in the Sun* as a feminist revision of Theodore Ward's *Big White Fog* and a catalyst to Joseph Walker's *The River Niger.* He shows how Hansberry corrects Ward's negative representation of women and counters *Fog's* Marxist politics by placing black aspirations within the American bourgeois context. He also examines Walker's exploration of the nature of black manhood and valorization of male dominance.

D39
Bell, Gay. "From a Resistance to Lesbian Theatre to a Lesbian Theatre of Resistance." *Resources for Feminist Research* 12.1 (1983): 30–34.

Reporting on the diversity of lesbian theatre in Quebec and English Canada, Bell differentiates between theatre that has simply permitted some lesbian characterization and theatre that directly presents the lesbian culture. Among the performances cited are *Alice Has Red Skin and Doesn't Wear Make-up* by Three and 7 the magic number 8; *As-tu-vu? Les maisons s'emportent!* by Le Théâtre des cuisines; satirical acting by Marcia Cannon; the collaborative *Sizzle City: Women's Nuclear Reactions* by Bell and others and *Pink Triangle Tears* by Cannon and others; *Satin Thigh* by Liberty Jane Carter; *La Terre est trop courte, Violette Leduc* by Jovette Marchessault; and the work of Le Théâtre expérimental des femmes.

D40
Ben-Zvi, Linda. "Susan Glaspell and Eugene O'Neill." *The Eugene O'Neill Newsletter 6.2* (1982): 21–29.

Arguing that Glaspell's role in O'Neill's life was far more extensive than that usually assigned by critics, Ben-Zvi points out her advice, support, and influence in his artistic development. In addition, she studies themes in Glaspell's own work, such as the drive of women protagonists to escape societally imposed roles and the sharing of female experience.

D41
"Betty Lambert, 1933–83." *Canadian Theatre Review* 39 (1984): 6–8.

This reprint of a *Simon Fraser Week* article appears in a CTR issue dedicated to Lambert, who taught at Simon Fraser University but was better known as one of the few Vancouver women playwrights consistently creating significant work. Lambert's success in having productions mounted is contrasted with her failure to overcome sexist critical reaction to her plays, particularly *Jennie's Story*.

D42
Billman, Carol. "Women and the Family in American Drama." *Arizona Quarterly* 36 (1980): 35–48.

Billman analyzes the stereotype of the submissive, powerless female perpetuated in American plays from the 1920s through the 1960s (particularly by O'Neill, Miller, Williams, and Albee), noting that even the few plays with resourceful female protagonists (e.g., Rachel Crothers' *He and She*) dramatize the pervasiveness of the idea that women belong in the home. She contrasts contemporary feminist drama, which re-examines women's role in the family (Myrna Lamb's *The Mod Donna*, Merriam/Wagner/Hoffsiss's *Out of Our Fathers' House*), places women outside the home (Megan Terry's *Calm Down Mother*, Ruth Wolff's *The Abdication*), or, emphasizing moral or political ideas, presents women less bound by social or biological roles (Terry's *Approaching Simone*), with this tradition. Her inventory includes a summary of feminist playwrights' dramatic techniques.

D43
Bolt, Carol. "An Interview with Carol Bolt." With Rota Lister. *Women Writers of the Commonwealth*. Spec. issue of *World Literature Written in English* 17 (1978): 144–53.

While most of the interview consists of a general overview of Bolt's career, the concluding comments touch on the Canadian playwright's creation of active female characters and interest in writing good roles for women.

D44
Bond, Jean Carey, ed. *Lorraine Hansberry: Art of Thunder, Vision of Light*. Spec. issue of *Freedomways* 19.4 (1979).

Of particular interest are Margaret B. Wilkerson's "Lorraine Hansberry: The Complete Feminist," Adrienne Rich's "The Problem with Lorraine Hansberry," Aishah Rahman's "To Be Black, Female and a Playwright," and an extensive bibliography. Other essays include Steven R. Carter's

"The John Brown Theatre: Lorraine Hansberry's Cultural Views and Dramatic Goals"; Jewell Handy Gresham's "Lorraine Hansberry as Prose Stylist"; Clayton Riley's "Lorraine Hansberry: A Melody in a Different Key"; Lonne Elder III's "Lorraine Hansberry: Social Consciousness and the Will"; Woodie King, Jr.'s, "Lorraine Hansberry's Children: Black Artists and *A Raisin in the Sun*"; Douglas Turner Ward's "Lorraine Hansberry and the Passion of Walter Lee"; Lerone Bennett, Jr., and Margaret G. Burroughs' "A Lorraine Hansberry Rap"; Demetria Brendan Royals' "The Me Lorraine Hansberry Knew"; Julian Mayfield's "Lorraine Hansberry: A Woman for All Seasons"; James Baldwin's "Lorraine Hansberry at the Summit"; John Oliver Killens' "Lorraine Hansberry: On Time!"; Alex Haley's "The Once and Future Vision of Lorraine Hansberry"; Nikki Giovanni's "An Emotional View of Lorraine Hansberry"; and Sarah E. Wright's "Lorraine Hansberry on Film."

D45
Bosworth, Patricia. "Some Uncommon Dramatists." *Working Woman*
   Aug. 1984: 138–41.

Bosworth briefly discusses Elizabeth Forsythe Hailey, Tina Howe, Sybille Pearson, and Wendy Wasserstein.

D46
Braudy, Susan. " 'Ladies and Gentlemen, My Mother Is Dying.' " *Ms.*
   Nov. 1974: 100–104.

Braudy describes the events leading up to the creation and production of Honor Moore's *Mourning Pictures,* which was produced at the Lenox Art Theatre in Massachusetts and Off-Broadway.

D47
Brown, Lorraine A. " 'For the Characters Are Myself': Adrienne Kennedy's *Funnyhouse of a Negro.*" *Negro American Literature Forum* 9 (1975): 86–88.

Brown explores the playwright's depiction of a world where the combination of blackness, femaleness, and education creates "insurmountable barriers to wholeness and psychic balance."

D48
Brown-Guillory, Elizabeth. "Black Women Playwrights: Exorcising Myths." *Phylon: The Atlanta University Review of Race and Culture* 48 (1987): 229–39.

Brown-Guillory analyzes the creation of credible images of blacks by Alice Childress, Lorraine Hansberry, and Ntozake Shange, who "present a vital slice of life." Although she deals with images of the black male in search of his manhood and the black male as walking wounded, she emphasizes the playwrights' depiction of the "evolving black woman," an ordinary but resilient woman "for whom the act of living is sheer heroism."

D49

Brown-Guillory, Elizabeth. "Contemporary Black Women Playwrights: A View from the Other Half." *Helicon Nine: The Journal of Women's Arts and Letters* 14–15 (1986): 120–27.

Dealing with the works of Hansberry, Shange, and Childress, this essay is a slightly different version of "Black Women Playwrights: Exorcising Myths," annotated in D48. *Terms:* female-male relationships; images of women, black, evolving black woman; images of women, black, black mammy; stereotypes, racial.

D50

Brunazzi, Elizabeth. "When the Rainbow Is Not Quite Enough." *Off Our Backs* Feb. 1979: 18.

Brunazzi recounts the process of bringing a production of Shange's *for colored girls who have considered suicide/when the rainbow is enuf* to the Alderson (West Virginia) federal prison for women in December 1978. She briefly looks at the images of black women in the play and the play's impact on the audience of inmates.

D51

Buchanan, Roberta. "Outport Reminders." *Feminism and Canadian Theatre.* Spec. issue of *Canadian Theatre Review* 43 (1985): 111–18.

Acknowledging the lack of feminist theatre companies in Newfoundland, Buchanan describes three indigenous works centering on the lives of women that would fit in with the goals of such groups as Monstrous Regiment: Rhonda Payne's *Stars in the Sky Morning,* Michael Cook's *Therese's Creed,* and Grace Butt's *Mom.* Other plays featuring the strong outport woman are mentioned.

D52

Butruille, Susan G. "Acting Out! Curtain Going Up on Women's History." *Ms.* Mar. 1984: 95–98.

This article delineates the wide range of current theatrical approaches to depicting women's history, from one-woman shows to readers' theatre, musicals, and historical reenactments. Among the many works discussed are the following: *Quilters* by Molly Newman and Barbara Damashek; *Women of the San Juan,* a readers' theatre production by the American Association of University Women in Durango, Colorado; and Elizabeth Shultis's *Seneca Falls, 1948,* a reenactment of the first Women's Rights Convention. Solo performances mentioned include Vinie Burrows' tribute to the women of the world and the portrayal of famous women by Barbara Rowe (Susan B. Anthony), Laurie James (Charlotte Perkins Gilman), Anne O'Connell (Fanny Kemble), Jehane Dyllan (Karen Silkwood), and others.

D53

Carlson, Susan. "Comic Textures and Female Communities 1937 and 1977: Clare Boothe and Wendy Wasserstein." *Modern Drama* 27 (1984): 564–73.

Carlson argues that Clare Boothe Luce's unintentional misogyny in *The Women* is produced by limitations that the traditional comic form and its attitudes toward double standards and social roles impose on female characters. She sets in contrast Wasserstein's *Uncommon Women and Others,* in which a more open form and efforts to combat comedy's sexist assumptions produce "a comic world where women can work within a female community to challenge social roles."

D54

Carter, Steven R. "Commitment Amid Complexity: Lorraine Hansberry's Life in Action." *MELUS* 7.3 (1980): 39–53.

Carter provides a detailed chronology to indicate the close relationship between Hansberry's life and her ideas. He then examines her political and social concerns, including her feminism, commitment to gaining justice for blacks, and dedication to the growth of socialism. *A Raisin in the Sun* is used to illustrate Hansberry's advocacy of power-sharing.

D55

Case, Sue-Ellen. "Gender as Play: Simone Benmussa's *The Singular Life of Albert Nobbs.*" *Women & Performance: A Journal of Feminist Theory* 1.2 (1984): 21–24.

Following a summary of Benmussa's theatrical career, Case explores gender issues and structural choices in her adaptation of George Moore's short story. She locates the central character as a victim of the patriarchal economy and contends that in portraying the male-identified Nobbs in relation to other women, Benmussa's distinctive use of drag makes all gender roles seem fictitious.

D56

Case, Sue-Ellen. "Judy Grahn's Gynopoetics: *The Queen of Swords.*" *Studies in the Literary Imagination* 21.2 (1988): 47–67.

Noting the problems in criticizing a play developed outside the context of the dominant discourse, Case applies a strategy that includes describing the separatist, grass-roots lesbian culture in which Grahn's work is embedded. Case's deconstruction of the patriarchal reception of myth and performance, and the violence and misogyny inscribed therein, underscores the necessity for this community's project of "neomythology" ("taking back the myths"). She analyzes *The Queen of Swords,* an empowering, gynocentric ritual whose neomythological characters "perform for women the dimensions of their choices and experiences," and contrasts the work's peaceful effect with the Aristotelian priorities of "pity and fear," pointing out similarities between Grahn's poetics and those of Sanskrit drama.

D57

Childress, Alice. Interview. "Alice Childress: A Pioneering Spirit." With Elizabeth Brown-Guillory. *Sage: A Scholarly Journal on Black Women* 4.1 (1987): 66–68.

The playwright talks about early influences, the writing process, and her career in the theatre.

D58

Churchill, Caryl. Interview. "Caryl Churchill: The Playwright Who Makes You Laugh About Orgasm, Racism, Class Struggle, Homophobia, Woman-Hating, the British Empire and the Irrepressible Strangeness of the Human Heart." With Judith Thurman. *Ms.* May 1982: 52–57.

Churchill's playwriting strategies in *Cloud 9* are featured in this overview of her life and work.

D59

Churchill, Caryl. Interview. "The Common Imagination and the Individual Voice." With Geraldine Cousin. *New Theatre Quarterly* 4.13 (1988): 3–16.

After recalling the early years of her career, Churchill talks about recurrent themes, the idea of being a "woman writer," and her collaborative work with Joint Stock. The processes involved in creating *Serious Money* and *A Mouthful of Birds* (with David Lan) are detailed. Churchill suggests the importance of women's realizing "their capacity for violence, if men are also to recognize their capacity for peacefulness."

D60

Churchill, Caryl. Interview. "A Fair Cop." With Lynne Truss. *Plays and Players* Jan. 1984: 8–10.

Churchill discusses the stages in her career and American responses to her plays. She comments on *Top Girls, Cloud Nine,* and *Softcops.*

D61

Clarke, Annette. "Downtown Views." *Feminism and Canadian Theatre.* Spec. issue of *Canadian Theatre Review* 43 (1985): 119–26.

Reporting on the downtown St. John's (Newfoundland) theatre scene, Clarke notes that despite a lack of feminist activity and the rarity of all-women casts, there is attention focused on women's experiences and imaginations. She cites the work of Lois Brown, Cathy Jones, and Janis Spence, who promote women's views of the world.

D62

Clarke, Cheryl, Breena Clarke, Gwendolen Hardwick, and Linda Powell. "*Narratives: A Dramatic Event.*" *Acting Up!* Spec. issue of *Heresies* 5.1 (1984): 74–76.

Cheryl Clarke (writer), Breena Clarke (director-actor), Hardwick (actor), and Powell (actor) separately discuss *Narratives,* a performance of poetry that replaces stereotyped images of black women, particularly lesbians, with more truthful representations. A brief excerpt is included.

D63

Cohn, Ruby. "Benmussa's Planes." *Theater* 13.1 (1981–82): 51–54.

Cohn profiles director-playwright Simone Benmussa and several of her productions, including *Portrait of Dora, The Secret Life of Albert Nobbs,* and *Appearances.*

D64

Conover, Dora Smith, and Lois Reynolds Kerr. "The Playwrights' Studio Group (Toronto): An Interview with Two Women Playwrights of the 1930's." With Patrick O'Neill. *Atlantis* 8.1 (1982): 89–96.

Conover and Kerr reminisce about an all-women group of producing playwrights.

D65

Coss, Claire. "On Jane Chambers: An Interview with Beth Allen and Jere Jacob." *Acting Up!* Spec. issue of *Heresies* 5.1 (1984): 83–84.

The playwright's life and work are discussed.

D66

Cowan, Cindy. "Messages in the Wilderness." *Feminism and Canadian Theatre.* Spec. issue of *Canadian Theatre Review* 43 (1985): 100–110.

While underscoring the necessity of networking for women in Nova Scotian theatre, Cowan recognizes that women must work with men or remain isolated because of the sparse population. She exemplifies the possibilities of a women's theatre in the work of the Mulgrave Road Co-op (a mixed male and female collective), relating how the actresses began to write plays in order to control what appeared on the stage.

D67

Curb, Rosemary K. "Fragmented Selves in Adrienne Kennedy's *Funny-house of a Negro* and *The Owl Answers.*" *Theatre Journal* 32 (1980): 180–95.

Curb analyzes Kennedy's creation of nightmare worlds in two plays set in the minds of female protagonists obsessed with blackness and whiteness, confused about their sexual identity, and torn between their sensual and intellectual aspects. She explains how Kennedy's use of multilayered imagery reveals themes of imprisonment, powerlessness, and death.

D68

Curb, Rosemary K. " 'Goin' through Changes': Mother-Daughter Confrontations in Three Recent Plays by Young Black Women." *Kentucky Folklore Record: A Regional Journal of Folklore and Folklife* 25 (1979): 96–102.

In her examination of *Black Girl* by J.E. Franklin, *Black Cycle* by Martie Charles, and *Toe Jam* by Elaine Jackson, Curb shows how the daughters in each play struggle "to break away from maternal values, prejudices, restrictions, fears, and ambitions."

D69

Curb, Rosemary K. "Re/cognition, Re/presentation, Re/creation in Woman-Conscious Drama: The Seer, the Seen, the Scene, the Obscene." *Staging Gender.* Spec. issue of *Theatre Journal* 37 (1985): 302–16.

Curb defines "woman-conscious drama" as "encompassing all drama by and about women characterized by multiple interior reflections of women's lives and perceptions." She analyzes specific plays to illustrate the three layers of women's consciousness of self: re/cognition—"the psychic mirroring of the seeing subject and the object" (Adrienne

Kennedy's *Funnyhouse of a Negro* and Martha Boesing's *River Journal*); re/presentation—"scenes of past history made present" (Joan Schenkar's *Signs of Life* and Wendy Kesselman's *My Sister in This House*); and re/creation—"a tribal revival of a lost past and/or . . . a present survival ritual" (*Daughters* by W.E.T.'s Clare Coss, Sondra Segal, and Roberta Sklar; Megan Terry's *Babes in the Bighouse;* Ntozake Shange's *for colored girls who have considered suicide/when the rainbow is enuf;* and Karen Malpede's *Sappho and Aphrodite*). Curb also addresses the subversive potential of woman-conscious drama.

D70
Curb, Rosemary [K.]. "An Unfashionable Tragedy of American Racism: Alice Childress's *Wedding Band.*" *MELUS* 7.4 (1980): 57–68.

Curb explores Childress's use of black women protagonists and race-related themes in her works, particularly *Wedding Band.* She considers Childress's realistic approach in that play.

D71
Diamond, Elin. "(In)Visible Bodies in Churchill's Theatre." *Feminist Diversions.* Spec. issue of *Theatre Journal* 40 (1988): 188–204.

With reference to *l'écriture féminine,* Diamond investigates issues of representation in Caryl Churchill's work, which demonstrates both "a commitment of the apparatus of representation . . . in order to say something *about* human oppression and pain" and consistent "attention to the powers of theatrical illusion, to modalities within representation that subvert the 'aboutness' we normally call the work's 'content.' " Delineating conceptual differences between performance and theatre, Diamond points out Churchill's increasing concern with "the ideological nature of the seeable," discusses her use of Brechtian techniques, and describes her adaptation of Foucault's writing on social discipline. Plays examined include *Traps, Vinegar Tom, Light Shining in Buckinghamshire, Cloud Nine,* and especially *Fen* and *A Mouthful of Birds* (with David Lan).

D72
Diamond, Elin. "Refusing the Romanticism of Identity: Narrative Interventions in Churchill, Benmussa, Duras." *Staging Gender.* Spec. issue of *Theatre Journal* 37 (1985): 273–86.

Diamond demonstrates how the three playwrights, concerned with the "historical human activity that confuses or conflates identity and gender," refuse their female protagonists a recognizable selfhood and in so doing reject both the logic of social narratives in which women are constrained and the perpetuation of a romanticized female who transcends constraints. She also articulates the ways in which the playwrights disrupt the narrativizing desire of the audience. Churchill's *Cloud Nine,* Benmussa's *The Singular Life of Albert Nobbs,* and Duras's *India Song* are analyzed.

D73
Diamond, Elin. "(Theoretically) Approaching Megan Terry: Issues of Gender and Identity." *Work by Women.* Spec. issue of *Art & Cinema* ns 1.3 (1987): 5–7.

Summarizing work in semiotics and psychoanalytic theory that demystifies cultural myths, Diamond argues that these discourses as well as material analyses are all needed "to conduct a gender critique that is not going to slip back into valorizing an ideologically normative identity." She suggests that a theatrical critique of gender "might alienate (make us re-see, re-think) the signs of masculinity and femininity that are verbally and gesturally reproduced" by the performer. After briefly surveying treatments of gender and identity by several contemporary women playwrights, Diamond examines Terry's gestic theatre, focusing on her use of transformational techniques.

D74
Dickerson, Glenda. "The Cult of True Womanhood: Toward a Womanist Attitude in African-American Theatre." *Feminist Diversions.* Spec. issue of *Theatre Journal* 40 (1988): 178–87.

Dickerson, a black feminist director and creator of "miracle plays" using nondramatic sources (myths, black history, poetry), reveals the process of consciousness-raising that led her from patriarchal to womanist theatre and her role of PraiseSinger, "a guardian of the archetypes of her culture's collective unconscious." She discusses her replacement of stereotypical black females with proud women of color.

D75
Dymkowski, Christine. "On the Edge: The Plays of Susan Glaspell." *Modern Drama* 31 (1988): 91–105.

Dymkowski analyzes Glaspell's preoccupation with the limits of experience and depiction of women "as outside the mainstream of life and thus capable of shaping it anew." Plays examined include *Trifles, The Outside, The Verge, Woman's Honor, Bernice,* and *Inheritors.*

D76

Endres, Robin Belitsky. "Notes Toward an Androgynous Theatre: Self-Profile." *Women and Performance*. Spec. issue of *Fireweed* 7 (Summer 1980): 8–13.

Recounting significant incidents from her personal life, Toronto playwright Endres contrasts "male" and "female" language and notes the insufficiency of the language of art and that of politics without one another. She contemplates her need to write to defy the spiritual death that accompanies exploitation and oppression and to "find images that will be charged with meaning *and* sentiment."

D77

Féral, Josette. "Writing and Displacement: Women in the Theatre." *Modern Drama* 27 (1984): 549–63.

Relying heavily on Luce Irigaray's theoretical writing, Féral articulates the simultaneity and contiguity that are characteristic of female discourse. Illustrating with five texts—*Portrait de Dora* and *Le Nom d'Oedipe* by Hélène Cixous, *Three Women* by Sylvia Plath, *La Table* by Michèle Foucher, and *The Daughters Cycle* by Clare Coss, Sondra Segal and Roberta Sklar—she confronts the questions of *what* women say in language (they tell their own stories; reexamine the world; reveal, refuse, and subvert all forms of repression) and *how* they use language (fragmentation, mobility and incompleteness of text, multiple characters, rejection of syntax).

D78

Fichera, Virginia M. "Simone de Beauvoir and 'The Woman Question': *Les Bouches inutiles*." *Yale French Studies* 72 (1986): 51–64.

Fichera analyzes this critically neglected 1945 play, which explores the relationship between power and gender in a society not unlike today's in assuming male experience as the human norm. Fichera asserts that the underlying objectives of this early venture into modern feminism "are to present, to critique, and ultimately to change relationships which are based on dominance rather than interdependence."

D79

Fido, Elaine Savory. "A Question of Realities: Zulu Sofola's *The Sweet Trap*." *Ariel: A Review of International English Literature* 18.4 (1987): 53–66.

Fido addresses the question of subjectivity in literature and criticism, declaring that African women writers and characters have been ignored because "the male writer/critic's *reality* did not often engage women's experience as a primary concern." Stressing Sofola's importance in dramatizing Nigerian women's conditions and in challenging audiences and critics by her complex presentation of issues, she acknowledges that Sofola is committed to tradition, but in a selective fashion "perfectly able to co-exist with her strong insistence on women's awareness and rights."

D80

Fifer, Elizabeth. "Put Language in the Waist: Stein's Critique of Women in *Geography and Plays.*" *University of Michigan Papers in Women's Studies* 2.1 (1975): 96–102.

Noting that Stein's series of plays about women reveals a substantial feminist strain, Fifer examines several themes, including narcissism, romantic love (lesbian and heterosexual), and aggression versus dependency. She also describes the ambiguous position of Alice Toklas in these plays as simultaneously a symbol of traditional womanhood (of which Stein is critical) and of Stein's liberated relationship.

D81

Fitzsimmons, Linda. " 'I Won't Turn Back for You or Anyone': Caryl Churchill's Socialist-Feminist Theatre." *Essays in Theatre* 6 (1987): 19–29.

Reading *Top Girls* and *Fen* as political texts, Fitzsimmons investigates Churchill's treatment of the notion of motherhood and femininity as constructed, not natural, and her depiction of women's oppression by patriarchy and capitalism. She argues that both plays optimistically advocate change "through collective action in class and female solidarity."

D82

Fletcher, Winona. "From Genteel Poet to Revolutionary Playwright: Georgia Douglas Johnson." *Women in Theatre.* Spec. issue of *Theatre Annual* 40 (1985): 41–64.

Fletcher studies Johnson's career within the context of choices all black American writers must make in dealing with artistic barriers forced upon them because of their race. Her analysis of Johnson's five plays of intense social protest—three about lynching and rape and two about slavery—rejected by the Federal Theatre Project and of the playreaders' evaluations of them enables Fletcher to consider why social protest from a black perspective failed to find a place in American drama of the 1930s.

D83

Flowers, Sandra Hollin. *"Colored Girls:* Textbook for the Eighties." *Black American Literature Forum* 15 (1981): 51–54.

Flowers determines that Shange presents a compassionate vision of black men and a perceptive understanding of the crisis between black men and women.

D84

Fo, Dario, and Franca Rame. "An Interview with Dario Fo and Franca Rame." With Steve Grant and Tony Mitchell. *Theater* 14.3 (1983): 43–49.

The playwrights discuss *Female Parts* and *Medea* and what these plays communicate about women.

D85

Fornes, Maria Irene. Interview. "I Write These Messages That Come." With Robb Creese. *Playwrights and Playwriting.* Spec. issue of *The Drama Review* 21.4 (1977): 25–40.

Fornes reflects on the creative process involved in writing *Fefu and Her Friends* and other works.

D86

Fornes, Maria Irene. Interview. "Maria Irene Fornes." With Bonnie Marranca. *Performing Arts Journal* 2.3 (1978): 106–11.

This interview centers on *Fefu and Her Friends.*

D87

Fornes, Maria Irene. Interview. "Seeing with Clarity: The Visions of Maria Irene Fornes." With Scott Cummings. *Theater* 17.1 (1985): 51–56.

Fornes talks about her writing techniques and career in theatre.

D88

Fornes, Maria Irene, and Tina Howe. "Women's Work: Tina Howe and Maria Irene Fornes Explore the Woman's Voice in Drama." *American Theatre* Sept. 1985: 10–15.

Jan Stuart's introduction comments on the status of women playwrights and briefly contrasts the careers of Howe and Fornes. In separate sections, each playwright discusses the creative process, her female characters, her relationship to feminism, and other pertinent topics.

D89

Fraticelli, Rina. "'Any Black Crippled Woman Can!' or A Feminist's Notes from Outside the Sheltered Workshop." *Women in Theatre.* Spec. issue of *Room of One's Own* 8.2 (1983): 7–18.

In an essay generally dealing with discrimination against women in the male-dominated Canadian theatre industry, Fraticelli reports on interviews with several women playwrights, noting their shared awareness of dismissive attitudes toward women's lives. She also mentions the growth of feminist cultural organizations throughout the country.

D90

Friedman, Sharon. "Feminism as Theme in Twentieth-Century American Women's Drama." *American Studies* 25.2 (1984): 69–89.

Arguing that feminism as theme is not only a call for women's rights in a male-dominated society but may also be "a statement about feminine consciousness," Friedman focuses on Susan Glaspell's *Trifles, Bernice,* and *The Verge;* Rachel Crothers' *A Man's World, He and She,* and *When Ladies Meet;* Lillian Hellman's *The Little Foxes* and *Another Part of the Forest;* and Lorraine Hansberry's *A Raisin in the Sun* and *The Drinking Gourd.*

D91

Gaboriau, Linda. "A Luminous Wake in Space." *Feminism and Canadian Theatre.* Spec. issue of *Canadian Theatre Review* 43 (1985): 91–99.

Profiling Jovette Marchessault, Gaboriau reveals how her plays "reflect (and transcend) the themes that have dominated feminist art and writing" for the past decade. Gaboriau notes Marchessault's celebration of famous women writers, use of myth and rejection of a patriarchally recorded history, treatment of lesbianism, and lyrical dialogue. A bibliography of Marchessault's theatrical works is included.

D92

Gems, Pam. Interview. "Women Are Uncharted Territory." With Michelene Wandor. *Spare Rib* 62 (Sept. 1977): 10 + .

Wandor's explanation of why women have seldom figured as playwrights throughout history precedes the interview. Gems discusses *Dusa, Fish, Stas and Vi* and other works.

D93

Gipson, Rosemary. "Martha Morton: America's First Professional Woman Playwright." *Theatre Survey* 23 (1982): 213–22.

Reviewing Morton's pioneering role for women in theatre, Gipson outlines her career from 1890–1915 and her determination to place independent female characters on stage. Gipson also writes about the large number of produced women playwrights following Morton, the American Dramatists Club's refusal to admit women members, and Morton's founding of The Society of Dramatic Authors.

D94

Goodman, Vera. "Britons Generate Excitement on New York Stage." *New Directions for Women* May–June 1983: 6+.

Goodman reports on roles for women in several British plays, including Caryl Churchill's *Top Girls,* Nell Dunn's *Steaming,* and David Hare's *Plenty,* and in one American play, William Mastrosimone's *Extremities.*

D95

Gottlieb, Lois C. "Obstacles to Feminism in the Early Plays of Rachel Crothers." *University of Michigan Papers in Women's Studies* 1.4 (1975): 71–84.

Gottlieb examines Crothers' ambivalent commitment to feminism as manifested in her early plays, including *Criss-Cross, The Rector, The Three of Us, Myself Bettina, A Man's World, Ourselves,* and *Young Wisdom.* Gottlieb points out that the conflict between the New Woman and her male love interest is basically a conflict between feminism and traditional femininity, and that Crothers' works tend to close the gap between the sexes by restricting the woman's freedom rather than by changing the man's attitudes.

D96

Gould, Karen. "Setting Words Free: Feminist Writing in Quebec." *Signs* 6 (1981): 617–42.

Placing Quebec feminists within a literary, social, and political context, Gould analyzes the invention of a feminist discourse. In the section of the essay devoted to theatre, she shows how playwrights have explored topics of social taboo regarding female experience and focused on the "tension between word/power and silence/weakness." Plays discussed include Marie Savard's *Bien à moi,* Denise Boucher's *Les Fées ont soif,* and the collaborative *La Nef des sorcières.*

D97

Guttman, Melinda Jo. Interview. "The Story of Anna O: Performing a Case History." With Katheryn Kovalcik-White. *Women & Performance: A Journal of Feminist Theory* 2.1 (1984): 75–80.

Guttman, creator of the solo performance piece *Anna O's Private Theatre,* talks about her reconstruction of the life of pioneer Jewish feminist and psychoanalytic patient Bertha Pappenheim.

D98
Hansberry, Lorraine. "Make New Sounds: A Conversation with Lorraine Hansberry." With Studs Terkel. *American Theatre* Nov. 1984: 4+.

This excerpt from a 1959 radio interview focuses on *A Raisin in the Sun.*

D99
Harbin, Billy J. "Familial Bonds in the Plays of Beth Henley." *Southern Women Playwrights.* Spec. issue of *The Southern Quarterly: A Journal of Arts in the South* 25.3 (1987): 81–94.

General comments on feminism and American women playwrights precede an examination of *Crimes of the Heart, The Miss Firecracker Contest, The Wake of Jamey Foster, The Debutante Ball,* and *The Lucky Spot.* Harbin explores Henley's depiction of separation and communion and analyzes food metaphors. He maintains that underlying the plays' whimsy and humor are themes related to the disintegration of traditional ideals.

D100
Harris, Valerie. "Recycling: Self-Profile." *Women and Performance.* Spec. issue of *Fireweed* 8 (Fall 1980): 12–18.

In an attempt to call on her past to guide her through her present period of creativity, playwright-journalist Harris intersperses selections from her journal dealing with the writing process and reactions to being produced with excerpts from her plays.

D101
Hart, Lynda. "Doing Time: Hunger for Power in Marsha Norman's Plays." *Southern Women Playwrights.* Spec. issue of *The Southern Quarterly: A Journal of Arts in the South* 25.3 (1987): 67–79.

The author's analysis of Norman's use of hunger imagery in *Getting Out* and *'night, Mother* underscores the interrelationships among food, mother-daughter struggles, and the protagonists' search for autonomy.

D102
Hewett, Dorothy. "Creating Heroines in Australian Plays." *Hecate* 5.2 (1979): 73–80.

Hewett discusses Australia's male-dominated theatre and the savage criticism of her work. Tracing recurrent images of women in her plays, she theorizes that she has not created what feminists would call a truly liberated woman "because I see the objective situation as too ambivalent, the dice too loaded."

D103

Hewett, Dorothy. "Dorothy Hewett: An Interview." With Pip Porter. *Hecate* 3.1 (1977): 6–15.

Topics include Hewett's childhood, political activism, and playwriting techniques.

D104

Hirshfield, Claire. "The Suffragist as Playwright in Edwardian England." *Frontiers* 9.2 (1987): 1–6.

Hirshfield locates the genre of the suffrage play within its social, political, and theatrical context. The ground-breaking *Votes for Women* by Elizabeth Robins is discussed, as is the work of the Actresses' Franchise League, the functions of which included presenting stage productions for fund-raising and propaganda purposes. Hirshfield briefly describes plays by a number of men and women sympathetic to the cause and outlines the significance of Alison Garland's *The Better Half*.

D105

Hoder-Salmon, Marilyn. "The Intimate Agony of Mary McDougal Axelson's *Life Begins.*" *American Studies* 18.2 (1977): 55–69.

Tracing the personal and professional life of Axelson, whose careers ranged from suffragist to social reformer, political activist, businesswoman, and writer, Hoder-Salmon particularly chronicles the production and reception of the 1930s' stage and film versions of *Life Begins.* She details how praise for the play, which takes place in a hospital maternity ward, was tempered by distaste for its subject.

D106

Hopkins, Elaine R. "Feminism and a Female Trinity in Denise Boucher's *Les Fées ont soif.*" *American Review of Canadian Studies* 14 (1984): 63–71.

Placing Boucher within the context of feminist rejection of patriarchal religious tradition, Hopkins analyzes the playwright's demythologization of the Virgin and Mary Magdalene and dramatization of women's liberation from stereotypes.

D107

Jillson, Teresa L. "Working Women's Words and the Conditions of Their Production(s)." *Journal of Dramatic Theory and Criticism* 2.2 (1988): 135–48.

This critique of Michèle Foucher's *La Table, parole de femmes* investigates "both the paradox of institutional production, and the problems of populism, identification, and projection which plague the political theatre." While Jillson recognizes the potential power of Foucher's refusal to make the working-class woman character either a type or an individual, she finds that the production cannot avoid "exoticizing the non-legitimized dominated other" for the middle-class audience. Jillson suggests that its weakness may reside in not pushing the techniques and critical implications of theatricalization far enough, leaving "room for universalization on the level of gender and for the projection of the audience into the lifestyle presented."

D108

Jones, Judith Zykofsky, and Janelle Reinelt. "Simone de Beauvoir as Dramatist: *Les Bouches Inutiles.*" *Modern Drama* 26 (1983): 528–35.

The writers demonstrate the interconnection between feminist issues and existentialist themes of freedom and responsibility in Simone de Beauvoir's only play.

D109

Jones, Sonia. "Alfonsina Storni's *El amo del mundo.*" *Revista/Review Interamericana* 12 (1982): 100–103.

Describing the 1927 play as a repository of Storni's feminist ideas, Jones discusses the negative reaction of critics who viewed it as an attack on men.

D110

Kearney, Eileen. "Teresa Deevy: Ireland's Forgotten Second Lady of the Abbey Theatre." *Women in Theatre.* Spec. issue of *Theatre Annual* 40 (1985): 77-90.

The author summarizes the playwright's life and career, particularly her association with the Abbey Theatre.

D111

Kennedy, Adrienne. Interview. "A Growth of Images." With Lisa Lehman. *Playwrights and Playwriting.* Spec. issue of *The Drama Review* 21.4 (1977): 41–48.

Kennedy talks about the ways in which she works and the inspiration for her plays.

D112
Keyssar, Helene. "Dramas of Caryl Churchill: The Politics of Possibility." *Massachusetts Review* 24 (1983): 198–216.

A slightly altered and updated version of this article appears as Chapter 4 in Keyssar's book, *Feminist Theatre.* See A8. *Terms:* capitalism, women and; collaborative/collective process; feminism(s), influence on/relationship to women's playwriting.

D113
Kilkelly, Ann Gavere. "Who's in the House?" *Women & Performance: A Journal of Feminist Theory* 3.1 (1986): 28–34.

In her exploration of Wendy Kesselman's revision of history in *My Sister in This House,* Kilkelly underscores the patriarchal structures, both social and religious, that deny selfhood to the characters.

D114
Klein, Kathleen Gregory. "Language and Meaning in Megan Terry's 1970s 'Musicals.'" *Modern Drama* 27 (1984): 574–83.

Klein examines Terry's concern with language's influence on gender roles in *American King's English for Queens.* Also discussed are *Babes in the Bighouse, Brazil Fado,* and *Tommy Allen Show.*

D115
Kolb, Deborah S. "The Rise and Fall of the New Woman in American Drama." *Educational Theatre Journal* 27 (1975): 149–60.

The author tracks the close relationship between the dramatic portrayal of the New Woman and changes in the women's rights movement from the 1890s through the 1920s. Three basic issues are delineated: the sexual double standard, women's economic independence, and the conflict between professional career and family. Illustrations are drawn from *A Man's World, He and She,* and other works by Rachel Crothers; *Margaret Fleming* by James Herne; *As a Man Thinks* by Augustus Thomas; *Why Marry?* by Jesse Lynch Williams; and *Craig's Wife* by George Kelly.

D116
Krouse, Agate Nesaule. "Doris Lessing's Feminist Plays." *World Literature Written in English* 15 (1976): 305–22.

Krouse argues that *Each His Own Wilderness* and *Play with a Tiger* are essential to understanding Lessing's feminism. While showing that an analysis of *Tiger,* which depicts the sex war and the disadvantages for women in marriage, enlarges appreciation of Lessing's nondramatic work, Krouse criticizes the play's reliance on negative male stereotypes. *Wilderness,* which Krouse considers more convincing in its presentation of feminist issues, is examined in terms of two closely connected sets of relationships: between women and men, and between women and children.

D117

Lambert, Betty. Interview. "A Conversation between Playwright Betty Lambert and Director Bonnie Worthington." *Women in Theatre.* Spec. issue of *Room of One's Own* 8.2 (1983): 54–66.

Reviewing her writing career, Lambert reveals the inspiration for her work, particularly *Jennie's Story* and its controversial ending in which the protagonist commits suicide. She distinguishes between "the highly individualized classical tragedy" and her attempt to establish a female tragic form.

D118

Lamont, Rosette C. "Rosalyn Drexler's Semiotics of Instability." *Theater* 17.1 (1985): 70–77.

Lamont's study of Drexler's work delineates the playwright's subversion of cultural stereotypes, destabilizing of common forms of discourse, and precarious balancing between reality and illusion. Noting Drexler's postmodern aesthetic, the author analyzes her plays with reference to such traditions as dadaism, while emphasizing the American optimism-pragmatism characterizing "her search for a transcendent kind of realism." She suggests that Drexler's works exemplify the Case-Forte definition of feminist drama. (See A21.)

D119

Landau, Penny. "Jane Chambers: In Memoriam." *Women & Performance: A Journal of Feminist Theory* 1.2 (1984): 55–57.

The author focuses on the lesbian playwright's zest for life, commitment to enhancing the self-respect of gay people, and creation of gay characters who are open about their sexuality.

D120

Lappin, Lou. "Gems Views History in a New Light: Sex, Power and Politics Are Connected in Her Plays." *American Theatre* Apr. 1987: 42–44.

Lappin's analysis of Gems' deconstruction and demythologizing of female heroines includes *Camille, Piaf,* and *Queen Christina.*

D121

Laughlin, Karen L. "Criminality, Desire, and Community: A Feminist Approach to Beth Henley's *Crimes of the Heart." Women & Performance: A Journal of Feminist Theory* 3.1 (1986): 35–51.

Laughlin studies the self-destructive nature of the crimes in Henley's play, the patriarchal mediation of the protagonists' desire, and the rejection of patriarchal forces in favor of female bonding. She also stresses the feminist implications of the work (despite compromises made by the playwright to gain a wide audience) and places Henley's concern with madness within a literary and historical tradition.

D122

Lebowitz, Andrea P. "Jackie Crossland: West Coast Woman of Theatre." *Women in Canadian Drama.* Spec. issue of *Canadian Drama* 5 (1979): 83–93.

In this profile of the playwright-director-actress, Lebowitz underscores Crossland's belief in the collaborative process and proposes that her work reflects the past decade's development of alternate West Coast drama. Concentrating on *Ruins of S__ PERMAR____,* which features two male characters, Lebowitz remarks on the play's underlying feminine sensibility and Crossland's insistence on an all-female production crew.

D123

Lester, Elenore. "*The Women:* Older but Not Wiser." *Ms.* Aug. 1973: 42–45.

The 1973 Broadway revival provides the impetus for this examination of Clare Boothe Luce's play. Lester reports on the play's production history, analyzes male critical reaction, and addresses the issue of Luce's feminism.

D124

Lester, Tanya. "On Playwright Lill and Dusty Documents." *Herizons* June–July 1984: 49.

The author outlines the steps taken by Wendy Lill in researching and writing *The Fighting Days,* a play adaptable for high school audiences, about suffragist newspaper columnist Frances Beynon.

D125

Lindfors, Viveca. "It's a Human Revolution: An Interview with Viveca Lindfors." With Gloria Orenstein. *Feminist Art Journal* 4.1 (1975): 23–30.

Actress-playwright Lindfors discusses the inadequacy of roles for older women; the influence of the women's liberation movement on her work; the process of compiling (with Paul Austin) her one-woman show, *I Am a Woman;* and discrimination against women in theatre.

D126

Lister, Rota Herzberg. "Beverly Simons and the Influence of Oriental Theatre." *Canadian Drama* 10 (1984): 218–26.

Explicating the symbolism and rituals in the Vancouver playwright's mature works, especially *Leela Means to Play,* Lister points out Simons' visions of universal patriarchy and her association of woman's role in *Leela* with death. She declares that Simons "has given us women's theatre, the theatre of cruelty, and now a new kind of global theatre."

D127

Lowy, Virginia. "Theater Company Gives New Life to Plays." *New Directions for Women* May–June 1980: 11.

Second Stage's upcoming production of Corinne Jacker's *Bits and Pieces* and the play's theme of self-realization are described, as well as the formation of the theatre company by Carole Rothman and Robyn Goodman.

D128

Lynd, Phyllis. *"That's a Heavy Crown, Mr. Jones." Feminist Art Journal* 5.4 (1976-77): 30–32.

Lynd recounts the genesis of the feminist musical revue that she wrote and produced. She specifies the issues dealt with in the work, including female-male relationships, sex roles, and marriage.

D129

Lyssa, Alison. "Feminist Theatre: A Monologue to Start a Discussion." *Australasian Drama Studies* 2.2 (1984): 27–40.

In this transcript of a talk given at Troupe Theatre Annual Writers' Workshop in Adelaide, Lyssa expresses the struggle of women playwrights to make their voices heard in a sexist society. She surveys current feminist drama in Australia and addresses the dilemma of working in the mainstream versus creating an alternative theatre in the community.

D130
Lyssa, Alison, and Sandra Shotlander. "Belles Lettres Interviews." With Rosemary [K.] Curb. *Belles Lettres* Sept.–Oct. 1986: 4–5.

Lyssa discusses *Pinball,* which centers on a lesbian's custody battle, and *The Boiling Frog,* an incitement to political action. Shotlander, author of *Framework* and *Blind Salome,* reflects on the effect of the feminist movement on her writing. Providing background information on these iconoclastic Australian playwrights as well as synopses of their works, Curb asserts that they deserve worldwide attention.

D131
Malpede, Karen. "An Interview with Karen Malpede." With Gloria Orenstein. *Women and Performance.* Spec. issue of *Fireweed* 8 (Fall 1980): 89–97.

Playwright Malpede describes several feminist and pacifist works produced by the New Cycle Theater and her involvement in the rehearsal process. Offering the reasons behind her choice of poetic language and historical material, she concludes that feminist art is re-imaging the world, "creating an entirely new moral, as well as aesthetic, sensibility."

D132
Mann, Maureen. "Ann Henry: A Canadian Paycock." *Women in Canadian Drama.* Spec. issue of *Canadian Drama* 5 (1979): 129-38.

The author elucidates Henry's use of the Winnipeg General Strike as a symbol of the problem of paternalism in Canadian societal and familial organization in *Lulu Street.* She details the ways in which Henry altered her autobiography, particularly the father-daughter relationship, in writing the play.

D133
Marohl, Joseph. "De-realised Women: Performance and Identity in *Top Girls.*" *Modern Drama* 30 (1987): 376–88.

After an overview of Churchill's themes and techniques, Marohl investigates *Top Girls'* dramatization of the impossibility of true social reform, particularly in regard to gender roles, within a system maintaining class distinctions. He focuses largely on the first scene, which emphasizes cultural relativity and links the ghost characters' accomplishments to concessions willingly made to their various patriarchies.

D134

Marranca, Bonnie. "The Real Life of Maria Irene Fornes." *Performing Arts Journal* 8.1 (1984): 29–34.

Marranca analyzes Fornes's technique, particularly her approach to realism as exemplified in *Mud*, and the social meaning of her work.

D135

Messenger, Ann. "B. A. Cameron/Cam Hubert: Poet of the Afflicted." *Women in Canadian Drama*. Spec. issue of *Canadian Drama* 5 (1979): 94–103.

Beginning with a lengthy review of Cameron's television scripts dealing with Indian culture, Messenger goes on to contrast the playwright's responses with the different demands of writing for TV and for the stage. Of particular interest here is her study of Cameron's later, women-centered theatrical works and the theme of self-awareness.

D136

Miller, Jeanne-Marie A. "Angelina Weld Grimké: Playwright and Poet." *CLA Journal* 21 (1978): 513–24.

The author shows how Grimké uses genteel black characters to protest against racial injustice in *Rachel* and *Mara*.

D137

Miller, Jeanne-Marie A. "Images of Black Women in Plays by Black Playwrights." *CLA Journal* 20 (1977): 494–507.

Miller surveys the varied treatment of black women in works by Alice Childress, Lorraine Hansberry, J. E. Franklin, Ron Milner, Ed Bullins, Imamu Amiri Baraka, and Adrienne Kennedy. She notes that the female-authored works (except Kennedy's) often present optimistic women characters, whereas the male-authored works depict women's happiness as dependent upon men.

D138

Miller, Judith G. "Jean Cocteau and Hélène Cixous: Oedipus." *Themes in Drama* 7 (*Drama, Sex and Politics*) (1985): 203–11.

Exploring the revision of the Oedipus myth using Freud's reworking as a foil in Cocteau's *La Machine infernale* and Cixous's *Le Nom d'Oedipe:*

Chant du corps interdit, Miller determines that although both playwrights "have affirmed their freedom from Freudian determinism through the self-conscious use of language," only Cixous offers a positive "hero/ine," giving the audience "the possibility of identifying with a kind of triumph."

D139
Milleret, Margo. "Entrapment and Flights of Fantasy in Three Plays by Leilah Assunção." *Luso-Brazilian Review* 21.1 (1984): 49–56.

Milleret discusses Assunção's dramatization of middle-class life as a suffocating social structure with unalterable sex roles and her use of fantastic events in which the individual is temporarily liberated. Three plays are analyzed: *Fala baixo senão eu grito, Jorginho, o machão,* and *Roda cor de roda.*

D140
Miner, Madonne M. " 'What's These Bars Doin' Here?'—The Impossibility of *Getting Out.*" *Women in Theatre.* Spec. issue of *Theatre Annual* 40 (1985): 115–36.

Miner views Norman's play as raising questions about subjecthood and identity construction in its critique of a capitalistic, patriarchal ideology that valorizes a single, stable "self." She argues that Norman consistently undercuts the characters' apparent freedom by showing how "free choices" actually testify to "the real boundaries which an ideology of individuality imposes upon us."

D141
Molette, Barbara. "They Speak: Who Listens? Black Women Playwrights." *Black World* Apr. 1976: 18–34.

Delineating the difficulties faced by black women in getting their plays produced, Molette cites the refusal of media brokers to present truths helpful in reducing oppression and contradicting black stereotypes. She surveys works addressing black issues by Angelina Grimké, May Miller, Mary Burrill, Lorraine Hansberry, and Alice Childress.

D142
Moore, Honor. "Theatre Will Never Be the Same." *Ms.* Dec. 1977: 36 + .

In assessing the proliferation of theatre by women in the 1970s, Moore provides an overview of the work of feminist groups and individual playwrights and analyzes some of the nontraditional forms emerging. Wendy Wasserstein's comic *Uncommon Women and Others;* Aishah Rahman's poetic *Unfinished Women Cry in No Man's Land While a*

Bird Dies in a Gilded Cage; and Los Angeles's Artists in Prison's ritualistic, collaborative piece, *Not as Sleepwalkers*, are among the plays discussed. In addition, Moore looks at employment discrimination against women in theatre.

D143

Morrow, Laura. "Orality and Identity in *'night, Mother* and *Crimes of the Heart*." *Studies in American Drama, 1945–Present* 3 (1988): 23–39.

In this comparison and contrast of plays by Marsha Norman and Beth Henley, Morrow shows how the female characters' identities are defined through their attitudes toward eating, drinking, smoking, and speaking.

D144

Moss, Jane. "Le Corps Spectaculaire: Le Théâtre au Féminin." *Modern Language Studies* 16.4 (1986): 54–60. Rpt. as "The Body as Spectacle: Women's Theatre in Quebec." *Women & Performance: A Journal of Feminist Theory* 3.1 (1986): 5–16.

Moss discusses *l'écriture féminine* in relation to Quebec feminists' representing of the female body on the stage "to be exposed, demystified, reclaimed, rehabilitated and reintegrated." Noting the explicitly sexual scenes celebrating the female libido, she offers examples from plays including Marie Savard's *Bien à moi* and the collective works *La Nef des sorcières* and *A ma mère, à ma mère, à ma mère, à ma voisine.*

D145

Moss, Jane. "Creation Reenacted: The Woman Artist as Dramatic Figure." *American Review of Canadian Studies* 15 (1985): 263–72.

Moss examines how Canadian women dramatists, using women writers as symbols of the difficulty of female expression, reenact the writing act for both their characters and themselves. She concludes that "the desire to write in a language which expresses female experience, sexuality, and imagination becomes the subject of this self-reflective *prise de parole* which is feminist dramatic discourse."

D146

Moss, Jane. "Les Folles du Québec: The Theme of Madness in Quebec Women's Theater." *The French Review* 57 (1984): 617–24.

Asserting that the repressive conditions faced by women in Quebec make them especially vulnerable to psychological problems, Moss suggests that feminist writers exorcise the fear of madness by bringing it out into the open. She analyzes Marie Savard's *Bien à moi,* the collective piece *La Nef des sorcières,* Denise Boucher's *Les Fées ont soif,* Jocelyne Beaulieu's *J'ai beaucoup change depuis. . . ,* and Jovette Marchessault's *La Saga des poules mouillées.*

D147

Mussman, Linda, and Ann Wilson. Interview. "Hearing and Seeing: Linda Mussmann and Ann Wilson on Creating Nonnarrative Theater." With Harmony Hammond. *Acting Up!* Spec. issue of *Heresies* 5.1 (1984): 89–93.

Each writer-director talks about her background and artistic processes. Mussmann, who first "hears" a text, discusses influences on her work (including Gertrude Stein and Eastern culture), rehearsal procedures, and the problems facing women artists. Wilson, who first "sees" images, discusses the use of architectural spaces, the role of dreams, economic realities, and her creation of *Anna O's Private Theater.*

D148

Newman, Kathy. "Susan Glaspell and *Trifles*: 'Nothing Here but Kitchen Things.' " *Trivia* 3 (1983): 88–94.

Newman explains how the "trivia" of female experience yields insight for meaningful thought and a heroic act of moral judgment in *Trifles.*

D149

Nielsen, Sigrid. "Women in Scottish Theatre." *Spare Rib* 101 (Dec. 1980): 20–23.

This discussion of the difficulties of creating women's theatre in Scotland includes interviews with playwright Marcella Evaristi (*Hard to Get*), actor Elizabeth MacInnan, cofounder of the 7:84 (Scotland) Theatre Company; playwright-director Pam Blackwood, founder of Central Players; and others.

D150

Niemi, Irmeli. "Modern Women Playwrights in Finland." *World Literature Today* 54 (1980): 54–58.

Niemi analyzes the subject matter, form, and structure in four works centering on women: Maaria Koskiluoma's realistic, biographical play, *The Life of Fredrika Runeberg;* Kerttu-Kaarina Suosalmi's *Vanha morsian (The Old Bride),* which centers around family issues; Eeva-Liisa Manner's *Poltettu oranssi (Burnt Orange),* a poem for the stage; and Pirkko Jaakola's radio play, *Kehtolauluja au-lapselle (Lullabyes [sic] for Illegitimate Children).*

D151

Novak, Sigrid Scholtz. "The Invisible Woman: The Case of the Female Playwright in German Literature." *Journal of Social Issues* 28.2 (1972): 47–57.

Novak discerns two major causes for the lack of historical recognition of German women playwrights, despite their impressive numbers and the quality of their work: the prejudice that women are incapable of crafting good plays and the underrating of their work because critics use male psychology for judging female characters. Drawing illustrations from Elsa Bernstein-Rosmer's *Achill* and *Nausikaa,* she discusses critics' resentment against female playwrights' reinterpretations of legends or folklore.

D152

O'Connor, Patricia W. "Mercedes Ballesteros' Unsung Poetic Comedy: *Las mariposas cantan.*" *Crítica Hispánica* 7.1 (1985): 57–63.

The author places Ballesteros' play within the *teatro de la felicidad* (or *teatro de evasión*) tradition and investigates reasons for critical neglect of the playwright.

D153

O'Connor, Patricia W. "Six *Dramaturgas* in Search of a Stage." *Gestos: Teoria y practica del Teatro Hispanico* 3.5 (1988): 116–20.

This study compares six promising women playwrights of the 1980s with commercially produced *dramaturgas* of the Franco years. O'Connor observes that the earlier playwrights, typically writing in melodramatic, sentimental modes, were more ideologically and technically conservative than their male counterparts. She finds that while the newer playwrights do not avoid strong subjects or idealize the family, they tend to utilize male protagonists and masculine discourse. She concludes that "in different ways and for different reasons, these young women, like their predecessors, are failing to speak with their own voices."

D154

O'Connor, Patricia W. "Spain's 'Other' Post-War Dramatists: The Women." *Letras Peninsulares* 1.1 (1988): 97–107.

O'Connor briefly chronicles the careers of seven successful *dramaturgas*—Dora Sedano, Julia Maura, Ana Diosdado, Mercedes Ballesteros, Maria Isabel Suárez de Deza, Carmen Troitiño, and Luisa-Maria Linares—and notes their virtual exclusion from the canon. Contrasting them with men playwrights, she describes these women as "more conservative ideologically, more puritanical linguistically, and less innovative technically." In addition, she acknowledges several women on the fringes of theatre.

D155
Page, Malcolm. "Sharon Pollock: Committed Playwright." *Women in Canadian Drama.* Spec. issue of *Canadian Drama* 5 (1979): 104–11.

Tracing the development of Pollock's art and political consciousness, Page concludes with a critique of *My Name Is Lisbeth,* an early version of Pollock's *Blood Relations.* He expresses disappointment that "the oppression of women in Victorian society, with a moral for the present," is not emphasized.

D156
Patraka, Vivian M. "Foodtalk in the Plays of Caryl Churchill and Joan Schenkar." *Women in Theatre.* Spec. issue of *Theatre Annual* 40 (1985): 137–57.

Patraka delineates the ways in which food and its related processes are used by Churchill *(Top Girls* and *Fen)* and Schenkar *(Cabin Fever* and *The Last of Hitler).* Demonstrating how "foodtalk" serves to collapse the division between what is inside and what is outside an individual, Patraka concludes that it can "encompass simultaneously culture and biological necessity, private and public labor, exploitation and personal desire, and psychic and economic reality."

D157
Patraka, Vivian M. "Notes on Technique in Feminist Drama: *Apple Pie* and *Signs of Life.*" *Women & Performance: A Journal of Feminist Theory* 1.2 (1984): 58–72.

After remarking on the exclusion from the contemporary canon of women playwrights who produce experimental or strongly feminist works, Patraka examines the parallels between *Apple Pie* and *Signs of Life* in terms of theme, form, and sensibility. She contrasts Lamb's "hot" (confrontational and explosive) and Schenkar's "cool" (analytical yet disturbing) techniques.

D158
Pevitts, Beverley Byers. "Autonomous Female Characters in Plays by Contemporary Women Playwrights." *Southern Theatre* 24.3 (1981): 12–16.

The author focuses on five plays that explore women's journey toward self-actualization: *Bits and Pieces* by Corinne Jacker, *I'm Getting My Act Together and Taking It on the Road* by Gretchen Cryer and Nancy Ford, *for colored girls who have considered suicide/when the rainbow is enuf* by Ntozake Shange, *Voices* by Susan Griffin, and *Getting Out* by Marsha Norman.

D159
Poteet, Susan H. "An Interview with Denise Boucher." *Fireweed* 5–6 (1979-80): 71–74.

Reviewing the furor caused by Boucher's *Les Fées ont soif,* Poteet assesses the play as an attack on male-created religions that oppress women. Boucher's interwoven comments and Poteet's paraphrases help clarify the playwright's positions regarding feminism and the challenging of authority. An excerpt from the play follows the article.

D160
Ravel, Aviva. Interview. "Talking with Aviva Ravel, on Priorities, Fairness, and Being Human." With Patricia Morley. *Women in Canadian Drama.* Spec. issue of *Canadian Drama* 5 (1979): 179–88.

In response to Morley's pointing out Ravel's focus on women's roles and choices in her plays and stories, Ravel comments that she never thinks of herself as a feminist (although she does identify with the movement). Ravel's use of humor, possessiveness about Montreal, and Jewish heritage are also discussed. A bibliography of her plays is included.

D161
Reinelt, Janelle. "Beyond Brecht: Britain's New Feminist Drama." *Theatre Journal* 38 (1986): 154–63.

Reinelt underscores the usefulness of Brechtian techniques for the feminist examination of material conditions of gender behavior and their interaction with other sociopolitical factors. Offering a short overview of socialist-feminist theatre in England, she distinguishes the ways in which two central issues—"the relationship of class oppression to sexual repression; and the ideological interpretation of production, reproduction, and procreation"—are dramatized through such Brechtian techniques as the "gest," historicization, and episodic structure. Three plays provide examples: Red Ladder Theatre's *Strike While the Iron Is Hot,* Claire Luckham's *Trafford Tanzi,* and Caryl Churchill's *Vinegar Tom.*

D162

Relke, Diana M. A. "Killed into Art: Marjorie Pickthall and *The Wood Carver's Wife." Canadian Drama* 13 (1987): 187–200.

Declaring the cultivation of femininity to be a suicidal act—a surrender of the self—Relke explores the cultural phenomena that shaped Pickthall's life and career. She argues that the subtext of *The Wood Carver's Wife,* wherein a sadistic husband turns his wife into an art object and religious icon, encodes "her sense of herself as a woman trapped in the gender conventions of her day and as a poet martyred to the artistic conventions and expectations which had alienated her from her own experience and pointlessly consumed her creative energies."

D163

Renée. Interview. "Feminist Writer Renee: All Plays Are Political." With Claire-Louise McCurdy. *Women's Studies Journal* [Women's Studies Association, New Zealand] 1.2 (1985): 61–72.

Discussing her determination to put women on stage, Renée describes *Wednesday to Come* and other plays. She also talks about her relationship with New Zealand's professional theatre and the new work of other women playwrights.

D164

Richards, Sandra L. "Conflicting Images in the Plays of Ntozake Shange." *Black American Literature Forum* 17 (1983): 73–78.

Richards examines the dialectic between "combat breath" (awareness of social determinants and commitment to change) and the will to divinity (transcendence of corporal existence to merge with cosmic forces), and the resultant roller coaster effect on the audience, in *spell #7* and *for colored girls who have considered suicide/when the rainbow is enuf.*

D165

Richards, Sandra L. "Nigerian Independence Onstage: Responses from 'Second Generation' Playwrights." *Theatre Journal* 39 (1987): 215–27.

In a study of playwrights' responses to challenges facing postindependence Nigeria, Richards' section on Zulu Sofola constitutes a feminist critique of her depiction of women's roles in precolonial Nigerian societies and the cultural confusion ensuing from the adoption of Western perspectives. Richards finds that although Sofola advocates adherence to a traditional African cosmology entailing an equilibrium among competing forces, she does not apply this cosmology to gender roles. Other sections concentrate on two less conservative men playwrights, Bode Sowande and Femi Osofisan.

D166

Ringwood, Gwen Pharis. "Women and the Theatrical Tradition." *Atlantis* 4.1 (1978): 154–58.

Ringwood reviews the scarcity of women playwrights in the past as well as their increased numbers in recent years. She reveals problems of self-censorship she has faced as a playwright; addresses the difficulties that women, torn between family duties and creativity, must overcome to write; and expresses her fascination with the communal aspects of theatre.

D167

"*The Rise of the Fates:* A Preview of New Production." *Sister* Oct.–Nov. 1977: 12.

This article briefly describes a new tradition in the L.A. wimmin's community: a performance of the religious comedy by Zsuzsanna E. Budapest at the annual Hallowmas festival.

D168

Ritter, Erika. Interview. "Erika Ritter: 'The Very Fact That I Survive Is Encouraging.'" With Constance Brissenden. *Women and Performance.* Spec. issue of *Fireweed* 7 (Summer 1980): 68–70.

As Ritter considers Charlie's options as a woman and artist in *Automatic Pilot,* she particularly notes the character's resistance to being viewed in terms of her work.

D169

Roll-Hansen, Diderik. "Dramatic Strategy in Christina Reid's *Tea in a China Cup.*" *Modern Drama* 30 (1987): 389–95.

Analyzing the techniques used in the Irish playwright's semi-autobiographical play, which portrays the uneasy relationship between Protestants and Catholics in Belfast, Roll-Hansen also comments on the theme of self-realization.

D170

Rubess, Baṇuta. "Aspazija: The Spiteful Poppy and Her Silver Veil." *Fireweed* 17 (1983): 67–79.

Rubess emphasizes the historical and artistic significance of this rediscovered Latvian playwright. Focusing on the legendary impact of *The*

Silver Veil during the 1905 revolution in the Russian Empire, Rubess distinguishes two political themes—"an encouragement of revolution and a radical investigation of female sexuality"—and explores the nature of women's power in the play. She also describes the 1982 Theatre Company's collaborative adaptation of Aspazija's work.

D171
Rushing, Andrea Benton. *"For Colored Girls,* Suicide or Struggle." *Massachusetts Review* 22 (1981): 539–50.

Rushing examines the play's ability to galvanize both black and white audiences and the extent to which it reflects black women's thinking and feeling. She underscores the autobiographical nature of the piece, manifested in the kinds of women depicted (single, alienated) and the isolation from black culture (extended family, church, literary and political history). Rushing contends that despite its artistic merits and affirmative ending, the play's meager African-American critical analysis remains disturbing; in fastening on men as the roots of black women's pain, Shange ignores other significant causes, including racism.

D172
Russell, Elizabeth. "Caryl Churchill: Sexual Politics and *Cloud Nine.*" *Revista Canaria de Estudios Ingleses* 12 (1986): 153–60.

Russell's study centers on the effects of character doubling and men in women's roles. She argues that while the effects may be funny in Act I (set in the nineteenth century), it is hard to laugh at Act II (set in the present) when one realizes that the Victorian values still linger. Russell maintains that although sexual liberation characterizes Act II's new morality, the presence of Victorian colonialism remains unchanged.

D173
Saddlemeyer, Ann. "Circus Feminus: 100 Plays by English-Canadian Women." *Women in Theatre.* Spec. issue of *A Room of One's Own* 8.2 (1983): 78–91.

This survey details the multitude of themes and forms employed by Canadian women playwrights. While most plays are mentioned only briefly, Sharon Pollock's *Blood Relations,* epitomizing "the strengths and originality of many of these plays about women imprisoned in a man-ordered universe," is analyzed more fully.

D174
Scott, Milcha, and Jeremy Blahnik. "An Excerpt from *Latina.*" *Frontiers* 5.2 (1980): 25–30.

A short introduction to the excerpt describes the work's genesis and includes a synopsis.

D175
Shafer, Yvonne. "The Liberated Woman in American Plays of the Past." *Players: The Magazine of American Theatre* 49 (1974): 95–100.

Surveying the various ways in which American plays of the first half of this century treated the theme of female independence, Shafer examines four works by Rachel Crothers, Sophie Treadwell's *Machinal,* S. N. Behrman's *Biography,* Guy Bolton's *Chicken Feed,* and Jesse Lynch Williams's *Why Marry?* Several "forgotten" plays are also briefly discussed for their treatment of women's difficulties in terms of economics, sex, careers, and marriage.

D176
Shange, Ntozake. "Genesis of a Choreopoem." Presented by Jeffrey Eliot. *Negro History Bulletin* Jan.–Feb. 1978: 797–800.

Shange recounts the creation of *for colored girls who have considered suicide/when the rainbow is enuf.*

D177
Shange, Ntozake. "An Interview with Ntozake Shange." With Henry Blackwell. *Black American Literature Forum* 13 (1979): 134–38.

Shange reflects on her writing, the need to establish a women's aesthetic, and related topics.

D178
Shange, Ntozake. "Ntozake Shange Interviews Herself." *Ms.* Dec. 1977: 35 + .

Shange talks about her current work and influences on her writing.

D179
Shewey, Don. "Gay Theatre Grows Up." *American Theatre* May 1988: 10 + .

This is an adaptation of the introduction to Shewey's book, *Out Front: Contemporary Gay and Lesbian Plays.* See G35. *Terms:* gay drama/theatre; lesbian drama/theatre.

D180
Skurnik, Jennifer A. "At Last, Lesbian Characters for the Stage." *Off Our Backs* Apr. 1983: 13 + .

The author discusses Jane Chambers' creation of lesbian roles in *A Late Snow, My Blue Heaven,* and *Last Summer at Bluefish Cove.* The article is preceded by Chambers' obituary.

D181
Skurnik, Jennifer. "San Francisco Mime Troupe Criticized." *Off Our Backs* Jan. 1983: 14.

Skurnik describes the controversy surrounding *Americans; or Last Tango in Huahuatenango,* including accusations of anti-Semitism and Jewish American Princess stereotyping, and the response by playwright Joan Holden.

D182
Smith, Beverly A. "Women's Work—*Trifles?* The Skill and Insights of Playwright Susan Glaspell." *International Journal of Women's Studies* 5 (Mar.–Apr. 1982): 172–84.

Smith explores the play's structure and symbolism, as well as its social insights, particularly the depiction of female bonding. She also looks at *Trifles* in relation to recent studies on wife battering and the trials of wives who strike back.

D183
Solomon, Alisa. "Witches, Ranters and the Middle Class: The Plays of Caryl Churchill." *Theater* 12.2 (1981): 49–55.

Solomon investigates socialist and feminist concerns in four plays by Churchill: *Owners, Vinegar Tom, Light Shining in Buckinghamshire,* and *Traps.*

D184
Spencer, Jenny S. "Norman's *'night, Mother:* Psycho-Drama of Female Identity." *Modern Drama* 30 (1987): 364–75.

In her psychoanalytical study of Norman's play, Spencer contends that the text produces for female audience members an experience similar to cathartic psychodrama (while leaving men relatively unmoved) because of the ways in which it highlights issues of female identity and autonomy, focuses on the mother-daughter relationship (demanding that female viewers identify with both characters simultaneously in a gender-specific manner), and controls the narrative movement. Spencer also explores the question of whether *'night, Mother* is a feminist play.

D185

Splater-Roth, Bobbie, and Fran Moira. "WAFT Comes Out: *The Franny Chicago Play.*" *Off Our Backs* Oct. 1974: 22–23.

The "Backstage" section of the article, written by Splater-Roth, describes her experience at a dress rehearsal for Judith Katz's play. She reports Katz as "explaining that she doesn't feel that the play turns on the fact that its characters are lesbians" and as emphasizing the importance of women seeing themselves on stage. In the "Upfront" section, Moira outlines the play's content and production. Moira concludes that the work reaffirms "our struggles for self-identity, our failures and our promise."

D186

Steadman, Susan M. "Comedy, Culture, Communion and Canvas: Breaking the Silence about Women Artists in Three Plays by Tina Howe." *Theatre Southwest* 14.3 (1987): 12–18.

Noting that until recently there have been few dramatic treatments of the process of female artistic creation and the effect of the resultant product on others, the author focuses on Howe's celebration of women artists in *Museum, The Art of Dining,* and *Painting Churches.*

D187

Stephens, Judith L. "The Compatibility of Traditional Dramatic Forms and Feminist Expressions." *Women in Theatre.* Spec. issue of *Theatre Annual* 40 (1985): 7–23.

Stephens acknowledges feminists' rejection of realistic, linear play structures and traditional dramatic protagonists, but urges consideration of "the usefulness of established forms before rejecting them as specifically male constructs, suited only to a patriarchal view of experience." Emphasizing the factors of conscious choice, decisive action, and change, she illustrates the possibilities for feminist expression in realism by analyzing Zona Gale's *Miss Lulu Bett* and Elmer Rice's *Street Scene.*

D188

Stone, Elizabeth. "Playwright Marsha Norman: An Optimist Writes about Suicide, Confinement and Despair." *Ms.* July 1983: 56–59.

This examination of Norman's career includes comments from the playwright. Topics range from giving voice to those usually unheard to issues of hope and control in the plays and the depiction of mother-daughter relationships.

D189

Sutherland, Cynthia. "American Women Playwrights as Mediators of the 'Woman Problem.'" *Modern Drama* 21 (1978): 319–36.

The author studies the work of several women playwrights who "chronicled the increasingly noticeable effects of free love, trial marriage, the 'double standard,' career, divorce, and war on women's lives" in the first third of this century. Among the plays discussed are Rachel Crothers's *A Man's World, He and She, Mary the Third,* and *When Ladies Meet;* Susan Glaspell's *Trifles* and *The Verge;* and Zona Gale's *Miss Lulu Bett.*

D190

Swanson, Michael. "Mother/Daughter Relationships in Three Plays by Caryl Churchill." *Theatre Studies* 31–32 (1984–85/1985–86): 49–66.

Swanson explicates Churchill's use of mother-daughter relationships and epic techniques to explore the evolution of women's role in society and the possibilities for change. The plays examined are *Cloud 9, Top Girls,* and *Fen.*

D191

Sykes, Alrene. "Dorothy Hewett: Playwright of Splendid Moments." *Women Writers of the Commonwealth.* Spec. issue of *World Literature Written in English* 17 (1978): 106–13.

Citing Hewett's contribution of some of the best acting roles for women in Australian drama, the author assesses the playwright's strengths and weaknesses. *The Chapel Perilous,* centering on the life of a rebellious woman, is analyzed, while other works are briefly discussed.

D192

Tener, Robert L. "Theatre of Identity: Adrienne Kennedy's Portrait of the Black Woman." *Studies in Black Literature* 6.2 (1975): 1-5.

Concentrating on *The Owl Answers,* Tener discusses the relationship of She's fragmented identities to her quest for a stable and unified self-image and the way Kennedy externalizes She's problem through the symbolism of the owl and the fig tree.

D193

Terry, Megan. "Interview: Megan Terry." With Jo Hynes. *Christopher Street* June 1978: 33–35.

The playwright talks about feminism in the theatre as well as her personal and professional history.

D194

Terry, Megan. "Two Pages a Day." *Playwrights and Playwriting*. Spec. issue of *The Drama Review* 21.4 (1977): 59–64.

Terry reflects on the act of writing.

D195

Thomas, Veona. "Negro Ensemble Company: Women Come Center Stage." *New Directions for Women* Mar.–Apr. 1984: 11.

This article concerns the company's devotion of a season to plays by women and the gender bias manifested in the New York critics' scathing reviews, particularly their response to Velina Houston's *American Dreams*.

D196

Wachtel, Eleanor. "Two Steps Backward from the One Step Forward." *Feminism and Canadian Theatre*. Spec. issue of *Canadian Theatre Review* 43 (1985): 12–20.

Wachtel comments on the lack of feminist theatre per se and the marginalization of women in Vancouver theatre despite their prominent role in its development. She finds especially depressing the lack of women playwrights living there and the scarcity of women's plays produced, except by the New Play Centre's workshops, festivals, and "Short Takes for Women" competition. With references to several notable women playwrights, she considers what a feminist theatre might mean.

D197

Wandor, Michelene. "The Fifth Column: Feminism and Theatre." *Women in Theatre*. Spec. issue of *Drama* 152 (1984): 5–9.

Wandor outlines the effect of the women's movement on British theatre. Differentiating among radical, bourgeois, and socialist feminisms, she analyzes the feminist dynamic in Nell Dunn's *Steaming*, Caryl Churchill's *Cloud Nine*, Claire Luckham's *Trafford Tanzi*, and Sarah Daniels' *Masterpieces*.

D198

Wasserstein, Wendy. "Uncommon Woman: An Interview with Wendy Wasserstein." With Esther Cohen. *Last Laughs: Perspectives on*

Women and Comedy. Ed. Regina Barreca. Spec. issue of *Women's Studies* 15 (1988): 257–70.

Wasserstein covers such subjects as theatrical comedy, women characters, and other female playwrights.

D199

Waterman, Arthur. "Susan Glaspell's *The Verge:* An Experiment in Feminism." *Great Lakes Review* 6.1 (1979): 17–23.

Examining the combined influence of Glaspell's traditional midwestern background and avant-garde milieu in *The Verge*, Waterman suggests that Glaspell's depiction of the obsessed heroine, who seeks to become a Nietzschean woman-artist, reaches beyond the feminist emphasis to questions of society's relationship with gifted eccentrics.

D200

White, Helen C. "Women in the Theatre in Aotearoa." *Hecate* 12.1–2 (1986): 158–65.

White describes the revolution in New Zealand theatre stemming from the impact of women's liberation, which, paralleling the Maori renaissance, has exploded "in a flowering of creativity that expresses both new freedom and old bitterness, celebration and frustration, popular energy and personal pain." Remarking that the "real woman" has been absent from patriarchal theatre, she cites the rise of the female playwright as the most significant development.

D201

Wilkerson, Margaret. "Diverse Angles of Vision: Two Black Women Playwrights." *Women in Theatre.* Spec. issue of *Theatre Annual* 40 (1985): 91–116.

Wilkerson explores the contrasting sensibilities and playwriting strategies of Lorraine Hansberry and Adrienne Kennedy. She examines Hansberry's criticism of American materialistic values in *A Raisin in the Sun* and her presentation of victimized women who educate the protagonist to his chauvinism and intolerance in *The Sign in Sidney Brustein's Window.* Wilkerson's analysis of Kennedy focuses on her imagistic, surrealistic approach and suggestion of the "terrifying relationship between private self and public history" in *Funnyhouse of a Negro* and *The Owl Answers.*

D202

Wilkerson, Margaret. "*A Raisin in the Sun:* Anniversary of an American Classic." *Theatre Journal* 38 (1986): 441–52.

The author looks at the social, historical, and artistic factors responsible for the continued relevance and popularity of Hansberry's work. Wilkerson comments on the playwright's prescience regarding both civil and women's rights, discusses the play's repudiation of materialism, and examines the restoration of originally omitted dialogue that illuminates the protagonists and strengthens the articulation of the basic theme.

D203
Willis, Sharon. "Hélène Cixous's *Portrait de Dora:* The Unseen and the Un-scene." *Staging Gender.* Spec. issue of *Theatre Journal* 37 (1985): 287–301.

Willis demonstrates how Hélène Cixous's play, which is among contemporary feminist rereadings of Freud's analysis of a case of hysteria, calls up for examination the theatrical frame and the staged body. She suggests that Cixous's splintering of Freud's narrative through fragmentation, juxtaposition, and interruption undermines the authority of the central voice and disrupts the spectator's usual position as subject outside the frame.

D204
Winston, Elizabeth. "Making History in *The Mother of Us All.*" *Mosaic* 20.4 (1987): 117–29.

Winston characterizes Stein's opera about Susan B. Anthony as a "disguised autobiography," in which Stein uses a code of names, literary allusions, and quotations to explore her personal and artistic development as well as the theme of women's relation to patriarchal tradition.

D205
Woddis, Carole. "Twenty Writers: Ten Women." *Plays and Players* May 1984: 14–17.

Woddis notes the difficulty women playwrights experience in gaining recognition and productions. Ten playwrights are profiled: Andrea Dunbar, Sarah Daniels, Marcella Evaristi, Berta Freistadt, Lenka Janiurek, Ayshe Raif, Sue Townsend, Jacqui Shapiro, Timberlake Wertenbaker, and Paulette Randall.

D206
Wolverton, Terry. "An Oral Herstory of Lesbianism." *Frontiers* 4.3 (1979): 52–53.

Wolverton, who conceived the collaborative piece that tells thirteen women's stories based on true experiences, briefly describes its creation. "Yellow Queen," an excerpt written and performed by Christine Wong, follows.

D207

Wolverton, Terry. "Theater as Community Ritual: An Interview with Terry Wolverton." With Bia Lowe. *Acting Up!* Spec. issue of *Heresies* 5.1 (1984): 48–49.

Wolverton discusses the collaborative process resulting in *An Oral Herstory of Lesbianism,* her solo work in *In Silence Secrets Turn to Lies/ Secrets Shared Become Sacred Truth,* and the ways in which she invites audience participation.

D208

Yarbro-Bejarano, Yvonne. "Cherríe Moraga's *Giving Up the Ghost:* The Representation of Female Desire." *Third Woman* 3.1–2 (1986): 113–20.

Explicating Moraga's exploration of the relationship between female sexuality—both lesbian and heterosexual—and the Chicano culture, Yarbro-Bejarano also articulates Moraga's vision of salvation through women's love for each other.

D209

Yarbro-Bejarano, Yvonne. "*Teatropoesía* by Chicanas in the Bay Area: *Tongues of Fire.*" *Revista Chicano-Riquena* 11.1 (1983): 78–94.

Drawing attention to the vitality of Chicanas in theatre despite the shrinking number of Chicano *teatros,* Yarbro-Bejarano concentrates on the *teatropoesía*'s fusion of poetry and theatre. After discussing the form's history, its present resurgence, and forthcoming projects, she focuses on *Tongues of Fire* (structured by Barbara Brinson-Pineda), a piece unified by the idea of the Chicana writer. She delineates themes that include the importance of history for the contemporary Chicana, the Chicana's changing self-image, and the cultivation of an authentic voice. Yarbro-Bejarano suggests that the organization of this project, involving a temporary banding and disbanding of participants, offers an alternative to permanent collectives.

D210

Zatlin, Phyllis. "Ana Diosdado and the Contemporary Spanish Theater." *Estreno: Cuadernos del Teatro Espanol Contemporaneo* 10.2 (1984): 37–40.

Citing Diosdado as the sole successful Spanish woman playwright, Zatlin examines several of her plays dealing with social problems. She proposes that two of her less successful works may have had their essence obscured through realistic staging. Writing about Diosdado's relationship to feminism, Zatlin argues that although her plays do not revolve around women's issues per se, they always include strong female characters.

Feminist Reassessment of Men's Playwriting

❖
❖

Books and Monographs

E1

Adelman, Janet. " 'Anger's My Meat': Feeding, Dependency, and Aggression in *Coriolanus.*" *Shakespeare, Pattern of Excelling Nature.* Ed. David Bevington and Jay L. Halio. Newark: University of Delaware Press, 1978. 108–24. (Rpt. in *Representing Shakespeare: New Psychoanalytic Essays.* Ed. Murray M. Schwartz and Coppélia Kahn. Baltimore, Md.: Johns Hopkins University Press, 1980. 129–49.)

Adelman argues that Coriolanus's establishment of a masculine identity is based on transforming his vulnerability, a condition inherent in feeding and associated with femininity, into phallic aggression and a sense of self-sufficiency. She investigates his failure to separate from his mother and sustain "his fantasy of self-authorship."

E2

Adelman, Janet. " 'Born of Woman': Fantasies of Maternal Power in *Macbeth.*" *Cannibals, Witches, and Divorce: Estranging the Renaissance.* Ed. Marjorie Garber. Selected Papers from the English Institute, 1985, ns 11. Baltimore, Md.: Johns Hopkins University Press, 1987.

Reading *Macbeth* as representing simultaneously the fantasy of an absolute, destructive maternal power and the fantasy of escape from it, Adelman contends that the reconstitution of autonomous manhood is achieved in the play's ending only by eliminating all female presence.

E3

Adelman, Janet. "Male Bonding in Shakespeare's Comedies." *Shakespeare's "Rough Magic": Renaissance Essays in Honor of C. L. Barber.* Ed. Peter Erickson and Coppélia Kahn. Newark: University of Delaware Press, 1985. 73–103.

Adelman focuses on Shakespeare's concern with "a male identity that locates itself via bonding with another man and recognizes in women a disturbance to the bond and to the identity so constituted." She demonstrates that even the middle comedies overtly concerned with heterosexual union and female friendship are shaped by the fantasies of male bonding. Among the works discussed are *The Comedy of Errors, Two Gentlemen of Verona, A Midsummer Night's Dream, As You Like It, Twelfth Night,* and *The Winter's Tale.*

E4

Baker, Susan Read. "Sentimental Feminism in Marivaux's *La Colonie.*" *To Hold a Mirror to Nature: Dramatic Images and Reflections.* Ed. Karelisa V. Hartigan. The University of Florida Department of Classics Comparative Drama Conference Papers 1. Washington, D.C.: University Press of America, 1982. 1–10.

Baker analyzes the structure and language of Marivaux's comedy to determine the nature and limits of his feminism.

E5

Bamber, Linda. *Comic Women, Tragic Men: A Study of Gender and Genre in Shakespeare.* Stanford, Calif.: Stanford University Press, 1982.

Taking issue with feminist critics who contend that Shakespeare's plays directly support feminist ideas, Bamber argues that the feminine in his plays is indeed Other, different from genre to genre but always external to the male Self, and for the most part, an embodiment of the world and not a projection of what has been repudiated by the Self. She contends that while Shakespeare's perspective is masculinist, it is not necessarily chauvinistic; he privileges the Self in tragedy and the Other in comedy, associating the feminine with what is most serious to or most challenges the Self. Bamber's comprehensive initial chapter outlines her thesis, while the following chapters center on *Antony and Cleopatra, Hamlet, Macbeth* and *Coriolanus,* comic heroines, and several of the history plays. A final chapter centers on the motif of the Return of the Feminine that is found in the romances (notably *The Winter's Tale*), with the significant exception of *The Tempest.*

E6

Barlow, Judith E. "O'Neill's Many Mothers: Mary Tyrone, Josie Hogan, and Their Antecedents." *Perspectives on O'Neill: New Essays.* Ed. Shyamal Bagchee. English Literary Studies Monograph Series 43. Victoria, B.C., Canada: University of Victoria, 1988. 7–16.

Barlow maintains that O'Neill's attitudes and those of his male characters toward female characters are determined by the extent to which the women fulfill the maternal function: nurturing others, subordinating their own dreams, and forgiving transgressions. She contrasts "failed" mothers (epitomized by Mary in *Long Day's Journey into Night*) with "good" mothers, noting that for O'Neill the ideal woman is a motherly virgin (Josie in *A Moon for the Misbegotten*).

E7

Belsey, Catherine. "Disrupting Sexual Difference: Meaning and Gender in the Comedies." *Alternative Shakespeares.* Ed. John Drakakis. London: Methuen, 1985. 166–90.

Belsey suggests that Shakespearean comedy calls into question "that set of relations between terms which proposes as inevitable an antithesis between masculine and feminine." She cites as the context for this disruption of sexual difference the sixteenth- and seventeenth-century contest between two meanings of family (as dynasty and as private, affective realm), which produced a "gap" in which emerged glimpses of alternative modes of being for women. In her subsequent examination of female transvestism in *Twelfth Night, As You Like It,* and *Two Gentlemen of Verona,* Belsey reads the plays as showing the possibility of speaking "from a position which is not that of a full, unified, gendered subject."

E8

Belsey, Catherine. *The Subject of Tragedy: Identity and Difference in Renaissance Drama.* London: Methuen, 1985.

Belsey specifies her three aims as (1) "to contribute to the construction of a history of the subject in the sixteenth and seventeenth centuries"; (2) to demonstrate the exclusion of women from the definition of the subject of liberal humanism; and (3) to bring together history and literature "to construct a history of the meanings which delimit at a specific moment what it is possible to say, to understand, and consequently to be." The book is divided into two parts, "Man" and "Woman." Tracing changes in the concept of subjectivity from medieval morality plays through the Renaissance, Part I offers chapters labeled "Unity," "Knowledge," and "Autonomy." Part II includes a chapter on "Alice Arden's

Crime" (and the play *Arden of Faversham*), with Belsey arguing that the real scandal lies not in Alice's procuring of her husband's murder but her "challenge to the institution of marriage." "Silence and Speech," dealing largely with domestic power and its relationship to women's right to speak ("for women to speak is to threaten the system of differences which gives meaning to patriarchy," notes Belsey), explores such works as *The White Devil, The Play of Patient Grissell,* and *The Tragedy of Mariam.* Investigating shifting views of love and marriage in "Finding a Place," Belsey cautions that "the installation of women as subjects through the redefinition of the family" does not guarantee equality.

E9

Berek, Peter. "Text, Gender, and Genre in *The Taming of the Shrew.*" *"Bad" Shakespeare: Revaluations of the Shakespeare Canon.* Ed. Maurice Charney. Rutherford N.J.: Fairleigh Dickinson University Press; London: Associated University Presses, 1988. 91–104.

Claiming that *The Taming of the Shrew* "leads the canon in bad qualities," Berek remarks on critical interpretations that attempt to exonerate Shakespeare or his characters from the worst antifeminism. He details the differences between the play and its bad quarto, *The Taming of a Shrew,* an even more sexist work, and speculates that *A Shrew* was not an earlier but a pirated version, reflecting Elizabethan audiences' attitudes toward gender. He also discusses the "bad genre" of farce and its relationship to patriarchal orthodoxy in *The Shrew.*

E10

Boa, Elizabeth. *The Sexual Circus: Wedekind's Theatre of Subversion.* Oxford, England: Basil Blackwell, 1987.

Boa contends that despite Wedekind's entrapment in the sexist ideas of his time, "the theatrical effect of the major plays, depending on production, undermines that very ideology." This in-depth study of sexual and generational relationships in four plays—*Spring Awakening, Earth Spirit, Pandora's Box,* and *The Marquis of Keith*—also focuses on Wedekind's attack on authoritarianism and conservative morality, themes of social mobility and individual freedom, and response to the impact of the market on the arts. In a separate chapter on the "woman question," Boa places the playwright within the context of German thought on family roles and sexuality. Other chapters deal with Berg's opera *Lulu,* critical readings of Wedekind, and Wedekind's relationship to the modern theatre.

E11

Bono, Barbara J. "Mixed Gender, Mixed Genre in Shakespeare's *As You Like It." Renaissance Genres.* Ed. Barbara Kiefer Lewalski. Harvard English Studies 14. Cambridge, Mass.: Harvard University Press, 1986. 189–212.

Bono constructs "a framework of contemporary feminist theory around a traditional genre-based analysis" of the play to respond to the debate over whether Shakespeare's preoccupation with strong female characters and feminine concerns evidences his period's feminism or provides "male projections of what women must be," ultimately supporting the structure of male dominance. Applying Chodorow's model for the formation of gender identity to Orlando's and Rosalind's roles in pastoral Arden, Bono explores the interaction between Orlando's masculine heroic discourse and Rosalind's feminine romantic "double-voiced" discourse, with which she criticizes and challenges the patriarchy even while she accommodates herself to it.

E12

Carlson, Susan. *Women of Grace: James's Plays and the Comedy of Manners.* Studies in Modern Literature 48. Ann Arbor, Mich.: UMI Research, 1985.

In her reevaluation of Henry James's dramatic achievement, Carlson calls for an understanding of the comedy of manners wherein manners *are* morals and women's superior social understanding arises from their compromised positions stemming from the sexual double standard. Her chapter on the manners tradition since the Restoration includes a discussion of gender-genre issues and conflicting critical views toward sexual equality in the comedies. After analyzing the role of women in selected plays from 1890 to 1915, she turns to James's consideration of the women-manners-morals relationship in such works as *The Americans, Tenants, Disengaged, The Album, The Reprobate, Guy Domville, The High Bid,* and *The Outcry,* citing as his major embellishment on the form the depiction of female generation-spanning friendships. Carlson also outlines post-1910 comedy's portrayal of the cultural breakdowns James had labored to forestall. Other playwrights examined include Congreve, Sheridan, Henry Arthur Jones, Maugham, Pinero, Wilde, Shaw, Granville-Barker, D. H. Lawrence, and Coward.

E13

Cherry, Caroline Lockett. *The Most Unvaluedst Purchase: Women in the Plays of Thomas Middleton.* Salzburg Studies in English Literature; Jacobean Drama Studies 34. Salzburg, Austria: Institut für Englische Sprache und Literatur, Universität Salzburg, 1973.

Contending that Middleton has been mistakenly labeled a misogynist, Cherry proposes that his realistic, sympathetic view of women makes his work useful in studying the theory and status of women in the Jacobean era. Cherry demonstrates how women, both dramatic subjects and vehicles for Middleton's moral vision, are treated differently from genre to genre. In illustrating the comedies' presentation of problems of women's action in a masculine, commercial, dehumanizing society, Cherry focuses on the oppression of women, antifeminist commonplaces (women as lustful, greedy, fickle, etc.), use of contrast, and dramatic types. Her analysis of the tragicomedies shows Middleton's treatment of women becoming less sociological and more psychological, with the characters facing situations involving difficult choices or strong shocks. Discussing the tragedies, wherein women's restricted position provides an opening for evil and destruction, she examines the centrality of women in *The Changeling* and *Women Beware Women.*

E14

Cunningham, Dolora. "Conflicting Images of the Comic Heroine." *"Bad" Shakespeare: Revaluations of the Shakespeare Canon.* Ed. Maurice Charney. Rutherford, N.J.: Fairleigh Dickinson University Press; London: Associated University Presses, 1988. 91–104.

Stating that Shakespeare departs radically from his handling of the comic heroine in *All's Well That Ends Well,* Cunningham investigates Helena's engineering of the love plot and challenging of dramatic and social conventions. She further explicates the demands made on the audience in accepting "the coexistence of puzzling contradictions between codes of behavior and attitudes toward human relations," and the play's lack of aesthetic unity.

E15

Dash, Irene G. *Wooing, Wedding, and Power: Women in Shakespeare's Plays.* New York: Columbia University Press, 1981.

Dash attacks biased criticism of Shakespeare's women which has resulted in simplified, stereotyped, or evasive interpretations. Underscoring their enormous variety (which has been submerged by critical concentration on male characters), she argues that the female characters' actions, for the most part, "spring from a realistic confrontation with life as they learn the meaning of self-sovereignty for a woman in a patriarchal society." In demonstrating how alterations to Shakespeare's writing by actor-managers and directors have corrupted the portrayal of women and the meaning of the plays, Dash proposes an "interrelationship between textual excision or emendation and attitudes toward women in the larger society of the time." Individual chapters detail oath-taking in *Love's Labour's Lost,* the challenge of accepted patterns of wooing in *The Taming of the Shrew,* adolescent sexuality in *Romeo and Juliet,* "a woman tamed" in *Othello,* courageous wives in *The Winter's Tale,* the paradox of power in the *Henry VI–Richard III* tetralogy, and the interweaving of a powerful woman's sexual and political roles in *Antony and Cleopatra.*

E16
Dreher, Diane Elizabeth. *Domination and Defiance: Fathers and Daughters in Shakespeare.* Lexington: University Press of Kentucky, 1986.

According to this psychological study of the tension-filled father-daughter relationships in twenty-one Shakespearean plays, each of the pair faces critical adult transitions against a backdrop of societal change. Dreher's historical perspective further clarifies the father-daughter generational struggle as a contrast between two conflicting paradigms, with fathers upholding the traditional concept of hierarchical obedience and daughters striving for the self-determination propounded by the progressive humanists and Puritans who redefined marriage, family, and women's role in society. Underscoring the dangers of sex role polarization, Dreher demonstrates how the outcome of the father-daughter struggle differs according to genre, with the tensions "resolved in comedy, exploded in tragedy, transcended in romance."

E17
Dusinberre, Juliet. *Shakespeare and the Nature of Women.* London: MacMillan; New York: Barnes & Noble, 1975.

Characterizing the drama from 1590–1625 as feminist in sympathy, Dusinberre traces the influence of humanistic ideals about women and Puritan attitudes toward marriage in the work of not only Shakespeare— who viewed in the individual woman or man "an infinite variety of union between opposing impulses"—but also Middleton, Marston, Webster, Heywood, Jonson, and others. In addition to the philosophical, cultural, and political background, she considers theatrical conditions, particularly the use of boy actors, which "spurred dramatists to look beyond the manner of femininity . . . into the real nature of women." There are four separate sections: "The Idea of Chastity" discusses virginity and virtue, the double standard, and art as the enemy of chastity; "The Problem of Equality" addresses women and authority (the chain of Degree, women's freedom of conscience, male authority in marriage) and women as property; "Gods and Devils" examines how both idolatry and satire of women "submerge the individual in the image"; and

"Femininity and Masculinity" explores issues of women's education, disguise, and politics and violence.

E18

Erickson, Peter. "The Order of the Garter, the Cult of Elizabeth, and Class-Gender Tension in *The Merry Wives of Windsor." Shakespeare Reproduced: The Text in History and Ideology*. Ed. Jean E. Howard and Marion F. O'Connor. New York: Methuen: 1987. 116–40.

Erickson observes that class and gender in *The Merry Wives of Windsor* are "strongly marked by a conservative valence" and in conflict with each other. He demonstrates that "the Order of the Garter reinforces class hierarchy, while the cult of Elizabeth, of which the Order is a part, reverses traditional gender hierarchy by affirming female authority." In addition, he illustrates that the play's female-controlled plotting parallels the Queen-dominated court politics, producing "a similar male uneasiness," and analyzes the role of female chastity in the exercise of power.

E19

Erickson, Peter. *Patriarchal Structures in Shakespeare's Drama*. Berkeley: University of California Press, 1985.

Exploring the versions of society emerging in Shakespeare's works, Erickson delineates the various outcomes of Shakespeare's examination of the conflict between male-female and male-male relationships. He analyzes the political and psychological implications of male bonding as the basis for patriarchal power; the interplay of state, family, and sexual politics; and the dichotomization of women as good or bad. Outlining Shakespeare's gradual shift toward the male characters' possible accommodation with women, he distinguishes between ruthless and benevolent patriarchies, cautioning that the latter still preclude fully independent female characters. Individual chapters investigate the coordinated themes of friendship and loving in *As You Like It,* whose promise of marital success contrasts with the renouncing of women in *Love's Labour's Lost;* exclusive male relationships (fathers, sons, brothers) in *Henry V;* maternal images and male ties in *Hamlet, Othello,* and *King Lear;* "heterosexual androgyny" in *Antony and Cleopatra;* and the limitations of reformed masculinity in *The Winter's Tale*.

E20

Ewbank, Inga-Stina. "Shakespeare's Portrayal of Women: A 1970's View." *Shakespeare: Pattern of Excelling Nature*. Ed. David Bevington and Jay L. Halio. Newark: University of Delaware Press, 1978. 222–29.

Ewbank asserts that Shakespeare was neither a feminist nor an anti-feminist, maintaining that his plays offer a nearly infinite variety of insight into the nature of women contained within his depiction of *human* relationships. She concentrates on Ophelia and Desdemona, contending that their submissiveness and apparent inarticulateness are not female stereotypes, but rather part of "Shakespeare's exploration of the relationship between language and tragic experience."

E21

Ferguson, Margaret W., Maureen Quilligan, and Nancy J. Vickers, eds. *Rewriting the Renaissance: The Discourses of Sexual Difference in Early Modern Europe.* Women in Culture and Society. Chicago: University of Chicago Press, 1986.

This interdisciplinary project, dedicated to understanding sex/gender arrangements in the early modern period, links explicitly feminist analyses with those whose primary commitments are psychoanalytic, Marxist, or deconstructive. The editors' introduction underscores three Renaissance phenomena important in reassessing gender and class differences: the development of capitalism, Elizabeth's rule, and changes in the structure of the family. Organized into three sections—"The Politics of Patriarchy: Theory and Practice," "The Rhetorics of Marginalization: Consequences of Patriarchy," and "The Works of Women: Some Exceptions to the Rule of Patriarchy"—the book includes a number of essays investigating plays by Shakespeare and Milton as well as pieces focusing on Renaissance art, women and work, and nondramatic writing.

E22

Fineman, Joel. "The Turn of the Shrew." *Shakespeare and the Question of Theory.* Ed. Patricia Parker and Geoffrey Hartman. New York: Methuen, 1985. 138–59.

Within the framework of the debate between Lacanian psychoanalytic theory and Derridean deconstruction, particularly in its feminist extensions, Fineman interrogates how an explicit discourse of subversion (the language of woman) actually resecures the very order (male authority) to which it seems opposed in *The Taming of the Shrew.*

E23

Foley, Helene P. "The Conception of Women in Athenian Drama." *Reflections of Women in Antiquity.* New York: Gordon and Breach, 1981. 127–68.

Foley investigates the methodological problems in the study of women in classical literature, focusing on the dichotomy between women's seeming confinement to the private sphere in real life emphasized in prose texts and their prominent role in Attic drama. Emphasizing the need to establish a methodology that allows interpretation of sex role conflicts in relation to the larger political, social, and philosophical issues they are used to explore, she analyzes two recent approaches: one stemming from a psychosociological perspective and the other based in structuralist anthropology and linguistics. She particularly explicates the application of structuralist readings that stress either the premise that female is to nature as male is to culture or (more promising, although problematic) that female is to domestic as male is to public.

E24

French, Marilyn. *Shakespeare's Division of Experience.* New York: Summit, 1981.

Assessing Shakespeare's work through her theory of gender principles, French defines the "masculine" principle as concerned with power, exaltation of the individual, and transcendence of nature and the "feminine" principle as identified with nature and divided into two aspects: the outlaw (sexuality, subversiveness) and the inlaw (compassion, altruism). French argues that Shakespeare moved from an early respect for masculine qualities and suspicion of feminine ones to a later fear of the power and capriciousness of the masculine and an idealization of particular aspects of the feminine. In addition to demonstrating how Shakespeare's male characters are *human* (e.g., experiencing, changing) while female characters act out *types,* thus occupying different conceptual realms, she roughly equates the gender principles with genres. The plays are examined in five sections: "Received Ideas" (power in the *Henry VI* plays and *Richard III,* marriage in *The Comedy of Errors* and *The Taming of the Shrew*), "The Inlaw Feminine Principle" (constancy in *Two Gentlemen of Verona, Love's Labour's Lost,* and *A Midsummer Night's Dream;* money in *The Merchant of Venice* and *The Merry Wives of Windsor;* emotion in *As You Like It* and *Twelfth Night;* chastity in *Much Ado About Nothing*), "Ideals Questioned" (female chaste constancy and male legitimacy in the problem plays: *Hamlet, Troilus and Cressida, All's Well That Ends Well,* and *Measure for Measure*), "Chaos Come Again: Ideals Banished" (male values in the late tragedies: *Othello, King Lear, Macbeth, Antony and Cleopatra, Coriolanus,* and *Timon of Athens*), and "A New Synthesis" (the spirit of reconciliation in the romances: *Pericles, Cymbeline, The Winter's Tale,* and *The Tempest*). She concludes that although Shakespeare never ceased searching for a means of reintegrating human experience "because he—and his tradition—saw experience in terms of polar opposites, his work has been important in perpetuating the very division he sought to reconcile."

E25

Garner, Shirley Nelson. *"The Taming of the Shrew:* Inside or Outside of the Joke?" *"Bad" Shakespeare: Revaluations of the Shakespeare Canon.* Ed. Maurice Charney. Rutherford, N.J.: Fairleigh Dickinson University Press; London: Associated University Presses, 1988. 105–19.

Reacting to the misogyny of Shakespeare's play, wherein the central joke is directed against a woman, Garner declares herself outside the community for whom the joke is intended and unable to participate in its humor. She observes that whatever the critical interpretation of Kate's final speech, it entails her losing her own voice and speaking the patriarchal language.

E26

Gohlke, Madelon [Madelon Sprengnether]. " 'I Wooed Thee with My Sword': Shakespeare's Tragic Paradigms." *Representing Shakespeare: New Psychoanalytic Essays.* Ed. Murray M. Schwartz and Coppélia Kahn. Baltimore, Md.: Johns Hopkins University Press, 1980. 170–87.

This essay dealing with *Hamlet, Othello, King Lear, Macbeth,* and *Antony and Cleopatra* appears in Lenz, Greene, and Neely's *The Woman's Part.* See E36. *Term:* violence, against women.

E27

Greenberg, Mitchell. "Stage Whispers: Corneille's Absolutism and the Voice of the *M/other.*" *Les Contes de Perrault/La Contestation et ses limites/Furetière.* Papers on French Seventeenth Century Literature 17. Ed. Michel Bareau, Jacques Barchilon, Domna Stanton, and Jean Alter. Paris: Wolfgang Leiner, 1987. 167–83.

In his analysis of patriarchy's coopting of the feminine in *Le Cid*, Greenberg argues that the play's "overinvestment in objects of representable masculinity hides (represses) the feminine component also necessary for propagation." While suggesting that patriarchy even eliminates the person of the mother "in a desperate attempt to place her outside of the representable world," he demonstrates how the invisible presence of the maternal figure permeates the drama.

E28

Hardwick, Elizabeth. "Ibsen's Women." *Seduction and Betrayal: Women in Literature.* New York: Random House, 1974. 31–83.

Offering a predominantly psychological analysis of the female characters in *A Doll's House, Hedda Gabler,* and *Rosmersholm,* Hardwick also touches upon acting problems in interpreting the roles of Nora and Hedda.

E29

Howard, Jean E. "Renaissance Antitheatricality and the Politics of Gender and Rank in *Much Ado About Nothing.*" *Shakespeare Reproduced: The Text in History and Ideology.* Ed. Jean E. Howard and Marion F. O'Connor. New York: Methuen, 1987. 163–87.

Howard relates the play's preoccupation with theatrical practices to Elizabethan antitheatrical tracts. She argues that the tracts, overtly focused on the nature, control, and "morality" of theatrical power, were "a site where anxieties about a changing social order were discursively produced and managed." Taking issue with the critical assumption that *Much Ado* is "above ideology," she analyzes how its representations of theatricality work to "reproduce class and gender differences within a social order dependent on these differences to justify inequalities of power and privilege."

E30

Ingram, Angela J. C. *In the Posture of a Whore: Changing Attitudes to "Bad" Women in Elizabethan and Jacobean Drama.* 2 vols. Salzburg Studies in English Literature; Jacobean Drama Studies 93. Salzburg, Austria: Institut für Anglistik und Amerikanistik, Universität Salzburg, 1984.

Ingram's descriptive work considers minor as well as major characters in plays by Beaumont and Fletcher (and their collaborators), Chapman, Dekker, Ford, Heywood, Jonson, Marlowe, Marston, Massinger, Middleton, Sackville and Norton, Shakespeare, Tourneur, Webster, and others. She argues that in most cases "bad" women's "indiscretion" is reduced to sexual matters and the disruption of the ideal pattern of womanhood. Delineating differences in characterization according to such variables as dramatic genre and the character's class, Ingram discusses treatment of women in the following categories: whores, bawds, shrews, citizens' wives, adulterous women, amazons, witches, revengers, politically or religiously disorderly women, and the Helen-image (Helen of Troy, Cressida, and Cleopatra). She concludes with a comparison and contrast of the playwrights' attitudes toward women.

E31

Jardine, Lisa. *Still Harping on Daughters: Women and Drama in the Age of Shakespeare.* Sussex, England: Harvester, 1983.

In reaction against previous feminist criticism of Shakespeare, both favorable and unfavorable, which analyzes his female characters as people, Jardine argues that his plays neither mirror society nor articulate Elizabethan views on "the woman question." The independent essays that make up the book deal with specific cultural issues intended to provide various perspectives on the stage representation of women. Using external evidence ranging from antitheatre pamphlets to poetry and diaries, Jardine examines Shakespeare and other Elizabethan and Jacobean playwrights, including Heywood, Jonson, Marlowe, Middleton, and Webster, within the context of the period's social, intellectual, political, and economic conditions. Topics include cross-dressing and Elizabethan eroticism; the double bind of the "liberating" possibilities for women (Protestantism, humanist education, marital partnership); wealth, inheritance, and what critics have referred to as "strong women"; the role of the shrew; dress as status; and Queen Elizabeth and the "saving stereotypes of female heroism," whereby the woman hero "is defined by . . . her being *other than* manly."

E32

Johnson, Marilyn L. *Images of Women in the Works of Thomas Heywood.* Salzburg Studies in English Literature; Jacobean Drama Studies 42. Salzburg, Austria: Institut für Englische Sprache und Literatur, Universität Salzburg, 1974.

Johnson examines Heywood's attitude toward women in both his dramatic and nondramatic works. After placing Heywood within the context of the Renaissance controversy over women, she devotes separate chapters to three character types: the adulteress, the good wife, and the chaste maiden. She finds that Heywood's morally constructive plays stress the women characters' virtues and show sympathy for their faults.

E33

Kahn, Coppélia. "The Cuckoo's Note: Male Friendship and Cuckoldry in *The Merchant of Venice.*" *Shakespeare's "Rough Magic": Renaissance Essays in Honor of C. L. Barber.* Ed. Peter Erickson and Coppélia Kahn. Newark: University of Delaware Press, 1985. 104–12.

Kahn explores the interdependence of two motifs involved in the ring plot: the conflict between male bonds and marriage and men's fear of cuckoldry after marriage.

E34

Kahn, Coppélia. *Man's Estate: Masculine Identity in Shakespeare.* Berkeley: University of California Press, 1981.

Combining psychoanalytic and feminist perspectives, Kahn seeks to discover "dilemmas of masculine selfhood revealed in the design" of Shakespeare's works. She defines two problems faced by the male characters in achieving manhood. The first concerns psychological processes: Having learned sexual identity in childhood by differentiating their masculinity from their mothers' femininity, men must in adulthood reunite with women to fulfill societal roles. The second involves a historical situation, patriarchy, that gives men control over women but makes men indirectly dependent on them for validation of their manhood. Successive chapters focus on particular crises: adolescence (the poem *Venus and Adonis* is discussed), identification with the father and masculine self-definition through aggression (the history plays), marriage as a passage to manhood (*Romeo and Juliet* and *The Taming of the Shrew*), cuckoldry *(Othello, Hamlet,* and *The Merry Wives of Windsor),* sexual confusion and the drive to prove masculinity through bloody exploits *(Macbeth* and *Coriolanus),* and maturation within the context of family and life cycle *(The Comedy of Errors, Twelfth Night, Pericles, The Winter's Tale,* and *The Tempest).*

E35
Kahn, Coppélia. "The Providential Tempest and the Shakespearean Family." *Representing Shakespeare.* Ed. Murray Schwartz and Coppélia Kahn. Baltimore, Md.: Johns Hopkins University Press, 1980. 217–43.

This essay, which examines *The Comedy of Errors, Twelfth Night, Pericles, The Winter's Tale,* and *The Tempest,* appears as Chapter 7 in Kahn's *Man's Estate.* See E34. *Terms:* family; father-daughter relationships; identity, male; sexuality, male.

E36
Lenz, Carolyn Ruth Swift, Gayle Greene, and Carol Thomas Neely. *The Woman's Part: Feminist Criticism of Shakespeare.* Urbana: University of Illinois Press, 1980.

The intentions behind this collection of essays, which examine both female and male characters and their relationship to social structures, are to free Shakespeare's women from stereotyped interpretations and restore the roles of women, often minimized in criticism and in production; to examine Shakespeare's women's relations to one another; to analyze the plays' patriarchal structures; and to explore the influence of genre on the portrayal of women. The introduction discusses the various critical approaches utilized in the articles, which include the following: Paula S. Berggren's "The Woman's Part: Female Sexuality as Power in Shakespeare's Plays"; Madonne M. Miner's " 'Neither Mother,

Wife, Nor England's Queen': The Roles of Women in *Richard III*"; Catharine R. Stimpson's "Shakespeare and the Soil of Rape"; John C. Bean's "Comic Structure and the Humanizing of Kate in *The Taming of the Shrew*"; Janice Hays' "Those 'Soft and Delicate Desires': *Much Ado* and the Distrust of Women"; Clara Claiborne Park's "As We Like It: How a Girl Can Be Smart and Still Popular"; Carole McKewin's "Counsels of Gall and Grace: Intimate Conversations Between Women in Shakespeare's Plays"; Gayle Greene's "Shakespeare's Cressida: 'A Kind of Self' "; Madelon Gohlke's " 'I Wooed Thee with My Sword': Shakespeare's Tragic Paradigms"; Coppélia Kahn's "Coming of Age in Verona"; Rebecca Smith's "A Heart Cleft in Twain: The Dilemma of Shakespeare's Gertrude"; Carol Thomas Neely's "Women and Men in *Othello*: 'What Should Such a Fool/Do with So Good a Woman?' "; Joan Larsen Klein's "Lady Macbeth: 'Infirm of Purpose' "; Marianne Novy's "Shakespeare's Female Characters as Actors and Audience"; Irene G. Dash's "A Penchant for Perdita on the Eighteenth-Century Stage"; Lorie Jerrell Leininger's "The Miranda Trap: Sexism and Racism in Shakespeare's *Tempest*"; and Charles Frey's " 'O Sacred, Shadowy, Cold, and Constant Queen': Shakespeare's Imperiled and Chastening Daughters of Romance." Also included is "Women and Men in Shakespeare: A Selective Bibliography."

E37

Levin, Carole. "I Trust I May Not Trust Thee: Women's Visions of the World in Shakespeare's *King John*." *Ambiguous Realities: Women in the Middle Ages and Renaissance*. Ed. Carole Levin and Jeanie Watson. Detroit, Mich.: Wayne State University Press, 1987. 219–34.

Levin argues that the women characters, although powerless to change events, are more insightful of their world and more honest than their male counterparts.

E38

Loeffelholz, Mary. "Two Masques of Ceres and Proserpine: *Comus* and *The Tempest*." *Remembering Milton: Essays on the Texts and Traditions*. Ed. Mary Nyquist and Margaret W. Ferguson. New York: Methuen, 1987. 25–42.

This inquiry into the relation of Prospero's interrupted betrothal masque in *The Tempest* to Milton's *Comus* considers such issues as maternal absence, women's silence, and the appropriation of female (pro)creativity by the patriarchy. Loeffelholz suggests that Shakespeare occupies the place of the mother in patriarchy (i.e., the parent with no proprietary rights to the daughter) in *Comus*.

E39

Loraux, Nicole. *Tragic Ways of Killing a Woman*. Trans. Anthony For-
ster. Cambridge, Mass.: Harvard University Press, 1987. Trans. of
Façons tragiques de tuer une femme. 1985.

Explaining that classical Greek tragedy granted to women's death a
completely different treatment from the banalities of real-life's intimate
mourning, Loraux further distinguishes between the violent deaths suffered by men and by women in drama. Directing her attention first to
suicide, she discerns that whether the tragic woman chooses the "wom-
anly" means of ending her life—the noose—or steals the man's way—
the sword—the act is performed offstage, behind the doors of that
closed space in which women belong, confirming their connection
with marriage and maternity. Next investigating the sacrifice of virgins,
she emphasizes the irony of the sacrifice's resemblance to marriage and
the unavailability of language to denote the glory of a woman. In the final section, Loraux determines from a word-by-word study of the texts
that tragedy endows men with an infinitely more diversified body than
women, insofar as access to death.

E40

McDonald, Margaret Lamb. *The Independent Woman in the Restoration Comedy of Manners*. Salzburg Studies in English Literature; Poetic Drama and Poetic Theory 32. Salzburg, Austria: Institut für
Englische Sprache und Literatur, Universität Salzburg, 1976.

In contrast to previous studies which concentrated on Restoration comedy's beau-rake, McDonald examines "the witty fair one" in the plays of
Wycherley, Etherege, Congreve, Dryden, Shadwell, Crowne, Sedley,
Southerne, Vanbrugh, Farquhar, and Cibber. After an introduction that
traces the evolution of the comic heroine in English drama, she devotes
two chapters to delineating the wide variety of Restoration heroines
characterized by wit and intelligence, an "aggressive will to power," and
a sense of their precarious role in an unstable society. While she sets up
the three categories of female fop, mischievous outwitter, and Truewit,
she admits that some heroines elude labeling. Other chapters deal with
the influence of Hobbes, the comic heroines' self-awareness, and the effect of the shift to sentimental comedy on the depiction of heroines.

E41

McKendrick, Malveena. *Women and Society in the Spanish Drama of
the Golden Age: A Study of the* Mujer Varonil. London: Cambridge
University Press, 1974.

In McKendrick's study of the *mujer varonil,* the woman departing from feminine norms of the sixteenth and seventeenth centuries, individual chapters define her various forms in the plays: the *bandolera;* the *mujer esquiva,* who shuns love and marriage; the amazon, the leader, and the warrior; the scholar and the career woman; the *bella cazadora;* and the avenger. In addition to describing feminist preoccupations in Lope, the greatest exponent of the *mujer varonil,* McKendrick draws on other playwrights, including Aguilar, Calderón, Castro, Cervantes, Cueva, Mira, Moreto, Tárrega, Tirso, Turia, Velez, Virués, Vicente, and Rojas Zorilla. Citing a variety of documentary sources, the introduction contrasts the depiction of the heroines with the common societal feminine ideal and with real-life women. The concluding chapter outlines the changing distribution of the various female character types over the period, grapples with lesbian implications in the plots, and hypothesizes about the appeal of the *mujer varonil* to male and female audience members.

E42

McLuskie, Kathleen E. " 'The Emperor of Russia Was My Father': Gender and Theatrical Power." *Images of Shakespeare.* Ed. Werner Habicht, D. J. Palmer, and Roger Pringle. Proceedings of the Third Congress of the International Shakespeare Association, 1986. Newark: University of Delaware Press; London: Associated University Presses, 1988. 174–87.

Explicating the use of the constructed category of "woman" and the concomitant absence of "women" in drama of the early modern period, the author analyzes *Othello* and *The Winter's Tale,* with particular attention to the female characters as the site of meanings generated by men and to the contradictions between visual and verbal signs.

E43

McLuskie, Kathleen. "The Patriarchal Bard: Feminist Criticism and Shakespeare: *King Lear* and *Measure for Measure." Political Shakespeare: New Essays in Cultural Materialism.* Ed. Jonathan Dollimore and Alan Sinfield. Ithaca, N.Y.: Cornell University Press, 1985. 88–108.

McLuskie articulates the limitations of the mimetic, essentialist model of feminist criticism and suggests, instead, focusing on "the narrative, poetic and theatrical strategies which construct the plays' meanings and position the audience to understand their events from a particular point of view." She examines "the tension between narrative and social meaning" concerning sexual relations in *Measure for Measure,* underscoring the way in which the text constructs the spectator as male. She also demonstrates the equation between human nature and male power in *King Lear* and the possibilities for reconstructing the text in a production that subverts its misogynist meaning.

E44

Marcus, Leah S. "Shakespeare's Comic Heroines, Elizabeth I, and the Political Uses of Androgyny." *Women in the Middle Ages and the Renaissance: Literary and Historical Perspectives.* Ed. Mary Beth Rose. Syracuse, N.Y.: Syracuse University Press, 1986. 135–53.

Marcus connects the sexual multivalence of several Shakespearean heroines with Elizabeth's political rhetoric, in which she defined herself as both male and female. She argues that the dramatic construct of a boy dressed as a woman, "who then expands her identity through male disguise in such a way as to mirror the activities which would be appropriate to her actual, hidden male identity . . . precisely replicates visually the composite self-image the Queen created through language." She discusses how Shakespeare's festive comedies helped reinforce Elizabeth's attempts to associate her androgynous nature with stability and renewal.

E45

Melville, Margarita B. "Female and Male in Chicano Theatre." *Hispanic Theatre in the United States.* Ed. Nicolas Kanellos. Houston, Tex.: Arte Publico, 1984. 71–79.

Melville's survey of Chicano plays of the 1970s examines family as well as female-male relationships, which she classifies into three groups: partnership, adversary with the male dominant, and adversary with the female dominant. Among the playwrights discussed are Luis Valdez, Carlos Morton, Ysidro R. Macías, and Estela Portillo-Trambley. Melville also comments on the development of *teatropoesía* as "a very appropriate female response" to the unsatisfactory depiction of male-female relationships in most Chicano drama.

E46

Millstone, Amy. "French Feminist Theater and the Subject of Prostitution." *The Image of the Prostitute in Modern Literature.* Ed. Pierre L. Horn and Mary Beth Pringle. New York: Ungar, 1984. 19–27.

Citing Dumas *fils' La Dame aux camélias* as the turning point in the dramatic treatment of female sexuality, Millstone concentrates on the concern with sexual exploitation expressed by playwrights such as Brieux between 1870 and 1914. She delineates three overlapping themes: the marriage of convenience as a form of prostitution, sexuality as a power struggle, and sexuality as a means of revenge against men.

E47

Murray, Timothy. "*Othello,* An Index and Obscure Prologue to the History of Foul Generic Thoughts." *Shakespeare and Deconstruction.* Ed. G. Douglas Atkins and David M. Bergeron. American University Studies, Series 4; English Language and Literature 57. New York: Peter Lang, 1988. 213–43.

Murray demonstrates how male fears of the power of mimesis underlie both antitheatrical prejudices in the Renaissance and the male characters' mistrust of Desdemona. He analyzes Desdemona's ability to reorder fixed sign systems to attain her goals and Bianca's discovery of a separate female life, which "threatens the patriarchal dependence on her presence as an engine for social definition through generic differentiation."

E48

Murray, Timothy. "*Othello*'s Foul Generic Thoughts and Methods." *Persons in Groups: Social Behavior as Identity Formation in Medieval and Renaissance Europe.* Ed. Richard C. Trexler. Papers of the Sixteenth Annual Conference of the Center for Medieval and Early Renaissance Studies. Medieval & Renaissance Texts & Studies 36. Binghamton, N.Y.: Medieval & Renaissance Texts & Studies, 1985. 67–77.

This is an abridged version of Murray's "*Othello,* An Index and Obscure Prologue to the History of Foul Generic Thoughts," annotated in E47. *Terms:* antitheatricalism, women and; discourse, female; misogyny; patriarchy.

E49

Neely, Carol Thomas. "Broken Nuptials in Shakespeare's Comedies." *Shakespeare's "Rough Magic": Renaissance Essays in Honor of C. L. Barber.* Ed. Peter Erickson and Coppélia Kahn. Newark: University of Delaware Press, 1985. 61–72.

A fuller version of this article constitutes the first chapter of Neely's *Broken Nuptials in Shakespeare's Plays.* See E50. *Terms:* courtship; female-male relationships; marriage; misogyny.

E50

Neely, Carol Thomas. *Broken Nuptials in Shakespeare's Plays.* New Haven, Conn.: Yale University Press, 1985.

Neely's exploration of the role of women in Shakespeare centers on an examination of marriage as the main paradigm within which women are defined. She considers how marriage and broken nuptials (irregular ceremonies, estrangements, etc.) influence Shakespeare's themes and structures and how gender relationships are shaped by and shape different genres. Neely's introduction outlines conflicting assessments from literary critics (about Shakespeare's women) and historians (about the status of Renaissance women) and explicates the period's contradictory attitudes toward women, sexuality, and marriage. The individual chapters, which focus on particular plays within the context of contemporaneous works, include "Broken Nuptials in Shakespeare's Comedies: *Much Ado About Nothing*," "Power and Virginity in the Problem Comedies: *All's Well That Ends Well*," "Women and Men in *Othello*," "Gender and Genre in *Antony and Cleopatra*," and "Incest and Issue in the Romances: *The Winter's Tale*."

E51

Newman, Karen. " 'And Wash the Ethiop White': Femininity and the Monstrous in *Othello*." *Shakespeare Reproduced: The Text in History and Ideology*. Ed. Jean E. Howard and Marion F. O'Connor. New York: Methuen, 1987. 141–62.

Investigating the play within the context of the Elizabethan and Jacobean culture's fascination with and fear of racial and sexual difference, Newman shows how both the desiring woman and the black man are identified with the monstrous. She also emphasizes political criticism's task to reread canonical texts in new ways "which disturb traditional interpretations and discover them as partisan, constructed, made rather than given, natural, and inevitable."

E52

Novy, Marianne. *Love's Argument: Gender Relations in Shakespeare*. Chapel Hill: University of North Carolina Press, 1984.

Novy focuses on two related conflicts in Shakespeare's works that involve the politics of gender: the tension between mutuality and patriarchy and the struggle between emotion and control. Dealing with plays that center on love between the sexes, she examines comedies, tragedies, and romances to determine genre differences in Shakespeare's exploration of these conflicts. She also considers the Elizabethan audience's ambivalence about gender relationships and draws parallels between stage conventions and social relations between the sexes. Separate chapters address mutuality in comedy (*Much Ado About Nothing, As You Like It, Twelfth Night*); the social order and game-playing (*The Taming of the Shrew*); the rivalry between two types of giving (*The*

Merchant of Venice); the roles of tragic women as actors and as audience to the hero; violence and gender *(Romeo and Juliet, Troilus and Cressida)*; mutuality and its destruction *(Othello)*; patriarchy, mutuality, and forgiveness *(King Lear)*; revisions of masculine stereotypes in the romances *(Cymbeline, The Winter's Tale, The Tempest)*; and Shakespeare's fascination with the image of gender as role and with gender-crossing.

E53
Novy, Marianne. "Sex, Reciprocity, and Self-Sacrifice in *The Merchant of Venice.*" *Human Sexuality in the Middle Ages and the Renaissance.* Ed. Douglas Radcliff-Umstead. University of Pittsburgh Publications on the Middle Ages and the Renaissance 4. Pittsburgh, Pa.: Pittsburgh Center for Medieval and Renaissance Studies, 1978. 153–66.

This article appears in a revised version as Chapter 4 in Novy's book, *Love's Argument.* See E52. *Terms:* sexuality, female; sexuality, male.

E54
Pitt, Angela. *Shakespeare's Women.* Totowa, N.J.: Barnes & Noble, 1981.

Intending her generously illustrated book for the nonspecialist, Pitt proposes to explore Elizabethan attitudes toward women, to examine various female roles bearing these attitudes in mind, and to trace the history of the characters on stage. An epilogue contains interviews with four noted Shakespearean actresses.

E55
Pomeroy, Sarah B. "Images of Women in the Literature of Classical Athens." *Goddesses, Whores, Wives, and Slaves: Women in Classical Antiquity.* New York: Schocken, 1975. 93–119.

After reviewing various hypotheses formulated to explain the discrepancy between real-life, disenfranchised Athenian women and the forceful heroines of many Greek tragedies, Pomeroy analyzes proper feminine and masculine behavior as proposed by the dramatists. She writes about the portrayal of the masculine woman as heroine in *Antigone,* Euripides' use of misogyny as a means of examining popular beliefs about women and his depiction of the horrors of patriarchy, and Aristophanes' negative characterization of women, particularly in *Lysistrata.* A final section deals with women in Plato's utopian works.

E56

Prandi, Julie D. *Spirited Women Heroes: Major Female Characters in the Dramas of Goethe, Schiller and Kleist.* American University Studies, Series 1; Germanic Languages and Literature 22. New York: Peter Lang, 1983.

In this study of a dramatic type that appears in several *Goethezeit* plays—the woman hero who in seeking self-realization comes into conflict with norms for feminine behavior—Prandi concentrates on Goethe's *Iphigenie* and *Die näturliche Tochter,* Schiller's *Maria Stuart* and *Jungfrau von Orleans,* and Kleist's *Penthesilea* and *Das Käthchen von Heilbronn.* Dividing the characters into two groups, those who refuse to act out female roles ("Amazons") and those who try to live within the boundaries of the period's expectations ("conventional" spirited women heroes), she identifies the social and cultural significance of the women's commonalities.

E57

Rose, Jacqueline. "Sexuality in the Reading of Shakespeare: *Hamlet* and *Measure for Measure.*" *Alternative Shakespeares.* Ed. John Drakakis. London: Methuen, 1985. 95–118.

Rose surveys twentieth-century critical analysis of these works, outlining "how psychoanalytic and literary criticism share with the literature they address a terrain of language, fantasy and sexuality—a terrain in which the woman occupies a crucial, but difficult, place." In particular, she points out the overlap of aesthetic and sexual failing (i.e., Gertrude's and Isabella's) that appears in commentaries on the plays.

E58

Rose, Mary Beth. *The Expense of Spirit: Love and Sexuality in English Renaissance Drama.* Ithaca, N.Y.: Cornell University Press, 1988.

To support her argument that drama is a participant in cultural change, Rose traces shifts in the Renaissance stage representations of love and sexuality and their parallels in moral and religious writings on women, eros, and marriage. She distinguishes the two dominant forms of sexual discourse—the dualistic sensibility that exalts or degrades women and eros, and the Protestant vision of marriage united with love as the foundation of an ordered society—and relates these conceptions to dramatic genre. Illustrating with plays by Lyly, Greene, and Shakespeare, Rose argues that romantic comedy evokes "potentially disruptive sexual tensions only to represent them as harmoniously assimilated within the existing social structure." Her study of Jacobean satire, particularly *Epicoene* and *The Roaring Girl*, investigates the linked struggles for social mobility and sexual equality. In an analysis of *Othello* and *The Duchess of Malfi,* she contrasts Elizabethan tragedy's heroism of public action and marginalization of women with Jacobean tragedy's "heroism of personal endurance," which centers on private life and depiction of women heroes. Concluding with tragicomedy (*Troilus and Cressida, The Two Noble Kinsmen,* and *The Knight of Malta*), Rose suggests that this form moves toward "redefining the relation between public and private life as separate but equal spheres."

E59

Sakellaridou, Elizabeth. *Pinter's Female Portraits: A Study of Female Characters in the Plays of Harold Pinter.* Totowa, N.J.: Barnes & Noble, 1988.

The author shows how Pinter's early depiction of women as masculinist archetypes gradually gives way to a fuller treatment of women as conscious and articulate human beings who function independently from the male characters' images of them. While arguing that Pinter's biased attitudes eventually transform into a gentler, androgynous vision, she notes his "lingering fondness . . . for closed male circles which lock out any female presence." In addition to Pinter's stage plays, Sakellaridou studies his television, radio, and film scripts.

E60

Scheman, Naomi. "Othello's Doubt/Desdemona's Death: The Engendering of Scepticism." *Power, Gender, Values.* Ed. Judith Genova. Edmonton, Alberta, Canada: Academic, 1987. 113–33.

Suggesting that for Othello or the skeptic, doubting "responds to an unease at the heart of the experiences of immersion in the world and connectedness to others," Scheman offers a rereading of several texts "that places the asymmetries of gender at the crux" of a profoundly disordered sixteenth-century Europe. Scheman relates Shakespeare's play to Descartes's *Meditations* in an attempt to locate reasons for changes in the ideas of nature and marriage during the period. She finds Othello to be an experimenter determined to control Desdemona to overcome his anxieties about female power.

E61

Schleiner, Winfried. "Deromanticizing the Shrew: Notes on Teaching Shakespeare in a 'Women in Literature' Course." *Teaching Shakespeare.* Ed. Walter Edens et al. Princeton, N.J.: Princeton University Press, 1977. 79–82.

Concentrating on the "wives willfully tested" motif, Schleiner distinguishes between works dealing with male-female relationships in the context of hierarchies of social rank and *The Taming of the Shrew*, which lacks disparity of rank or wealth between the protagonists but evidences a central sense of male-female hierarchy. She also contrasts the absence of romance in *Shrew* with its manifestations in *As You Like It.*

E62

Schotz, Myra Glazer. "The Great Unwritten Story: Mothers and Daughters in Shakespeare." *The Lost Tradition: Mothers and Daughters in Literature.* Ed. Cathy N. Davidson and E. M. Broner. New York: Ungar, 1980. 44–54.

Schotz first explores the absence of mothers and the male fear of the feminine in *Macbeth* and *King Lear.* She then analyzes Shakespeare's separation of a consolidated feminine archetype into mother and daughter (as embodied in the Demeter-Persephone myth) in the late romances, with *Pericles* providing a transition between the misogynistic *King Lear* and *The Winter's Tale,* in which revulsion toward female sexuality is acknowledged and overcome, and restoration of the powerful mother-daughter cathexis is welcomed.

E63

Schuler, Marilyn V. "Goddess vs. 'Gyn/Ecologist': A Comparative View of *Antigone* and *La Folle de Chaillot.*" *Myths and Realities of Contemporary French Theater: Comparative Views.* Ed. Patricia M. Hopkins and Wendell Aycock. Lubbock: Texas Tech Press, 1985. 141–51.

Schuler demonstrates that despite their similarities as protests during the Occupation and use of a woman as a symbolic agent combatting forces destructive to society and the future, Anouilh's and Giradoux's plays offer diametrically opposite representations of women. She argues that *Antigone* is classical and patriarchal, whereas *La Folle de Chaillot* offers an example of "gyn/ecology" (a woman-centered strategy for human survival).

E64

Shepherd, Simon. *Amazons and Warrior Women: Varieties of Feminism in Seventeenth-Century Drama.* New York: St. Martin's, 1981.

Shepherd suggests a seventeenth-century feminism "that questions assumptions about gender, challenges some of the norms and values of patriarchy," and sometimes provides alternatives or opposition. Drawing heavily on *The Fairie Queene,* he delineates two female images— warrior women, who rely on verbal wit or moral views, and Amazons, whose strength is used in pursuit of nonvirtuous or lustful goals—which he traces throughout Elizabethan and Jacobean drama. With frequent reference to the plays' political, religious, social, and literary contexts, Shepherd addresses such specific topics as women's position vis-a-vis work; the influence of Puritanism, particularly regarding marriage and adultery; the "roaring girls," whose real-life models adopted male dress and behavior; the tough/lecherous and the innocent tavern wenches; and the virgin martyrs. Several chapters consider interlocking themes of female sexuality, tyranny, corruption, and revenge; others focus on Shakespeare's witty women and on *Swetnam the Woman-Hater Arraigned by Women*. Playwrights studied include Chapman, Dekker, Fletcher, Marston, Massinger, Middleton, Tourneur, and Webster.

E65

Showalter, Elaine. "Representing Ophelia: Women, Madness, and the Responsibilities of Feminist Criticism." *Shakespeare and the Question of Theory*. Ed. Patricia Parker and Geoffrey Hartman. New York: Methuen, 1985. 77–94.

Showalter's threefold approach to tracing the iconography of Ophelia in the visual arts, psychiatry, literature, and stage production outlines the representational links between female insanity and sexuality, demonstrates the interaction between psychiatric theory and cultural representation, and proposes that feminist revisions of Ophelia stem as much from actresses' freedom as from critics' interpretation. She concludes that Ophelia's representation "changes independently of theories of the meaning of the play or the Prince, for it depends on attitudes toward women and madness."

E66

Sinfield, Alan. "Kinds of Loving: Women in the Plays." *Self and Society in Shakespeare's* Troilus and Cressida *and* Measure for Measure. Ed. J. A. Jowitt and R. K. S. Taylor. Bradford Centre Occasional Papers 4. Bradford, England: University of Leeds Centre for Adult Education, 1982. 27–44.

Sinfield examines Shakespeare's mingling of inherited literary codes of love (Romantic and Ovidian) in *Troilus and Cressida* and his expression of contradictory contemporary attitudes toward marriage and mutuality in *Measure for Measure*.

E67

Singh, Sarup. *The Double Standard in Shakespeare and Related Essays: Changing Status of Women in Sixteenth and Seventeenth Century England*. Delhi, India: Konark, 1988.

The first part of this tripartite study of restrictions on women's behavior includes chapters explicating Elizabethan society's views on chastity and examining several Shakespearean texts. Singh argues against Harbage's declaration that Shakespeare's works present a single standard of sexual morality, and distinguishes between our modern reactions and Shakespeare's audience's expectations of women's and men's codes of sexual conduct. The second part, focusing on women's education, surveys the sixteenth-century humanist view of this phenomenon as a means of establishing companionship between husband and wife and describes the decline of higher education for women in the following century. In the third part, devoted to the Restoration comedy of manners, Singh delineates the handicaps under which women suffered in the period, including the shortage of marriageable males. He shows that although the playwrights point to adultery as a natural consequence of mercenary marriages, adulterous women are judged differently from adulterous men. However, he finds that Restoration comedy stresses "that once women acquire intellectual maturity and self-possession . . . men would look upon them as individuals whose self-respect is as important as their own" and companionate marriage would result.

E68
Snow, Edward. "Language and Sexual Difference in *Romeo and Juliet.*" *Shakespeare's "Rough Magic": Renaissance Essays in Honor of C. L. Barber.* Ed. Peter Erickson and Coppélia Kahn. Newark: University of Delaware Press, 1985. 168–92.

Snow suggests that the play's language is most concerned not with the passion-social order opposition but, rather, with the difference between the sexes, and that "its subtler affirmations have to do not with romantic love but female ontology." Contrasting the protagonists' modes of desire and their attitudes toward death, he shows how the differences in language "consistently favor Juliet's imaginative world."

E69
Sprengnether, Madelon [Madelon Gohlke]. "Annihilating Intimacy in *Coriolanus.*" *Women in the Middle Ages and the Renaissance: Literary and Historical Perspectives.* Ed. Mary Beth Rose. Syracuse, N.Y.: Syracuse University Press, 1986. 89–111.

Sprengnether's essay is framed by pre-oedipal object-relations theory, in which femininity is primary, whereas masculine identity must be achieved and is "always at risk of becoming lost or diffused back into the original feminine matrix." Arguing that the male hero's ambivalent response to femininity shapes Shakespearean tragedy, the author studies the plays' structures of heteroerotic and homoerotic bonding. She demonstrates how the fantasy of destructive maternal omnipotence, under-lying if less clearly articulated in the earlier tragedies, is explored in *Coriolanus.*

E70

Vanita, Ruth. "Men's Power and Women's Resistance—Wife Murder in *Much Ado, Othello, Cymbeline* and *The Winter's Tale.*" *Women/Image/Text: Feminist Readings of Literary Text.* Ed. Lola Chatterji. New Delhi, India: Trianka, 1986.

Vanita discerns common patterns in four Shakespearean plays in which wife murder acts as a powerful metaphor, exemplifying the power relations between men and women. She detects a progressive restructuring of the situation, which involves a growing recognition of the problem's complexity and rejection of simple solutions, culminating with *The Winter's Tale*'s implication that "not just one man but the entire scenario, the whole stage needs to change."

E71

Vanovitch, Katherine. *Female Roles in East German Drama 1949–1977: A Selective History of Drama in the G.D.R.* European University Studies, Series 1; German Language and Literature 483. Frankfurt am Main, Germany: Peter Lang, 1982.

This analysis of the diverse images of womanhood in East German drama considers women characters both for their function in the plays and in the context of a shifting social environment. Vanovitch provides two background chapters, one summarizing Marxist classics and the historical influences affecting the SED (Sozialistische Einheitspartei Deutschlands) policy on women's status, the other describing the post-war theatrical climate. She then treats fourteen male playwrights in chronological order, pointing out their insights into patriarchal discrimination against women but noting their tendency to use female experience for its allegorical function. Such recurring themes as women's careers in a socialist society, domesticity, and motherhood are analyzed in the works of Baierl, Braun, Gozell, Hacks, Hammel, Hauser, Kerndl, Müller, Pfaff, Sakowski, Strahl, Strittmatter, Schütz, and Wolf.

E72

Weintraub, Rodelle, ed. *Fabian Feminist: Bernard Shaw and Women.* University Park: Pennsylvania State University Press, 1977.

Twenty essays exploring the causes and effects of Shaw's feminism and its manifestations in his work, are grouped into the following sections: literary and mythic influences on Shaw's writing, political and economic influences, sex roles in the plays, Shaw's depiction of liberated women, and the influence of Shaw's feminism on three generations of real-life women (Florence Farr, Clare Boothe Luce and Megan Terry). Five nondramatic pieces by Shaw supporting feminism and an extensive bibliographical checklist are also included. In his introduction, which reflects upon Shaw's advocacy of women's right to liberate themselves from traditional subservient roles and his belief that Fabianism must supplant capitalism to effect women's equality, Weintraub argues that much of Shaw is relevant to the contemporary feminist movement.

E73

Williamson, Marilyn L. *The Patriarchy of Shakespeare's Comedies.* Detroit, Mich.: Wayne State University Press, 1986.

Williamson employs a feminist-historicist methodology informed by Foucault's theories of power and sexuality. She emphasizes that as Shakespeare's audiences changed, "his approach, even to a given genre, modified too, and along with those alterations in subgenres came differing representations of women and patriarchy." The first section focuses on three comedies of courtship (*The Merchant of Venice, As You Like It,* and *Twelfth Night*), plays which satisfy male fantasies of marriage to superior women as advancement for merit and deal with anxieties about women's power through the theme of cuckoldry. In the section on the problem plays, Williamson relates *All's Well That Ends Well* and *Measure for Measure* to the dramas of enforced marriage and disguised rulers, subgenres that "form part of a culture preoccupied with problems of sexuality and the restraint of desire by authority." In the final section she asserts that the romances mythologize the father-ruler's power "by making it seem natural and inevitable." She distinguishes *The Tempest* from *Pericles, Cymbeline,* and *The Winter's Tale,* however, contending that its critique of Stuart political ideology demystifies patriarchal authority. In the epilogue Williamson observes the significance for today's feminists of Shakespeare's treatment of male control over female sexuality and generativity.

E74

Woodbridge, Linda [L. T. Fitz]. *Women and the English Renaissance: Literature and the Nature of Womankind, 1540–1620.* Urbana: University of Illinois Press, 1984.

This literary criticism and social history, which addresses the problem of separating life from art, is divided into three parts: an examination of the formal controversy about women, which Woodbridge sees as "largely a literary game, with very tenuous roots in real contemporary attitudes"; a study of female transvestism and changing sex roles; and a demonstration of how these two strains converged to produce new literary conventions and views of reality. Works by Shakespeare (whose transvestite heroines she assesses as revealing his basic conservatism about sex roles), Beaumont and Fletcher, Dekker, Jonson, Heywood, Marston, Middleton, Webster, and other playwrights are discussed, with a separate chapter devoted to the anonymous *Swetnam the Woman-Hater Arraigned by Women*. Two chapters of particular interest deal with "Pistolas in the Playhouse," the influence of females in the audience on the stage representation of women from about 1610, and the dramatic convention of the stage misogynist, a figure paradoxically used in the defense of women.

E75

Yates, W. E. "Nestroy, Grillparzer, and the Feminist Cause." *Viennese Popular Theatre: A Symposium*. Ed. W. E. Yates and John R. P. McKenzie. Exeter, England: University of Exeter, 1985. 93–107.

Yates argues that despite Nestroy's satirical treatment of women and marriage, his plays, no less than Grillparzer's, evidence sympathy for the underprivileged position of women in nineteenth-century Austria.

Periodicals, Serials, and Annuals

E76

Abrams, Richard. "Gender Confusion and Sexual Politics in *The Two Noble Kinsmen*." *Themes in Drama* 7 (*Drama, Sex and Politics*) (1985): 69–76.

Abrams analyzes the breakdown of strict sexual differentiation in the play. He suggests that the kinsmen's vanity and lack of curiosity about Emilia as an individual suggest "the moral inequality of the traditionally powerful (men) vs. the politically disenfranchised (women)."

E77

Adams, Elsie B. "Shaw's Ladies." *Shaw Review* 23 (1980): 112–18.

Adams explores the theme of ladyhood in the plays of Shaw, who uses "lady" in both elevating and derogatory senses, but most frequently as a class marker. She illustrates Shaw's contempt for the lady's role (sheltered, proper, hypocritical, lacking serious purpose) by examining women characters actively rebelling against it in several plays, including *Misalliance*, *Fanny's First Play*, and *Too True to Be Good*. She also analyzes Shaw's depiction of the hazards of ladyhood in *Pygmalion*.

E78

Adamson, W. D. "The Calumny Pattern in Shakespeare." *REAL: The Yearbook of Research in English and American Literature* 4 (1986): 33–66.

The author investigates Shakespeare's reenactment of "the conflict between the innocent sexual unselfconsciousness of the women and the sexually paranoid 'infected knowledge' of the men" in five plays: *Much Ado About Nothing*, *Hamlet*, *Othello*, *Cymbeline*, and *The Winter's Tale*. Adamson notes the flawed attitudes regarding sex and women not only in the male characters but also in the contemporary culture.

E79

Alexander, Bonnie L. "Cracks in the Pedestal: A Reading of *A Woman Killed with Kindness*." *Massachusetts Studies in English* 7.1 (1978): 1–11.

Demonstrating that Heywood's play foreshadows how the emerging middle-class would formulate ideas about women's nature and proper sphere, Alexander examines issues of economics, social behavior, and female sexuality. She finds the "fallen woman" character of Anne more appropriate to a Victorian novel than an Elizabethan play, and challenges the notion that women's lot has much improved to this day.

E80

Andresen-Thom, Martha. "Thinking about Women and Their Prosperous Art: A Reply to Juliet Dusinberre's *Shakespeare and the Nature of Women*." *Shakespeare Studies* 11 (1978): 259–76.

Andresen-Thom examines possible reasons for Shakespeare's presentation of the "ego-ideal" of the independent, eloquent woman. She explores the relationship of women's silence and wit to male ideals of woman, with illustrations from plays including *Much Ado About Nothing* and *Othello*. She also emphasizes the difficulty of ascertaining the precise relationship of fiction to social fact, and argues that Dusinberre ignores the reality for Renaissance writers of older fiction's images of women and paradigms of male-female relationships.

E81

Aquino, Deborah T. Curren. "Toward a Star That Danced: Woman as Survivor in Shakespeare's Early Comedies." *Shakespeare and Renaissance Association of West Virginia: Selected Papers* 11 (1986): 50–61.

Suggesting that it is mainly the female characters' survival instincts and facility to adapt that ensure the plays' happy endings, Aquino offers examples from *Love's Labour's Lost, A Midsummer Night's Dream, The Comedy of Errors,* and other works. She particularly distinguishes between women's and men's verbal strategies, pointing out women's greater sensitivity to propriety and creative combination of boldness and prudence.

E82

Asp, Carolyn. " 'Be Bloody, Bold and Resolute': Tragic Action and Sexual Stereotyping in *Macbeth*." *Studies in Philology* 78 (1981): 153–69.

Asp investigates how Lady Macbeth's attempts to renounce her femininity and adopt a male mentality produce a dichotomy between role and nature that results in her mental disintegration, and how Macbeth's acceptance of a false masculinity, tempting him to exercise godlike power through violence, ultimately seals his doom.

E83

Asp, Carolyn. "In Defense of Cressida." *Studies in Philology* 74 (1977): 406–17.

The author analyzes Cressida as the embodiment of *Troilus and Cressida*'s central metaphysical question regarding whether value is intrinsic in objects or projected onto objects by observers. Asp argues that the pathos of Cressida's situation as a pawn in a male world stems from her own assumption that she lacks intrinsic value.

E84

Asp, Carolyn. "Subjectivity, Desire, and Female Friendship in *All's Well That Ends Well*." *Literature and Psychology* 32.4 (1986): 48–53.

Using paradigms from psychoanalytic theory that are congruent with Renaissance ideas of the female, Asp interprets Helena "as coming to independent womanhood by surmounting attitudes and theories of female deprivation and inferiority." She explicates how Helena breaks out of strictures applied to women through her assertion of desire, refusal of objectification, and bonding with other female characters.

E85

Baines, Barbara J., and Mary C. Williams. "The Contemporary and Classical Antifeminist Tradition in Jonson's *Epicoene*." *Renaissance Papers* 1977: 43–58.

The authors contend that *Epicoene* offers a more comprehensive attack on women than other Jacobean plays displaying antifeminist sentiments. Detailing Jonson's use of Ovid and Juvenal in his satire of women who reject traditional roles, they suggest that his contempt is not based on the characters' desire for liberty "but on their desire for sexual license and power over men."

E86

Baruch, Elaine Hoffman. "Ibsen's *Doll House*: A Myth for Our Time." *Yale Review* 69 (1980): 374–87.

Baruch proposes that Ibsen's play can be seen as a myth of the contemporary feminist consciousness. Delineating the ways in which he questions the underpinnings of sexual politics, she discusses such issues as assumptions about romantic love and marriage, home as prison, sex/gender roles, biology versus social conditioning, and the relationship of the individual to family and state. In addition, she considers the tragic aspects of *A Doll House*, which she compares to Sophocles' *Antigone*, and the play's ambivalences.

E87

Bassnett, Susan. "Sexuality and Power in the Three Parts of *King Henry VI*." *Shakespeare-Jahrbuch* 124 (1988): 183–91.

Comparing the strategies of Elizabeth I at Tilbury and Margaret Thatcher in Moscow, Bassnett underscores their double bind: A woman holding political power, associated with the masculine, must still retain signs of femininity. She suggests that in the late sixteenth century, with the erosion of humanist social idealism's enlightened attitude toward women's role, their increasing marginalization in public life is traceable in Shakespeare's highly popular *Henry VI* plays. She maintains that in these works concerned with political instability women are associated with attitudes, emotions, and actions exemplifying unwomanliness, unqueenliness, and various violations of the natural order.

E88

Belkin, Roslyn. "Prisoners of Convention: Ibsen's 'Other' Women." *Journal of Women's Studies in Literature* 1 (1979): 142–58.

Belkin argues that despite Ibsen's understanding of society's oppression of women, all of his female characters (except, to some extent, Nora of *A Doll's House*) are convention-bound and seek fulfillment through men rather than struggling for independence. *When We Dead Awaken*, *An Enemy of the People*, *Hedda Gabler*, and *Rosmersholm* are among the works examined.

E89

Belsey, Catherine. "Alice Arden's Crime." *Renaissance Drama* ns 13 (1982): 83–102.

This study of *Arden of Faversham* within its historical context is an earlier version of Chapter 5 in Belsey's book, *The Subject of Tragedy*. See E8. *Terms:* criminality, female; divorce; marriage.

E90

Berg, Elizabeth. "Impossible Representation: A Reading of *Phèdre*." *Romanic Review* 73 (1982): 421–37.

Challenging phallocentric criticism's traditional interpretation of *Phèdre* through Hippolyte's eyes, Berg aligns herself with Racine's title character. Underscoring Phèdre's dilemma in having to hide herself in order to show herself, she dissects a system of representation that gives man an image while effacing or disfiguring woman. Her analysis draws attention to the entangled, asymmetrical relationship between *les voiles* (Phèdre's veils), part of the stage setting, and *la voile* (Hippolyte's sail), a symbol. This asymmetry is repeated in the main characters, who do not exist in the same space (are incommensurable) yet are doubles. Berg's conclusions involve the irreconcilability of classicism and the representation of women.

E91

Berger, Harry. "Against the Sink-a-Pace: Sexual and Family Politics in *Much Ado About Nothing*." *Shakespeare Quarterly* 33 (1982): 302–13.

Berger explores the characters' attitudes toward love and marriage. He also investigates the gender ideology of the play, including the concept that male deception and inconstancy are God-given gifts.

E92

Berggren, Paula S. " 'Womanish' Mankind: Four Jacobean Heroines." *International Journal of Women's Studies* 1 (July–Aug. 1978): 349–62.

The author argues that the powerless, economically dependent, and sexually vulnerable heroines of *The White Devil, The Duchess of Malfi, The Changeling,* and *Women Beware Women* "define a Jacobean view of the human condition." She also contrasts Webster's and Middleton's attitudes toward the willful female.

E93

Beston, Rose Marie. "Women in Australian Drama: *White with Wire Wheels* and *Jugglers Three*." *Literary Half-Yearly* 18.1 (1977): 41–50.

Regarding contemporary Australian plays as revealing documents of a male-dominated society, Beston compares two prominent playwrights whose works are marked by hostility both between men and between men and women. She contends that Jack Hibberd (*White with Wire Wheels*) demonstrates a sympathetic understanding of women's subordinate position, whereas David Williamson (*Jugglers Three*) offers no corrective viewpoint to his male characters' antagonism toward women.

E94

Birdwell, Christine. "The Passionate Purity That Led to Domesticity: Heroines of Repertoire Comedy-Drama." *Journal of American Culture* 10.2 (1987): 49–53.

Birdwell shows how the chaste, morally superior heroines of comedy-drama between 1900 and 1940 reflect the coexistence of old and new attitudes toward women. She underscores the plays' reinforcement of the conservative, multigenerational audience's vision of the desirable community. George Broadhurst's *Bought and Paid For*, Ted and Virginia Maxwell's *The Hoodlum*, *Tildy Ann* (no author given), and Bob Feagin's *The Governor's Lady* are discussed.

E95

Bita, Lila. "The Position of Women in Greek Drama." *Southern Theatre* 21.3 (1978): 3–7.

Reminding readers that they must interpret characters such as Clytemnestra and Medea—women who "have shaped . . . our concept of the feminine"—through the masculine consciousness of their creators, Bita applies modern psychology to her analysis. She notes that men's fear of women's power over them can be alleviated by possessing women as victims, a self-defeating process resulting in dreams of feminine vengeance.

E96

Blair, Rhonda. "A White Marriage: Rozewicz's Feminist Tragedy." *Slavic and East European Arts* 3.1 (1985): 13–21.

In her analysis of *A White Marriage*, a play that runs counter to the heavily androcentric Polish theatre in its focus on a feminist tragic hero, Blair describes the protagonist's struggle to define herself in a hostile environment and her eventual defeat.

E97

Boa, Elizabeth. "Der Gute Mensch von Barnhelm: The Female Essence and the Ensemble of Human Relations in Lessing's *Minna von Barnhelm*." *Publications of the English Goethe Society* 54 (1984): 1–36.

Boa approaches the play in the context of eighteenth-century ideas and ideals concerning women. She also assesses how it measures up in its period as an emancipatory work and how it reads in relationship to today's feminist debate. Among her assertions is that the play shows masculinity and femininity as embedded in social conditions.

E98
Boose, Lynda E. "The Comic Contract and Portia's Golden Ring." *Shakespeare Studies* 20 (1988): 241–54.

Boose argues that the fulfillment of the "comic contract" through the formulaic closure of marriage not only dramatizes a model of social harmony but "more importantly . . . re-presents the ultimate wedding between play and audience and thus fulfills the generic obligations of comic form." Demonstrating that Shakespeare questions the terms of both indentures, she focuses on the comic heroine, "the figure on whose body both contracts are written," as his "most potent strategy for appropriating the debt structure and subverting both its contractual terms."

E99
Boose, Lynda E. "The Father and the Bride in Shakespeare." *PMLA* 97 (1982): 325–47.

Investigating Shakespeare's use of the marriage ceremony as a dramatic substructure in depicting father-daughter relationships, Boose notes that the ritual seems designed to control the problem dramatized in the actions of most of Shakespeare's fathers, who want, consciously or unconsciously, "to retain, withhold, lock up, and possess" their daughters.

E100
Borker, David, and Olga K. Garnica. "Male and Female Speech in Dramatic Dialogue: A Stylistic Analysis of Chekhovian Character Speech." *Language and Style* 13.4 (1980): 3–28.

Focusing on the evolution of a specific character type in two plays by Chekhov, the authors analyze Masha Shamrayeva in *The Seagull* and Masha Kulygina in *Three Sisters*. They compare the speech patterns of these characters with one another and with those of other characters to determine the extent to which sex differentiation is reflected in male and female language usage. Applying their methodology to Turgenev's *A Month in the Country* as well, they find that Chekhov creates a more androgynous (or at least individualized character) speech.

E101

Bower, Martha. "The Cycle Women and Carlotta Monterey O'Neill."
The Eugene O'Neill Newsletter 10.2 (1986): 29-33.

Contending that in contrast to most of O'Neill's female characters, the
women in the Cycle plays "achieve a self-determination, an independence of spirit and an uncharacteristic ability to succeed" in the male
business world, Bower also maintains that the pattern of sex role reversal in these plays seems to coincide with the playwright's relationship
with Carlotta Monterey.

E102

Brown, Janet, and Pamela Loy. "Cinderella and Slippery Jack: Sex Roles
and Social Mobility Themes in Early Musical Comedy." *International Journal of Women's Studies* 4 (Nov.–Dec. 1981): 507–16.

The authors demonstrate how musical comedy of the early twentieth
century, excelling at the depiction of popular cultural fantasies, offered
the "tired businessmen" audience reassurance against fears of mass im-
migration, changing morals, and women's increased independence.
Brown and Loy's content analysis reveals that in contrast to physically
active male characters who rise in status through luck or bravery, the essentially passive females rise through beauty plus hard work in humble
service positions.

E103

Busette, Cedric. "Libido and Repression in García Lorca's Theatre."
Themes in Drama 7 (*Drama, Sex and Politics*) (1985): 173–82.

Asserting that Lorca's plays, which deal with freedom on a number of
levels, "constitute a plea for recognition of the victimized status of
women," Busette focuses on the long-suffering women in *Blood Wedding*, *Yerma*, *The House of Bernarda Alba*, and *Mariana Pineda*.

E104

Carlson, Susan. "Women in *As You Like It*: Community, Change, and
Choice." *Essays in Literature* 14 (1987): 151–69.

Taking the position that Shakespeare's comedy presents more restrictions than possibilities for its women, Carlson weighs the illusory female freedom of *As You Like It*'s middle section, manifested in
Rosalind's linguistic skill and friendship with Celia, against the ending's
return to the "'norm'-al" world. Carlson's examination of the play's
conclusion considers the relationship between marriage and social
change.

E105

Carlson, Susan L. "Women in Comedy: Problem, Promise, Paradox."
  Themes in Drama 7 (*Drama, Sex and Politics*) (1985): 159–71.

Carlson maintains that comedy's bottom-line message is the preservation of the known social order and that the promise of power and freedom offered its women characters is at best a paradox. She illustrates
her arguments with an analysis of Maugham's *The Constant Wife*. Her
conclusion focuses on contemporary female playwrights' experimentation with forms and the creation of nonsexist dramas that joyously celebrate life.

E106

Case, Sue-Ellen. "Classic Drag: The Greek Creation of Female Parts."
  Staging Gender. Spec. issue of *Theatre Journal* 37 (1985): 317–27.

Case summarizes the scholarship that resulted in the current feminist
view that images of women in classical plays represent a patriarchally
constructed fiction ("Woman") that actually suppresses the experiences
of real-life women. In tracing the development of a Greek theatre that
denied women the power of representation, she examines the Athenian
economic and legal practices that reduced women to objects of exchange and the creation of cultural institutions that became allied with
this oppression of women through the construction of polar categories
of gender privileging the masculine. Case provides a feminist reading
(against the text) of *The Oresteia* trilogy and establishes that Aristotle's
Poetics excludes women both from the category of tragic subject and
from the dramatic experience itself.

E107

Charney, Maurice, and Hanna Charney. "The Language of Madwomen
  in Shakespeare and His Fellow Dramatists." *Signs* 3 (1977): 451–60.

Analyzing the depiction of madwomen in *Hamlet* and other Elizabethan plays, the authors delineate the signs of madness (e.g., loose hair,
singing, childlike speech, preoccupation with repressed sexuality, broken syntax, lyrical free association) demanded by the period's conventions. They conclude that stage madness "releases the emotional and
imaginative powers that the saner women . . . are required to suppress."

E108

Cholakian, Patricia Francis. "The Itinerary of Desire in Molière's *Le Tar-
  tuffe*." *Theatre Journal* 38 (1986): 165–79.

With reference to the writing of Freud/Lacan and Derrida, Cholakian
identifies Molière's female characters as fictitious male constructs

embodying the message that "women function most desirably when reduced to silence." In addition to distinguishing the female stereotypes who populate Orgon's family—phallic mother, hysterical daughter, and narcissistic wife—she analyzes the vocal servant Dorine, who refuses to accept her traditional place in the patriarchal hierarchy but ceases to function as a speaking subject when she is revealed as a desirable woman. Cholakian argues that Dorine, representing Molière's viewpoint, serves the playwright's desire "to reinforce his comedy's patriarchal message."

E109
Cholakian, Patricia Francis. " 'The Woman Question' in Molière's *Misanthrope*." *The French Review* 58 (1985): 524–32.

Cholakian's investigation of *Le Misanthrope*'s female characters reveals discourse as their main tool in masking themselves to compensate for their inferior status in relationship to men. She demonstrates how the women, lacking autonomous identity and validating their existence only through male admiration, deprive language of its denotive meaning and overload it with connotative meaning, resulting in a breakdown of communication between the sexes.

E110
Clark, Larry D. "Female Characters on the New York Stage in the Year of Suffrage: Enter Advocacy, Quietly, Stage Left." *Theatre History Studies* 7 (1987): 51–60.

After surveying the traditional, boring roles allotted women in most of the plays produced in 1920, Clark examines two works that transcend the female stereotype to "create women who face important issues in unpredictable ways": *He and She* by Rachel Crothers and *Jane Clegg* by St. John Ervine.

E111
Clark, Sandra. "*Hic Mulier, Haec Vir*, and the Controversy over Masculine Women." *Studies in Philology* 82 (1985): 157–83.

Clark provides the literary and historical background for the controversy, which reached its height in the early 1620s. *The Roaring Girl* by Dekker and Middleton and *Love's Cure, or The Martial Maid* by Fletcher (and possibly Massinger) are among the plays examined.

E112
Cohen, Derek. "The Revenger's Comedy: Female Hegemony in *The Country Wife*." *Atlantis* 5.2 (1980): 120–30.

Exploring the dramatic uses of women and the meanings of their responses to Horner, Cohen underscores the play's theme of sexual subjugation.

E113

Cohen, Walter. " 'None of Woman Born': Shakespeare, Women, and Revolution." *Shakespeare-Jahrbuch* 124 (1988): 130–41.

Combining Marxist and feminist approaches, Cohen views Shakespeare from the perspective of the English Revolution to clarify both the relationship between women and the Revolution and that between Shakespeare's tragedies and the Revolution. Cohen concentrates on *Macbeth*, which "ratifies patriarchal aristocracy," declaring that the play's misogynistic rhetoric and logic, associated with male fears of female sexuality and assertiveness, "are ultimately directed against the potentially revolutionary practices of poor women." He generalizes that the tragedies anticipate the Revolution's left wing more closely on class than on gender matters.

E114

Conroy, Peter V. "Marivaux's Feminist Polemic: *La Colonie*." *Eighteenth-Century Life* 6.1 (1980): 43–66.

Conroy maintains that despite a disappointing ending in which no political or social results are produced by the women's fight for equality, Marivaux's play powerfully presents issues of women's rights and exposes potential traps that must be avoided by groups seeking change.

E115

Conroy, Peter V. "Marivaux's *The Colony*." *Signs* 9 (1983): 336–60.

Conroy's introduction to his translation of *The Colony* stresses the playwright's sensitivity to women's rights.

E116

Cook, Carol. " 'The Sign and Semblance of Her Honor': Reading Gender Difference in *Much Ado About Nothing*." *PMLA* 101 (1986): 186–202.

In contrast to critical readings, which find *Much Ado*'s sexual conflict resolved "in a thematic movement that privileges the feminine and provides moral closure," Cook argues that Messina's masculine ethos survives unchanged at the end. Cook's psychoanalytical examination of the cuckold jokes as an expression of male anxiety about women's potential power reveals their telling as a means of restoring the male prerogative. She also contrasts Beatrice's unthreatening appropriation of masculine language and wit with Hero's silence and vulnerability, which pose painful reminders to the men "of the sexual difference that is really a mirror."

E117
Cook, Carol. "Unbodied Figures of Desire." *Theatre Journal* 38 (1986): 34–52.

Dissecting the skewed relation between desire and its objects, which infects both the love and the war plots of *Troilus and Cressida*, Cook focuses on such issues as the operations by which women are produced as objects, Helen and Cressida as fetishized signs, and the impossibility of representing that which provokes desire. She also discusses the structure of homosexual desire inherent in the play, the instability of identity, and Cressida's recognition of the textuality of her existence.

E118
Curtin, Kaier. "Roaring Twenties Scandal: Yiddish Lesbian Play Rocks Broadway." *Lilith* 19 (1988): 13–14.

This piece on Sholom Asch's *The God of Vengeance* (*Gott fun Nekoma*) is excerpted from Curtin's book, *We Can Always Call Them Bulgarians*. See A5. *Term:* images of women, lesbian.

E119
Curtis, Julia. "A Virgin and a Whore: Fantasies of Witkiewicz." *Slavic and East European Arts* 3.1 (1985): 51–54.

Curtis's study of the principal female characters in *Tropical Madness* and *The Madman and the Nun* reveals that both are basic female stereotypes of Western culture who function in the plot as sexual decoys.

E120
Daalder, Joost. "Shakespeare's Attitude to Gender in *Macbeth*." *A.U.M.L.A.: Journal of the Australasian Universities Modern Language Association* 70 (1988): 366–85.

Cautioning against the notion of a universal Renaissance attitude toward women, Daalder holds that Shakespeare's own view is complex but not indecisive; rather, his plays express a belief in vital physical differences between the sexes that consequently cause significant psychological distinctions. She considers the symbolic significance of the play's discrepancy regarding Lady Macbeth's having had a child as well as Macbeth's preoccupation with children and its relationship to his violence.

E121

Dammers, Richard H. "The Female Experience in the Tragedies of Nicholas Rowe." *Women and Literature* 6.1 (1978): 28–35.

Dammers argues that Rowe shares modern playwrights' sensitivity toward women and their unfair treatment in a repressive society. Plays discussed include *The Tragedy of Jane Shore*, *The Royal Convert*, and *The Fair Penitent*.

E122

Das, Manini. "The World or I: Ibsen's Nora." *Manushi* 2 (Mar.–Apr. 1979): 59.

Declaring that the problems presented in *A Doll's House* are still relevant today, the author suggests using the play as a starting point for discussion by women's groups.

E123

Dash, Irene G. "A Penchant for Perdita on the Eighteenth-Century English Stage." *Studies in Eighteenth-Century Culture* 6 (1977): 331–46.

This essay on *The Winter's Tale* is reprinted with revisions in Lenz, Greene, and Neely's *The Woman's Part*. See E36. *Terms:* family, women's roles in, wives; images of women, dependent.

E124

Daugherty, Margaret. "Women in Euripides' Moral Quest." *San Jose Studies* 4.1 (1978): 73–81.

Daugherty contends that Euripides, disillusioned with Greek worship of the rational and usually aggressive male figure, deliberately used women as his main characters to serve as "beacons for what man is capable of being: inner directed, compassionate, creative, sincere." Plays examined include *Medea*, *The Trojan Women*, and *Helen*.

E125

Davidson, Clifford. "Women and the Medieval Stage." *Women in the Middle Ages*. Spec. issue of *Women's Studies* 11 (1984): 99–113.

Davidson maintains that despite the pervasive antifeminism of the Middle Ages, often displayed in the English cycle plays, certain female characters, particularly the Virgin Mary and St. Anne, were presented with enormous admiration, and saint plays about other women (e.g., the Digby *Mary Magdalene*) displayed a larger range of feminine experience. He also reexamines the belief that women were excluded from

dramatic activity, pointing to the playwriting of Hrotsvitha and Hilde-
garde of Bingen and the participation of others within the convent, and
citing the evidence of actresses in the English vernacular plays.

E126

Deats, Sara Munson. "*Edward II*: A Study in Androgyny." *Ball State
University Forum* 22.1 (1981): 30–41.

Deats analyzes the combination of "masculine" and "feminine" traits in
Isabella and other characters in Marlowe's play.

E127

Dejanikis, Mimi. "Women Against Pornography Protest *Lolita* Adaptation." *Off Our Backs* Apr. 1981: 13.

The author outlines the objections of Women Against Pornography to
Edward Albee's adaptation of the Vladimir Nabokov novel. Under attack
are the "Lolita syndrome" (eroticized images of little girls in the media)
and the play's misrepresentation of the effects of sexual abuse.

E128

Dolan, Jill. " 'What, No Beans?' Images of Women and Sexuality in Burlesque Comedy." *Journal of Popular Culture* 18.3 (1984): 37–47.

Dolan applies a psychoanalytical analysis to burlesque humor's underlying preoccupations with women and sex to support her contention that
"by reducing relations between men and women to extremely unsubtle,
routinized, recognizable categories, burlesque comedy helped men as-
suage their guilt, frustration and fear." She divides the comic bits' focus
into six well-illustrated categories: wives (in sketches involving money
or arguments), the rural/city split, mothers and mothers-in-law, adultery, overt sex, and men killing women.

E129

Drucker, Trudy. "Lillo's Liberated Women." *Restoration and 18th Century Theatre Research* 1.2 (1986): 42–43.

Drucker briefly surveys several female characters who use their intelligence in managing their lives.

E130

Drucker, Trudy. "Sexuality as Destiny: The Shadow Lives of O'Neill's
Women." *The Eugene O'Neill Newsletter* 6.2 (1982): 7–10.

Classifying recurrent female types in O'Neill's work, Drucker proposes
that his "inability to distinguish virgin from whore reflects the generally

faulty sense of identity shared by most of his women." She contrasts his narrowly sexual view of women, whose aspirations and achievements are focused on relationships with men, to the male characters' ability to function in work and dream in every imaginable sphere.

E131
DuBois, Page. "A Disturbance of Syntax at the Gates of Rome." *Stanford Literature Review* 2 (1985): 185–208.

DuBois draws a parallel between the double bind of the woman scholar, who must break from her male teachers, and that of Coriolanus, heir of a single parent of the opposite sex. She describes how *Coriolanus* questions the principle of linear order, with "breaks in descent, in lineage, breaks in city walls, breaks in bodies." She also places Shakespeare's critique of matriarchal power in a historical context.

E132
DuPlessis, Rachel Blau. "In the Bosom of the Family: Contradiction and Resolution in Edward Albee." *Minnesota Review* ns 8 (1977): 133–45.

Focusing mainly on *Who's Afraid of Virginia Woolf?*, *The American Dream*, and *A Delicate Balance*, DuPlessis investigates the ways in which Albee privatizes social problems pertaining to work, power, and success—problems for which no solutions are offered—and transforms them into sexual and family strife capable of being resolved through male domination.

E133
Durán, Gloria. "*Orchids in the Moonlight*: Fuentes as Feminist and Jungian Playwright." *World Literature Today* 57 (1983): 595–98.

Durán states that for the first time in Fuentes' work female archetypes are examined from women's viewpoints rather than from the perspective of a male protagonist. She also reports on the shortcomings of the American Repertory Theatre's production of *Orchids*.

E134
Eaton, Sara. "Beatrice-Joanna and the Rhetoric of Love in *The Changeling*." *Theatre Journal* 36 (1984): 371–82.

Eaton demonstrates how Middleton and Rowley's play connects the male problem of knowing women, the confusion between feminine being and seeming, to the rhetoric of Courtly Love, and in so doing "displays its linguistic exchanges as a drama of sexual revenge leaving the deaths of impure women to be 'prized.' " In her discussion of Beatrice-

Joanna, Eaton analyzes the character's mirroring of male desires and discourse.

E135
Erickson, Peter. "Patriarchal Structures in *A Winter's Tale*." *PMLA* 97 (1982): 819–29.

This article is an earlier version of Chapter 5 in Erickson's book, *Patriarchal Structures in Shakespeare's Drama*. See E19. *Terms:* male bonding; mother-son relationships; patriarchy; sexual politics.

E136
Erickson, Peter. "Sexual Politics and the Social Structure in *As You Like It*." *Massachusetts Review* 23 (1982): 65–83.

This article is an earlier version of Chapter 1 in Erickson's book, *Patriarchal Structures in Shakespeare's Drama*. See E19. *Terms:* patriarchy; sexual politics.

E137
Fawcett, Mary Laughlin. " 'Such Noise as I Can Make': Chastity and Speech in *Othello* and *Comus*." *Renaissance Drama* ns 16 (1985): 159–80.

Fawcett investigates how both Shakespeare's tragedy and Milton's masque treat the connection between women's speech and chastity. She details five parallel "inward structures": the positing of chastity as an essence; the effect of the idea of chastity on the central female character's sense of autonomy and how the male antagonist limits her sphere; the woman's movement from echoism to a larger verbal arena; the replacement of the muted central woman at the climax by another woman who speaks for her; and the appropriation of the chastity-speech theme by the male artist.

E138
Ferris, Dianne. "Elizabeth I and *Richard II*: Portraits in 'Masculine' and 'Feminine' Princes." *International Journal of Women's Studies* 4 (Jan.–Feb. 1981): 10–18.

The author argues that Elizabeth's belying of the female stereotype and the rationale for male rule created societal tensions reflected in early Shakespearean plots denigrating independent women. Focusing on *Richard II*, whose title character is a paradigm of feminine frailty, she notes: "If Shakespeare's hidden message was that women do not belong on the throne, Elizabeth could read it as well as any man in England."

E139

Finke, Laurie A. "Painting Women: Images of Femininity in Jacobean Tragedy." *Theatre Journal* 36 (1984): 357–70.

In an exploration of the dialectical notions of femininity—woman as ideal and as memento mori—in Tourneur's *Revenger's Tragedy*, Webster's *Duchess of Malfi*, and Ford's *'Tis Pity She's a Whore*, Finke contends that the plays reflect the authors' simultaneous participation in and calling into question "the Renaissance's cultural repression of the feminine and its concomitant assertion of masculine power." She distinguishes the ways in which the Jacobean heroine is victim of two kinds of "painting": man painting woman ("killing her into art") and woman painting herself (to conform to men's image of her).

E140

Fischetti, Renate. "A Feminist Reading of Brecht's Pirate Jenny." *Communications from the International Brecht Society* 14.2 (1985): 29–33.

Assessing Brecht's patriarchal view of women and reinforcement of sexist stereotypes in the *Threepenny Opera* and other works, the author argues that "his work stopped short of recognizing that the ills of capitalist society are tied to the ills of patriarchy."

E141

Fitz, L. T. [Linda Woodbridge]. "Egyptian Queens and Male Reviewers: Sexist Attitudes in *Antony and Cleopatra* Criticism." *Shakespeare Quarterly* 28 (1977): 297–316.

Fitz claims that almost all critical approaches to the play have been colored by sexist assumptions and shows how these attitudes have distorted Shakespeare's meaning. Specific biases cited include the following: the comparison of Cleopatra with only female characters and the view of Cleopatra as the archetypal woman; the damning of her character because of her frank sexuality; judgment of Cleopatra's and Antony's respective actions according to a double standard; and the assumption that Antony is the sole protagonist.

E142

Forsyth, Louise. "First Person Feminine Singular: Monologues by Women in Several Modern Quebec Plays." *Women in Canadian Drama*. Spec. issue of *Canadian Drama* 5 (1979): 189–203.

Forsyth cites the significance of Michel Tremblay's eleven-play cycle as marking a new phase in Quebec theatre, bringing new insight into the Quebec family and the push for self-determination. She notes that all

Tremblay's characters in *Les Belles Soeurs* and *Damnée Manon sacrée Sandra* are female, and that he gives the female monologue importance as a mode of dramatic expression. Subsequently, Forsyth considers the varied ways in which monologues are employed by Antonine Maillet (*La Sagouine*), Jean Barbeau (*Solange*), Claude Roussin (*Une Job*), Michel Garneau (*Quatre à quatre*), Serge Mercer (*Elle*), and Jean-Claude Germain (*Les Hauts et les bas de la vie d'une diva: Sara Ménard par eux-mêmes*). She uses this study to analyze themes that include women's victimization in "the violence inherent in a social system based on privilege," the Church's role in perpetuating the status quo, suppression of female sexual desire, and the solitude of the Quebec family that results from "a pervasive atmosphere of distrust and hatred." She also examines the exploration of creativity in female monologues with a theatre stage for their setting.

E143
Frey, Charles. "Shakespeare's Imperiled and Chastening Daughters of Romance." *South Atlantic Bulletin* 43.4 (1978): 125–40.

This essay, which deals with *Pericles*, *Cymbeline*, *The Winter's Tale*, *The Tempest*, *The Two Noble Kinsmen*, and *Henry VIII*, appears with revisions in Lenz, Greene, and Neely's *The Woman's Part*. See E36. *Terms:* chastity, female; family, women's roles in, daughters; father-daughter relationships; marriage; nature, women and; patriarchy.

E144
Friedman, Edward. "The Thorns on the Roses: A Reading of Benavente's *Rosas de Otoño*." *International Journal of Women's Studies* 4 (Mar.–Apr. 1981): 168–72.

Friedman argues that although Benavente's protagonist, the suffering wife Isabel, has been seen as a symbol of female superiority, the character of Maria Antonia, who demands a system of sexual equality, offers an opposing perspective and provides the basis for an ironic interpretation of the play.

E145
Furst, Lilian R. "No Bed of Roses: The Women in the *Rosenkavalier*." *Jahrbuch fur Internationale Germanistik* 16.1 (1984): 116–20.

Challenging dominant male interpretations of Hofmannsthal's play, Furst explicates how the iconography of roses and beds denotes two prevailing attitudes toward women: the idealization of womanhood in the moral sphere and the subjugation and exploitation of women on the social level. She determines that Hofmannsthal's sentimental depiction of women paradoxically represents another form of victimization, as they are obliged "to fulfil the expectation imputed to them through superhuman acts of renunciation and self-sacrifice in the name of human generosity."

E146

Garner, S[hirley] N[elson]. "Shakespeare's Desdemona." *Shakespeare Studies* 9 (1976): 233–52.

Garner attempts to correct critical misreadings of Desdemona based on the assumption that she ought to be perfect. Maintaining that the tragedy's meaning depends on a clear vision of Desdemona's complexities, in addition to those of Othello and Iago, she analyzes Desdemona's sensuality and courage in marrying Othello as well as her gradual decline into passivity.

E147

Gohlke, Madelon [Madelon Sprengnether]. " 'And When I Love Thee Not': Women and the Psychic Integrity of the Tragic Hero." *Hebrew University Studies in Literature* 8 (1980): 44–65.

Asserting that the patriarchal organization of Shakespeare's works makes them "susceptible to sensitive reading through patriarchally organized systems of interpretation," Gohlke uses psychoanalytic theory to study how tragic heroes "invest women with the capacity either to organize or to disorganize their psychic universe." In each play examined, she finds that the woman's unreadability combined with her infidelity (real or imagined) produces anxiety, disorientation, or madness in the hero. She also addresses the problems of the feminist reader in working with texts and interpretive approaches that privilege masculinity and marginalize femininity.

E148

Gossett, Suzanne. " 'Best Men Are Molded Out of Faults': Marrying the Rapist in Jacobean Drama." *Women in the Renaissance*. Spec. issue of *English Literary Renaissance* 14 (1984): 305–27.

Gossett relates alterations between 1594 and 1624 in the depiction of rape to changes in social mores and dramatic form. Distinguishing between the unambiguous moral condemnation of rape in the conventionally plotted tragedies and the subsequent tragicomedies' view of rape as a sexual impulse controllable by marriage, she observes that "rape becomes a comic error cured by being brought into the social order." She notes the traditional pattern's restoration at the end of the period.

E149

Gourlay, Patricia Southard. " 'O My Most Sacred Lady': Female Metaphor in *The Winter's Tale.*" *English Literary Renaissance* 5 (1975): 375–95.

The author analyzes the ideal qualities represented by Hermione, Paulina, and Perdita, "who suggest the subversive and creative power of love, art, and nature" and triumph over what the masculine social order takes for its truth.

E150

Greco, Norma A. "Sexual Division and Revision in *The Merchant of Venice.*" *Pennsylvania English* 9.1 (1982): 39–45.

Greco suggests that the play is about the need for the individual to unite "masculine" and "feminine" elements within the self and for society to integrate the inner sphere of the emotions and spirit into the public realm.

E151

Green, Douglas E. "The 'Unexpressive She': Is There Really a Rosalind?" *Journal of Dramatic Theory and Criticism* 2.2 (1988): 41–52.

Arguing against the possibility of escaping from Shakespeare's "masculine imagination" or Elizabethan theatrical conventions privileging the male, Green reveals the falsity of Rosalind's apparent freedom and underscores her function as a commodity of exchange. He further submits that Rosalind is a male projection, inhabiting the stage "solely as a variable object of desire"; or, if she does exist in the world of the play, it is as mediator and fulfiller of desires as they accord with patriarchal institutions.

E152

Greene, Gayle. " 'This That You Call Love': Sexual and Social Tragedy in *Othello.*" *Journal of Women's Studies in Literature* 1 (1979): 16–32.

Locating the source of Othello's and Desdemona's tragedy in the accepted ideals of masculinity and femininity that circumscribe both, Greene examines the flaws in the couple and their love. She says that by not defying Othello, Desdemona is an accomplice in their destruction.

E153

Greene, Gayle. "Women on Trial in Shakespeare and Webster: 'The Mettle of [Their] Sex.' " *Topic: A Journal of the Liberal Arts* 36 (*The Elizabethan Woman*) (1982): 5–19.

Characterizing Shakespeare as essentially conservative in the roles he allots women in the various genres, Greene contends that women in the tragedies "are even more relational, incidental, and carry heavier symbolic burdens than in comedy." She contrasts Shakespeare's tragic vision with Webster's "greater intimation of chaos," suggesting that perhaps "this is what is necessary to disrupt the hierarchical ideal and allow woman prominence in so significant a genre as tragedy; that is, woman assumes prominence in significant spheres when the very notion of significance has been drained." Her analysis of the bold heroines of *The White Devil* and *The Duchess of Malfi* illustrates Webster's wider, less conventional conception of female value and behavior.

E154

Greene, Gayle, and Carolyn Ruth Swift, eds. *Feminist Criticism of Shakespeare*. Spec. issue of *Women's Studies* 9.1 (1981).

Greene's brief introduction notes the contradictory aspects of Shakespeare's depiction of women and men. Three of the articles directly concern theory: Carol Thomas Neely's "Feminist Modes of Shakespearean Criticism: Compensatory, Justificatory, Transformational," Marianne Novy's "Demythologizing Shakespeare," and Greene's "Feminist and Marxist Criticism: An Argument for Alliances." The relationship of comedy to the power of patriarchy is investigated in Shirley Nelson Garner's "*A Midsummer Night's Dream*: 'Jack Shall Have Jill;/Nought Shall Go Ill'" and Peter B. Erickson's "The Failure of Relationship between Men and Women in *Love's Labor's Lost*." David Sundelson's "Misogyny and Rule in *Measure for Measure*" explores male fear of female power, and Judith Wilt's "Comment on David Leverenz's 'The Woman in *Hamlet*'" surveys the banishment of the female and her return as fury or healer in selected plays.

E155

Greene, Gayle, and Carolyn Ruth Swift, eds. *Feminist Criticism of Shakespeare II*. Spec. issue of *Women's Studies* 9.2 (1982).

In her introduction, Greene comments on the essays' investigation of the gender-genre relationship and the place of feminist criticism in determining Shakespeare's connection to the received ideas of his culture. Marilyn L. Williamson's "Doubling, Women's Anger, and Genre" examines Shakespeare's doubling of passive heroines with assertive women of lower social status. Martha Andresen-Thom's "Shrew-Taming and Other Rituals of Aggression: Baiting and Bonding on the Stage and in the World" analyzes the transformation from aggression to bonding between men and women in *Shrew*. Anne Parten's "Re-Establishing Sexual Order: The Ring Episode in *The Merchant of Venice*" suggests that the business of the rings "acts as focus for the unresolved—and potentially explosive—issue of the heroine's power." Also included are Madelon Gohlke's " 'All That Is Spoke Is Marred': Language and Consciousness in *Othello*," which argues that the portrayal of tragic male and female characters stems from Shakespeare's exploration of male sexual anxiety; " 'Behind a Dream': Cleopatra and Sonnet 129," wherein Barbara L. Estin asserts that Cleopatra begins "with a knowledge that love jeopardizes security and concludes in the triumph of having taken its risk"; and Peter B. Erickson's review of Marilyn French's *Shakespeare's Division of Experience*. Georgianna Ziegler provides "A Supplement to the Lenz-Greene-Neely Bibliography on 'Women and Men in Shakespeare.' "

E156
Greiner, Norbert. "Mill, Marx and Bebel: Early Influences on Shaw's Characterization of Women." *Shaw Review* 18 (1975): 10–17.

A revised version of this essay appears in *Fabian Feminist: Bernard Shaw and Women*, edited by Rodelle Weintraub. See E72. *Terms:* feminism(s), influence on/relationship to men's playwriting; marriage; sex/gender roles.

E157
Grennan, Eamon. "The Women's Voices in *Othello*: Speech, Song, Silence." *Shakespeare Quarterly* 38 (1987): 275–92.

Determining that *Othello* is not only a play *of* voices but also *about* voices, Grennan argues that the women characters' speech, song, and silence are critical elements in understanding the moral experience of the work.

E158
Guilfoyle, Cherrell. " 'Ower Swete Sokor': The Role of Ophelia in *Hamlet*." *Comparative Drama* 14 (1980): 3–17.

Examining the strands of the Mary Magdalen legends woven into Ophelia's words and actions, the author shows how this imagery illuminates the succor the pure Ophelia can offer through atonement as well as Hamlet's delusion of female wantonness. Particular attention is drawn to Ophelia's mad scene.

E159
Hess, Linda. "The Poet, the People, and the Western Scholar: Influence of a Sacred Drama and Text on Social Values in North India." *Feminist Diversions*. Spec. issue of *Theatre Journal* 40 (1988): 236–53.

Hess's study of the Ramlila, an Indian sacred drama based on the work of the sixteenth-century poet-saint Tulsidas and presented in a month-long production in Ramnagar, concentrates on messages regarding gender and caste. She includes samples of interviews exploring audience reception of text and performance, and comments on her role as a cross-cultural scholar.

E160

Hoover, Claudette. "Goneril and Regan: 'So Horrid as in Woman.' " *San Jose Studies* 10.3 (1984): 49–65.

Opposing the critical view of Lear's elder daughters as symbols rather than individualized characters or even dramatic types, Hoover shows how Shakespeare drew from various sources in their creation, rejecting some feminine characteristics and exploiting others. She argues that similar to Lear, "whose imagination is shackled by myths about the nature of women, we succumb (however periodically and briefly) to the myths, dramatic traditions, and stereotypes that the playwright evokes, and we share Lear's dismay when we discover that the seductively familiar proves inadequate" to explain Goneril's and Regan's evil.

E161

Hopwood, Alison. " 'Hey What's That From?'—Edward Albee's *Who's Afraid of Virginia Woolf?*" *Atlantis* 3.2 (Part 1) (1978): 100–111.

The author proposes that the numerous allusions to myth, history, and literature and the parallels to action in other plays combine to reveal the patriarchal ideology that underlies Albee's drama. She contends that the central action of the play is George's assertion of supremacy.

E162

Howard, Jean E. "Crossdressing, the Theatre, and Gender Struggle in Early Modern England." *Shakespeare Quarterly* 39 (1988): 418–40.

Positioning herself within materialist feminism, Howard examines female cross-dressing both in real-life practice and on the stage. She declares that while cross-dressing threatened the patriarchal social order, its subversive potential was recuperated in several ways and its meaning varied according to circumstances. She investigates the ideological implications of cross-dressing and whether constructions of woman that challenge her subordinate place in the sex/gender system are presented in the following works: Jonson's *Epicoene*, Middleton and Dekker's *The Roaring Girl*, and Shakespeare's *Twelfth Night, The Merchant of Venice,* and *As You Like It.*

E163

Huebert, Ronald. " 'An Artificial Way to Grieve': The Forsaken Woman in Beaumont and Fletcher, Massinger and Ford." *ELH* 44 (1977): 601–21.

The Maid's Tragedy, The Duke of Milan, and *The Broken Heart* illustrate Huebert's thesis that the actions of the abandoned woman in Jacobean and Caroline tragedy affect the shape of the plays and that her voice is at least partly "a cry of protest against a social order and a masculine world that expects and condones only stereotypical female behavior." He opines that while this character is a theatrical convention, she is not merely a stereotype, despite persistent critical treatment of the "forsaken maid" as an amorphous class.

E164

Hume, Robert D. "Marital Discord in English Comedy from Dryden to Fielding." *Modern Philology* 74 (1977): 248–72.

Hume suggests that the playwrights' attitudes toward marriage offer a key to the shifting ideologies underlying the transition from seventeenth- to eighteenth-century comedy. Surveying numerous works, he discerns two different structures in marital discord comedy: one "comprising a movement to reconciliation, higher harmony, personal and social felicity" and the other, more rare, springing from "a recognition of the intractability of the problem" and moving only to impasse. He concludes by contrasting Dryden's skepticism in *Marriage à la Mode* (1671) and Fielding's realistic optimism in *The Modern Husband* (1732).

E165

Hunter, Dianne. "Doubling, Mythic Difference, and the Scapegoating of Female Power in *Macbeth*." *Psychoanalytic Review* 75 (1988): 129–52.

Fusing psychoanalytic feminist and contextual criticism to explore Shakespeare's analogies between psychological dynamics and political processes, Hunter perceives *Macbeth* as a patriarchal myth associating "the dissolution of differences that inheres in father-son succession with illegitimate violence, preoedipal fluidity, and sterile female power." She states that by portraying the unnaturalness of gender confusion, *Macbeth* mediates the masculinist contradiction that "man depends on woman for birth but must get rid of her in order to be (re)born."

E166

Hurst, Mary L. "Shakespeare, Chaucer, and 'False Cressida': A Reinterpretation." *Shakespeare and Renaissance Association of West Virginia: Selected Papers* 8 (1983): 1–8.

Hurst delineates the way in which Shakespeare's treatment of Cressida differs from that of Chaucer and others and finds that he provides his character with the spirit and strength to survive despite her vulnerability in a male-dominated world.

E167

Hyslop, Gabrielle. "Deviant and Dangerous Behavior: Women in Melodrama." *Journal of Popular Culture* 19.3 (1985): 65–77.

Contending that Pixérécourt's melodramas aim at imposing the values of the dominant social class, Hyslop shows how his patriarchal outlook affects the depiction of women (i.e., their moral purity binds family and society, they act within primarily domestic situations, and they tend to be physically weak). She contrasts the predominant heroine-victim image with those active heroines who move in the public arena, noting that despite their deviant, powerful behavior, male dominance is upheld.

E168

Jackson, Gabriele Bernhard. "Topical Ideology: Witches, Amazons, and Shakespeare's Joan of Arc." *Women in the Renaissance II.* Spec. issue of *English Literary Renaissance* 18 (1988): 40–65.

Jackson argues against previous readings of *Henry VI*'s (Part I) Joan as a harsh caricature and emphasizes how the play's topicality complicates this picture. Citing Shakespeare's characteristic presentation of "unexplained and suggestive discontinuities"—in this case, allowing Joan to perform inconsistent ideological functions in the various phases of her portrayal—she dissects the play and its ambiguous use of culturally powerful images within the context of contemporary history: the English expedition to France, the controversy over women's nature, the vogue for stage Amazons, the real-life fad of women's cross-dressing, Queen Elizabeth's appearance in armor in Tilbury, and King James's Scots witchcraft trials.

E169

Jardine, Lisa. "Cultural Confusion and Shakespeare's Learned Heroines: 'These Are Old Paradoxes.' " *Shakespeare Quarterly* 38 (1987): 1–18.

Through a study of *All's Well That Ends Well* and *The Merchant of Venice*, plays in which heroines use specialized knowledge in traditionally male fields, Jardine investigates the ambivalence about "woman's place" in Renaissance intellectual life. She discerns two versions of the cultural response to the educated woman: "the version of her as powerfully chaste and loyal in her emblematic capacity as woman *virilis animi*" and "the version of her as threateningly unruly and disorderly in her indecorous articulateness and sexual 'knowingness.'"

E170
Jordan, Constance. "Gender and Justice in *Swetnam the Woman-Hater.*" *Renaissance Drama* ns 18 (1987): 149–69.

Maintaining that the anonymously authored *Swetnam*'s purpose was not only to silence the misogynist but also to criticize patriarchalism "as a system of thought and social order," Jordan focuses on the concept of androgynous justice explored in the play.

E171
Juneja, Renu. "Eve's Flesh and Blood in Jonson's *Bartholomew Fair.*" *Comparative Drama* 12 (1978–79): 340–55.

The author examines the centrality and complexity of the women characters and Jonson's sympathetic understanding of the social realities faced by women, particularly regarding marriage.

E172
Juneja, Renu. "Widow as Paradox and Paradigm in Middleton's Plays." *Journal of General Education* 34 (1982): 3–19.

Juneja argues that Middleton's presentation of widows, whether manipulated or manipulating, reflects his concern with the social and cultural causes of their behavior and forces the audience to question its assumptions about women. He reviews the ways in which Middleton dramatizes the widow-hunt and the treatment of the widow as a commodity in *A Trick to Catch the Old One; The Widow; No Wit, No Help like a Woman's; More Dissemblers besides Women;* and *Women Beware Women.*

E173
Kahn, Coppélia. "Coming of Age in Verona." *Modern Language Studies* 8.1 (1977–78): 5–22.

This essay on *Romeo and Juliet* appears with revisions in Lenz, Greene, and Neely's *The Woman's Part* (see E36) and in Chapter 4 of Kahn's *Man's Estate* (see E34). *Terms:* family; patriarchy; sexuality, female; violence, masculinity and.

E174

Kahn, Coppélia. " 'Magic of Bounty': *Timon of Athens*, Jacobean Patronage, and Maternal Power." *Shakespeare Quarterly* 38 (1987): 34–57.

In an essay inspired by psychoanalytically oriented feminist criticism and the new historicism, Kahn explores the play's "core fantasy" of maternal bounty and betrayal. She explicates the ways in which this fantasy is made intelligible through the grammar afforded by the period's practice of patronage, entailing gift-giving and usury.

E175

Kahn, Coppélia. "*The Taming of the Shrew*: Shakespeare's Mirror of Marriage." *Modern Language Studies* 5.1 (1975): 88–102. (Rpt. in *The Authority of Experience: Essays in Feminist Criticism*. Ed. Arlyn Diamond and Lee R. Edwards. Amherst: University of Massachusetts Press, 1977. 84–100.)

This essay appears in an altered version in Chapter 4 of Kahn's book, *Man's Estate*. See E34. *Terms:* father-daughter relationships; images of women, shrew; marriage; patriarchy; stereotypes, male; women, dehumanization of, woman as object/currency, etc.; violence, female; violence, masculinity and.

E176

Kehler, Dorothea. "Echoes of the Induction in *The Taming of the Shrew*." *Renaissance Papers* (1986): 31–42.

In recovering a subversive subtext of *Shrew*, Kehler traces two themes initiated in the Induction: the "elusiveness and exorbitant price of love" and the societally approved views of woman as property, child, and beast.

E177

Kenny, Shirley Strum. "Elopements, Divorce, and the Devil Knows What: Love and Marriage in English Comedy, 1690–1720." *South Atlantic Quarterly* 78 (1979): 84–106.

Kenny finds comedy's new interest in marriage—an emphasis on values in courtship and mutuality—a reflection of real-life developments at the turn of the eighteenth century. She argues that the subject effected changes in the nature of comedy, including a shift from satire to a more compassionate view of life. Among the playwrights surveyed are Cibber, Congreve, Farquhar, Steele, and Vanbrugh.

E178
Kimbrough, Robert. "Androgyny Seen Through Shakespeare's Disguise."
   Shakespeare Quarterly 33 (1982): 17–33.

Defining androgyny as "a psychic striving for an ideal state of personal wholeness," Kimbrough states that the impulses toward a recognition and realization of androgyny run throughout Shakespeare's plays. *As You Like It* and *Twelfth Night* provide illustration.

E179
Kimbrough, Robert. "Macbeth: The Prisoner of Gender." *Shakespeare Studies* 16 (1983): 175–90.

Arguing that androgyny is an ideal goal, Kimbrough claims that Shakespeare's work attempts to break down barriers between the sex-genders. Demonstrating that despite Macbeth and Lady Macbeth's alienating behavior, a bond is maintained with the audience, he contends that "we are moved through pity to understand and to fear the personal and social destructiveness of polarized masculinity and femininity."

E180
Konrad, Linn B. "Father's Sins and Mother's Guilt: Dramatic Responses to Darwin." *Themes in Drama* 7 (*Drama, Sex and Politics*) (1985): 137–49.

An assessment of the treatment of issues of heredity and environment in Ibsen's *Ghosts* and Daudet's *The Obstacle* leads the author to conclude that the mother figures can be seen as a warning about the failure to realize potential for a full life.

E181
Kowsar, Mohammad. "In Defense of Desire: Chimène's Role in *Le Cid* Reconsidered." *Theatre Journal* 34 (1982): 289–301.

Kowsar disagrees with the notion that Corneille's heroine is immobilized between love and duty; rather, she operates "from the platform of desire by actively and critically examining the code of conduct by which the race of patriarchs justifies itself." He suggests that the improbable, hysterical behavior that violates her characterization's consistency results from the playwright's concession to popular taste.

E182
Kuhn, Anna K. "Peter Hacks' *Ein Gespräch im Hause Stein über den abwesenden Herrn von Goethe*: A Feminist Reinterpretation of the *Geniebegriff*?" *Germanic Review* 60 (1985): 91–98.

In this essay on Hacks' play dealing with the relationship between Charlotte von Stein and Goethe, the author demonstrates how von Stein's condemnation of male behavior, although insightful regarding the inequity between the sexes, is only superficially feminist. In addition to pointing out ways in which Hacks ironically calls into question von Stein's reliability, she also remarks on women's status in the German Democratic Republic in real life and in drama.

E183

Leinwand, Theodore B. " 'This Gulph of Marriage': Jacobean City Wives and Jacobean City Comedy." *Women's Studies* 10 (1984): 245–60.

Examining the comedies' city wives within the context of Jacobean ideology about women, Leinwand notes how the plays simultaneously expose and participate in contemporary prejudices. Discussed are *Westward Ho* by Dekker and Webster, *The Roaring Girl* by Dekker and Middleton, and *The Woman's Prize, or The Tamer Tamed* by Fletcher.

E184

Lennox, Sara. "Brecht, Feminism and Form: Theses toward a Feminist Reutilization of Brecht." *Communications from the International Brecht Society* 13.1 (1983): 16–19.

Lennox calls for a feminist reutilization of Brecht to "elaborate those dimensions of his work which challenge and subvert dominant structures of instrumental reason." She suggests that feminist productions of Brecht "act the characters against the grain," supplementing them with dimensions other than Brecht's conceptions, and stress the tendencies toward a counter-discourse.

E185

Lennox, Sara. "Women in Brecht's Work." *New German Critique* 14 (1978): 83–96.

While Lennox points out the limitations of Brecht's characterization of women and concern with women's issues, emphasizing that even in terms of Brecht's own dramatic theories his plays seem to perpetuate women's oppression, she finds that his works contain in rudimentary form and contrary to his conscious intentions elements demonstrating women's subversive potential.

E186

Lester, Elenore. "Ibsen's Unliberated Heroines." *Scandinavian Review* 66.4 (1978): 58–66.

Lester contends that although feminism engaged Ibsen's intellect, it did not inform his most profound artistic images. Her survey of Ibsen's plays, with particular attention to *The Vikings at Helgeland, Rosmersholm*, and *Hedda Gabler*, shows that rather than seeking an independent existence, most of his major female characters live *through* men.

E187

Leverenz, David. "The Woman in Hamlet: An Interpersonal View." *Signs: Journal of Women in Culture and Society* 4 (1978): 291–308. (Rpt. in *Representing Shakespeare: New Psychoanalytic Essays*. Ed. Murray Schwartz and Coppélia Kahn. Baltimore, Md.: Johns Hopkins University Press, 1980. 110–28.)

Determining that the play's patriarchal order "has cracked all the mirrors for self-confirmation," Leverenz relates Hamlet's confusion to the dichotomies characterizing his world (and ours): male-female, role-self, reason-nature, mind-body, and language of power-language of feeling.

E188

Lowe, Lisa. " 'Say I Play the Man I Am': Gender and Politics in *Coriolanus*." *Kenyon Review* 8.4 (1986): 86–95.

Lowe dismisses both the critical interpretation of *Coriolanus* as a metaphor for England's political problems and the feminist psychoanalytic focus on the mother-son dyad as too narrow. She investigates the coexistence of political and gender dramas in the play "as a description of how social and political conflicts are both reflected in, and informed by, gender conflict within the family." Lowe suggests that Coriolanus and Volumnia, as well as other members of the community, "assume, perform, and develop the violent warrior ethos which already circulates" within the play's language.

E189

Luckyj, Christina. "Great Women of Pleasure: Main Plot and Subplot in *The Duchess of Malfi*." *Studies in English Literature, 1500–1900* 27 (1987): 267–83.

The author reviews past critical and performance interpretations in her reassessment of the role of Julia. She contends that the Julia subplot transcends functions of either foil or parody, serving instead as a mirror for the main action. She further argues that Webster's linking of Julia and the Duchess underscores women's vulnerability in a hostile male world and challenges antifeminist stereotypes about female sexuality.

E190

Lug, Sieglinde. "The 'Good' Woman Demystified." *Communications from the International Brecht Society* 14.1 (1984): 3–16.

In her analysis of Brecht's discrediting of clichés about women, Lug looks at the stereotype of woman's pure goodness, woman's role as polar opposite to that of man, and the myth of motherhood with all its emotional connotations. *The Good Person of Sezuan, Mother Courage*, and *The Caucasian Chalk Circle* are examined.

E191

MacCurdy, Raymond R. "Women and Sexual Love in the Plays of Rojas Zorrilla: Tradition and Innovation." *Hispania* 62 (1979): 255–65.

MacCurdy outlines the manifestation of Rojas's feminism in the rebellion of his heroines against forced marriages, their rejection of the honor code's double standard, and their assertion of intellectual and spiritual equality with men. Arguing for Rojas's ability to adopt a woman's viewpoint, MacCurdy analyzes several characters' free expression of sexuality. He illustrates Rojas's "feminist and erotic tendencies" with an examination of *La vida en el ataúd*, focusing particularly on its linking of love and death.

E192

McEachern, Claire. "Fathering Herself: A Source Study of Shakespeare's Feminism." *Shakespeare Quarterly* 39 (1988): 269–90.

Criticizing previous avenues of feminist inquiry into Shakespeare as positing a mimetic-deterministic relationship between art and society, and noting recent trends toward investigating the contradictory play of cultural texts, McEachern recommends working toward a historicized notion of gender and the consideration of literary text as an agent of change. She proposes to examine Renaissance patriarchy by studying fathers and daughters, including Shakespeare's literary fathers and his father and daughter characters. Detailing Shakespeare's modifications of sources for *Much Ado About Nothing* and *King Lear*, she shows how he explores the profound contradiction underlying patriarchy: the conflict between family and political loyalties. She argues that in separating his identity from that of his literary authority, Shakespeare (like his daughter characters) "defies the control of patriarchy."

E193

McLennan, Kathleen A. "Woman's Place: *Marriage* in America's Gilded Age." *Staging Gender*. Spec. issue of *Theatre Journal* 37 (1985): 345–56.

McLennan's reading of Steele MacKaye's 1872 drama reveals not only the playwright's revolt against the conventions of melodrama but also his critique of the Genteel Tradition, laissez-faire capitalism, and Social Darwinism, all of which combined to suppress women and imprison them in the ideology of domesticity. *Marriage*'s attempt to redefine "womanliness" and "manliness" is assessed.

E194

McLuskie, Kathleen. "Drama and Sexual Politics: The Case of Webster's Duchess." *Themes in Drama* 7 (*Drama, Sex and Politics*) (1985): 77–91.

The author demonstrates how the form and structure of *The Duchess of Malfi*, in which the "descriptions of character and moral judgments pronounced in set speeches are tested by realistic action which exposes their internal contradiction," question the ideology of oppression. She also analyzes how production attempts that emphasize emotional realism militate against the audience's understanding of the play's sexual politics.

E195

Mandl, Bette. "Absence as Presence: The Second Sex in *The Iceman Cometh*." *The Eugene O'Neill Newsletter* 6.2 (1982): 10–15.

Mandl maintains that the invisibility of the offstage significant female characters, Evelyn and Rosa, brings into relief their purpose in O'Neill's play and intensifies their "otherness." She suggests that in this work, "the women tend to be merely representative of that which men struggle with and against in enacting their destinies."

E196

Matlack, Cynthia S. "'Spectatress of the Mischief Which She Made': Tragic Woman Perceived and Perceiver." *Studies in Eighteenth-Century Culture* 6 (1977): 317–30.

This discussion of pathetic tragedy, particularly by Rowe and Otway, centers around the polarization of female roles and the union of eroticism and didacticism. Matlack points out that sexual liaison violating a father's authority largely determines the plot and the culpable woman's tragic fate.

E197

Mattes, Eleanor. "'The Female Virtuoso' in Early Eighteenth Century English Drama." *Women and Literature* 3.2 (1975): 3–9.

Mattes surveys several plays, including Thomas Wright's *The Female Vertuoso's*, which ridicule women's scientific curiosity and caricature the ways in which the virtuosa deviates from her expected female role. She notes that although Susanna Centlivre's *The Basset-Table* presents an exception to the unsympathetic portrait of these women, the playwright's attitude is tolerant rather than supportive.

E198

Maus, Katharine Eisaman. "Horns of Dilemma: Jealousy, Gender, and Spectatorship in English Renaissance Drama." *ELH* 54 (1987): 561–83.

In the context of the period's conception of the theatrical experience, particularly as expressed in the antitheatricalists' fusion of aesthetic and erotic excitement and the traditional association of female promiscuity and theatrical display, Maus examines the complex connection between jealous male characters' voyeurism and theatrical spectatorship.

E199

Mellick, Margo J. V. "Mid-Victorian Plays: A Source for Divergent Female Images." *Theatre Studies* 23 (1976-77): 31–39.

Mellick calls for setting aside preconceptions about serious Victorian drama, its audiences, and its images of women who, she argues, are not universally idealized. Classifying four categories of divergent heroines, she concentrates on the female characters who play traditional male roles and the phenomenon of sex role reversal.

E200

Miller, Jeanne-Marie A. "More Than a Servant in the House: Black Female Characters in American Drama, A Sketch." *Theatre News* Apr. 1978: 6–7.

Citing works by both white and black playwrights, Miller discusses negative stereotypes and more favorable images of black women on stage, the impact of the 1960s civil rights movement on playwriting, and the need for dramas realistically depicting the lives of black middle-class women.

E201

Miller, Milton. "A Contrary Blast: Milton's Dalila." *Themes in Drama* 7 (*Drama, Sex and Politics*) (1983): 93–108.

Noting the extremely varied critical interpretations of the contradictory Dalila of *Samson Agonistes*, Miller states that Milton's characterization not only touches on the Renaissance figure of the temptress but also incorporates the dimension of the seventeenth-century women with

225

"newly perceived possibilities of an independent moral status." Shakespeare's Cleopatra is used for comparison and contrast.

E202
Moss, Jane. "Living with Liberation: Quebec Drama in the Feminist
    Age." *Atlantis* 14.1 (1988): 32–37.

Moss focuses on Jean Barbeau's *Les Gars*, a reexamination of the relationship between the sexes that exemplifies how male dramatic discourse of the 1980s has changed in response to feminism. Also discussed is an earlier antifeminist work, *Citrouille*. In addition, Moss surveys recent plays by several other men in which new male roles are explored.

E203
Mowat, Barbara A. "Images of Woman in Shakespeare's Plays." *Southern
    Humanities Review* 11 (1977): 145–57.

Mowat distinguishes three superimposed images of Shakespeare's women: an unbiased image created by their actions and words, what other characters say about them and their depiction in relationship to significant males, and a shifting image corresponding to Shakespeare's personal view. Concentrating on the second category, Mowat traces male characters' fantasies and fears about women, often viewed as mythically powerful. Delineating differences among the genres, she demonstrates how at times the male image of woman ("other") is comically or grotesquely different from the real woman, while at other times it relates ambiguously to or coincides with the figure it reflects.

E204
Myrsiades, Linda Suny. "The Female Role in the Karaghiozis Performance." *Southern Folklore Quarterly* 44 (1980): 145–63.

This study of Greek shadow puppet theatre emphasizes the restricted range and number of female roles. Myrsiades draws three sets of distinctions: between female figures in comedy and those in history or tragicomedy, between the depiction of women in older plays borrowed from a Turkish prototype and in performances after Karaghiozis became hellenized, and between the rural folk view and the newer urban-cosmopolitan view of women. She examines at length the dominant role of Karaghiozaina (the nagging wife).

E205
Neely, Carol Thomas. "Women and Issue in *The Winter's Tale*." *Philological Quarterly* 57 (1978): 181–94.

This is an earlier version of Chapter 5 in Neely's book, *Broken Nuptials in Shakespeare's Plays*. See E50. *Terms:* nature, women and; pregnancy/childbirth; sexuality, female.

E206

Neely, Carol Thomas. "Women and Men in *Othello*: 'What Should Such a Fool/Do with So Good a Woman?' " *Shakespeare Studies* 10 (1977): 133–58.

This article is reprinted with revisions in Lenz, Greene, and Neely's *The Woman's Part*. See E36. Chapter 3 of Neely's book, *Broken Nuptials in Shakespeare's Plays*, offers a somewhat different version. See E50. *Terms:* friendship, female; identity, male; love, romantic; sexuality, female.

E207

Nelson, Doris. "O'Neill's Women." *The Eugene O'Neill Newsletter* 6.2 (1982): 3–7.

Nelson establishes that O'Neill defines his male characters' humanity through their social roles and his female characters solely through their biological roles or relationships to men. After considering issues of work and domesticity in several plays, she concentrates on Nina's search for fulfillment in *Strange Interlude*.

E208

Newman, Karen. "Portia's Ring: Unruly Women and Structures of Exchange in *The Merchant of Venice*." *Shakespeare Quarterly* 38 (1987): 19–33.

Newman finds that the play exemplifies both the exchange system described by Lévi-Strauss, in which the exchange of women is the basis of social life, and the French feminist critique of that system, which "exposes it as a strategy for insuring hierarchical gender relations." In tracing the movements of Portia's ring as it accumulates meanings and associations and examining how Portia transgresses the ideal of a lady to become an "unruly woman," Newman delineates *Merchant*'s interrogation of the Elizabethan sex/gender system.

E209

Newman, Karen. "Renaissance Family Politics and Shakespeare's *The Taming of the Shrew*." *English Literary Renaissance* 16 (1986): 86–100.

In a study of the troubled gender relations characterizing Elizabethan and Jacobean society, Newman connects historians' findings regarding anxieties about rebellious women to Katherine's threat to male authority, a threat posed through language. Newman asserts that discourse is power, both in the real world and in the play's fictional space. She further argues that although *Shrew* demonstrates Elizabethan patriarchal ideology, "*representation* gives us a perspective on that patriarchal system which subverts its status as natural."

E210
Nornhold, Susan E. "Portrait of a Woman: A Predictable Drama." *English Journal* Mar. 1985: 52–53.

The author briefly reviews the negative depiction of women in selected American plays from the 1920s through the 1960s.

E211
Novy, Marianne. "'And You Smile Not, He's Gagged': Mutuality in Shakespearean Comedy." *Philological Quarterly* 55 (1976): 178–94.

This article is reprinted with revisions as Chapter 2 in Novy's book, *Love's Argument*. See E52. *Terms:* love, romantic; mutuality.

E212
Novy, Marianne. "Giving, Taking, and the Role of Portia in *The Merchant of Venice*." *Philological Quarterly* 58 (1979): 137–54.

This article is reprinted with revisions as Chapter 4 in Novy's book, *Love's Argument*. See E52. *Terms:* love, romantic; marriage; mutuality; sexuality, male; sexuality, female.

E213
Novy, Marianne. "Patriarchy and Play in *The Taming of the Shrew*." *English Literary Renaissance* 9 (1979): 264–80.

This article is reprinted with revisions as Chapter 3 in Novy's book, *Love's Argument*. See E52. *Terms:* family, women's roles in, wives; marriage; patriarchy.

E214
Novy, Marianne. "Patriarchy, Mutuality and Forgiveness in *King Lear*." *Southern Humanities Review* 13 (1979): 281–92.

This article is reprinted with revisions as Chapter 8 in Novy's book, *Love's Argument*. See E52. *Terms:* father-daughter relationships; mutuality; patriarchy; sex/gender roles.

E215

Novy, Marianne. "Shakespeare and Emotional Distance in the Elizabethan Family." *Theatre Journal* 33 (1981): 316–26.

Portions of this article appear in the introduction to Novy's book, *Love's Argument*. See E52. *Terms:* cross-dressing/gender crossing; family; love, romantic; sex/gender roles.

E216

Nussbaum, Laureen. "The Evolution of the Feminine Principle in Brecht's Work: Beyond the Feminist Critique." *German Studies Review* 8 (1985): 217–44.

Nussbaum attempts to paint a more complete picture of Brecht's women than that offered by Sara Lennox (see E185). Although acknowledging the limited roles of women in his early writing, she argues that after he embraced Marxism, he entrusted the charge to work for change to mother figures, who he felt "are often more able and willing than men to sacrifice in a productive and concretely down-to-earth way in order to nurture and foster growth."

E217

O'Brien, Susan. "The Image of Women in Tony-Award-Winning Plays, 1960–1979 [sic]." *Journal of American Culture* 6.3 (1983): 45–49.

Noting the ambivalent attitude toward women in the Tony-award winners of the 1960s, O'Brien discusses three of these plays that examine women's potential for self-realization: Williams' *The Night of the Iguana*, Hellman's *Toys in the Attic*, and Pinter's *The Homecoming*.

E218

Okerlund, Arlene N. "In Defense of Cressida: Character as Metaphor." *Women's Studies* 7 (1980): 1–17.

Okerlund reviews recent shifts in critical attitudes toward the characters in *Troilus and Cressida*, contending that stereotypical or simplified interpretations ignore the play's complex structure. Distinguishing Cressida, an initially innocent young woman who becomes a faithless dissembler and ultimately perpetuates her society's corruption, as the play's central metaphor, Okerlund suggests that her role "incarnates the process of evil in the world." She maintains that Cressida has provided a scapegoat to excuse evils that continue to plague society.

E219

Osherow, Anita R. "Mother and Whore: The Role of Woman in *The Homecoming*." *Modern Drama* 17 (1974): 423–32.

Osherow focuses on the dichotomized concept of woman in Pinter's play, wherein the men of the family respond to both Ruth and the dead Jesse as both mother and whore. She claims that Ruth becomes dominant by assuming this dual role and thereby achieves a kind of freedom.

E220
Paran, Janice. "Redressing Ibsen: Directors Fornes, Near and Mann Emancipate His Proto-Feminist Plays from Their Victorian Bonds." *American Theatre* Nov. 1987: 14–20.

Three women directors' interpretations of and production approaches to Ibsen's *A Doll's House* and *Hedda Gabler* are discussed.

E221
Park, Clara Claiborne. "As We Like It: How a Girl Can Be Smart and Still Popular." *The American Scholar* 42 (1973): 262–78.

This article, which concentrates on *Much Ado About Nothing, As You Like It,* and *The Merchant of Venice,* is reprinted with revisions in Lenz, Greene, and Neely's *The Woman's Part.* See E36. *Term:* images of women, intelligent.

E222
Parten, Anne. "Falstaff's Horns: Masculine Inadequacy and Feminine Mirth in *The Merry Wives of Windsor.*" *Studies in Philology* 82 (1985): 184–99.

Parten demonstrates how the play's climactic scene is shaped by the same attitudes and traditions that produced such ceremonies as the skimmington, a folk ritual that expressed a community's hostility toward a man who allowed an inversion of the normal sexual hierarchy.

E223
Paster, Gail Kern. "Leaky Vessels: The Incontinent Women of City Comedy." *Renaissance Drama* ns 18 (1987): 43–65.

Paster analyzes the representations of women needing to urinate in Jonson's *Bartholomew Fair* and Middleton's *A Chaste Maid in Cheapside* as manifestations of the contemporary construction of woman: "the weaker vessel as leaky vessel." She argues that the female characters, particularly in *Cheapside*, "reproduce a virtual symptomology of woman that insists on the female body's moistures, secretions, and productions as a shameful token of uncontrol."

E224

Pearson, D'Orsay W. "Male Sovereignty, Harmony and Irony in *A Midsummer Night's Dream.*" *The Upstart Crow* 7 (1987): 24–35.

Relating the ironic dual vision of feminine obedience embodied in the "Sermon on the State of Matrimony" to Shakespeare's comedy, Pearson contends that whereas the play's structure reinforces the rightness of male dominance as a source of harmony, individual male-female relationships suggest that "masculine sovereignty, or its illusion, results from trickery, from fiat, or from feminine will achieved."

E225

Pennington, Eric. "*La doble historia del doctor Valmy*: A View from the Feminine." *Symposium: A Quarterly Journal in Modern Foreign Literatures* 40 (1986): 131–39.

The author maintains that in addition to an outcry against torture, Antonio Buero Vallejo's play is an indictment of a savage patriarchy's treatment of women. He assesses Mary's killing her husband as a politically symbolic act of liberation and hope.

E226

Popovich, Helen. "Shelf of Dolls: A Modern View of Ibsen's Emancipated Women." *CEA Critic* 39.3 (1977): 4–8.

Popovich perceives that despite Ibsen's reputation for advocating women's emancipation, his women characters maintain traditional female roles and are defined by their relationship to male characters. *A Doll's House, Ghosts,* and *Hedda Gabler* are among the plays examined.

E227

Prandi, Julie D. "Goethe's Iphigenie as Woman." *Germanic Review* 60 (1985): 23–31.

Prandi offers a revision of the idealized saintly picture of Iphigenie and illustrates the extent to which sex-typed models of humanity are presented in *Iphigenie auf Tauris*.

E228

Rackin, Phyllis. "Androgyny, Mimesis, and the Marriage of the Boy Heroine on the English Renaissance Stage." *PMLA* 102 (1987): 29–41.

Analyzing five comedies that feature transvestite heroines in plots centering on marriage—Lyly's *Gallathea*; Shakespeare's *Merchant of Venice, As You Like It*, and *Twelfth Night*; and Jonson's *Epicoene*—Rackin investigates the connection between changing conceptions of the dramatists' art and increasingly rigid and negative ideas of gender and femininity. She also explores differences between Lyly's and Jonson's works, which "resolve the tensions between real sex and illusory gender," and those of Shakespeare, which sustain sexual ambiguity throughout.

E229
Rackin, Phyllis. "Anti-Historians: Women's Roles in Shakespeare's Histories." *Staging Gender*. Spec. issue of *Theatre Journal* 37 (1985): 329–44.

Rackin's delineation of the ways in which Shakespeare's women characters oppose and subvert the authority of the masculine historical record focuses on two works: *Henry VI*, Part I, which dramatizes the issue of physical reality vs. historical record as a conflict between English men and French women, and sustains historical myth against feminine challenge; and *King John*, which incorporates feminine forces, exposes the arbitrary nature of patriarchal succession, and re-presents historiography as a questionable construct.

E230
Ranald, Margaret Loftus. "Women and Political Power in Shakespeare's English Histories." *Topic: A Journal of the Liberal Arts* 36 (*The Elizabethan Woman*) (1982): 54–65.

Concentrating on three historical female characters, Margaret of Anjou, Constance of Brittany, and Katherine of Aragon, each of whom underscores a different aspect of women's roles as wives and mothers, Ranald argues that their only power lies in their command of language.

E231
Reiss, Timothy J. "Corneille and Cornelia: Reason, Violence, and the Cultural Status of the Feminine. Or, How a Dominant Discourse Recuperated and Subverted the Advance of Women." *Renaissance Drama* ns 18 (1987): 3–41.

In this study of the debate about the relation between gender and reason and its connection to the urgent discussions about the unstable political and social order (1540–1650), Reiss shows how several of Corneille's plays both articulate "the political optimism about women's rationality" and represent "the contours of its failure."

E232
Rhome, Frances Dodson. "Shakespeare's Comic Women: Or Jill Had Trouble with Jack!" *Ball State University Forum* 35.2 (1984): 20–28.

Rhome views Shakespeare's heroines' actions as expressing the period's changing attitudes toward women. While acknowledging that his comic heroines never exceed the bounds of what an Elizabethan audience would deem acceptable for a woman, she reveals how his treatment of female characters reflects a sense of emancipation and self-sufficiency. She also notes women's role as the agents of happiness and order.

E233

Richards, Sandra L. "Negative Forces and Positive Non-Entities: Images of Women in the Dramas of Amiri Baraka." *Theatre Journal* 34 (1982): 233–40.

Richards examines Baraka's male-dominated, misogynistic plays, wherein women fall into three general categories: the aggressive, evil white women; the neurotic, self-destructive black woman; and the bland mouthpiece for political ideology. She discusses the failure of his female characters to achieve self-definition and directorial opportunities to temper some of the plays' biases. The works studied include *Dutchman, The Slave, Madheart, Experimental Death Unit #1,* and *What Was the Relationship of the Lone Ranger to the Means of Production?*.

E234

Richmond, Velma Bourgeois. "Renaissance Sexuality and Marlowe's Women." *Ball State University Forum* 16.4 (1975): 36–44.

Remarking on the stereotyped portrayal of women in most of Marlowe's plays, Richmond argues that their more complex treatment in *Tamburlaine, Part I* and *Part II* reflects the residual values of Christianity and women's increasing importance in Elizabethan times. She underscores the contrast between the dominant world of male aggression and the women's valuing of gentleness and world view ordered toward eternity.

E235

Richmond, Velma Bourgeois. "Shakespeare's Women." *Midwest Quarterly* 19 (1977): 330–42.

Richmond sets her overview of Shakespeare's plays within a historical context and contends that he is "very much in favor of marriage." She suggests that his recognition of the private-public dichotomy and celebration of the personal "are perhaps his firmest embracing of the feminine," and points to the romances as "the final triumph of feminine roles."

E236

Riefer, Marcia. "'Instruments of Some More Mightier Member': The Constriction of Female Power in *Measure for Measure.*" *Shakespeare Quarterly* 35 (1984): 157–69.

Riefer observes that most of the comic heroines preceding Isabella function as surrogate dramatist figures who manipulate the plot and that the kind of powerlessness Isabella experiences is anomalous in Shakespearean comedy. The author traces the destruction of Isabella's sense of self through her encounters with patriarchal authority. She concludes that the play "ultimately demonstrates . . . the incompatibility of sexual subjugation with successful comic dramaturgy."

E237

Roberts, Jeanne Addison. "Making a Woman and Other Institutionalized Diversions." *Shakespeare Quarterly* 37 (1986): 366–69.

Roberts expresses concern with the effects of teaching the Shakespeare plays traditionally chosen for secondary school, which she considers as "indoctrinating young minds with the sacred writ . . . of patriarchal tradition, of immersing students in such powerful texts, observed through male eyes, focused on male problems and experience, and developed into a critical tradition shaped almost exclusively by male critics." She suggests teaching different plays, critically examining Shakespearean ideologies, and other strategies.

E238

Rogers, Elizabeth S. "The Abandoned Woman as Subject for Comedy in López Rubio and Mihura." *The USF Language Quarterly* 20.1–2 (1981): 44–48.

Rogers argues that López Rubio's *La venda en los ojos* and Mihura's *La bella Dorotea*, both depicting the pain of abandonment and society's insensitivity to women's conditions, contain the seeds of social awareness, although masked by absurdist humor, self-conscious theatricality, and optimistic endings involving true love.

E239

Rogers, Katharine M. "Masculine and Feminine Values in Restoration Drama: The Distinctive Power of *Venice Preserved.*" *Texas Studies in Language and Literature* 27 (1985): 390–404.

Contending that Otway's "unusual confidence in feminine values," which he does not use to elicit tears but affirms as valid in balance with masculine ones, distinguishes his play from other "she-tragedies," Rogers contrasts *Venice Preserved* with Nathaniel Lee's *Lucius Junius*

Brutus, Dryden's *All for Love*, and Otway's earlier play, *The Orphan*. She determines that "by the time he wrote *Venice Preserved*, he saw a larger significance in the victimization of women and...the consequences of neglecting the values they represent."

E240

Rose, Jacqueline. "Hamlet: The *Mona Lisa* of Literature." *Critical Quarterly* 28.1–2 (1986): 35–49.

This altered version of "Sexuality in the Reading of Shakespeare: *Hamlet* and *Measure for Measure*" in *Alternative Shakespeares* (see E57) also appears as Chapter 5 in Rose's book, *Sexuality in the Field of Vision* (London: Verso-New Left, 1986). *Terms:* criticism, bias in, gender bias; psychoanalytic theory; sexual difference; sexuality, female.

E241

Rose, Mary Beth. "Moral Conceptions of Sexual Love in Elizabethan Comedy." *Renaissance Drama* ns 15 (1984): 1–29.

This article, which deals with works by Lyly, Greene, and Shakespeare, appears in a revised version as the first chapter in Rose's book, *The Expense of Spirit*. See E58. *Terms:* desire, heterosexual; marriage; sexuality, female; sexuality, male.

E242

Rose, Mary Beth. "Women in Men's Clothing: Apparel and Social Stability in *The Roaring Girl*." *Women in the Renaissance*. Spec. issue of *English Literary Renaissance* 14 (1984): 367–91.

A revised version of this article appears as Chapter 2 in Rose's book, *The Expense of Spirit*. See E58. *Terms:* cross-dressing/gender-crossing; independence, female; sex/gender roles.

E243

Scoble, Fran Norris. "In Search of the Female Hero." *English Journal* Feb. 1986: 85–87.

Scoble urges changing the typical curriculum by including works by and about women, and by applying new perspectives to traditional offerings such as *Romeo and Juliet*. Defining the ability to choose while aware of risk as symbolizing maturity, she emphasizes how female and male students will benefit from reading about courageous, caring women.

235

E244
Segal, Charles. "The Menace of Dionysus: Sex roles and Reversals in Euripides' *Bacchae*." *Arethusa* 11 (1978): 185–202.

Segal analyzes the challenge to the ideals of the *polis* presented by Dionysus and by women, both of whom are associated with irrationality, occupy an ambiguous place between the human and the bestial, and are connected with the mysterious processes of nature. He suggests that Pentheus's tragedy "lies in the implicit recognition that the narrowly masculine orientation of this society is as destructive of male as of female self-realization."

E245
Shafer, Yvonne. "The Liberated Woman in Ibsen's *The Lady from the Sea*." *Women in Theatre*. Spec. issue of *Theatre Annual* 40 (1985): 65–76.

Examining Ibsen's study of marriage and women's need for freedom in *The Lady from the Sea*, Shafer comments on the contemporaneousness of Ibsen's concerns and the play's psychological elements.

E246
Shafer, Yvonne. "Restoration Heroines: Reflections of Social Change." *Restoration and 18th Century Theatre Research* 2.1 (1987): 38–53.

Shafer enumerates changes in the lives of seventeenth-century women, including their improved level of education, opportunities for earning a livelihood, and greater independence, particularly in choosing husbands. In her argument that women's increased freedom was mirrored in the comedies, she discusses works by Etherege, Wycherley, Congreve, Ravenscroft, and others.

E247
Shapiro, Susan C. "Shakespeare's View of Motherhood." *The CEA Forum* 8.4 (1978): 8–10.

Asserting that Shakespeare avoids female stereotypes except that of motherhood, Shapiro describes several of his "unnatural" women characters who take on masculine roles and fail to fulfill the motherhood ideal. She also remarks on Shakespeare's lack of exploration of "good" mothers' influence on their children's lives.

E248
Shaw, David. "*Les Femmes Savantes* and Feminism." *Journal of European Studies* 14 (1984): 24–38.

Shaw disputes criticism of Molière's play as antifeminist. Viewed within the context of the period and its attitudes toward the role of women, Shaw states, the satire is not aimed at the feminist movement but at a small group of pretentious middle-class women. He also underscores Molière's sympathy with women's rights regarding marriage.

E249

Sjogren, Christine O. "The Status of Women in Several of Lessing's Dramas." *Studies in Eighteenth-Century Culture* 6 (1977): 347–59.

Maintaining that Lessing's female characters reflect the position of women in the Age of Enlightenment, Sjogren finds that *Miss Sara Sampson* and *Emilia Galotti* express his criticism of society's oppression of women. *Minna von Barnhelm* is also briefly discussed.

E250

Snow, Edward. "Sexual Anxiety and the Male Order of Things in *Othello.*" *English Literary Renaissance* 10 (1980): 384–412.

Snow investigates the "pathological male animus toward sexuality," which underlies not only Othello's jealousy but also "the social institutions with which men keep women and the threat they pose at arm's length." He considers the play's tragedy to be Desdemona's inability to break out of "the restraints and Oedipal prohibitions that domesticate woman" to the patriarchal order.

E251

Snyder, Susan. "*All's Well That Ends Well* and Shakespeare's Helens: Text and Subtext, Subject and Object." *Women in the Renaissance II.* Spec. issue of *English Literary Renaissance* 18 (1988): 66–77.

Suggesting that the "gaps and disjunctions" associated with Helena's shifts between assertion and self-abnegation reflect the difficulty of representing a heroine as an actively desiring subject, Snyder connects the Helena of *All's Well* to the Helena of *A Midsummer Night's Dream*, explicating how their name "ironically contradicts its prototype" (i.e., Helen of Troy as pursued object). She proposes two interpretations of *All's Well*: a "safe" reading, which defuses the heroine's potential subversiveness by imputing agency to God, and a feminist interpretation, wherein female solidarity provides empowerment.

E252

Spivack, Charlotte. "The Duchess of Malfi: A Fearful Madness." *Journal of Women's Studies in Literature* 1 (1979): 122–32.

Tracing the ways in which Webster's courageous title character defies her tyrannical brothers, resists attempts to drive her into madness, and transfigures three male characters, Spivack declares that she "fulfills both the elementary and transformative nature of the feminine archetype."

E253
Stanton, Domna C. "Power or Sexuality: The Bind of Corneille's Pulchérie." *Women and Literature* 1 (1980): 236–47.

The author explores the phallocentric assumptions underlying the heroine's entrapment within the double bind of phallic power and feminine sexuality.

E254
Staton, Shirley F. "Female Transvestism in Renaissance Comedy: 'A Natural Perspective That Is and Is Not.'" *Iowa State Journal of Research* 56.1 (1981): 79–89.

Arguing for the interdependency of dramatic structure and Renaissance gender assumptions, Staton shows how cross-dressing is used in either of two ways: to free the heroine from conventional limitations by fusing feminine and masculine traits (Lyly's *Gullathea*, Shakespeare's *Merchant of Venice, As You Like It,* and *Twelfth Night*) or to reinforce patriarchal gender paradigms (Greene's *James IV*, Beaumont and Fletcher's *Philaster*, Shakespeare's *Two Gentlemen of Verona* and *Cymbeline*). She notes that all the plays discussed end with the heroine's unmasking and the restoration of the paternalistic world.

E255
Stephens, Judith L. "*Why Marry?* The New Woman of 1918." *Theatre Journal* 34 (1982): 183–96.

In analyzing Jesse Lynch Williams's protagonist, Stephens applies four characteristics commonly assigned to women (preoccupation with love, irrationality and emotionality, selfishness or selflessness, and passivity) as standards of comparison, then integrates these traits with four traditional dramatic criteria (motivation, deliberation, decision, and action). She concludes that Helen, although inadequate as a "New Woman," possibly represents a transitional character.

E256
Sturrock, June. "*Othello*: Women and 'Woman.'" *Atlantis* 9.2 (1984): 1–8.

Assessing Shakespeare's dramatic and ironic use of the English tradition of antifeminism in *Othello*, Sturrock shows how the women characters "compel our admiration partly for their command of the very virtues which Iago and the satirists believe them to lack."

E257

Templeton, Joan. "The Bed and the Hearth: Synge's Redeemed Ireland." *Themes in Drama* 7 (*Drama, Sex and Politics*) (1985): 151–57.

The author describes Synge's heroines as victims whose conflicts embody the possibilities for freedom from a restrictive society.

E258

Tiefenbrun, Susan. "Blood and Water in *Horace*: A Feminist Reading." *Papers on French Seventeenth Century Literature* 10.19 (1983): 617–34.

With two representative scenes from Corneille's tragedy for analysis, the author proposes to demonstrate how the blood and water metaphoric system generates the play's language; facilitates the perception of the female characters, Sabine and Camille, as symbols of the two sides of the Cornelian ethic; and "constitutes the source of a gender-related idiolect."

E259

Traub, Valerie. "Jewels, Statues, and Corpses: Containment of Female Erotic Power in Shakespeare's Plays." *Shakespeare Studies* 20 (1988): 215–38.

Traub draws on work by feminist, psychoanalytic, and new historical critics who have investigated the meanings of masculine anxiety toward female power in Shakespeare's plays to analyze the dramatic strategy of containment, which entails the metaphorical displacement of sexually threatening women into corpses, jewels, or statues, in *Hamlet*, *Othello*, and *The Winter's Tale*. She determines that Shakespeare "perpetuates defensive structures of dominance instituted by men."

E260

Vanita, Ruth. "Strengthening the 'Strong Man–Helpless Woman' Stereotype." *Manushi* 5 (May–June 1980): 26–27.

Reporting on four street plays on rape presented by three theatre groups in various Delhi (India) locations, Vanita expresses unhappiness at the depiction of women as victims and the reactions of predominantly male audiences. She distinguishes the one script written by a woman from the male-authored works that reflect patriarchal norms, noting its greater number of articulate females and highlighting of myths about rape.

E261

Vinkler, Beth Joan. "Character and Space in Two Tragedies by Bernardo Santareno." *Gestos: Teoria y practica del Teatro Hispanico* 3.6 (1988): 99–107.

In her study of *António Marinheiro (O Édipo de Alfama)* and *O Crime de Aldeia Velha*, Vinkler points out structural parallels to Greek tragedy. Detecting that in both plays a choral character conspires to destroy a female rebel to preserve the status quo, she explicates how Santareno's choice of women protagonists, personifying the interior space threatened by the outside, reinforces his expression of Portuguese society's repressiveness under Salazar's rule.

E262

Vlasopolos, Anca. "Authorizing History: Victimization in *A Streetcar Named Desire*." *Theatre Journal* 38 (1986): 322–38.

Vlasopolos contends that *Streetcar*, similar to earlier "problem plays" in its raising of questions concerning genre and ethics, as well as performance and audience response, makes explicit the issue of "the narrative authority of history-makers and story-tellers versus the dramatic representation of the victims of that authority." In her delineation of Blanche's "fall from authority" and the violence involved in her victimization, she discusses the undermining of Blanche's discourse by the play's action and Stanley's success in inscribing not only Blanche's past but her future. She concludes that *Streetcar*'s force "is to disquiet us so that perhaps we might hear, if not speak for, those whom history has silenced."

E263

Wayne, Valerie. "Refashioning the Shrew." *Shakespeare Studies* 17 (1985): 159–87.

Wayne demonstrates how both the Wakefield Master and Shakespeare transform the traditional shrew figure from "an unregenerate agent for discord" into "a regenerative agent for concord." She notes how their adaptation of this character calls into question the structures of patriarchal society and hierarchical marriage.

E264

Weintraub, Rodelle. "The Irish Lady in Shaw's Plays." *Shaw Review* 23 (1980): 77–89.

Weintraub suggests that Shaw's wife, Irish millionairess Charlotte Payne Townshend, provided a model for the independent women in many of his plays, including *Captain Brassbound's Conversion, Getting Married, Misalliance,* and *In Good King Charles's Golden Days.*

E265
Wexler, Joyce. "A Wife Lost and/or Found." *The Upstart Crow* 8 (1988): 106–17.

Declaring that through Derrida's "strategy of reversing and displacing polarities and his description of undecidability, feminist criticism can offer revisionary readings of classic texts," Wexler applies deconstructive techniques to *The Winter's Tale.* Shifting the emphasis from the strength of the hero to that of his wife, she addresses issues including Leontes' phallogocentrism, the representation of women's truth by silence, and particularly the significance of production choices in staging the play's textually undecidable ending.

E266
White, Helen. "Paths for a Flightless Bird: Roles for Women on the New Zealand Stage Since 1950." *Australasian Drama Studies* 3.2 (1985): 105–43.

In introducing her chronologically arranged essay, White remarks on the recent flowering of woman-oriented plays in New Zealand and differentiates between women's theatre ("a vehicle for women's communication and creativity") and feminist theatre. She surveys plays from 1950–65 (mostly male-authored), noting the dominance of realism, the centrality of male characters, and the few true-to-life depictions of married women that reveal their domestic imprisonment. She subsequently focuses on 1965-75, when the dominant successful mode was comedy and satire in which women's parts tended to be stereotypical and reflect their "otherness." While citing some exceptions, White stresses the rare appearance of women's viewpoints challenging traditional conceptions of "women's roles." The final section, covering 1975–84, traces themes of parenthood, the increased range of theatrical styles, and the inclusion of women's experience in drama. She also comments on the necessary versatility of women actors.

E267
Williamson, Marilyn L. "'When Men Are Ruled by Women': Shakespeare's First Tetralogy." *Shakespeare Studies* 19 (1987): 41–59.

Williamson argues that Shakespeare and the chroniclers of the Wars of the Roses mitigated the horror of civil war "by displacing much of the opprobrium for the conflicts on a series of women."

E268
Wood, John A. "The 'Female Eunuch': An Eighteenth-Century Ideal." *McNeese Review* 26 (1979–80): 40–46.

To examine the indoctrination into subservience and "neutering" of women in English society and drama between 1675 and 1725, Wood considers three plays: Wycherley's *The Country Wife*, Cibber's *Love's Last Shift*, and Steele's *The Conscious Lovers*. He theorizes that sexist playwrights of sentimental drama popularized an image of society's ideal woman "to a degree it might not have otherwise known" and thus "share responsibility with those they pandered to" for creating a myth that has debilitated women.

E269
Worthington, Bonnie. "Ryga's Women." *Women in Canadian Drama*. Spec. issue of *Canadian Drama* 5 (1979): 139–43.

The author offers insights into George Ryga's "vision of woman as a socially impotent animal" in *Sunrise on Sarah* and *The Ecstasy of Rita Joe*.

E270
Zeitlin, Froma I. "The Dynamics of Misogyny: Myth and Myth-Making in the *Oresteia*." *Arethusa* 2 (1978): 149–84.

Zeitlin contends that Aeschylus presents civilization as a product of conflict between opposing forces, particularly the male-female, achieved through a hierarchization of values. Demonstrating that the *Oresteia* poses social evolution as a movement from female to male dominance, Zeitlin explicates the "basic dilemma posed by the female—the indispensable role of women in fertility for the continuity of the group by the reason of her mysterious sexuality and the potential disruption of that group by its free exercise" and the establishment of patriarchal marriage as a means of subordinating women and reaffirming patrilineal succession.

E271
Zeitlin, Froma I. "Playing the Other: Theater, Theatricality, and the Feminine in Greek Drama." *Representations* 11 (1985): 63–94.

In an investigation of the connections between Athenian tragedy and the culturally defined "feminine" in society's sex/gender system, Zeitlin systematically discusses four theatrical elements: the representation of the body on stage; the architectural space that "suggests a relational tension between inside and outside"; the plot; and theatrical mimetism, in terms of role-playing and disguise. In reference to the last-named element, she suggests that "the final paradox may be that theater uses the feminine for the purposes of imagining a fuller model for the masculine self, and 'playing the other' opens that self to those often banned emotions of fear and pity." Sophocles' *Trachiniae*, Euripides' *Bacchae*, and other plays are used in illustration. The essay concludes with discussions of Aristophanes' lampooning of Euripides' "feminized" tragedies and Plato's views on drama and gender.

E272
Zeitlin, Froma I. "Travesties of Gender and Genre in Aristophanes' *Thesmophoriazousae.*" *Critical Inquiry* 8 (1981): 301–28. (Rpt. in *Writing and Sexual Difference*. Ed. Elizabeth Abel. Chicago: University of Chicago Press, 1982. 131–57.)

Exploring the play from the dual perspectives of the topos of role inversion ("women on top") and the self-reflectiveness of art concerned with the nature of mimesis, Zeitlin maintains that Aristophanes poses an "intrinsic connection between the ambiguities of the feminine and those of art." She addresses issues of gender and genre, transvestism, parody, art and the literary tradition, and eros and art.

Performers/Performance Issues/ Performance Art

Books and Monographs

F1

Auerbach, Nina. *Ellen Terry: Player in Her Time.* New York: Norton, 1987.

This comprehensive study of Terry's life and art traces Terry from nineteenth-century child actress in "boy" parts through her later reign as leading lady of the Lyceum and her role as supporter of her children's unorthodox projects in a new era marked by modernism, feminism, and visionary theatrical experiment. In addition to describing Terry's relationships with such brilliant real-life players as her offspring (Edward Gordon Craig and Edith Craig), Henry Irving, Christopher St. John, and George Bernard Shaw, Auerbach discusses at length Terry's interpretation of Lady Macbeth, Ophelia, and other Shakespearean characters. Throughout, Auerbach demonstrates the connection between Victorian gender stereotyping and the portrayals of women expected and permitted onstage. Other topics woven into the biography include social attitudes toward the theatre, female cross-dressing on the Victorian stage, and suffrage plays.

F2

Auster, Albert. *Actresses and Suffragists: Women in the American Theater, 1890–1920.* New York: Praeger, 1984.

Auster concentrates on the increased participation and influence of women in theatre, both as performers and audience, in his social history of American theatre during a period of intellectual and cultural transformation. Tracing the personal and political links between actresses and feminists, Auster argues that actresses both wittingly and unwittingly used the stage and their fame to help in the struggle for women's rights and emancipation. Individual chapters deal with the following actresses: Mary Shaw, whose experience with the Professional Woman's League blossomed into a life of artistic and political activism that included championship of the realistic "women's plays" of Ibsen and Shaw, writing feminist sketches, and efforts to create a Woman's National Theater; Lillian Russell, the "American beauty" who outspokenly supported the suffrage movement; and Ethel Barrymore, who appeared in such plays as *The Twelve Pound Look,* which advocated women's independence.

F3

Griffiths, Viv. *Using Drama to Get at Gender.* Studies in Sexual Politics 9. Manchester, England: Sociology Dept., University of Manchester, 1986.

The author reports on a project that used improvisation and role-play along with informal discussion to discern the distinctive aspects of girls' experience of adolescence. Participants, who included fifty-one thirteen- and fourteen-year-old West Indian, Asian, and white girls, explored such areas as parent-daughter relationships, likes and dislikes about being a girl, and plans for the future. Griffiths notes class and ethnic differences, as manifested in the girls' performances.

F4

Hill, Holly. *Playing Joan: Actresses on the Challenge of Shaw's Saint Joan.* New York: Theatre Communications Group, 1987.

The twenty-six American, Canadian, and British actresses interviewed reflect on Joan as a historical figure and as Shaw's heroine.

F5

Holledge, Julie. *Innocent Flowers: Women in the Edwardian Theatre.* London: Virago, 1981.

Holledge offers an account of British actresses committed to women's rights who determined to change the roles of women both in real life and on stage. Part I, which describes the early influence of the women's movement on actresses, details their championship of the "new drama" (Ibsen, Shaw, and others) and the playwriting efforts of such actresses as Cicely Hamilton and Elizabeth Robins. Part II focuses on the work of the Actresses' Franchise League, whose active producing arm encouraged women's playwriting and erased the line between professional and amateur theatre. Holledge also examines the short-lived Women's Theatre

Company. Part III is devoted to producer-director-designer Edy Craig and the Pioneer Players. Three short propaganda plays are included: *Jim's Leg* by L. S. Phibbs, *10 Clowning Street* by Joan Dugdale, and *Miss Appleyard's Awakening* by Evelyn Glover.

F6

Johnson, Claudia D. *American Actress: Perspective on the Nineteenth Century.* Chicago: Nelson-Hall, 1984.

This study of seven extraordinary nineteenth-century actresses—Mary Ann Duff, Fanny Kemble, Charlotte Cushman, Anna Cora Mowatt, Laura Keene, Adah Isaacs Menken, and Lotta Crabtree—considers contemporary attitudes toward theatre and women's role in society. Johnson elaborates on the damaged reputation of women involved with theatre, an institution that afforded one of the few areas for financial independence (often an economic necessity) and opportunities to compete professionally with men. She comments that at the root of American fears of the dangers of theatre "was the same apprehension that led Victorians to wrap up their women, body and soul: fear of the creative principle that, in the hands of artist or woman, could summon up devilishness to threaten nineteenth-century order."

F7

Klein, Maxine. *Theatre for the 98%.* Boston: South End, 1978.

Klein presents a scathing indictment of establishment theatre's sexism, racism, ageism, class bias, and homophobia, and argues for a celebratory communal people's theatre. She includes discussion of exemplary theatres (such as the Caravan Theatre and her own Little Flags Theatre Collective), scenarios, guidelines for starting a company, and suggestions for dealing with traditional scripts.

F8

Roth, Moira, ed. *The Amazing Decade: Women and Performance Art in America, 1970–1980.* Los Angeles: Astro Artz, 1983.

This volume includes a detailed essay by Roth, which explores the history and nature of women's performance art, its relationship to the women's movement, and three significant aspects of the form: the autobiographical/narrative, the mystical/ritualistic, and the political, with models for feminist activism based on the work of Leslie Labowitz and Suzanne Lacy. In her forecast of new directions, Roth describes Nancy Buchanan's focus on political paranoia and the threat of nuclear holocaust. A year-by-year chronology of "History/Women's History/ Women's Performance Art" precedes profiles and photographs of the following performers and collectives, in addition to those named above: Laurie Anderson, Eleanor Antin, Jacki Apple, Ida Applebroog, Judith Barry, Judy Chicago (with Suzanne Lacy, Sandra Orgel, and Aviva Rahmani), Betsy Damon, Norma Jean Deak, Mary Beth Edelson, Feminist Art Workers, Simone Forti, Tina Girouard, Donna Henes, Lynn Hershman, Poppy Johnson, Joan Jonas, Alison Knowles, Meredith Monk, Linda Montano, Pauline Oliveros, Adrian Piper, Yvonne Rainer, Rachel Rosenthal, Martha Rosler, Carolee Schneemann, Jill Scott, Bonnie Sherk, Theodora Skipitares, Barbara T. Smith, Mierle Laderman Ukeles, The Waitresses, Faith Wilding, Hannah Wilke, and Martha Wilson.

F9

Staples, Shirley. *Male-Female Comedy Teams in American Vaudeville, 1865–1932*. Theater and Dramatic Studies 16. Ann Arbor, Mich.: UMI Research Press, 1984.

Staples argues that vaudeville's transformation from stag entertainment to star-studded family fare with an emphasis on domestic humor was largely brought about by the presence of women in the audience and on the stage. She claims that the male-female acts' treatment of relations between the sexes revealed much about the social scripts for men and women in contemporary America and mirrored tensions about the women's rights movement. Although she states that "by redefining their stage roles, and by acquiring new responsibility as laughmakers, women in the male-female teams were asserting new rights for women," she also notes the sexist implications of the humor. Many vaudeville acts, now mostly unknown, are chronicled, and a separate chapter provides an in-depth analysis of George Burns and Gracie Allen.

Periodicals, Serials, and Annuals

F10

Adams, Patricia. "Dorothy Tutin and J. C. Trewin: An Essay on the Possibilities of Feminist Biography." *Theatre Studies* 31–32 (1984–85/1985–86): 67–102.

Adams investigates the implications of current critical work in feminism, deconstruction, narratology, and psychoanalysis for the theatrical biographer dealing with "a subject/Object as socially and culturally overloaded (one might say overdetermined) as the Actress." Suggesting that biographers dealing with performance criticism must turn the spotlight on the journalistic critics themselves to discover their subjectivity and how they create an image construct around the actress as object and spectacle, she provides a detailed analysis of J. C. Trewin's reviews of Tutin's performances from 1953 to 1970.

F11
Aitken, Maria. Interview. "The Woman." With Carole Woddis. *Plays and Players* Nov. 1986: 7–8.

Aitken expresses admiration for Clare Boothe Luce's work, which she considers as "based on a real perception of the predicament of women at that time," and delight in the humorous, bitchy role in which she appeared in a revival of *The Women*. She maintains that the play and production process (even with a male director) are compatible with feminism.

F12
Ashcroft, Peggy. "Playing Shakespeare." *Shakespeare Survey* 40 (1988): 11–19.

Based on a conversation with Inga-Stina Ewbank, this jointly edited, informal article contains Dame Peggy's reflections on her career. Concluding with a discussion of Shakespeare's understanding of women, she expresses amazement that women can consider him antifeminist.

F13
Aston, Elaine. "Male Impersonation in the Music Hall: The Case of Vesta Tilley." *New Theatre Quarterly* 4.15 (1988): 247–57.

The nature of Tilley's hidden appeal when she performed in male attire and the gender messages encoded are analyzed. Aston distinguishes between the earlier theatrical use of breeches roles to heighten femininity and the 1890s impersonator's suppression of femininity to perfect the illusion of maleness, arguing that successful impersonation had the potential to subvert gender power roles and identities. She describes Tilley's "clothes-conscious" dressing (the dandy and the soldier) and contemplates her allure for women, who viewed her as an "androgynous image of a beautiful youth."

F14
Berry, Ralph. "*Measure for Measure* on the Contemporary Stage." *Humanities Association Review* 28 (1977): 241–47.

Berry contrasts productions since 1970 with those which came before. He suggests a cultural context for the shift in the depiction of Isabella, noting that neither a contemporary audience nor an actress will perceive marriage as the automatic close to the play.

F15

Blair, Rhonda. "Shakespeare and the Feminist Actor." *Women & Performance: A Journal of Feminist Theory* 2.2 (1985): 18–26.

Blair details the dual problems encountered by a feminist in creating a Shakespearean role: both the female character and the actor's work as an artist are treated as "other." The author draws upon her own experiences in performing Desdemona in *Othello* and Isabella in *Measure for Measure*.

F16

Carlisle, Carol J. "The Critics Discover Shakespeare's Women." *Renaissance Papers* (1979): 59–73.

Carlisle examines the interaction of literary, theatrical, and social trends in the eighteenth and nineteenth centuries, which produced a change from critical neglect of Shakespeare's women to their being considered worthy of attention. Among the actresses discussed, Helen Faucit is noted for her combination of the real and the ideal in her portrayals and written interpretations.

F17

Carr, C. "The Mirror Turned Lamp." *Artforum* Jan. 1987: 80–85.

Lily Tomlin's work with playwright Jane Wagner, the "culture-types" who populate *The Search for Signs of Intelligent Life in the Universe*, and Tomlin's character-hopping on stage, television, and records, are the topics covered.

F18

Cima, Gay Gibson. "Acting through the Barricades: A Search for Prototypes of Feminist Theatre." *Turn-of-the-Century Women* 3.2 (1986): 42–46.

Adapting Annette Kolodny's three "crucial propositions" of feminist literary criticism to the study of theatre history, Cima focuses on British theatre in the 1890s, particularly the career of actress-manager Elizabeth Robins. She describes how Robins and other women not only explored new repertory and acting techniques but also attempted to establish alternatives to the hierarchical, patriarchal system.

F19

Cocuzza, Ginnine. "First Person Plural: A Portfolio from the Theatre of Angna Enters." *Women & Performance: A Journal of Feminist Theory* 1.1 (1983): 36–39.

Brief descriptions accompany photographs of Enters' dance-mime performances of the 1920s and 1930s.

F20

Daly, Ann, ed. "Tanztheater: The Thrill of the Lynch Mob or the Rage of a Woman?" *The Drama Review* 30.2 (1986): 46–56.

This abridged transcript from a 1985 symposium, "German and American Dance: Yesterday and Today," contains comments by Anna Kisselgoff (moderator), Jochen Schmidt, Reinhild Hoffmann, Nina Wiener, Nancy Goldner, and others. *Tanztheater* and American experimental dance are contrasted, with many examples of the former drawn from the work of Pina Bausch. Daly's postscript scrutinizes Bausch's depiction of the violence against women and women's acquiescent powerlessness.

F21

Damon, Betsy. "An Interview with Betsy Damon." With Vivian Patraka. *Work by Women*. Spec. issue of *Art & Cinema* ns 1.3 (1987): 16–17.

Damon reflects on aspects of her performance art, including the use of ritual and archetypal images. She also discusses the nature of performance art, the creation of "female space," strategies of empowerment in art, and related matters.

F22

Dolan, Jill. "The Dynamics of Desire: Sexuality and Gender in Pornography and Performance." *Theatre Journal* 39 (1987): 156–74.

A revised version of this article appears as Chapter 4 in Dolan's book, *The Feminist Spectator as Critic*. See A6. *Terms:* acting/actors, lesbian; desire, lesbian; images of women, lesbian; performance art and artists; pornography; sexuality, female; feminist theatres and theatre groups.

F23

Dragu, Margaret. "More Life on the Road: Self-Profile." *Women and Performance*. Spec. issue of *Fireweed* 7 (Summer 1980): 14–17.

The Toronto-based performer grapples with the impossibility of labeling her collaborative touring piece, her feelings about working in film, and the pervasiveness of "marketing" in the arts and in real life.

F24

Dworkin, Susan. "Whose Role Is It Anyway? Mary Tyler Moore and Other Actresses Are Playing Roles Written for Men." *Ms.* Aug. 1980: 81–82.

Dworkin writes about the performances of Moore in *Whose Life Is It Anyway?* and Olympia Dukakis and Judy Delgado in *Waiting for Godot*. A sidebar features four other female actors and the male roles they would like to play.

F25
Fernie, Lynne. "Ms. Unseen." *Feminism and Canadian Theatre*. Spec. issue of *Canadian Theatre Review* 43 (1985): 59–72.

The author presents the career of director Svetlana Zylin as a case study illuminating "the systemic marginalization and silencing of talented women directors in Canada." Among the topics addressed is the actor-director relationship, with Fernie noting that female directors often prefer actors to retain more independence and aesthetic judgment than do male, father-figure directors. A chronology of excerpts from newspaper reviews of Zylin's work is included.

F26
Finley, Karen. Interview. "Karen Finley: A Constant State of Becoming." With Richard Schechner. *TDR, The Drama Review: A Journal of Performance Studies* 32.1 (1988): 152–58.

Finley talks about *The Constant State of Desire*, reactions to her work, her approach to writing, and her performance process.

F27
Finley, Karen. Interview. "Performance Strategies: Karen Finley." With Marc Robinson. *Performing Arts Journal* 10.3 (1987): 42–46.

Robinson's comments on *The Constant State of Desire*'s apparent lack of structure precede Finley's discussion of her performing technique and aims, which include denouncing myths about women.

F28
Fisher, Berenice. "Learning to Act: Women's Experience with 'Theater of the Oppressed.'" *Off Our Backs* Oct. 1986: 14–15.

The author describes the appropriation of Augusto Boal's "theatre of the oppressed" by feminists in France and Holland. In addition to outlining the various ways in which the techniques of forum theatre, image or statue theatre, and invisible theatre involve the audience in the presentation of women's oppression, she defines several problem areas, including tension between professionals and nonprofessionals, emphasis on individual rather than collective experience, and assumptions of audience homogeneity.

F29

Forte, Jeanie. "Rachel Rosenthal: Feminism and Performance Art." *Women & Performance: A Journal of Feminist Theory* 2.2 (1985): 27–37.

Tracing Rosenthal's career from her early autobiographical pieces which addressed eating compulsions, sexuality, and the search for personal authenticity, to her more recent orientation toward social issues, including ecology and nuclear threat, Forte emphasizes Rosenthal's illumination of gender as a cultural construction. Forte points to her performance art as a paradigm for feminist performance: "woman-identified, politically alive, gender deconstructing, assertive, and . . . thoroughly moving."

F30

Forte, Jeanie. "Women's Performance Art: Feminism and Postmodernism." *Feminist Diversions*. Spec. issue of *Theatre Journal* 40 (1988): 217–35.

Forte assesses women's performance art of the 1970s as a deconstructive project operating to dismantle the Western system of representation based on the culturally constructed category of "Woman." She details the ways that performance artists subvert the denial of women as "speaking subjects" through the use of autobiographical material and the reclaiming of female sexuality. She concludes by raising issues for women's performance art in the 1980s.

F31

Friedlander, Mira. "On the Cutting Edge." *Feminism and Canadian Theatre*. Spec. issue of *Canadian Theatre Review* 43 (1985): 52–58.

Friedlander highlights examples of the feminist development of new theatrical forms, ranging from the Hummer Sisters' technological performances to stand-up comic–performance artist Sheila Gostick, for whom comedy is life; the more mainstream Clichettes' satirical combination of politics and art; and Lillian Allen's blend of poetry, music, and prose. The production company Womynly Way's efforts to provide entertainment for women by women and commitment to the larger community are also discussed.

F32

Goldberg, Marianne. "Transformative Aspects of Meredith Monk's *Education of the Girlchild*." *Women & Performance: A Journal of Feminist Theory* 1.1 (1983): 19–28.

The author explores the ritual dimensions of *Girlchild*, a collaborative effort by Monk and her experimental performance group, The House. Interviews with company members provide insights into the creative process resulting in the depiction of the spiritual journal of a community of women. Goldberg includes a description of the nonlinear, image-filled performance.

F33

Gossett, Suzanne. "'Man-Maid, Begone!': Women in Masques." *Women in the Renaissance II*. Spec. issue of *English Literary Renaissance* 18 (1988): 96–113.

Gossett investigates different demands placed on the audience's consciousness by the masques of Queens Anne and Henrietta: one for professional actors (playing male or female speaking or singing roles), whose identities were to be ignored, and another for masquers, recognition of whose identities was central to the production's meaning. Tracing changes from Jacobean performances, in which women participated only as silent dancers, to Caroline innovations, when women's voices were heard on stage and courtiers played parts formerly reserved for professionals, Gossett argues that "neither poets nor audience could always make the necessary dissociations between actor or part, or adjust to having real women on the stage." She also examines the masques' messages about proper female behavior and societal ambivalence about women.

F34

Griffiths, Linda. Interview. "An Eye to Listen." With Kate Lushington. *Women and Performance*. Spec. issue of *Fireweed* 8 (Fall 1980): 64–71.

The Canadian performer–playwright's reflections on her successful one-woman, three-character play, *Maggie and Pierre*, includes details on how developing the role of Margaret Trudeau awakened Griffiths' narcissism and broadened her definition of feminism. In addition, she remarks on her approach to portraying the male characters.

F35

Grossmann, Mechthild. Interview. "Mechthild Grossmann: The Art of Anti Heroes." With Carol Martin. *The Drama Review* 30.2 (1986): 98–106.

Martin's discussion of *Wo meine Sonne scheint* (*Where My Sun Shines for Me*), conceived (with Helmut Schäfer) and performed by Grossmann, and the elements of *tanztheater* precedes the interview. Grossmann talks about performance choices, the implications of cross-dressing and the ways in which gender stereotypes are presented, the pairing of glamour and politics, her work with Pina Bausch, and her reservations about the women's movement.

F36

Hamer, Mary. "Shakespeare's Rosalind and Her Public Image." *Theatre Research International* 11 (1986): 105–18.

The author examines the development of expectations surrounding the portrayal of *As You Like It*'s Rosalind, who since the mid-eighteenth century has come to be perceived as an ideal of femininity, "in which weakness and potency are reconciled, feminine allure and mystery reassuringly garbed in masculine attire."

F37

Hirshfield, Claire. "The Actresses' Franchise League and the Campaign for Women's Suffrage, 1908–1914." *Theatre Research International* 10 (1985): 129–53.

Tracing the history of the League, Hirshfield outlines its goals, organization, membership, accomplishments, relationship to other suffrage societies, and internal dissension regarding militancy. She comments that the actresses choosing "the uncertain path of activism were in part inspired by an understandable distaste for the insipid heroines they had often portrayed."

F38

Holledge, Jules, and Jane Comfort. "The Lost Theatre." *Spare Rib* 55 (Feb. 1977): 33–36.

A revised and expanded version of this article on the Actresses' Franchise League appears in Part II (Chapters 3 and 4) of Holledge's book, *Innocent Flowers: Women in the Edwardian Theatre*. See F5. *Terms:* feminism(s), influence on/ relationship to women in theatre; pageants; suffrage drama; women playwrights.

F39

Jenkins, Linda Walsh, and Susan Ogden-Malouf. "The (Female) Actor Prepares." *Theater* 17.1 (1985): 66–69.

Asserting that "if the journey toward production can be liberated from gender oppression, perhaps the product itself will be so as well," the authors survey a number of women in academic and professional theatre to determine how they merge feminist theory, art, and praxis in the preproduction process. Specific topics addressed include cross-gender casting, gender awareness in actor training, and dramaturgy and playwriting.

F40

Keshishian, Hrut. "Kudiyattam: An Ancient Acting Tradition for Women." *Acting Up!* Spec. issue of *Heresies* 5.1 (1984): 87–88.

The author explains the participation of women in Kerala, India, as actresses and musicians in *Kudiyattam*, a stylized art form permitting extemporaneous performance. In particular she describes the role of the Nangyar, who nightly coordinates the performance, and contrasts her traditional and contemporary roles within the temple and society.

F41

Klett, Renate. "In Rehearsal with Pina Bausch." *Acting Up!* Spec. issue of *Heresies* 5.1 (1984): 13–16.

Klett reports on the improvisational rehearsals for *Kontakthof* at the Wuppertaler Tanztheater and comments on Bausch's complex, nonlinear form and female perspective.

F42

Kulp, Denise. "Whatever's for Us: Lesbians in Pop Culture." *Off Our Backs* June 1986: 24–25.

The author discusses Lily Tomlin's humorously presented lesbians and feminists in *The Search for Signs of Intelligent Life in the Universe*, written by Jane Wagner. She also analyzes lesbian characters in a made-for-TV movie and a film.

F43

Kwon, Yung-Hee Kim. "The Female Entertainment Tradition in Medieval Japan: The Case of *Asobi*." *Feminist Diversions*. Spec. issue of *Theatre Journal* 40 (1988): 205–16.

This historical study concerns professional singers of low social status during the eleventh and twelfth centuries.

F44

Lacy, Suzanne, and Lucy R. Lippard. "Political Performance Art." *Acting Up!* Spec. issue of *Heresies* 5.1 (1984): 22–25.

Performance artist Lacy and cultural activist Lippard explore the nature and process of creating performance art, the relationship between its aesthetics and political intent, the role of ritual and communion, and related topics.

F45

Lampe, Eelka. "Rachel Rosenthal: Creating Her Selves." *TDR, The Drama Review: A Journal of Performance Studies* 32.1: 170–90.

Lampe's article on Rosenthal's performance art is divided into the performance sequence (training, workshop, rehearsal, etc.), the macrostructure (a piece's overall organization), and the microstructure (performance technique). Lampe describes Rosenthal's use of ritual, provides a detailed description of *Traps*, traces influences on her work, and demonstrates her use of personae to break through limitations posed by gender positioning in traditional representation. Lampe also illustrates her own schema of the performing/not-performing continuum by Rosenthal's performance in *Gaia, Mon Amour*.

F46

Leigh-Hunt, Barbara, and Caroline Embling. Interview. "Acting Women: Questioning Roles: Questioning Myths?" With Malcolm Hay. *Women in Theatre*. Spec. issue of *Drama* 152 (1984): 15–17.

Issues surrounding women who act in the male-dominated theatre are explored in two contrasting interviews. Leigh-Hunt, while acknowledging the lack of opportunities for actresses and other women practitioners, feels that a "positive discrimination" policy would be dangerous. Embling disagrees, asserting that she can put more of herself in a play dealing with women's concerns, and expresses the desire to work with a women's theatre group.

F47

Lippard, Lucy R. "Lacy: Some of Her Own Medicine." *TDR, The Drama Review: A Journal of Performance Studies* 32.1 (1988): 71–76.

Lippard examines the spiritual and healing aspects of Suzanne Lacy's performance art and the role of the dinner party form in her work. Moira Roth's selected bibliography on Suzanne Lacy follows the article. Two other pieces on Lacy, one by Roth and one by Rothenberg, appear in this issue of *TDR* and are annotated in F60 and F61.

F48

Lock, Georgina. "Street Credibility." *Spare Rib* 157 (Aug. 1985): 22.

Street performer Lock describes her experiences with feminist busking. She suggests that "a feminist message is already implicit when social expectation is disrupted by a woman who shamelessly shows what she's made of on the street with clarity, energy, concentration and a lot of wit and humor when faced with hecklers."

F49

Londré, Felicia. "Ermolova's Revolutionary Realism Before and After the Revolution." *Women in Theatre*. Spec. issue of *Theatre Annual* 40 (1985): 25–39.

Surveying the actress's career, Londré notes Ermolova's reputation as an interpreter of heroic, tragic women, her revelation of untapped psychological depth in Shakespeare's characters, and her concern "to reveal a simple everyday heroism in the lives of ordinary contemporary Russian women."

F50

Loy, Pamela, and Janet Brown. "Red Hot Mamas, Sex Kittens and Sweet Young Things: Role Engulfment in the Lives of Musical Comedy Performers." *International Journal of Women's Studies* 2 (Sept.–Oct. 1982): 338–47.

The authors point out the ironic situation in which women, attracted to the independence of life in the theatre, attain success through portraying stereotypical figures from male fantasy. Tracing the careers of three stars of early twentieth-century vaudeville and musical comedy— Sophie Tucker (Red Hot Mama), Anna Held (Sex-Kitten), and Julia Sanderson (Sweet Young Thing)—they demonstrate how each responded to the societal view of her "public deviance" by maintaining her onstage image in offstage life.

F51

MacIntyre, Margaret, and David Buchbinder. "Having It Both Ways: Cross-Dressing in Orton's *What the Butler Saw* and Churchill's *Cloud Nine*." *Journal of Dramatic Theory and Criticism* 2.1 (1987): 23–39.

Distinguishing between attitudes toward transvestism in society and those toward theatrical cross-dressing, the authors' survey of the latter practice "suggests that any form of cross-dressing has the potential to interrogate culturally derived notions of gender and gender-role, but that in the past such notions were usually confirmed, not challenged, by the act of cross-dressing." They argue that in contrast to Orton's farce, which underscores the cultural construction of gender while remaining faithful to the conservative tradition, Churchill's feminist play both acknowledges and works against that tradition, demanding that the audience reevaluate issues surrounding gender.

F52

McLuskie, Kathleen. "The Act, the Role and the Actor: Boy Actresses on the Elizabethan Stage." *New Theatre Quarterly* 3.10 (1987): 120–30.

The author articulates the complex issues and conflicting views surrounding the representation of women in the Elizabethan theatre, discussing the antitheatricalists' indictment of cross-dressing, representation produced by emblem and symbol vs. internally constructed notions of character, the conventions governing distinctions between men and women both on stage and off, and related subjects. She argues that it was the ideological, anxiety-producing focus on the nature of women "rather than simple sexual attraction or disruptive metatheatrical confusion which determined the relationship between the audience and the boy actors." Implications for modern performance and criticism are addressed.

F53

Maus, Katharine Eisaman. " 'Playhouse Flesh and Blood': Sexual Ideology and the Restoration Actress." *ELH* 46 (1979): 595–617.

Maus examines the inadequacy of contemporary justifications of the new acceptability of actresses in the context of Restoration ideology. Tracing the similarities between Renaissance antitheatricalists and antifeminists, who blamed the seductiveness of the actor or woman for private or social disorder, she notes the persistence of assumptions connecting theatre and female sexuality. She argues that as the disruptive theatrical model of human relations, which defines women in terms of their seductive difference from men, displaces the hierarchical ideal, which defines women (and boys) in terms of their inferiority to men, "transvestite role-playing involves a much greater rupture of decorum."

F54

Merrill, Lisa. "Feminist Humor: Rebellious and Self-Affirming." *Last Laughs: Perspectives on Women and Comedy.* Ed. Regina Barreca. Spec. issue of *Women's Studies* 15 (1988): 271–80.

Investigating conventions of the comedic form, Merrill suggests that women's "lack of humor" is actually "a refusal to comply with the premise of a joke" detrimental to their fundamental interests. Merrill contrasts traditional humor to feminist comedy, which affirms rather than denigrates female experience. Her examples include such one-woman shows as Lily Tomlin's *The Search for Signs of Intelligent Life in the Universe*. Merrill also emphasizes feminist comedy's positing of a female spectator.

F55

O'Dell, Kathy. "The Performance Artist as Masochistic Woman." *Arts Magazine* Summer 1988: 96–98.

The author assesses the work of Ulrike Rosenbach, Gina Pane, and Vito Acconci in relation to psychoanalytic theory and gender-coded systems of representation.

F56

Orloff, Kossia. "Women in Performance Art: The Alternate Persona." *Acting Up!* Spec. issue of *Heresies* 5.1 (1984): 36–40.

In her examination of feminist performance art, Orloff discusses Carolee Schneemann's gynocentric pieces challenging patriarchal myths and exploding cultural taboos. She also analyzes the work of Eleanor Antin, Colette, Lynn Hershman, and Theodora Skipitares, particularly focusing on their creation of alternate personae through whom they call societal values into question.

F57

Parsons, Estelle. "*Orgasmo Adulto Escapes from the Zoo*: An Interview with Estelle Parsons." With Julie Malnig, Judy C. Rosenthal, and Anne B. Wyma. *Women & Performance: A Journal of Feminist Theory* 2.1 (1984): 49–62.

Parsons discusses feminism as it relates to her acting career, Italian actor-playwright Franca Rame (coauthor with Dario Fo of *Orgasmo Adulto Escapes from the Zoo*), the monologues that make up *Orgasmo*, and the response of audience members and critics.

F58

Phelan, Peggy. "Feminist Theory, Poststructuralism, and Performance." *TDR, The Drama Review: A Journal of Performance Studies* 32.1 (1988): 107–27.

Exploring issues of women's representation and the economy of exchange between performer and spectator, Phelan focuses on three artistic expressions: the gotipua (dance) performance of an eleven-year-old boy at the 1986 ISTA Conference; Yvonne Rainer's film, *The Man Who Envied Women*; and Angelika Festa's performance art piece, *Untitled Dance with Fish and Others*. She suggests that "by taking the notion that women are not visible within the dominant narratives of history and the contemporary customs of performance literally, Rainer and Festa prompt new considerations about the central 'absence' integral to the representation of women in patriarchy."

259

F59
Raven, Arlene, and Deborah Marrow. "Eleanor Antin: What's Your Story?" *Chrysalis* 8 (1979): 43–51.

The authors see artist Antin as part of a hidden narrative tradition, within which outsiders and the oppressed hand down stories containing encoded messages. Maintaining that her narratives reveal "a travelogue of the journey toward the self," revealing its "essential transformational nature," they survey her work. A major portion of the article deals with *Angel of Mercy*, a performance art piece inspired by Florence Nightingale.

F60
Roth, Moira. "Suzanne Lacy: Social Reformer and Witch." *TDR, The Drama Review: A Journal of Performance Studies* 32.1 (1988): 42–60.

Roth traces the shift in Lacy's work from an earlier focus on action-oriented feminist performance to a more general focus on women's history and community, with pageantlike gatherings of women celebrating women. She discusses ritual and archetypal connections in Lacy's work, particularly as related to older women and the figures of the witch and the crone, and Lacy's fascination with the macabre. Roth also applies Lacy's own three criteria of success to her works: the quality of experience for participants and audience, potential as models for future application, and assessment of the life span of the processes set in motion. Roth's selected bibliography on Lacy appears in this issue of *TDR*, as do two related articles by Lippard and Rothenberg. See F47 and F61.

F61
Rothenberg, Diane. "Social Art/Social Action." *TDR, The Drama Review: A Journal of Performance Studies* 32.1 (1988): 61–70.

Rothenberg, an anthropologist, reports on the preparation processes and development of volunteer organizations leading to the performances of Suzanne Lacy's *Whisper, the Waves, the Wind* in La Jolla and *Crystal Quilt* in Minneapolis. A selected bibliography on Lacy appears in this issue of *TDR*, as do two other related articles by Lippard and Roth. See F47 and F60.

F62
Safa-Isfahani, Kaveh. "Female-Centered World Views in Iranian Culture: Symbolic Representations of Sexuality in Dramatic Games." *Signs* 6 (1980): 33–53.

The author examines the *baziha*, a type of Iranian folk drama predominantly played by and for women and performed on festive occasions. Safa-Isfahani details themes related to female sexuality, including women as active and articulate erotic subjects, and themes dealing with marriage issues, including choice of mate and fears of husband-loss. The *baziha* are also considered within their cultural context.

F63

Senelick, Laurence. "The Evolution of the Male Impersonator on the Nineteenth-Century Popular Stage." *Essays in Theatre* 1 (1982): 30–44.

Senelick remarks on feminist theatre's recent resuscitation of the male impersonator as "a kind of totem" and the fact that male impersonation has received less attention from theatre historians than female impersonation. After noting the artistic legitimacy of breeches roles, which "never required a convincing impersonation of a male," he defines the true male impersonator as seeking to convey an illusion of masculinity, and ties the phenomenon to opportunities for women in America and the expression of lesbian wish-fulfillment.

F64

Sharma, D. D. "Participation of Women in Sanskrit Plays." *Panjab University Research Bulletin (Arts)* 7.1–2 (1977): 163–68.

Sharma outlines the contradictory evidence surrounding the question of women's performing in ancient India and the problems faced by directors in dealing with female characters. Gleaning that in later times the women who exhibited their stage talents were courtesans and professional actresses, who were considered immoral, Sharma concludes that social inhibitions were responsible for depriving talented women from participating in theatre.

F65

Sklar, Roberta. Interview. "Roberta Sklar: Toward Creating a Women's Theatre." With Cornelia Brunner. *Women and Performance*. Spec. issue of *The Drama Review* 24.2 (1980): 23–40.

Sklar recounts her early work in the experimental theatre of the 1960s, her increasing interest in nonlinear structure, and her participation in the Open Theatre. She discusses issues of sexism both outside and inside the theatre, her growing understanding of "the personal is political," and her brief departure from theatre after disillusionment over *The Mutation Show*. Sklar goes on to describe the Women's Unit (which evolved out of her class at Bard), the development of feminist acting techniques, the relationship of feminist theatre to its audience, her work with the Womanrite Theatre Ensemble, and the collaboration with Sondra Segal and Clare Coss at the Women's Experimental Theater. Brunner's analysis of W.E.T.'s *The Daughters Cycle Trilogy* is included.

F66

Stevenson, Juliet. Interview. "A Woman's Role." With Carole Woddis. *Plays and Players* Oct. 1987: 14–16.

Stevenson, a leading actress with the Royal Shakespeare Company, comments on the limited roles available for women, dealing with male directors, revising stereotyped interpretations of Shakespeare's female characters, and the experience of working with a group of women and a woman director.

F67

Swinton, Tilda. Interview. "Man to Man." With Anthony Vivis and Tinch Minter. *Drama* 166 (1987): 18–19.

Swinton reflects on her performance in Manfred Karge's *Man to Man*, translated by Vivis, and the discomfort experienced by men in the audience in response to her nonerotic onstage image.

F68

Swinton, Tilda. Interview. "Tilda Swinton." With Barbara Emmett. *Spare Rib* 192 (June 1988): 12–15.

Swinton discusses her work on stage, particularly her androgynous performance in the one-woman play, *Man to Man*, and in film. She also talks about political activism.

F69

Venables, Clare. "The Woman Director in the Theatre." *Theatre Quarterly* 10.38 (1980): 3–7.

Among the issues addressed are the underrepresentation of women directors, the relationship of the women's movement to the position of women in theatre, the problems of working with male-centered plays, the director as mother-figure, and inhibitions on her creativity.

F70

Wehle, Philippa. "Pina Bausch's Tanztheater—A Place of Difficult Encounter." *Women & Performance: A Journal of Feminist Theory* 1.2 (1984): 25–36.

Wehle examines Bausch's vision of "women's yearnings for refuge in an imaginary paradise of solace and safety" in four works: *Kontakthof, Ein Stück von Pina Bausch, Walzer,* and *Tanzabend: Nelken.*

F71

Weiss, Kate. "Trust and Risk: An Interview with Kate Weiss." With Peggy Thompson. *Women in Theatre.* Spec. issue of *Room of One's Own* 8.2 (1983): 70–77.

Director Weiss notes the opportunities her improvised soap operas afford actresses to provide input and play other than stereotyped roles.

F72

Zatlin, Phyllis. "Women Directors in Spain: Josefina Molina." *Women & Performance: A Journal of Feminist Theory* 3.1 (1986): 52–58.

Zatlin focuses on Molina's work, including her adaptation and direction of Delibes' novel *Five Hours with Mario,* whose misogynist approach is replaced by a feminist one, and her staging of *The Witches' Revolt* by Benet i Jornet.

F73

Zeig, Sande. "The Actor as Activator: Deconstructing Gender through Gesture." *Feminist Issues* 5.1 (1985): 21–25. (Rpt. in *Women & Performance: A Journal of Feminist Theory* 2.2 [1985]: 12–17.)

Zeig focuses on the ability of lesbian actors to influence contemporary theatre through gender-neutral presentation. She postulates that although gestures, "a particular aspect of the oppression of women," are genderized according to two sex class systems, rehabilitation of one's personal gestural system is possible. She describes techniques (developed with Monique Wittig) applicable to controlling gesture production.

Selected Play Collections

❖
❖

G1

Aykroyd, Juliet, et al. *Female Voices.* London: Playwrights' Press, 1987.

Plays included are *The Clean-up* by Juliet Aykroyd, *The Ungrateful Dead* by Anne Caulfield, *Casino* by Elizabeth Gowans, *Corryvrecken* by Claire Schrader, and *Alarms* by Susan Yankowitz.

G2

Barlow, Judith E., ed. *Plays by American Women: The Early Years.* New York: Avon, 1981.

This anthology intends to bring to the fore "neglected but not negligible" playwrights. Barlow contends that women have been excluded from the canon not because of their technique or choice of dramatic form but because of male critical bias against the female perspectives and centrality of women characters. Barlow's chronologically organized introduction places the lives and works of the five playwrights featured in the volume within the context of developments in American society and theatre and discusses other women dramatists as well. Plays included are *Fashion* by Anna Cora Mowatt, *A Man's World* by Rachel Crothers, *Trifles* by Susan Glaspell, *Miss Lulu Bett* by Zona Gale, and *Machinal* by Sophie Treadwell.

G3

Barlow, Judith E., ed. *Plays by American Women: Nineteen Hundred to Nineteen Thirty.* Rev. ed. New York: Applause, 1985.

This revised edition of *Plays by American Women: The Early Years* (see G2) has a nearly identical introduction; Anna Cora Mowatt is still discussed, but the examination of *Fashion* has been deleted, and a brief study of Georgia Douglas Johnson and other black women playwrights has been added. Plays included are *A Man's World* by Rachel Crothers, *Trifles* by Susan Glaspell, *Miss Lulu Bett* by Zona Gale, *Plumes* by Johnson, and *Machinal* by Sophie Treadwell.

G4
Benmussa, Simone. *Benmussa Directs.* London: John Calder, 1979.

Benmussa's introductory material illuminates the creative processes resulting in her productions of two works, the texts of which are contained here: *Portrait of Dora* by Hélène Cixous, translated by Anita Barrows, and Benmussa's *The Singular Life of Albert Nobbs,* translated by Barbara Wright.

G5
Bessai, Diane, and Don Kerr, eds. *Newest Plays by Women.* Prairie Plays Series 7. Edmonton, Alta., Canada: NeWest, 1987.

An overview of the playwrights and comments on their depiction of paternalism are provided in Bessai's introduction. Plays included are *Play Memory* by Joanna M. Glass, *The Occupation of Heather Rose* by Wendy Lill, *Inside Out* by Pamela Boyd, and *Whiskey Six Cadenza* by Sharon Pollock.

G6
Boesing, Martha. *Journey along the Matrix: Three Plays by Martha Boesing.* Minneapolis: Vanilla, 1978.

Phyllis Jane Wagner's introduction emphasizes the way in which Boesing calls on feelings as a basis for political action. She discusses the plays included here—*The Gelding, River Journal,* and *Love Song for an Amazon*—with reference to Wagner's own experiences with sexual politics and the collaborative efforts of At the Foot of the Mountain.

G7
Churchill, Caryl. *Plays: One.* London: Methuen, 1985.

Churchill reviews her playwriting career in the introduction and prefaces each play with brief remarks. Plays included are *Owners, Traps, Vinegar Tom, Light Shining in Buckinghamshire,* and *Cloud Nine.*

G8
Considine, Ann, and Robyn Slovo, eds. *Dear Proud: From Second Wave Young Women Playwrights.* London: Women's Press, 1987.

This collection of plays and extracts from submissions to the Second Wave Festival of Young Women Playwrights at the Albany Empire Theatre is introduced by Considine, who states that the festival's aim "is to celebrate and encourage new writing for the theatre from black and white working-class young women whose voices are not often heard." Works included are *Shopping Spree* by Marie Wilson, *Foreshore* by Briony Binnie, *Back Street Mammy* and *No Place Like Home* by Roselia John Baptiste, *Dear Proud* by Angie Milan, *Ishtar Descends* by Nandita Ghose, *When Last I Did See You* by Lisselle Kayla, *A Slice of Life* by Pauline Jacobs and the Bemarro Theatre Group, *A Netful of Holes* (compiled) by Cathy Kilcoyne and Robyn Slovo, and *Fallen* by Polly Teale (developed with Carole Pluckrose).

G9
Davis, Jill, ed. *Lesbian Plays*. London: Methuen, 1987.

Davis's introduction, which includes a discussion of the political implications of homosexuality, justifies the publication of this first British anthology of lesbian plays separate from those of either feminists or gay men. Plays included are *Any Woman Can* by Jill Posener, *Double Vision* by The Women's Theatre Group with Libby Mason, *Chiaroscuro* by Jackie Kay, and *The Rug of Identity* by Jill W. Fleming. Each play has an afterword by its author. Also included are lists of plays performed by Gay Sweatshop, the Women's Theatre Group, the Theatre of Black Women, and Hard Corps.

G10
Dreher, Sarah. *Lesbian Stages*. Norwich, Vt.: New Victoria, 1988.

Dreher introduces five plays by detailing her involvement in theatre, the autobiographical nature of her work, and her approach to writing. Each selection is preceded by wide-ranging notes on such topics as the play's development, Dreher's intentions, production problems encountered, and audience reactions. Plays included are *Alumnae News: The Doris Day Years; Base Camp; Backward, Turn Backward; This Brooding Sky;* and *Hollandia '45.*

G11
Fornes, Maria Irene. *Maria Irene Fornes: Plays*. New York: PAJ, 1986.

Susan Sontag's preface offers a brief overview of Fornes's work. Plays included are *Mud, The Danube, The Conduct of Life,* and *Sarita.*

G12

France, Rachel, ed. *A Century of Plays by American Women*. New York: Richards Rosen, 1979.

In her introduction, France defines her objective as being to bring American women playwrights into the critical mainstream, refutes the idea of a female sensibility, and traces the contributions of women playwrights within the context of social and political change through the decades. Plays included are *Criss-Cross* by Rachel Crothers, *How the Vote Was Won* by Cicely Hamilton and Christopher St. John, *The Mothers* by Edith Ellis, *The Outside* by Susan Glaspell, *Aftermath* by Mary Burrill, *Three from the Earth* by Djuna Barnes, *The Eldest* by Edna Ferber, *Plumes* by Georgia Douglas Johnson, *Winter's Night* by Neith Boyce, *Can You Hear Their Voice?* by Hallie Flanagan and Margaret Ellen Clifford, *Auf Wiedersehen* by Sada Cowan, *Journey for an Unknown Soldier* by Doris Frankel, *On the Way Home* by Esther Hawley, *The Mother of Us All* by Gertrude Stein, *Dope* by Maryat Lee, *The Trap Is a Small Place* by Marjean Perry, *Ex-Miss Copper Queen on a Set of Pills* by Megan Terry, *Skywriting* by Rosalyn Drexler, *Dr. Kheal* by Maria Irene Fornes, *Slam the Door Softly* by Clare Boothe Luce, *The Independent Female* by Joan Holden, *Lament for Three Women* by Karen Malpede, and *Pimp* by Martha Boesing.

G13

Friedl, Bettina, ed. *On to Victory: Propaganda Plays of the Woman Suffrage Movement*. Boston: Northeastern University Press, 1987.

Friedl's general introduction traces the history of suffrage propaganda performances in the United States beginning with the early parlor theatricals of the nineteenth century. Noting that productions of women's pageants, tableaux, and suffrage drama "helped to integrate the previously separate spheres of the theater and the American home," she outlines both suffragism's growing reliance on drama as a means of rallying support and the contributions of professional actresses to the cause. The introduction to the selections, which include both feminist and antifeminist works, goes beyond plot summary to an analysis of the plays' arguments in their historical context. Plays included are *Woman's Rights* by William B. Fowle, *The Spirit of Seventy-Six* by Ariana Randolph Wormeley Curtis and Daniel Sargent Curtis, *Lords of Creation* by Ella Cheever Thayer, *When the Women Vote* by Eleanor Freeman, *The New Woman* by George Rugg, *A Very New Woman* by Alice E. Ives, *Something to Vote For* by Charlotte Perkins Gilman, *Bridget's Sisters* by Catharine Waugh McCulloch, *A Voting Demonstration* by Kate Mills Fargo, *A Suffragette Baby* by Alice C. Thompson, *Election Day* by Emily Sargent Lewis, *A Suffrage Rummage Sale* by Mary Winsor, *An Anti-*

Suffrage Monologue by Marie Jenney Howe, *Cinderelline* by Florence Kiper, *The Woman of It* and *The Parrot Cage* by Mary Shaw, *On to Victory* by Hester N. Johnson, *Back of the Ballot* by George Middleton, *Melinda and Her Sisters* by Mrs. O. H. P. Belmont and Elsa Maxwell, and *Unauthorised Interviews* by Alice Duer Miller.

G14

Glaspell, Susan. *Plays.* Ed. C. W. E. Bigsby. Cambridge, England: Cambridge University Press, 1987.

Bigsby's critical biography of Glaspell precedes four plays: *Trifles, The Outside, The Verge,* and *Inheritors.*

G15

Hatch, James W., ed., and Ted Shine, consultant. *Black Theater, U.S.A.: Forty-five Plays by Black Americans 1847–1974.* New York: Free Press, 1974.

Two sections of this anthology, the selections for are intended to represent stages in the evolution of black playwriting, are of particular relevance. The first section, "Early Plays by Black Women," includes *Rachel* by Angelina Grimké, *Mine Eyes Have Seen* by Alice Dunbar Nelson, *They That Sit in Darkness* by Mary Burrill, *For Unborn Children* by Myrtle Smith Livingston, *The Church Fight* by Ruth Gaines-Shelton, *Undertow* by Eulalie Spence, and *The Purple Flower* by Marita Bonner. The second pertinent section, "Modern Black Women," includes *The Drinking Gourd* by Lorraine Hansberry, *Wine in the Wilderness* by Alice Childress, *The Owl Answers* by Adrienne Kennedy, and *Job Security* by Martie Charles.

G16

Hoffman, William M., ed. *Gay Plays: The First Collection.* New York: Bard-Avon, 1979.

Hoffman's introduction, which outlines the history of homosexuality and theatrical representation, distinguishes between gay plays (in which the central figure is homosexual or homosexuality is the main theme) and gay theatre ("a production that implicitly or explicitly acknowledges that there are homosexuals on both sides of the footlights"). An account by Jane Chambers on the problems of mounting *A Late Snow* is included. Of the eight plays contained in this volume, three focus on lesbian issues: *Confessions of a Female Disorder* by Susan Miller, *A Late Snow* by Chambers, and *The Killing of Sister George* by Frank Marcus.

G17

Kendall, ed. *Love and Thunder: Plays by Women in the Age of Queen Anne.* London: Methuen, 1988.

Kendall details the conditions supporting the production of many plays by women in late seventeenth- and early eighteenth-century London. She also delineates the ways in which the women's plays differ from those by men and notes such common themes as the depiction of intense female friendships. A brief biography of the playwright and critical commentary precede each of the works in this anthology: *The Adventures of Venice* by Susanna Centlivre, *The Spanish Wives* by Mary Pix, *Love at a Loss; or, Most Votes Carry It* by Catharine Trotter, and *Antiochus the Great; or, The Fatal Relapse* by Jane Wiseman.

G18

Kennedy, Adrienne. *Adrienne Kennedy in One Act.* Minneapolis: University of Minnesota Press, 1988.

Plays included are *Funnyhouse of a Negro, The Owl Answers, A Lesson in Dead Language, A Rat's Mass, Sun, A Movie Star Has to Star in Black and White,* and two Greek adaptations: *Electra* and *Orestes.* Kennedy provides a brief preface.

G19

Klein, Maxine, Lydia Sargent, and Howard Zinn. *Playbook.* Boston: South End, 1986.

The preface describes the works as part of a political theatre that reflects the oppressive and liberational sides of life. Plays included are *Daughter of Earth* and *I Read about My Death in* Vogue *Magazine* by Lydia Sargent; *Emma* by Howard Zinn; and *The Furies of Mother Jones, Split-Shift, New Rise of the Master Race,* and *Windfall* by Maxine Klein.

G20

Kourilsky, Françoise, and Catherine Temerson, eds. *Plays by Women: An International Anthology.* New York: Ubu Repertory Theater: 1988.

Five playwrights who write in French but come from various cultural backgrounds are represented in this English-translation collection. Plays included are *A Picture Perfect Sky* by Denise Bonal (France), *Jocasta* by Michèle Fabien (Belgium), *The Girls from the Five and Ten* by Abla Farhoud (Quebec, Canada), *You Have Come Back* by Fatima Gallaire-Bourega (Algeria), and *Your Handsome Captain* by Simone Schwarz-Bart (Guadeloupe).

G21

Kriegel, Harriet, ed. *Women in Drama: An Anthology.* New York: New American Library, 1975.

Kriegel's introduction correlates the dramatic portrayal of women with their actual roles in the societies of ancient Greece, Elizabethan England, nineteenth- and twentieth-century Europe, and contemporary America. In addition to discussing the anthologized works, Kriegel examines the treatment of women by such canonized playwrights as Eugene O'Neill, Tennessee Williams, and Edward Albee. Plays included are *Medea* by Euripides, *Lysistrata* by Aristophanes, *Women Beware Women* by Thomas Middleton, *The Lady from the Sea* by Henrik Ibsen, *Miss Julie* by August Strindberg, *Mrs. Warren's Profession* by George Bernard Shaw, *Trifles* by Susan Glaspell, and *Approaching Simone* by Megan Terry.

G22

LaTempa, Susan, ed. *New Plays by Women.* Berkeley, Calif.: Shameless Hussy, 1979.

LaTempa notes that these diverse, short plays from all over the United States serve to introduce the writers, "not to stand as their definitive work." Plays included are *Mash Notes to an Old Codger* by Toni Press, *Baron's Night,* or *Catch as Catch-Can* by L. M. Sullivan, *The Life of the Party* by LaTempa, *The Railroad Women* by Helen Ratcliffe, *Laundromat* by Madeline Puccioni, *The Shanglers* by Betsy Julia Robinson, and *St. Mael and the Maldunkian Penguins* by Susan Boyd.

G23

McDermott, Kate, ed. *Places, Please! The First Anthology of Lesbian Plays.* San Francisco: Spinsters/Aunt Lute, 1985.

McDermott's introduction, which recounts her efforts to locate plays for this collection, offers a definition of lesbian drama as a script written by a lesbian, "which consciously, and explicitly, claims through a Lesbian character a Lesbian perspective of the play's events." Brief editorial comments precede each of the plays included: *Dos Lesbos* by Terry Baum and Carolyn Myers, *8 × 10 Glossy* and *Ruby Christmas* by Sarah Dreher, *Going Up* by Julia Willis, *Immediate Family* by Baum, *Out of Bounds* by Mariah Burton Nelson, and *Soup* by Ellen Gruber Garvey.

G24

Malpede, Karen. *A Monster Has Stolen the Sun and Other Plays.* Marlboro, Vt.: Marlboro, 1987.

Judith Malina's preface characterizes Malpede's plays as presenting the struggle of women to change the ancient formula of love and death to one of love and birth. Malina comments on the ritual aspects of the works and Malpede's pacifism. In addition to the title play, *The End of War* and *Sappho and Aphrodite* are included.

G25

Miles, Julia, ed. *Women Heroes: Six Short Plays from the Women's Project.* New York: Applause, 1987.

Miles' brief introduction reveals the process through which these plays were developed and underscores the diversity in the playwrights' choices of women heroes. Plays included are *Colette in Love* by Lavonne Mueller, *Personality* by Gina Wendkos and Ellen Ratner, *Emma Goldman: Love, Anarchy and Other Affairs* by Jessica Litwak, *Parallax (In Honor of Daisy Bates)* by Denise Hamilton, *How She Played the Game* by Cynthia Cooper, and *Millie* by Susan J. Kander.

G26

Miles, Julia, ed. *The Women's Project: Seven New Plays by Women.* New York: PAJ, 1980.

Miles discusses the development of the Women's Project at the American Place Theatre as a response to the general inhospitality of the stage to women playwrights and directors. Plays included are *Acrobatics* by Joyce Aaron and Luna Tarlo, *In the Midnight Hour* by Kathleen Collins, *Property* by Penelope Gilliatt, *Letters Home* by Rose Leiman Goldemberg, *Killings on the Last Line* by Lavonne Mueller, *Separate Ceremonies* by Phyllis Purscell, and *Signs of Life* by Joan Schenkar.

G27

Miles, Julia, ed. *The Women's Project 2: Five New Plays by Women.* New York: PAJ, 1984.

Miles applauds the increased visibility of women in theatre, points out the accomplishments of the Women's Project at the American Place Theatre, and refers to the "feminine aesthetic" issue and the rediscovery of a history of women playwrights. Plays included are *The Brothers* by Kathleen Collins, *Little Victories* by Lavonne Mueller, *Territorial Rites* by Carol K. Mack, *Heart of a Dog* by Terry Galloway, and *Candy and Shelley Go to the Desert* by Paula Cizmar.

G28

Morgan, Fidelis. *The Female Wits: Women Playwrights on the London Stage, 1660–1720.* London: Virago, 1981.

271

Morgan states that her aim is to present a representative collection of the best work of the first English women playwrights. The introductory material provides historical background and profiles of the playwrights. Editorial comments precede each of the plays in this collection: Aphra Behn's *The Lucky Chance, or: An Alderman's Bargain,* Catharine Trotter's *The Fatal Friendship,* Delariviere Manley's *Royal Mischief,* Mary Pix's *The Innocent Mistress,* and Susanna Centlivre's *The Wonder: A Woman Keeps a Secret.* The appendixes include the anonymously authored *The Female Wits,* a chronology, a glossary, and bibliographies.

G29

Moore, Honor, ed. *The New Women's Theatre: Ten Plays by Contemporary American Women.* New York: Vintage-Random House, 1977.

Seeking to place recent plays by women within their historical tradition, Moore's introduction examines Hrotsvitha, *commedia dell'arte,* and Aphra Behn, before turning to the work of several Americans, including Lillian Hellman and Gertrude Stein. She also discusses gender bias in criticism, the birth of feminist theatre, and the ways in which women are writing plays about female experience. A brief sketch of the dramatist precedes each of the plays included: *Bits and Pieces* by Corinne Jacker, *Window Dressing* by Joanna Russ, *Breakfast Past Noon* by Ursule Molinaro, *Birth and After Birth* by Tina Howe, *Mourning Pictures* by Honor Moore, *Wedding Band* by Alice Childress, *The Abdication* by Ruth Wolff, *The Ice Wolf* by Joanna Halpert Kraus, *I Lost a Pair of Gloves Yesterday* by Myrna Lamb, and *Out of Our Fathers' House,* arranged by Eve Merriam, Paula Wagner, and Jack Hoffsiss.

G30

Owens, Rochelle. The Karl Marx Play *and Others.* New York: Dutton, 1974.

In her short introduction, Owens discusses the patronizing ways in which women artists are treated, why she writes plays, and theatre as a life-sustaining force. Plays included are *The Karl Marx Play, Kontraption, He Wants Shih!, Farmer's Almanac, Coconut-Folk-Singer,* and *O.K. Certaldo.* Each work, except for the last two, is preceded by an author's note.

G31

Remnant, Mary, ed. *Plays by Women: Volume Five.* New York: Methuen, 1986.

Noting the lack of women's playwriting in print until the 1980s, Remnant's introduction stresses the importance of publication to the preservation of women's plays, which often operate as social and political documents. Plays included are *Queen Christina* by Pam Gems, *A Raisin in the Sun* by Lorraine Hansberry, *Piper's Cave* by Rona Munro, and *Money to Live* by Jacqueline Rudet. Each piece is followed by an afterword by its author (except for *Raisin,* which has an afterword by Yvonne Brewster) and a list of the playwright's stage works.

G32

Remnant, Mary, ed. *Plays by Women: Volume Six.* London: Methuen, 1987.

Writing about the negative reactions to feminist theatre by male critics, Remnant focuses on responses to the plays of Sarah Daniels, whose work is informed by radical lesbian politics. Plays included are *About Face* by Cordelia Ditton and Maggie Ford, *More* by Maro Green and Caroline Griffin, *Origin of the Species* by Bryony Lavery, *Pax* by Deborah Levy, and *Ficky Stingers* by Eve Lewis. Each play has an afterword by its author(s).

G33

Remnant, Mary, ed. *Plays by Women: Volume Seven.* London: Methuen, 1988.

After commenting on the continuing discrimination against women in theatre practice and the increased number of women writing plays, Remnant's introduction surveys recent productions of works by individual women and feminist companies. Plays included are *Thatcher's Women* by Kay Adshead, *Adult Child/Dead Child* by Claire Dowie, *Stamping, Shouting and Singing Home* by Lisa Evans, *Night (L'Homme gris)* by Marie Laberge, translated by Rina Fraticelli, and *Effie's Burning* by Valerie Windsor. Each play has an afterword by its author.

G34

Shange, Ntozake. *Three Pieces.* New York: St. Martin's, 1981.

In her foreword, Shange envisions future possibilities for black theatre and talks about writing in a racist society. Plays included are *spell #7, a photograph: lovers in motion,* and *boogie woogie landscapes.*

G35

Shewey, Don, ed. *Out Front: Contemporary Gay and Lesbian Plays.* New York: Grove, 1988.

In an introduction entitled "Pride in the Name of Love: Notes on Contemporary Gay Theatre," Shewey describes the traditional (distorted) and more current stage images of gay life and differentiates between mass-media's portrayal of gays/lesbians and contemporary theatre made *by* homosexuals. He traces the history of gay theatre and its relationship to the off–off-Broadway and gay liberation movements. He also comments on the structural innovation of contemporary feminist and lesbian playwriting. Among the plays included are *Execution of Justice* by Emily Mann, *The Well of Horniness* by Holly Hughes, and *A Weekend near Madison* by Kathleen Tolan.

G36

Spender, Dale, and Carole Hayman, eds. *How the Vote Was Won and Other Suffragette Plays.* London: Methuen, 1985.

Spender's introduction reviews the history of the British suffrage movement, including the contributions of women working in theatre. The efforts of the Actresses' Franchise League, which aimed both at gaining enfranchisement of women and at reconstructing the male-dominated theatrical profession, are detailed. Additional comments by Spender precede each play, and performance notes are provided by Hayman. Plays included are *How the Vote Was Won* by Cicely Hamilton and Christopher St. John, *Votes for Women* by Elizabeth Robins, *Lady Geraldine's Speech* by Beatrice Harraden, A *Chat with Mrs Chicky* and *Miss Appleyard's Awakening* by Evelyn Glover, *A Woman's Influence* by Gertrude Jennings, and *The Apple* by Inez Bensusan.

G37

Sullivan, Victoria, and James Hatch, eds. *Plays by and about Women.* New York: Random House, 1973.

Discussing their selection of twentieth-century plays by women, the editors point out that although the anthology is not strictly feminist, each play "deals in some fashion, either positively or negatively, with the nature of women in Western society from a female point of view." They suggest measuring the distance women have traveled in self-awareness through tracking the images in the plays. Plays included are *Overtones* by Alice Gerstenberg, *The Children's Hour* by Lillian Hellman, *The Women* by Clare Boothe (Luce), *Play with a Tiger* by Doris Lessing, *Calm Down Mother* by Megan Terry, *The Advertisement* by Natalia Ginzburg, *Rites* by Maureen Duffy, and *Wine in the Wilderness* by Alice Childress.

G38

Terry, Megan, et al. *High Energy: Musicals from the Omaha Magic Theatre.* New York: Broadway Play, 1983.

Plays included are *American King's English for Queens,* book and lyrics by Megan Terry, music by Lynn Herrick; *Running Gag,* book and structure by Jo Ann Schmidman, lyrics by Megan Terry, music by Marianne de Pury and Lynn Herrick; and *Babes in the Bighouse,* book and lyrics by Megan Terry, structure by Jo Ann Schmidman, music by John J. Sheehan.

G39
Terry, Megan, and Rochelle Lynn Holt. *Two by Terry Plus One.* Schulenburg, Tex.: Clark, 1984.

Plays included are Terry's companion one-acts, *Pro Game* and *The Pioneer,* and Holt's *Walking into the Dawn: A Celebration.* Notes by Holt describe her play's development and production at the Omaha Magic Theatre.

G40
Wandor, Michelene. *Five Plays.* London and New York: Journeyman/Playbooks, 1984.

Plays included are *To Die among Friends, The Old Wives' Tale, Whores D'Oeuvres, Scissors,* and *Aid Thy Neighbour.*

G41
Wandor, Michelene, ed. *Plays by Women: Volume One.* London: Methuen, 1982.

Wandor's introduction sketches the history of women playwrights and their exclusion from the dramatic canon. She also outlines the social conditions favorable to women's surfacing as playwrights, traces the influence of feminism on theatre practice, and examines the image of the woman theatre worker. Plays included are *Vinegar Tom* by Caryl Churchill, *Dusa, Fish, Stas and Vi* by Pam Gems, *Tissue* by Louise Page, and *Aurora Leigh* by Wandor. Each play is followed by an afterword by its author and a list of her stage works.

G42
Wandor, Michelene, ed. *Plays by Women: Volume Two.* London: Methuen, 1983.

In her introduction, Wandor relates the feminist slogan, "the personal is political," to the included plays: *Rites* by Maureen Duffy, *Letters Home* by Rose Leiman Goldemberg, *Trafford Tanzi* by Claire Luckham, and *Find Me* by Olwen Wymark. Each play is followed by an afterword by its author and a list of her stage works.

G43

Wandor, Michelene, ed. *Plays by Women: Volume Three.* London: Methuen, 1984.

Wandor comments on the underrepresentation of women's plays in print and the relationship of feminism to women's playwriting. Plays included are *Aunt Mary* by Pam Gems, *Red Devils* by Debbie Horsfield, *Blood Relations* by Sharon Pollock, and *Time Pieces* by Lou Wakefield and the Women's Theatre Group. Each play has an afterword by its author(s) and a list of her (their) stage works.

G44

Wandor, Michelene, ed. *Plays by Women: Volume Four.* London: Methuen, 1985.

Wandor argues for a policy of "positive discrimination" to ensure an increase in the number of women playwrights. Plays included are *Objections to Sex and Violence* by Caryl Churchill, *Rose's Story* by Grace Dayley, *Blood and Ice* by Liz Lochhead, and *Pinball* by Alison Lyssa. Each play has an afterword by its author and a list of her stage works, where applicable.

G45

Wandor, Michelene, ed. *Strike While the Iron Is Hot: Three Plays on Sexual Politics.* London: Journeyman, 1980.

Wandor delineates the development of the women's liberation movement and gay activism and their effect on theatre in the 1970s. Characterizing the anthologized plays as representing three strands in socialist/feminist/gay theatre, she summarizes the histories of the theatre companies producing the works. Comments by a group member precede each of the plays included: *Strike While the Iron Is Hot* by Red Ladder Theatre, *Care and Control* by Gay Sweatshop and Michelene Wandor, and *My Mother Says I Never Should* by the Women's Theatre Group.

G46

Wilkerson, Margaret B., ed. *Nine Plays by Black Women.* New York: Mentor-New American Library, 1986.

Wilkerson's introduction, which traces the tradition of black women playwrights in America back to the early twentieth century, cites the contributions of Angelina Grimké, Georgia Douglas Johnson, and others, in addition to the anthologized playwrights. After outlining early struggles against stereotypes through "race propaganda" plays, "folk art" plays, and historical drama, Wilkerson comments on the impact of the civil rights and women's movements on playwriting, and points out recent trends. Additional notes by Wilkerson precede each of the plays included in this volume: *A Black Woman Speaks* by Beah Richards, *Toussaint* (excerpt) by Lorraine Hansberry, *Wedding Band* by Alice Childress, *The Tapestry* by Alexis DeVeaux, *Unfinished Women Cry in No Man's Land While a Bird Dies in a Gilded Cage* by Aishah Rahman, *spell #7: geechee jibara quik magic trance manual for technologically stressed third world people: A Theater Piece* by Ntozake Shange, *The Brothers* by Kathleen Collins, *Paper Dolls* by Elaine Jackson, and *Brown Silk and Magenta Sunsets* by P. J. Gibson.

Reports: Conferences, Festivals, and Organizations

❖
❖

H1

Bassnett, Susan. "The Magdalena Experiment: New Directions in Women's Theatre." *The Drama Review* 31.4 (1987): 10–17.

Reporting on Magdalena, the first international festival of women in experimental theatre, held in Wales in August 1986, Bassnett differentiates between two distinct phases: the first, open to the public, involved performances brought by individuals and groups, discussions, and workshops; the second was an unstructured period of training and improvisation culminating in a final performance. Bassnett underscores the significance of the participants' investigation of whether there is a specifically female theatre.

H2

Bassnett, Susan. "Perceptions of the Female Role: The ISTA Congress." *New Theatre Quarterly* 3.11 (1987): 234–36.

After explaining the structure of the five-day 1986 program—demonstrations, performances, and "reflections"—Bassnett focuses on the wide-ranging discussions elicited by the pervasive unresolved question of gender roles. She comments that "unfortunate assumptions were being made, not only about the female role in general but also about the ways in which concepts of femininity are constructed in different societies." The core paper of the conference by ISTA director Eugenio Barba follows Bassnett's essay.

278

H3

Bassnett, Susan. "Women Experiment with Theatre: Magdalena 86."
New Theatre Quarterly 3.11 (1987): 224–34.

Bassnett provides additional perspectives on the three-week festival in
Cardiff, Wales, detailed in "The Magdalena Experiment" (see H1). Emphasizing that the international project was essentially a *process* for the
women involved, she identifies the underlying question: What kind of
experimental theatre could be created by women working together at a
time when European experimental theatre in general, still relatively un-
affected by the women's movement, had reached a plateau? She offers a
critique of the wide-ranging performances brought to the festival, the
contributions of the training sessions, and the problems of a public "final performance."

H4

Bernhard, Betty. "Documenting a Process: Women's Conference on the
Arts." *Women & Performance: A Journal of Feminist Theory* 1.2
(1984): 14–20.

Bernhard describes a conference for, by, and about women to discuss
the female aesthetic and its manifestation in various arts, held at Heceta
Head Lighthouse (Oregon) in July 1983. Included are suggestions for future women's conferences.

H5

Bovasso, Julie, Megan Terry, Rosalyn Drexler, Rochelle Owens, and Maria Irene Fornes. Interview. "Five Important Playwrights Talk about
Theatre without Compromise and Sexism." *Mademoiselle* Aug.
1972: 288+.

Five of the six members of the Women's Theatre Council (which also includes Adrienne Kennedy), a nonprofit corporation of women playwrights established to nurture innovative playwrights and reach
disadvantaged audiences, converse about their organization's future
plans as well as their past experiences with discrimination against
women in theatre.

H6

Bush, Corky. "Three Generations of an Oral History-Readers Theater
Project: Telling Our Life Stories." *Frontiers* 7.1 (1983): 80-84.

One of the cofounders of the Rural Women's History Project at the University of Idaho, Moscow, Bush recounts the undertaking, which en-
tailed interviewing rural women about their lives and values, writing
character sketches based on selected interviews, and performing the

279

resultant minidramas for audiences of other rural women, who were in turn interviewed. Bush states that the dramatizations, which provided a mirror for rural women and reassured them against fears of exploitation or trivialization, were the key to the endeavor's success.

H7

Carney, Kay, and Julianne Boyd. "Directors and Designers Report on Sex Discrimination in the Theatre." *Women & Performance: A Journal of Feminist Theory* 1.2 (1984): 46–57.

This report results from a survey conducted by the Directors' Caucus of the League of Professional Theatre Women/New York. The issues addressed include why women are not moving to Broadway jobs, what women directors feel is responsible for their underrepresentation at higher-paying levels, how they perceive themselves and their careers, and how they think others perceive them.

H8

Case, Sue-Ellen, and Ellen Donkin. "FIT: Germany's First Conference for Women in Theatre." *Women & Performance: A Journal of Feminist Theory* 2.2 (1985): 65–73.

The authors provide an account of the May 1984 Frauen im Theater conference in Berlin. In addition to a brief description of the presentations, the article includes a discussion of the rift between women representing the German professional theatre and those involved in amateur theatre or the feminist movement per se. The professional histories of playwrights Gerlind Reinshagen and Friederike Roth are contrasted.

H9

Crawford, Pauline. "Drama as a Communications Tool." *Giving and Taking: An Anthology.* Spec. issue of *ISIS Women's World* 4 (Dec. 1984): 47.

Crawford relates her sharing of the basic workshop techniques used by Sistren to raise consciousness about oppression at the Women's International Cross-Cultural Exchange Programme on "Communication" (Geneva, Switzerland, 1984).

H10

Curb, Rosemary K. "Scenes of the Times." *Women's Review of Books* June 1986: 10–11.

Curb's report on the March 1986 Boston Women in Theatre Festival serves as a springboard for her vision of a women's theatre of "wild passion, transcendence, transformation." Among the twenty offerings during the five-day period, those highlighted by Curb include: storyteller Rhiannon's singing-clowning-improvisation piece; Maria Irene Fornes's *Mud*, presented by the Omaha Magic Theatre; a collaborative effort by At the Foot of the Mountain and Spiderwoman, *Neurotic Erotic Exotics;* Susan Galbraith's *Holding Patterns,* presented by the Performers Ensemble of Boston; and the London-based Clean Break Theatre's production of *Decade*. Curb also notes the limited lesbian offerings and the unusual onstage visibility of men at a women's festival.

H11

Cyrelson, Florane. "Womanstyle Sets a Theatrical First." *New Directions for Women* 5.3 (1976): 9+.

Cyrelson describes the summer 1976 Philadelphia festival in which women's theatre companies from all over the United States and Canada participated. Among the groups mentioned are the Washington Area Feminist Theatre, Reality Theatre (Boston), and Kuku Ryku Theatre Lab (New York).

H12

Dace, Tish. "The Third Annual Women in Theatre Festival." *Women & Performance: A Journal of Feminist Theory* 3.2 (1987/1988): 188–91.

Reporting on the panel discussions (on women playwrights, alternative theatre forms, and criticism), workshops, and performances at the March 1987 Boston festival, Dace focuses on Susan Yankowitz's *Alarms*, Janice Perry (a.k.a. Gal) in *Are There Any Questions?,* and Arina Isaacson's *A Matter of the Heart.*

H13

Day, Susan. "Political Perversity at WOW Spring Festival." *Womanews* June 1986: 14.

This preview of WOW's month-long festival underscores its vast continuum of artistic media and intent, as well as its refusal to limit women's expression to one political stance or performance genre. A partial listing of scheduled events is included and an invitation issued to those wishing to present a short performance piece during the work-in-progress Variety Nights.

H14

Dolan, Jill. "Women's Theatre Program ATA: Creating a Feminist Forum." *Women & Performance: A Journal of Feminist Theory* 1.2 (1984): 5–13.

Dolan's analysis of the fourth annual WTP conference (Minneapolis, August 1983) notes the continuing marginality of feminists and lesbians and emphasizes the organization's need for a political perspective and a common vocabulary. Delineating underlying but generally unaddressed issues such as gender portrayal, feminist acting styles, and lesbian stereotyping, Dolan uses selected performances as examples: At the Foot of the Mountain's *Antigone Too,* written and directed by Martha Boesing; Sande Zeig's excerpts from Monique Wittig's *The Constant Journey;* the Split Britches Company's *Split Britches*; Patricia Montley's *Sisters*; and Jane Chambers' *Quintessential Image.*

H15
Dunderdale, Sue. "The Status of Women in the British Theatre." *Woman in Theatre.* Spec. issue of *Drama* 152 (1984): 9–11.

Dunderdale relates the history of the Conference of Women Theatre Directors and Administrators. Summarizing the results of its 1983 survey to determine the representation of women directors, administrators, and playwrights in publicly funded theatres, she concludes that "the more money and more prestige a theatre has, the less women will be employed in decision making positions."

H16
"Edinburgh Festival Preview." *Spare Rib* 181 (Aug. 1987): 18–21.

An annotated list of more than thirty plays, cabaret performances, and music and film events scheduled for the 1987 festival is provided. Also featured is an interview by Monique Griffiths with the Vusisizwe Players, who depict the exploitation of black women in South Africa in *Wathint' Abafazi Wahint' Imbokotho (You Strike the Woman, You Strike the Rock).*

H17
"Edinburgh Fringe." *Spare Rib* 193 (Aug. 1988): 36–38.

In addition to a list of more than twenty performances by women scheduled at the 1988 Scottish festival, this preview article includes self-profiles by three groups: Sensible Footwear, the Alexander Sisters, and Cambridge Better Half Theatre Company.

H18
Freydberg, Elizabeth Hadley. "Black Women and Feminism: One More Time (How Many More Times?)." *Theatre News* 13.7 (Fall 1981): 22.

The author records her participation in and reactions to the American Theatre Association's preconvention conference for women, "The New

Girl Network" (San Diego, August 1980). She comments that "the same exclusiveness and development of pockets of privilege which plague American society as a whole were building in this women's group."

H19

Goodman, Vera. "Playwrights' Plight Triggers Dramatic Action." *New Directions for Women* Jan.–Feb. 1981: 6+.

Concentrating on the underrepresentation of women playwrights, male control of theatre, and gender bias in criticism, Goodman reports on the Action for Women in Theatre research on hiring practices and the formation of the Committee for Women within the Dramatists Guild. Several suggestions for improving the status of women playwrights are offered.

H20

Goodman, Vera. "Theater Women Celebrate Women." *New Directions for Women* July–Aug. 1981: 17+.

Goodman reports on "Women Playwrights on Stage: Their Lives Reflected in Their Work," a 1981 conference presented by the Dramatists Guild Committee for Women, with participants Betty Comden, Phyllis Newman, June Havoc, Eve Merriam, Micki Grant, and others.

H21

Goodman, Vera. "Women of Color Stage Protest at Confab." *New Directions For Women* July–Aug. 1982: 8+.

Goodman writes about the "Third World Women in American Theatre," a 1982 conference sponsored by the Dramatists Guild Committee for Women and the Women's Project at the American Place Theatre. Among the events detailed is the panel titled "What Is She Saying?" in which Tisa Chang, Maria Irene Fornes, Kathleen Collins, and members of Spiderwoman participated.

H22

Jensen, Katherine. "Three Generations of an Oral History-Readers Theater Project: Woman as Subject, Oral History as Method." *Frontiers* 7.1 (1983): 84–87.

Jensen describes the Wyoming Women's Oral History Project, which was modeled on the Idaho Rural Women's History Project. See H6.

H23

Kendall. "On a Stage of One's Own." *Women's Review of Books* July–Aug. 1987: 22–23.

Questioning the analysis of "three and only three strains of feminism in theatre" expressed by Michelene Wandor (in *Carry on, Understudies*) and Jill Dolan at the California Themes in Drama Conference on Women in Theatre (Riverside, February 1987), Kendall reports on the Women in Theatre Festival (Boston, March 1987). She describes productions of *Alarms* by Susan Yankowitz, produced by Monstrous Regiment, and *Patience and Sarah* by Isabel Miller, produced by WOW Cafe, as well as a panel discussion on alternative theatre. She also discusses "Hometown Heroes": An Evening with Marsha Norman and Ann Pitoniak at Stage West (Springfield, Mass., March 1987).

H24
Malnig, Julie. "The Women's Project: A Profile." *Women & Performance: A Journal of Feminist Theory* 1.1 (1983): 71–73.

Malnig briefly examines Julia Miles's work with the Women's Project at the American Place Theatre and her creation of the League of Professional Theatre Women/New York.

H25
Martin, Stephanie. "A Festival of Rainbow Women in the Arts." *Herizons* Apr. 1985: 9.

Martin reports on the fall 1984 Toronto festival intended to highlight the contributions that women of color have made to the arts. She notes the event's inclusion of theatrical presentations, dance, music, and poetry readings as well as the educational workshops that provided an opportunity for creative interaction among participants from various cultural backgrounds and artistic fields.

H26
Miles, Julia. "The Women's Project: An Interview with Julia Miles." With Nadine Honigberg. *Theater* 17.1 (1985): 57–62.

Miles talks about the Women's Project at the American Place Theatre, including its inception, the process of play selection, and some of the work by playwrights produced there.

H27
Munk, Erika. "The Rites of Women." *Performing Arts Journal* 10.2 (1986): 35–42.

Munk dissects the September 1986 International School of Theatre Anthropology (ISTA) conference, "The Female Role as Represented on the Stage in Various Cultures," intended to present cross-gender work in a multitude of styles to help participants unravel the ramifications of gender codification and examine theatrical expression of sexual attitudes. Criticizing the failure of the conference to deal with these issues, to question significant assumptions (such as gender polarization), or to explore relevant social and political contexts, Munk cites certain aspects of Western experimental theatre that adversely influenced the event's structure and content. She concludes that an authoritarian, antifeminist theatre cannot address a subject like female representation "without first questioning its own practice."

H28
Ravindran, T. K. Sundari. "A Report of the Drama Workshop." *Giving and Taking: An Anthology*. Spec. issue of *ISIS Women's World* 4 (Dec. 1984): 44–46.

Ravindran describes exercises designed for work with local women's groups to identify issues, collective script development, games to help overcome inhibition, storytelling as a tool for conveying nonracist, nonsexist values, and simulation games dealing with issues such as classism, all of which were presented at the Women's International Cross-Cultural Exchange Programme on "Communication" (Geneva, Switzerland, 1984).

H29
Rothschild, Mary Aickin. "Three Generations of an Oral History- Readers Theater Project: Using Oral History to Find the 'Common Woman': An Arizona Project." *Frontiers* 7.1 (1983): 87–90.

The author describes "The Lives of Arizona Women: Past and Present," for which women representing different religious, ethnic, and geographical groups and different familial situations were interviewed, as "a linear descendent of the Idaho and Wyoming projects." See H6 and H22.

H30
Shaheed, Farida. "Creating One's Own Media: WAF in Pakistan." *ISIS International Women's Journal* 2 (Dec. 1984): 82.

Placing the Women's Action Forum (*Khawateen Mahaz-e-Amal*), a lobbying group formed to raise consciousness of women's oppression in both passed and proposed legislation, within its historical context, Shaheed focuses on the organization's use of the *jalsa*. She defines a *jalsa* as more than a meeting yet less than a rally, comprising speeches, poems, skits, songs, and resolutions adopted at the end, and summarizes the reasons behind the *jalsas'* success and the audiences' sense of sisterhood.

H31

Shewell, Debbie. "Women in Entertainment." *Women in Theatre.* Spec. issue of *Drama* 152 (1984): 14.

Shewell details Women in Entertainment's commitment to creating opportunities for women in the arts, its exploration of women's culture, and its development of workshop projects for professionals and outreach programs to respond to the needs of women in the community. The 1982 month-long "Women Live" festival, "a focus to which women could respond actively as creators and consumers," is noted as pointing up the difficulties faced by women in the entertainment industry.

H32

Solomon, Alisa. "Redressing Imbalances: Boston's Women in Theatre Festival Aims for a Wider Audience." *American Theatre* June 1987: 31–32.

This article describes the attempts of the organizers of the Women in Theatre Festival to redress the underrepresentation of women in American theatres, and summarizes the workshops, panels, and performances at the March 1987 event.

H33

Sullivan, Esther Beth. "West Coast Woman [sic] and Theatre Conference." *Theatre Journal* 40 (1988): 540–43.

Sullivan reports on the second West Coast Women and Theatre Conference (January 1988), dedicated to women's empowerment in theatre. She comments on the plurality of the opening night cabaret, citing especially Genny Lim's *XDoubleX*. Assessing the "Women of Color" session, she notes an underlying adherence to "womanism" rather than "feminism." She also writes about the session on "Women's Rage" and analyzes Anna Deavere Smith's one-woman performance, *On the Road: Voices of Bay Area Women in Theatre.*

H34

Woddis, Carole. "Second Wave Festival." *Plays and Players* Feb. 1987: 30–31.

Woddis provides information about the submission procedures, panels, and productions associated with the Deptford Albany Empire's 1986 three-week festival of plays by young women.

APPENDIX I

Resources: Bibliographies and Directories

❖
❖

Books

I1

Arata, Esther Spring. *More Black American Playwrights: A Bibliography.* Metuchen, N.J.: Scarecrow, 1978.

A continuation of the earlier work by Arata and Rotoli (see I2), this bibliography covers about 490 playwrights, 190 of whom were also included in the first volume. A listing of all periodicals and newspapers used in the compilation is included, as are authors and titles of reviews.

I2

Arata, Esther Spring, and Nicholas John Rotoli. *Black American Playwrights, 1800 to the Present: A Bibliography.* Metuchen, N.J.: Scarecrow, 1976.

This reference work covers 530 playwrights and is divided into three sections: a listing of black playwrights and their works, including criticisms and reviews of the authors and their publications and awards; a selected, general bibliography; and an index of play titles.

I3

Armistead, J. M. *Four Restoration Playwrights: A Reference Guide to Thomas Shadwell, Aphra Behn, Nathaniel Lee, and Thomas Otway.* Boston: Hall, 1984.

Armistead's annotated bibliography lists in chronological fashion the titles of books and articles about Behn written from 1675 through 1981. Of particular interest is the section in the introduction entitled "Trends in Behn Criticism."

14

Batchelder, Eleanor. *Plays by Women: A Bibliography*. New York: Wo-
    manbooks, 1977.

This combination reference work and catalog (published by a New York
City bookstore for women), intended to increase women playwrights'
visibility, lists both individually published plays and anthologies containing plays by women. Batchelder's introduction includes an explanation of the somewhat arbitrary selection process, acknowledges the
unfortunate exclusion of recent (unpublished) plays by women's theatre
groups, and provides directions for use and search tips.

15

Coven, Brenda. *American Women Dramatists of the Twentieth Cen-
    tury: A Bibliography*. Metuchen, N.J.: Scarecrow, 1982.

A selected bibliography on the general topic of women dramatists is followed by 133 bibliographies of playwrights who have had at least one
play successfully produced in New York (on Broadway or off-
Broadway). Each playwright's listing includes play titles, biographical
information, criticism, and reviews.

16

Frost, Wendy, and Michele Valiquette. *Feminist Literary Criticism: A
    Bibliography of Journal Articles, 1975–1981*. New York: Garland,
    1988.

The lengthy introductory essay traces the development of feminist criticism in the period and explores two divergent strands: that within the
alternative feminist culture and that within the academy. Separate author and subject indexes provide access to the entries, which are mostly
grouped by century and subdivided into prose, poetry, drama, miscellaneous, and multiple genres. Other sections cover multiple time periods,
folklore and oral tradition, language and gender, pedagogy and research, and theory. Entries are followed by descriptive key words and a
list of authors and works discussed.

17

Hatch, James V., and OMANii Abdullah, eds. *Black Playwrights 1823–
    1977: An Annotated Bibliography of Plays*. New York: Bowker,
    1977.

The editors cite more than 2700 plays by about 900 black Americans,
including several pertinent to the study of feminist drama. Each entry
features all or most of the following information: author's name, play title, date, genre, description, cast requirements, length, production his-

tory, publication details, library source, and whom to contact for permission.

I8

Helbing, Terry, ed. *Gay Theatre Alliance Directory of Gay Plays*. New York: JH, 1980.

Helbing's compilation alphabetically lists some 400 plays with major gay characters or predominant gay themes. Although male gay plays are in the majority, many lesbian plays are included. The introduction comments on recurrent themes such as the gay relationship and coming out. In addition to a plot synopsis, information is included on the type of play, number of acts, male and female characters, settings, production and publication history, amateur royalties, etc. One appendix lists "lost" plays and another lists gay theatre companies (as of December 1979).

I9

Heys, Sandra. *Contemporary Stage Roles for Women: A Descriptive Catalog*. Westport, Conn.: Greenwood, 1985.

Although this work is intended to highlight accessible plays with strong female roles, Heys cautions that the pervasive nature of negative female stereotypes means that few plays completely avoid them. In addition to providing encouragement for revising scripts and specific advice for strengthening and salvaging weak roles, Heys discusses redesigning male roles for portrayal by women. The first section, an alphabetical listing by title, includes play synopses and descriptions of female roles. The following sections catalogue the plays according to age groupings, character types, unusual physical characteristics, and roles specifically for minorities. Appendixes classify the plays by gender distribution and offer agent and publisher information.

I10

Humm, Maggie. *An Annotated Critical Bibliography of Feminist Criticism*. Boston: Hall, 1987.

Humm's purpose is "to provide a core collection of women-centered materials which can support feminist research, policy and studies." She divides the entries into eight categories; of particular interest here are "Arts, Film, Theatre, Media, Music," and "Literary Criticism." The book contains two indexes, one of subjects and one of contributors.

I11

Miller, Jeanne-Marie A. "Black Women Playwrights from Grimké to Shange: Selected Synopses of Their Works." *All the Women Are White, All the Blacks Are Men, but Some of Us Are Brave: Black Women's Studies.* Ed. Gloria T. Hull, Patricia Bell Scott, and Barbara Smith. Old Westbury, N.Y.: Feminist Press, 1982. 280–96.

Preceding biographical-bibliographical notes on twenty playwrights, Miller's essay notes the frequent use of the one-act form in the early works, the mostly realistic treatment of the black experience, and the female perspective from which they tell the black woman's story. Works by Childress, Hansberry, Kennedy, Sanchez, and others are discussed.

I12

O'Donnell, Mary Ann. *Aphra Behn: An Annotated Bibliography of Primary and Secondary Sources.* New York: Garland, 1986.

O'Donnell divides the materials into two parts: primary sources, including Behn's complete works, works she edited or translated, works written or edited by others that include works by Behn, attributions with some validity, and other attributions or works containing attributions; and secondary sources, including more than 600 books, articles, and essays. The brief introduction provides an overview of Behn's career.

I13

Peterson, Bernard L., Jr., ed. *Contemporary Black American Playwrights and Their Plays: A Biographical Directory and Dramatic Index.* New York: Greenwood, 1988.

In an encyclopedic format, this book covers famous and less well-known playwrights, screenwriters, television scriptwriters, etc. In addition to biographical information, entries include annotated lists of works, production histories, and locations of published or unpublished scripts. The appendix features additional playwrights whose scripts are in special repositories and other contemporary black American playwrights.

I14

Schwartz, Narda Lacey. *Articles on Women Writers: A Bibliography.* Vol. 1. Santa Barbara, Calif.: ABC-Clio, 1977.

This bibliography of works dealing with more than 600 women writers, including playwrights from English-speaking countries, uses materials published between 1960 and 1975 in popular and scholarly periodicals. Citations from *Dissertation Abstracts International* are included.

I15

Schwartz, Narda Lacey. *Articles on Women Writers, 1976–1984: A Bibliography.* Vol. 2. Santa Barbara, Calif.: ABC-Clio, 1985.

This continuation of Schwartz's earlier work (see I14) involves more than 1000 women writers.

I16

White, Barbara. *American Women Writers: An Annotated Bibliography of Criticism.* New York: Garland, 1977.

Concentrating on criticism that treats at least three individual writers or women writers as a distinct group, White divides her bibliography into ten sections: biography, special groups (minority, lesbian, regional), special topics (genre, theme), literary history, contemporary assessments, feminine sensibility, problems faced by women because of their gender, phallic criticism, feminist literary criticism, and miscellaneous. White's introduction examines the historically contradictory criticism of women writers and related topics.

Periodicals, Serials, and Annuals

I17

Anthony, Geraldine, and Tina Usmiani. "A Bibliography of English Canadian Drama Written by Women." *Women Writers of the Commonwealth.* Spec. issue of *World Literature Written in English* 17 (1978): 120–43.

Works by more than 200 playwrights are included.

I18

Bach, Gerhard. "Susan Glaspell (1876–1948): A Bibliography of Dramatic Criticism." *Great Lakes Review* 3.2 (1977): 1–34.

Bach maintains in his introduction that the collected criticism suggests that "Glaspell rises above the large group of secondary playwrights specifically for her increasing ability to connect and intertwine the *drama of ideas* with the *drama of emotion.*" Most entries are annotated.

I19

Curb, Rosemary. "Catalog of Feminist Theatre—Part 2." *Chrysalis* 10 (1979): 63–75.

This annotated list of 29 feminist theatres offers information on their founding, participants, productions, etc. Theatres dormant for at least a year or for which there is no recent information are separately categorized. Curb's introductory essay on the first decade of feminist theatre in the United States reviews the ways in which the theatres started, their aesthetic and political diversity, their structure and working processes, audience reactions, and the similarity of material used, such as feminist versions of Greek myths and the celebration of female ancestors.

I20
Curb, Rosemary, Phyllis Mael, and Beverley Byers Pevitts. "Catalog of Feminist Theatre—Part 1." *Chrysalis* 10 (1979): 51–62.

The authors provide lengthy, critical annotations in their bibliography of feminist drama, encompassing anthologies, published plays, produced but unpublished plays, and alternative theatre projects. A list of sources for additional information is included. The introductory essay by Mael, which discusses the increase in women playwrights and the diversity of feminist drama, appears in modified form in *Kansas Quarterly* as "Beyond Hellman and Hansberry." See A45.

I21
Gillespie, Patti [P.]. "A Listing of Feminist Theatres." *Women's Theatre.* Spec. issue of *Theatre News* Nov. 1977: 22–24.

Gillespie's compilation of more than 80 theatres in the United States, Canada, and England "includes groups representing a wide range of theatrical, political, and sexual ideologies but sharing some degree of affiliation with feminism."

I22
Goodman, Vera. "Feminist Theatres." *New Directions for Women* July–Aug. 1982: 8.

This is a briefly annotated list of 15 theatres.

I23
Lister, Rota Herzberg. "Canadian Plays in English about Older Women: A Bibliography." *Resources for Feminist Research* 11.2 (1982): 238–40.

An annotated bibliography of plays by both women and men featuring female characters who are middle-aged or older is preceded by Lister's introduction, which notes that however battered by her circumstances, none of the characters is totally vanquished.

124

"More Feminist Theaters." *New Directions for Women* Mar.–Apr. 1983: 7.

Six theatre companies are detailed.

125

Navaretta, Cynthia. "A Guide to All the Arts—for a Modern Mona." *Ms.* Dec. 1975: 87–90.

The section on theatre includes feminist theatre groups, action groups, and publications and resources.

126

Perinciolo, Lillian. "Feminist Theatre: They're Playing in Peoria." *Ms.* Oct. 1975: 101–4.

A brief description of each group accompanies this selective catalog of feminist theatres in the United States.

127

Spedding, Carole, comp. "A Guide to Women's Theatre Groups." *Spare Rib* 80 (Mar. 1979): 18–21.

Suggestions on how to book a touring theatre company, pay for a production, publicize the event, and help the company on the day of performance precede an annotated directory of groups in England, Wales, and Ireland.

128

Wolfe, Irmgard H. "Marsha Norman: A Classified Bibliography." *Studies in American Drama, 1945–Present* 3 (1988): 148–75.

Following a concise overview of Norman's career and critical reaction to her work, Wolfe divides the materials into the following categories: Norman's works (nonfiction, book reviews, novel, plays, screenplays), interviews, criticism, reviews, and biographical and informational sources.

APPENDIX II

Special Issues of Journals and Periodicals, Including Selected Annuals

❖
❖

J1

Acting Up! Women in Theater and Performance. Spec. issue of *Heresies* 5.1 (1984).

While most articles are annotated in the appropriate chapters (see B69, D62, D65, D147, D207, F40, F41, F44, F56), Stephanie Skura's interview with Meredith Monk; Susan Mosakowski's interview with seven women involved in marketing, grant-getting, and producing; a panel organized by Daryl Chin dealing with funding and alternative performance; and other brief pieces also are included. The issue features numerous photographs from feminist productions. Among the scripts or excerpts are the following: Bonnie Greer's *Vigil Part II*; Clare Raulerson's *Script for a Women [sic] in Prison Performance*; *Women in Research* by Cindy Carr, Lenora Champagne, and Patricia Jones; Jessica Hagedorn's *Crayon Bondage*; W.E.T.'s *The Daughters Cycle*; Stephanie Skura's *Some Kind of Dance*; Jovette Marchessault's *Saga of the Wet Hens*; Vanalyne Green's *Trick or Drink*; and Jacqueline Allen's *Nudes in Repose*.

J2

Barranger, Milly S., ed. *Southern Women Playwrights*. Spec. issue of *Southern Quarterly* 25.3 (1987).

In her introduction, Barranger notes the ways in which the works of Childress, Norman, Henley, and others are distinctly southern and female-centered. In addition to the annotated articles (see D36, D99, D101), this issue contains W. Kenneth Holditch's "Another Part of the Country: Lillian Hellman as Southern Playwright," Virginia Spencer Carr's "Carson McCullers: Novelist Turned Playwright," Polly Holliday's "I Remember Alice Childress," Lisa J. McDonnell's "Diverse Similitude: Beth Henley and Marsha Norman," and Linda L. Hubert's "Humor and Heritage in Sandra Deer's *So Long on Lonely Street*."

J3

Bond, Jean Carey, ed. *Lorraine Hansberry: Art of Thunder, Vision of Light*. Spec. issue of *Freedomways* 19.4 (1979).

See D44.

J4

Case, Sue-Ellen, ed., and Enoch Brater, co-ed. *Feminist Diversions*. Spec. issue of *Theatre Journal* 40.2 (1988).

See A26, D71, D74, E159, F30, and F43.

J5

Chin, Daryl, ed. *Work by Women*. Spec. issue of *Art & Cinema* ns 1.3 (1987).

Pertinent articles are annotated. See A20, A29, D73, and F21. Additional pieces of interest include interviews with Pat Oleszko and Linda Hartinian, and texts, excerpts, or descriptions of *Ruined: A Beach Opera* by Jessica Hagedorn, *Trick or Drink* and *This Is Where I Work* by Vanalyne Green, *Outrage* by Sue Heinemann, and *Sophie Heightens the Contradictions* by Sally Banes.

J6

Crum, Jane Ann, ed. *Theater* 17.1 (1985).

Although this marks the first *Theater* issue based on gender, the Afterword by Crum and regular editor Joel Schechter states that no special title was given because "some of these people prefer to see themselves as artists first, and not be judged by gender." Annotated articles include D34, D87, D118, F39, and H26. The issue also contains an interview with Theodora Skipitares and the script of *The Age of Invention*; the script of *An Open Couple—Very Open* by Franca Rame and Dario Fo; Susan Mason's interview with Kristin Linklater; Crum's interview with lighting designers Peggy Clark Kelley, Jennifer Tipton, and Danianne Mizzy; Scott Cummings' interview with Dolly Jacobs; Ruby Cohn's "Ariane Mnouchkine: Twenty-One Years of Théâtre du Soleil"; Judith Graves Miller's "*Donna Giovanni*: Staging Ambiguous Desire"; Jan

Breslauer's review of Helene Keyssar's *Feminist Theatre*; and Kenneth Bernard's "Some Observations on Meredith Monk's Revival of *Quarry.*"

J7

Falconieri, John V., ed., and Beverley Byers-Pevitts, spec. issue co-ed. *Women in Theatre*. Spec. issue of *Theatre Annual* 40 (1985).

Beverley Byers-Pevitts provides a brief introduction that comments on themes in feminist drama and the multiplicity of critical approaches. See D82, D110, D140, D156, D187, D201, E245, and F49.

J8

Greene, Gayle, and Carolyn Ruth Swift, eds. *Feminist Criticism of Shakespeare*. Spec. issue of *Women's Studies* 9.1 (1981).

See E154.

J9

Greene, Gayle, and Carolyn Ruth Swift, eds. *Feminist Criticism of Shakespeare II*. Spec. issue of *Women's Studies* 9.2 (1982).

See E155.

J10

Julian, Ria, ed. *Women in Theatre*. Spec. issue of *Drama* 152 (1984).

Articles already annotated are A24, B11, B51, D197, F46, H15, and H31. Other articles of note focus on various women theatre practitioners. Margaret Sheehy asks "Why Aren't There More Women Directors?" and Sheila Hancock and Nancy Meckler offer different perspectives on their roles as directors. Amanda Fiske and Di Seymour discuss theatrical design and differences between working with male and female directors. Also included are pieces on Peggy Ashcroft, composers Lindsay Cooper and Stephanie Nunn, and administrators Sue Storr and Sally Barling.

J11

Kinney, Arthur F., ed., and Kirby Farrell, co-ed. *Women in the Renaissance*. Spec. issue of *English Literary Renaissance* 14.3 (1984).

See E148 and E242 for annotated articles. This issue also features a preface by Kathleen E. McLuskie, a bibliography on women writers from 1485 to 1603 by Elizabeth H. Hageman, Dale B. J. Randall's essay on chastity-testing and its problematic use in *The Changeling*, and a number of essays examining various types of writing by women.

J12

Kinney, Arthur F., ed., and Kirby Farrell and Elizabeth H. Hageman, co-eds. *Women in the Renaissance II*. Spec. issue of *English Literary Renaissance* 18.1 (1988).

The preface by Hageman, who also contributes a bibliography of "Recent Studies in Women Writers of the English Seventeenth Century (1604–1674)," contends that most recent work on Renaissance women "is overtly feminist in its tone and implications," because it is written by scholars seeking to modify the traditional assumptions about women's nonparticipation in Renaissance literary life. In addition to the annotated essays (see A46, E168, E251, F33), Jacqueline Disalvo's piece on Milton and witchcraft may be of interest.

J13

Kirby, Michael, ed. *Women and Performance*. Spec. issue of *The Drama Review* 24.2 (1980).

Kirby's introduction clarifies that although this issue deals with feminist work, it is not the primary focus. See A22 and F65 for the articles that fall within the parameters of this bibliography. Other pieces deal with Ellen Stewart and La Mama, Joan Holden and the San Francisco Mime Troupe, performance artist Laurie Anderson, designer Vanessa James, Linda Mussman's Time and Space Limited Theatre, Anne Bogart, and Yvonne Rainer. Anderson's script of *Americans on the Move, Parts 1 and 2* is also included.

J14

Lister, Rota [Herzberg]. *Women in Canadian Drama*. Spec. issue of *Canadian Drama* 5.2 (1979).

As noted in an editorial emphasizing the entrapment of Canadian women in roles not of their own making, this issue covers not only women writing on women playwrights but also women writing on men, men writing on women, men writing on women writing on women, etc. See D122, D132, D135, D155, D160, E142, and E269 for the annotated articles. The following also appear: an essay on Gwen Pharis Ringwood's social protest plays that focus on Canadian Indians and the problems of bigotry and materialism in contemporary society; articles in French on the theatre of Marcel Dubé, Anne Hébert's *Le Temps sauvage*, and Denise Boucher's *Les Fées ont soif*; scripts of Ringwood's *The Stranger* and *Murmurs*; an English translation of a radio play by Marie-Claire Blais; and numerous reviews.

J15
Moy, James S., ed., and Timothy Murray, co-ed. *Staging Gender*. Spec.
    issue of *Theatre Journal* 37.3 (1985).

See D69, D72, D203, E106, E193, and E229.

J16
Redmond, James, ed. *Themes in Drama* 7 (*Drama, Sex and Politics*)
    (1985). (Also published as: Redmond, James, ed. *Drama, Sex and
    Politics*. Themes in Drama 7. Cambridge, England.: Cambridge Uni-
    versity Press, 1985.)

Essays chosen for annotation and included in the periodicals sections,
as explained in the introduction to this bibliography, are C21, D138,
E76, E103, E105, E180, E194, E201, and E257. Other articles, more peripheral, include studies on Aristophanes, Büchner, Euripides, David
Hare, García Lorca, Machiavelli, Marlowe, Greek and Roman comedy,
and pornography.

J17
Wallace, Robert, ed. *Feminism and Canadian Theatre*. Spec. issue of
    Canadian Theatre Review 43 (Summer 1985).

In addition to the annotated articles (see A43, A60, B12, B31, B38, B52,
D51, D61, D66, D91, D196, F25, F31), this issue offers "En de multiples
scènes," a chronology of Quebec feminist plays with notes in French by
Lorraine Camerlain, the script of *This Is for You, Anna*, and a piece on
artistic director Janet Amos. In his introduction, which emphasizes the
collaborative effort and contributions of women that went into *Feminism and Canadian Theatre*, Wallace admits that although he considers himself proto-feminist, "I believe my position as a man prevents
me from fully appreciating the circumstances that instruct the feminist
perspective."

J18
Winsten, Lynne R. *Women's Theatre*. Spec. issue of *Theatre News* 10.2
    (Nov. 1977).

See A38, B29, and I21. Also of interest are articles outlining the goals of
the newly formed Women's Theatre Program and various research projects involving women in theatre, a tribute to women leaders of the
American Theatre Association, pieces on performers, play reviews, and
purpose statements by At the Foot of the Mountain and Karen Malpede
of the New Cycle Theater.

J19

Women in Theatre. Spec. issue of *Room of One's Own* 8.2 (1983).

In addition to D89, D117, D173, and F71, the issue contains Margaret Hollingsworth's *Islands*. In introductory notes, Eleanor Wachtel comments on the underrepresentation of women playwrights and directors.

J20

Women and Performance. Spec. issue of *Fireweed* 7 (Summer 1980).

See B50, B53, D76, D168, and F23 for fully annotated articles. The editorial by Rina Fraticelli, Rhea Tregebov, and the Fireweed Collective underscores that "the creation of women by women now allows for the body of performance literature to include *self-fictions*: fictions only once removed from their source." Of interest are Susan Poteet's description of *Parce que c'est la nuit* by Le Théâtre expérimental des femmes; Constance Brissenden's interview with director Kathryn Shaw; Martha Fleming's piece on the video art of storyteller Lisa Steele, followed by the transcripts of two (live) performance pieces (*Mrs. Pauly* and *Hello, My Name Is Sandy*); and scenes from Nightwood Theatre's *The True Story of Ida Johnson* and Erika Ritter's *Automatic Pilot*.

J21

Women and Performance. Spec. issue of *Fireweed* 8 (Fall 1980).

This second *Fireweed* issue on women and performance includes, in addition to the annotated material (B58, D100, D131, F34), interviews and pieces by women in dance, film, visual and video art, and an excerpt from D. Ann Taylor's *The Bible As Told To*.

APPENDIX III

Selected Works Published after 1988

Books

Austin, Gayle. *Feminist Theories for Dramatic Criticism.* Ann Arbor, Mich.: University of Michigan Press, 1990.

Bassnett, Susan, comp. *Magdalena: International Women's Experimental Theatre.* Oxford, England: Berg, 1989.

Ben-Zvi, Linda, ed. *Women in Beckett: Performance and Critical Perspectives.* Urbana: University of Illinois Press, 1990.

Brater, Enoch, ed. *Feminine Focus: The New Women Playwrights.* New York: Oxford University Press, 1989.

Callaghan, Dympna. *Woman and Gender in Renaissance Tragedy: A Study of* King Lear, Othello, The Duchess of Malfi *and* The White Devil. Atlantic Highlands, N.J.: Humanities, 1989.

Case, Sue-Ellen, ed. *Performing Feminisms: Feminist Critical Theory and Theatre.* Baltimore, Md.: Johns Hopkins University Press, 1990.

Ferris, Lesley. *Acting Women: Images of Women in Theatre.* New York: New York University Press, 1989.

Finney, Gail. *Women in Modern Drama.* Ithaca, N.Y.: Cornell University Press, 1989.

Hart, Lynda. *Making a Spectacle: Feminist Essays on Contemporary Women's Theatre*. Ann Arbor: University of Michigan Press, 1989.

McLuskie, Kathleen. *Renaissance Dramatists*. Atlantic Highlands, N.J.: Humanities, 1989.

Loomba, Ania. *Gender, Race, Renaissance Drama*. Cultural Politics Series. Manchester, England: Manchester University Press, 1989.

Novy, Marianne, ed. *Women's Re-Visions of Shakespeare*. Urbana: University of Illinois Press, 1990.

Robinson, Alice M., Vera Mowry Roberts, and Milly S. Barranger, eds. *Notable Women in American Theatre: A Biographical Dictionary*. New York: Greenwood, 1989.

Rutter, Carol. *Clamorous Voices: Shakespeare's Women Today*. New York: Routledge/Theatre Arts, 1989.

Schlueter, June, ed. *Feminist Rereadings of Modern American Drama*. Rutherford, N.J.: Fairleigh Dickinson University Press; London, Associated University Presses, 1989.

Schlueter, June, ed. *Modern American Drama: The Female Canon*. Rutherford N.J.: Fairleigh Dickinson University Press; London, Associated University Presses, 1990.

Play Collections

Champagne, Lenora, ed. *Out from Under: Texts by Women Performance Artists*. New York: Theatre Communications Group, 1990.

Churchill, Caryl. *Plays: Two*. London: Methuen, 1990.

Davis, Jill, ed. *Lesbian Plays II*. London: Metheun, 1989.

Miles, Julia, ed. *WomensWork: Five New Plays from the Women's Project*. New York: Applause, 1989.

Perkins, Kathy A., ed. *Black Female Playwrights: An Anthology of Plays Before 1950*. Bloomington: Indiana University Press, 1989.

Bibliography

Boos, Florence, and Lynn Miller, eds. *Bibliography of Women and Literature*. Vol I: Articles and Books (1974–1978) by and about Women from 600 to 1975. Vol. II: Supplement. Articles and Books (1979–1981) by and about Women from 600 to 1975. New York: Holmes & Meier, 1989. Forthcoming: Vol. III: (1981–1985).

Special Issues of Periodicals and Annuals

Brater, Enoch, ed., and W. B. Worthen, co-ed. *Women and/in Drama*. Spec. issue of *Theatre Journal* 42.3 (1990).

Cody, Gabrielle, and Liza Henderson, eds. *Engendering Theater*. Spec. issue of *Theater* 20.2 (1989).

Kolin, Philip C., and Colby H. Kullman, eds. *Studies in American Drama, 1945–Present* 4 (1989). While there is no special title, the issue is devoted to American women playwrights.

Redmond, James, ed. *Themes in Drama* 7 (*Women in Theatre*): Cambridge, England: Cambridge University Press, 1989.

Savona, Jeannette Laillou, and Ann Wilson, eds. *Women in the Theatre*. Special issue of *Modern Drama* 32.1 (1989).

Wilson, Ann, ed. *Sexuality, Gender and Theatre*. Spec. issue of *Canadian Theatre Review* 59 (Summer 1989).

Women and Performance continues to publish. Issue 4.1 (1988–89), is devoted to *Feminist Americana*. Of particular interest is issue 4.2 (1989), celebrating the tenth anniversary of the Women and Theatre Program. Issue 5.1 (1990) is subtitled *Feminist Ethnography and Performance*.

Name Index

❖
❖

This index includes the names of both women and men in drama/performance/theatre, such as playwrights, performance artists, directors, producers, and designers. Also within this alphabetized list are the names of theatres, theatre companies, organizations, conferences, and festivals. The letter and number following a name refer to an entry code, not a page number.

Variations on names due to different translations, discrepancies unclarified through the centuries, a woman's adoption of a huband's last name, or the use of pseudonyms, are handled through a cross-reference system. The main entry is the name under which the person is best known in terms of theatrical practice. For example, the Latvian playwright Aspazija would be located in two places, as follows:

Main entry: Aspazija (Elza Rozenberga)
See reference: Rozenberga, Elza. *See* Aspazija

When necessary, I have consulted the Library of Congress authority file, the Modern Language Association's International Bibliography, and other available sources, such as biographical dictionaries and encyclopedias of theatre. For example, the name of Hrotsvitha of Gandersheim, the tenth-century German nun who wrote six Latin plays, appears in several forms in the criticism. The user seeking information on this playwright will find the following as she or he searches for "Hro":

Hrotsvitha von Gandersheim (also Hrotsvit, Hrotsvita, Hroswitha, Roswitha)

As these variations in the "Hro" spellings are so slight, with no intervening names in the index, common sense precludes the need for separate listings and cross-referencing. However, if the user looks up "Roswitha," she or he will be referred to "Hrotsvitha."

Although I am not always entirely comfortable with the Library of Congress or Modern Language Association choices (for example, Clare

303

Boothe Luce is listed in both sources under "Luce," her married name, although many critics refer to her as "Boothe"), they have often provided valuable guidelines. In Clare Boothe Luce's case, I have followed their lead. However, if most of the current research on a historical figure concurs in a name's spelling, I have chosen to maintain the practice, even if it conflicts with the Library of Congress authority file. A case in point is the seventeenth-century playwright whose main entry here is "Manley, Delariviere." At times she has been called "Mrs. Mary Delariviere Manley" (the "Mary" is now contested) and at other times "Delariviere" has been spelled in such variations as "de la Riviere."

For the Anglo-American names of theatre groups, I have eliminated for the most part any use of a preceding "the" (which writers sometimes employ with an uppercase "T," sometimes with a lowercase "t," and sometimes omit altogether). For a theatre company whose name is in a foreign language, an article such as "Le" appears at the beginning of the entry. The name is alphabetized according to the first letter following the article or contraction thereof.

If "theater" or "theatre" is spelled consistently one way, I have followed suit. Where inconsistencies exist, I have generally opted for "theatre."

When necessary to distinguish between identical names or when additional information has been deemed helpful in the understanding of the entry, I have added it. For example:

Magdalena (Wales festival)
Women's Theatre Group (Australia)

If a woman playwright has authored an article and it is about another playwright or a feminist company, or is theoretical in nature, the article is not indexed under her name. If, however, she discusses her own writing, then her name *will* be followed by the appropriate code in the Name Index. Similar rules govern other theatre practitioners.

Title Index

Titles of plays and performance art pieces that have received substantive discussion in an article or book are listed here. As noted in the Introduction, plays by feminist groups that are discussed more than in passing—although perhaps not as fully as a play by an individual, well-known playwright—have not been subjected to as stringent criteria.

If the user has not found sufficient information under a title, she or he should check the Name Index for the playwright(s), performance artist(s), or theatre group responsible for the creation of the work.

Foreign plays are indexed under their English titles *and* cross-referenced from their original titles when both versions have been used in the annotated item(s). For example:

> Main entry: The Secret Life of Albert Nobbs (La Vie singulière d'Albert Nobbs; *also* The Singular Life of Albert Nobbs)
> *See* reference: La Vie singulière d'Albert Nobbs. *See* The Secret Life of Albert Nobbs

When bibliographic entries have used *only* foreign-language titles for a particular play and these titles have not been translated, even parenthetically, I have made no attempt to do so. Therefore, access to studies of such works must be gained through the original title or through the use of another index.

If a work in translation is widely available and well-known in English, such as Ibsen's *A Doll House,* only the English title is given. Alternative translations with slight differences, such as *A Doll's House,* are provided in parentheses. Thus, the entry would read:

> A Doll House (*also* A Doll's House)

Preference is given to the original rather than to updated forms of titles, with the modern spelling parenthetically supplied if used by some critics; for example, a work by the seventeenth-century playwright, Aphra Behn, would appear in the index as:

The Forc'd Marriage (*also* The Forced Marriage, or The Jealous Bridegroom)

A similar indication is used when a play originally written in English has alternative titles, such as *Cloud Nine* (Caryl Churchill's original British play) and *Cloud 9* (the American version, which differs *slightly* in production and publication, but is essentially the same play).

The code letter and number following a title designate an entry, not a page number.

Categorical Index

The following extensive index contains a cataloging of the drama/performance/theatre of different countries and time periods; feminist theatre companies by location and specialization; lesbian plays; and women playwrights by nationality including a selected ethnic breakdown of American women playwrights. Works in which the sole focus is on theory and criticism without a substantive discussion of a play, playwright, group, etc., are not indexed here.

Code letters and numbers following headings refer to bibliographic entries, and not to pages.

Drama/Performance/Theatre by Geographical Location and Period

Not every country is subdivided into two or more time periods. Such divisions are used only as realistically necessary.

English drama/performance/theatre presents the most subheadings. Unlike the Modern Language Association, which assigns authors and works by centuries, the system here entails categories that correspond to material changes in theatrical practice as well as in the dramatic texts. To illustrate: There is a separate section for "English, Restoration (c. 1660–1700)," the period distinguished not only for a change in the English government (the return of Charles II to the throne) but also for changes in theatrical production (including the use of actresses) and playwriting style. (There is room for dispute in this area, of course. The 1690s are treated in the criticism variously as "Restoration theatre" *and* as the start of eighteenth-century dramatic practice. Some scholars consider 1688 the cutoff point, based on political and social considerations: the beginning of William and Mary's reign and a revived conservatism.)

In general, an entry is indexed under the nationality of the playwright or practitioner discussed. For instance, Nancy Cotton's work on

Katherine of Sutton, who lived in the fourteenth century, would be listed under both English women playwrights and medieval English drama/performance/theatre. However, if the production aspects are emphasized in a bibliographic item, a variety of categorical terms may be applied. Holly Hill's *Playing Joan,* a collection of interviews with actresses who have portrayed George Bernard Shaw's heroine, is indexed under twentieth-century English, Canadian, and American drama/performance/theatre because of its concentration on acting and directing elements. (It is also indexed under Irish drama/performance/theatre because of *Shaw's* nationality, following the practice of both the Modern Language Association and the Library of Congress.)

Entries that cover more than four different nations or eras are listed under "multiple countries and time periods."

Feminist Theatres and Theatre Companies

The problems for the bibliographer are manifold when it comes to categorizing a theatre or theatre group as feminist. (See the Introduction for a detailed discussion.) Groups have formed, dissolved, and occasionally re-formed, with changes in their degree of affiliation with the label and aims of feminist theatre, to say nothing of changes in their names. Some companies have only gradually become feminist, whereas others have shifted in their feminist focus.

Perhaps the most important understanding for users of the Categorical Index is that I have been liberal in my inclusions of "feminist" (and "women's") theatres.

While the geographical breakdown of feminist theatres and theatre companies is a simple matter, other subheadings under "specialized" have proven more difficult to determine. For example, under lesbian feminist theatres and theatre companies, entries are included only if the theatre or group is feminist and specifically concentrates on lesbian issues. However, I did include Gay Sweatshop (which is neither an all-female nor an originally feminist group), because the influence of feminism caused it to branch out into two basically autonomous companies, one of women and one of men. Needless to say, some of these decisions have been extremely challenging, particularly in cases where the theatre no longer exists and documentation, aside from the bibliographic entries, is difficult or impossible to obtain. The term "multicultural," used sparingly, refers to what Sue-Ellen Case in *Feminism and Theatre* calls "coalition theatre": a group of women from various ethnic backgrounds working together to concentrate on issues affecting and reflecting minority women.

Lesbian Plays

The main entry "lesbian plays" includes bibliographic entries that examine works with major lesbian characters or predominant lesbian themes (and not plays that only peripherally touch on homosexuality). An item listed here does not necessarily mean that the author(s) of the work studied is lesbian; nor is discussion of all work by lesbian playwrights included here, if a particular play does not fall within the guidelines stated above.

Women Playwrights

All attempts have been made to use both authoritative sources *and* common sense in classifying by nationality. For example, Elizabeth Robins is an American-born actress, playwright, and suffragette who moved to England and whose dramatic contributions and campaigning for women's rights are associated with British theatre and politics. Despite her American roots, I have elected to index her under English women playwrights and twentieth-century English drama/performance/theatre. Similarly, Maria Irene Fornes was born in Cuba but emigrated to the United States, where she has been a prolific playwright and director of her own work. She is listed in *Who's Who of American Women* and *Notable Women in the American Theatre,* and analyzed in many essay collections centering on American writers. Therefore, she is categorized as an American woman playwright.

If an article or book deals with women playwrights from more than three nations, it is indexed under worldwide women playwrights; no attempt is then made to indicate the corresponding countries and time periods. Such situations often arise in indexing bibliographies of criticism of women's writing.

Selected terms have been included to provide access to specific bodies of work dealing with minority playwrights in the United States. As African-American women playwrights have received much attention in recent years, a separate category acts as a locating device. The increasing study of Chicana and Latina playwrights is reflected in a combined heading, as many items deal with the work of both. Codes following "women of color" refer to items in which the conditions and work of a variety of minority women (Asian, Hispanic, etc.) are discussed in the same entry. In all the above cases, critical works are indexed both under American women playwrights and under the minority designation.

Subject Index

The headings and subheadings included in this selective index have been derived from the works annotated in the bibliography as well as from input by active and knowledgeable feminist theorists specializing in drama/performance/theatre. Not all terms are employed by critics in the same fashion, nor are all expressions included in the critical discourse provided with a separate heading. Therefore, the Subject Index is characterized by plentiful cross-referencing. For example, while there is a listing for "power, female," there is no listing for "power, male." As the "see" reference suggests, the user should look under "patriarchy," "oppression of women," "sexual politics," and other pertinent terms. In addition, certain terms are used mainly when individual authors stress them, particularly "sexual politics," a concept that underlies and informs the feminist project.

Both broad and specific terms are used. Broad terms are marked by an asterisk (*), which indicates that the entry is general, covering numerous playwrights or comprehensive issues. For example, under "*feminist drama," the subheading "forms" provides access to items that survey the various ways in which feminist playwrights and troupes have experimented with form or that deal with a sizable number of representative plays. (To obtain the most specific information about a particular play's form, it is best to consult the Title Index.) Other broad headings include "black drama/theatre," "Chicana/Chicano drama/ theatre," and "lesbian drama/theatre." (Again, for more direct access to a particular work, the Name or Title index should be used. In addition, the Categorical Index includes subheadings for African-American women playwrights, Chicana/Latina women playwrights, and lesbian plays.)

I combined "drama" and "theatre" in such broad headings as "gay (male) drama/theatre" and "lesbian drama/theatre" because separate headings for drama and theatre proved repetitive in most cases. However, "feminist drama" and "feminist theatre," as the main focuses of this bibliography, are separately listed, and each includes a variety of subheadings.

A significant and frequently employed Subject Index term is "sex/gender roles," adapted in part from Gayle Rubin's influential coining of the term "sex-gender system" (discussed in the Introduction to this book), and in part from Simone de Beauvoir's famous observation that "One is not born, but rather becomes, a woman." In other words, "sex roles" are learned, not biologically determined. Although gender is the more applicable term to describe "role"—or, in fact, the entire system under which men (biological) and women (biological) traditionally function—in the Subject Index I have combined "gender" and "sex" with a slash to help the user find the pertinent studies. My decision is based on the varying ways writers have used the term(s) through the period under study, not out of ignorance of the distinction.

"Sexual difference" has been employed by a wide range of critics in differing contexts. For the most part, references to items under "sexual difference" concern those based in psychoanalytic theory and biology. The term "sex/gender roles" has been applied to writings dealing more with the gender ideology (e.g., expectations of how a "woman" or "man" should act) in a given society.

Subject Index terms such as "work, women and" are used only insofar as they are discussed in the source in relation to drama/performance/theatre. For example, in the collection *Rewriting the Renaissance,* several essays discuss women's part in the Renaissance economy but have nothing to do with theatre; therefore, in annotating this book, the term "work, women and" has not been assigned. On the other hand, criticism dealing with Rachel Crothers' depictions of women's struggles between career and domestic life would necessarily be cited under the heading "work, women and."

As in the preceding indexes, the code letters and numbers following headings and subheadings refer to bibliographic entries, not to page numbers.

feminist drama—forms *(continued)*
D157, D173, D187, E105,
G35, G45, I20
non-verbal elements, B11
rhetorical aspects, A2, A4, A10,
B28, B29
themes in, A1, A2, A3, A8, A10,
A14, A16, A40, A45, A56,
B7, B11, B12, B40, B43,
B49, B55, B58, B73, D19,
D42, D77, D90, D157,
D173, G29, G33, I19, I20, J7
use of participants' real-life
experiences, A8, B49, B54
See also dream enactment;
lesbian drama/theatre;
performance art and artists;
music; myth; ritual. *See also*
specific themes such as
women's history. *Consult* the
Play Index for individual
feminist plays. *Consult* the
Name Index for specific
feminist playwrights and
feminist theatre groups.
*feminist theatre
agitprop, A1, A14, A16, B9, B11,
B55
critical response to, B7, B40,
G32
definitions of, A1, A4, A10, A36,
A40, A57, A60, B7, B39,
B73, D196, I19
history of, A10, A36, A53, A58,
B7, B28, B29, B39, B55,
D19, D197, G29, I19
See also audience(s), feminist
theatre and; avant-garde
theatre of the 1960s,
relationship to feminist
theatre; black theatre
movement, compared to
feminist theatre; feminist
drama; feminist theatres and

theatre groups; lesbian
drama/theatre; male
participation in feminist
theatre; performance art and
artists; political theatre of
the 1930s, compared to
feminist theatre
feminist theatres and theatre groups,
A1, A2, A3, A4, A6, A8, A9,
A10, A14, A16, A25, A30, A36,
A52, A53, A58, A60, A61,
B1–B76, C8, D7, D9, D19,
D39, D77, D142, D149, D209,
E266, F22, F25, F31, F32, F65,
G6, G9, G33, G43, G45, H9,
H10, H11, H13, H14, H16, H17,
H23, I19, I21, I22, I24, I25,
I26, I27, J1, J17, J18, J20.
Consult the Name Index for
specific groups and the
Categorical Index for
geographical location or
specialized nature
feminization of theatre, F2
fidelity/infidelity, C15, C26,
D162, E17, E24, E30, E32, E33,
E34, E36, E40, E46, E50, E52,
E59, E64, E67, E70, E71, E73,
E79, E91, E93, E112, E116,
E147, E154, E155, E164, E166,
E177, E183, E193, E198, E222,
E246, E250, E259, E263, E265,
F62
food/hunger imagery, D19, D80,
D101, D143, D156, E19
frame (i.e., theatrical frame), A33,
D203
freedom, illusory, D140, E88, E104,
E105, E151
friendship, female, A4, A8, B15, C6,
C16, C19, D33, D53, D121,
D158, D182, E3, E12, E17, E36,
E50, E59, E74, E84, E104,
E154, E155, E206, F3, G17.

E158, E187, E234. *See also* madness, women and

man-hating feminist, E202

masculine, C6, E17, E23, E41, E55, E64, E74, E111, E160, E168, E183

moral custodian, E71, E94, E124, E144, E167

mulatto. *See under* black woman (above)

narcissistic, E108, E133

older, A49, B49, D126, D163, D173, F60, I23

outport woman, D51

outsider, A15, D75, D102, E95, F59

patient, E8, E14, E31, E32, E40, E73, E74, E254

"phallic woman," E108, E131

powerful, E15, E55, E73, E155, E254

powerless, D42, E37, E92, E236, E267, E269

prude, E109

red hot Mama, F50

resilient, D2, D48, D210, E15, E166

revenger, C16, E30, E41, E64, E87, E95, E126, E191

rural, A4, D66, I16, I122

saint, E125

self-sacrificing, C6, C16, C19, C27, D170, E55, E56, E63, E88, E103, E144, E145, E180, E185, E216, E254

sex-kitten, D109, F50

shrew, E15, E25, E30, E31, E34, E40, E61, E74, E125, E155, E175, E209, E263

social mover, E12

sphinx, E72

spinster, D20, D187

submissive, C6, C7, C27, D20, D42, E8, E16, E79, E146, E152, E153, E154, E155

subversive, D170, E30, E149, E229

sweet young thing, F50

sweetheart, E216

Venus armata, E201

victim, A23, B17, B75, C24, D157, D162, D200, D201, E92, E103, E116, E121, E142, E163, E166, E167, E196, E230, E238, E239, E249, E257, E260, E261, E262, E266, E269

virgin/virginal, C13, C14, D106, E6, E24, E32, E39, E64, E119

virtuous, C10, C16, E13, E17, E24, E31, E32, E78, E94, E137, E167, E171, E196, E230, E254, E256, E268

warrior, E41, E64, E168, E244

whore, C13, C14, D10, D106, E13, E30, E46, E72, E119, E139, E207, E216

widow, E15, E74, E171, E172

witch, E2, E30, E168, E267, F60

witty, C6, E40, E64, E80, E116, E166, E178, E183, E246

See also family, women's roles in; sex/gender roles; stereotypes, female

incest, D22, D138, D207, E13, E16, E24, E50, E62, E95, E99, E261

incontinence (i.e., bladder), E223

independence, female, A10, B4, C8, D10, D19, D48, D90, D95, D110, D115, D175, D204, E14, E15, E31, E58, E71, E77, E88, E209, E217, E242, E245, E246, F2, G21. *See also* autonomy, search for; images of women,